The Jewish State

The Jewish State

A Century Later

Alan Dowty

UNIVERSITY OF CALIFORNIA PRESS

Berkeley   Los Angeles   London

University of California Press
Berkeley and Los Angeles, California

University of California Press, Ltd.
London, England

© 1998 by
The Regents of the University of California

Library of Congress Cataloging-in-Publication Data

Dowty, Alan, 1940–
    The Jewish state : a century later / Alan Dowty.
      p. cm.
    Includes bibliographic references and index.
    ISBN 0–520–20941–9 (cloth : alk. paper)
    1. Israel—Politics and government.   2. Democracy—Israel.
  3. Jews—Politics and government.   4. Democracy—Religious, aspects—
Judaism. 5. Judaism and state—Israel. 6. Jews—Israel—Identity.
  7. Zionism—History. 8. Palestinian Arabs—Israel—Politics and
government. I. Title.
JQ1830.A58D69   1998
320.95694—dc21   97–6603
                                            CIP

Printed in the United States of America
9 8 7 6 5 4 3 2 1

The paper used in this publication is both acid-free and totally chlorine-
free (TCF). It meets the minimum requirements of American Standard
for Information Sciences—Permanence of Paper for Printed Library
Materials, ANSI Z39.48–1984.

To the generation of the second century:
Merav, Tamar, Gidon, David, Rachel, and Rafi

Children are living messages we send to a time we will not see.
AUTHOR UNKNOWN

Then from this center the spirit of Judaism will go forth to the great circumference, to all the communities of the Diaspora, and will breathe life into them and preserve their unity; and when our national culture in Palestine has attained that level, we may be confident that it will produce men in the country who will be able, on a favorable opportunity, to establish a State which will be a Jewish State, and not merely a State of Jews.

AHAD HA'AM
"THE JEWISH STATE AND THE JEWISH PROBLEM" (1897)

CONTENTS

MAPS AND TABLES

PREFACE

Having divided my adult life between residence in Israel and the United States, I often find myself explaining Israel or Israelis to non-Israelis (Jewish and non-Jewish alike), or conversely trying to convey to Israelis how things are seen from elsewhere. For what it is worth, I have tried to utilize this dual perspective in the work at hand, tapping into the vigorous debates among Israelis themselves while attempting to keep a broader view in mind. Whether such an "inside-outside" perspective has been useful is for others to judge, but at least I hope this book will provide a bridge between attentive publics that have not always paid attention to each other.

Acknowledgment for assistance must be extended to many colleagues and friends on both sides of the ocean. At various stages Ari Rosenthal, at Haifa University, and Caio Blinder and Carmela Lutmar, both at Notre Dame, gave valuable help as research assistants. Menachem Hofnung, at the Hebrew University, has been especially kind in providing comments and suggestions as well as handling numerous queries that arose in the course of the work. Others who have aided in one way or another include: Hatem Abu-Ghazeleh, Majid Al-Haj, Asher Arian, Myron Aronoff, Shlomo Aronson, Shlomo Avineri, Ya'akov Bar-Siman-Tov, Gad Barzilai, Avraham Ben-Zvi, Michael Brecher, Aryeh Carmon, Shlomo Deshen, Avraham Diskin, Eliezer Don-Yehiya, Daniel Elazar, André Eshet, Ze'ev Eytan (z"l), Morley Feinstein, Michael Francis, Menachem Friedman, Hillel Frisch, Yitzhak Galnoor, Yosef Gorny, Emanuel Gutmann, Alo「uph Hareven, Tamar Hermann, Tom Idinopulos, Efraim Inbar, Rachel Israeli, Elihu Katz, Edy Kaufman, Baruch Kimmerling, Aharon Klieman, Ran Kochan, Rebecca Kook, Shlomit Levi, Sam Lehman-Wilzig, Hana Levinsohn, Charles Liebman, Arend Lijphart, Noah Lucas, Ian Lustick, Greg Mahler, Ze'ev Maoz, Peter Medding, Gil Merom, William V. O'Brien, Ilan Pappé, Yoav Peled, Ilan Peleg, Yoram Peri, Elie

Rekhess, Susan Hattis Rolef, Allen Schapiro, Ozer Schild, Michal Shamir, Gabi Sheffer, Michael Signer, Rita Simon, Hanoch Smith, Sammy Smooha, Sasson Sofer, Arnon Soffer, Ehud Sprinzak, Russell Stone, Ilan Troen, Mina Tsemach, Shevach Weiss, Gadi Wolfsfeld, Ephraim Ya'ar, Natan Yanai, Avner Yaniv (z"l), Yael Yishai, and Yair Zalmanovitch.

Anyone familiar with many of these names will know at once that I could not possibly have accepted all their advice, as they represent a full spectrum of clashing approaches and interpretations of Israeli politics and society. I have tried to draw upon each school of thought for what it had to offer, finding that each has its unique insights and contributions. The result, I hope, is a synthesis that encompasses these insights without engaging in scholarly quarrels in which the general reader may have little interest. If critics are frustrated trying to place this book easily in one camp or another, then I will feel that I have not totally failed in this regard.

I am grateful to the University of Haifa, Tel Aviv University, and the Hebrew University in Jerusalem for hosting me as a visitor at various times. The University of Notre Dame also gave me a semester's freedom for writing, and the Institute for the Study of the Liberal Arts at Notre Dame supplied a summer stipend for a research assistant.

Earlier versions of parts of the book have been published in *Middle East Review* (Fall 1988), *Jewish Political Studies Review* (Fall 1990), *Mosaic* (Spring 1991), *Shofar* (Fall 1991); in Shao-chuan Leng, ed., *Coping with Crisis: How Governments Deal with Emergencies* (University Press of America, 1990); in Menachem Mor, ed., *Jewish Sects, Religious Movements, and Political Parties* (Creighton University Press, 1992); in S. Ilan Troen and Noah Lucas, eds., *Israel: The First Decade of Independence* (State University of New York Press, 1994); and in Gabriel Ben-Dor and David B. Dewitt, eds., *Confidence Building Measures in the Middle East* (Westview Press, 1994).

PART ONE

The Shaping
of Israeli Democracy

ONE

Democracy in Israel

Can a state be both Jewish and democratic? Over a century since the Zionist idea began to gather momentum, argument continues over what it means for a state to be Jewish. To those hostile to the very concept, it is clear that Jewishness is antithetical to democracy: "To the extent that Israel is a Jewish state, it cannot be a democratic state."[1]

Such a view essentially equates "Jewish" with race or religion. A state employing racial criteria would clearly be exclusivist (racist), while a state based on religious principles would by definition be theocratic. Some unsympathetic critics attach both definitions to Israel; they bracket Jews with Christians and Muslims (all living under "religious authority and religious law" in Israel), while arguing at the same time that a "sovereign state of the Jewish people" is the same as a "sovereign state of the White people" or of the Anglo-Saxon people.[2] Most Jews, however, reject the simple equation of Jewishness with race or religion. Jews in Israel and elsewhere clearly comprise a mixed racial group; furthermore, one can either cease to be a Jew or decide to become a Jew by personal choice, without regard to genetics. And while there is a Jewish religion, nonobservant Jews are still considered Jews. Israel demonstrates that a "Jewish" state can operate largely by secular rather than religious law—precisely the major criticism of Israel made by religious Jews.

What, then, is the commonly accepted meaning of "Jewishness"? For most Jews, or for that matter for most outside observers, it is a common national or ethnic identity as a historically developed community of people with distinctive cultural, linguistic, and other attributes. This includes a distinctive Judaic religion, which makes Jews unusual, though not unique, among ethnic groups. Jews are a people, a nation (in the original sense of the word), an *ethnos*. While the sense of peoplehood has been diluted in modern liberal assimilationist societies such as that of the United States, or even reduced in some cases to religious expressions alone or to nothing at all, this characterization of Jews in history is still valid. It has been true for most Jews, in most places, at most times.

Consequently, a Jewish state, as simply a state with a largely Jewish population and a dominantly Jewish culture, is not necessarily any more undemocratic than any state structured around a dominant ethnic group or groups (in other words, than several dozen states in the world today). The question is, first, whether the dominant group or groups practice democracy among themselves, and second, whether they extend it to citizens from other ethnic groups. This is a question to be answered by observation, not by plays on words or a priori assumptions. Finland is not undemocratic simply because it contains a significant Swedish minority while at the same time maintaining its Finnish character. One must examine the actual functioning of Finnish politics. Likewise, a Jewish state is not by definition undemocratic or democratic. We have to observe the Israeli political system as it operates in order to pass judgment. That is what this book attempts to do.

But isn't ethnicity much more important in Israel than in progressive, social-democratic, postnationalistic Finland? To be sure, the importance of ethnicity does vary. On one end of the spectrum is the perfectly liberal modern secular state, ethnically neutral in laws and political behavior, and committed to universalistic norms that transcend the narrow confines of race, creed, or national origin (whether such a state actually exists is another question). At the other end is the state that clings to its ethnic identity explicitly, adopting a particularistic orientation rooted not in general principles but in its own traditions and values. This tension between the pull of universalism and the demands of particularism is familiar to anyone who knows Zionist history, because it has always been a basic point of contention. Was the Jewish state to be "a state like other states," by which advocates usually meant something on the progressive European model? Or was it to be something uniquely Jewish, an expression of the Jewish people's own history, traditions, and way of life? Or some synthesis of the two? Though Jewish history seems to have been intensely particularistic, universalist ideas were well represented in Zionism. The debate accompanied the movement from its very first days.[3]

The argument has implications for how one judges the Israeli political system. Those impressed by the particularism or uniqueness of the Jewish people sometimes use this as a basis for judging Israel by a different set of standards. This group includes both critics and sympathizers. Many outside observers, including professed friends, would hold Israel to a higher standard than other states, on grounds of the unique historical experience of Jews or the unique moral importance of Israel as a haven from antisemitism. Some Israelis and Israel supporters, on the other hand, argue that the same history of persecution makes it understandable, and excusable, for Israel to be judged more leniently (Jews having, so often, been the victims of widespread violation of international norms by others).

Both of these arguments are rejected here. Even if we decide that Israeli political traditions and institutions are quite different, bearing little in common with the histories of other peoples, this does not justify invoking different standards. The circumstances under which nations function should be taken into account (for example, the seriousness of threats to security). But to cite the uniqueness of a people's character or past as cause for either unique condemnation or unique approbation is to enter the treacherous terrain of the double standard. Therefore, wherever Israel falls on the particularist-universalist spectrum, the working assumption here is that Israeli democracy must be judged by the same standards applied elsewhere—no more and no less.

But where does Israel fall on this spectrum? Is it true that Jewish history and traditions are biased toward particularism? Actually the apostles of pure universalism should find much to like in Theodor Herzl's original vision of the Jewish state. The title of Herzl's 1896 manifesto that galvanized the emergence of the Zionist movement, *Der Judenstaat*, usually translated as *The Jewish State*, is more accurately rendered as *The Jews' State*. There was little that was "Jewish" either in the arguments for the state—basically as a response to antisemitism—or in the nature of the state itself. As later depicted in his utopian novel *Altneuland* (or *Old-New Land*), Herzl's "Jews' state" was basically an empty framework into which he poured various progressive ideas then current in Europe and in which Jews, Muslims, and even Christian Europeans could feel equally comfortable.[4] Needless to say, many Zionist thinkers (especially Ahad Ha'am, the proponent of "spiritual" Zionism) condemned the near-total absence of Jewish content in Herzl's background, thinking, and program. But for Herzl, who dominated the movement in its early years, the aim was indeed "a state like other states" (though perhaps even more progressive).

Nor was Herzl alone in failing to find inspiration in purely Jewish themes; in a sense, Zionism itself was a reaction to the particularism of Jewish life. Though nationalist in content, the movement for a Jewish state was very much part of the currents then sweeping Europe. As Shlomo Avineri observes, "in all these founders of modern Zionism there appears again and again the same phenomenon: they did not come from the traditional, religious background. They were all products of European education, imbued with the current ideas of the European intelligentsia."[5] In copying the nationalism of other peoples, proponents of a Jewish state were revolting against the powerlessness, passivity, and pious quietism they associated with the ghettoized Jewish life of recent centuries: "Jewish nationalism was then one specific aspect of the impact of the ideas and social structures unleashed by the French Revolution, modernism, and secularism. . . . For the Zionism Revolution is very basically a permanent revolution against those powerful forces in Jewish history, existing at least partially within the Jewish people, which have turned the Jews from a self-reliant people into a community living at the margin of and sometimes living off alien communities."[6]

Zionism was thus not merely an act of assertion against external threats, but also a revolution against age-old patterns of Jewish existence and an attempt to establish "normal" social, political, cultural, and occupational patterns that would make Jews more like other nations. Much of early Zionism—at least in its ideology—should therefore meet the approval of those whose ideal is Western secular liberal democracy, shorn of particularism. The "tragedy of Zionism," writes Bernard Avishai, is "that Labor Zionism is a good revolution that long ago ran its course, that it stopped short of its liberal-democratic goals, and that recent efforts to reinvigorate Zionism in Israel have only brought Israelis more misfortune."[7] In this view, shared by many veteran Israelis, positive aspects of early Zionism, such as the pioneering settlement ethic, have been appropriated in recent years by a narrower and more particularistic version of Zionism: "the question . . . is whether democratic tendencies—some of which, to be sure, were inherent in historic Labor Zionism—will prevail against the anachronistic institutions which Labor Zionists once made; prevail against the new Zionist ideology of a Greater Israel."[8] Democracy failed to take root in Israel because it was eventually overwhelmed by resurgent Jewish particularism: "Israeli schools have taught children much more about the tribes of Israel than about the Enlightenment. . . . "[9] This was even reflected in the Hebrew language itself, claims Avishai, since Hebrew has no word for democracy except the "borrowed" word *demokratia*, which, he feels, strikes the Israeli ear as "alien" or "affected."[10]

The fact that many early Zionists sought to divorce themselves from Jewish history does not, of course, mean that they always succeeded in disentangling themselves from its grip. Discussion of this point is central to much of what follows. But it should be noted at the outset that even had Zionists, against all odds, started with an entirely clean slate and had simply copied wholesale the European models they admired, this would still not necessarily have secured democracy. Of course liberal universalism seems much more hospitable to democracy than nationalistic doctrines, especially with regard to treatment of minorities. This was certainly something that Jews were especially well situated to appreciate, since the increasingly tenuous position of minorities in the new nations of Europe was one of the primary motivations for Zionism itself. But this is no simple one-to-one relationship; just as national self-expression can conceivably be achieved democratically, so also universalistic norms are no absolute guarantee of democratic practice.

In the first place, no state can claim to have achieved a true universalism in its politics; the idea of true neutrality toward all citizens, with blindness toward all ethnic, religious, cultural, linguistic, and other attributes, is a chimera. No state exists in a demographic or cultural vacuum; all reflect the human reality from which they are constructed. The prevailing values of a society, the distinctive history through which its people have passed, the very language or languages in which its public affairs are conducted—all these are particulars that give each state its own character. And all states, even the most liberal and progressive, consider the preservation of this national character to be a legitimate and even obligatory function of government. All contemporary states, for example, carefully and selectively limit immigration in order to ensure, among other things, against massive demographic change.[11]

In the second place, not all universalist ideas are necessarily democratic in content. It should be sufficient to recall socialist internationalism, which does indeed purport to transcend ethnicity and religion but which has laid the groundwork for totalitarian rule based theoretically on dictatorship of one class over others. Traditional nondemocratic regimes never achieved the penetration and control of society achieved by Marxism-Leninism in the name of universal laws of history.

Particular traditions and practices can of course be either democratic or nondemocratic; by definition, particularism offers no single pattern in this regard or others. While we suspect that an inward-looking state might be less likely to respect internal differences, there is no a priori reason to assume this. Some peoples claim to have deeply grounded democratic traditions of their own, that may in the end be a firmer foundation for tolerance than alien doctrines from outside. Typically, a people's history includes precedents for both popular rule and authoritarianism. Certainly Jewish history includes both democratic and oligarchic tendencies.

In other words, both the "Jewishness" of Israel and the outside influences (ideologies and models) that have operated upon it have an ambivalent relationship to democracy. Both include strands that could lead in either direction. As Benyamin Neuberger has put it: "Israel's political tradition is a mix of democratic and nondemocratic traditions because its major components such as the Jewish religion and the Judaic historical traditions, but also the modern ideologies of socialism and nationalism, contain both liberal-democratic and authoritarian elements."[12]

That the "Jewish" dimension of Israel should contain both democratic and nondemocratic elements should come as no surprise, since the same could probably be said of most traditions. The real surprise comes when one puts the oligarchic strands of traditions and ideologies together with the objective conditions hostile to democracy that impinged on the Zionist movement and on Israel. Considering the highly unfavorable circumstances attending its emergence, how did Israel achieve any democracy?

OBSTACLES TO DEMOCRACY

The central puzzle of Israeli politics is, in fact, how the state has managed to maintain a stable democratic system. The obstacles to such an achievement were enormous. Consider the following ten influences on the development of the State of Israel:

Relatively few of the Jewish immigrants to Palestine or to Israel over the last century came from countries with a viable democratic tradition. A quick survey of official statistics shows that only about 10 percent of those who entered Palestine or Israel from 1919 to 1987 came from countries with democratic governments at the time (and the pre-1919 figure would be even lower).[13] Not only were the countries of origin undemocratic but typically the Jewish communities there lived in a state of hostility toward official authority; Jews did not look to governments for protection but regarded them in "us–them"terms, with fear and antagonism.

Most immigrants came as refugees, with a life experience molded by disaster and political perceptions dominated by a sense of insecurity and vulnerability. Another rough survey of official figures shows that about three-quarters of those who arrived over the years would probably meet the standard definition of refugee: those fleeing because of "a well-founded fear of being persecuted for reasons of race, religion, nationality, membership of a particular social group or political opinion."[14]

Those who came were plunged into a situation of permanent war, requiring full mobilization of manpower and resources, overwhelming dependence on the military, and a constant state of high readiness for emergency. All able-bodied males between the ages of eighteen and fifty-one are subject to military service, and most women are also drafted for two years. Contiguous Arab states have a combined advantage over Israel of 18 to 1 in population and 12 to 1 in size of armed forces.

The country is plagued by serious threats to internal cohesion, not only from a significant minority identified ethnically with the enemy but also by deep communal, religious, ideological, and political cleavages within the Jewish community itself. It has become a commonplace, if untested, observation that, without the unity enforced by the Arab-Israeli conflict, Israel would tear itself apart in internal squabbles.

The economic pressures created by security needs, by the rapid absorption of large numbers of immigrants, and by conflicting development demands often seem beyond the capacity of the political system. The Israeli system is in a permanent state of overload. "The simultaneous striving for several major objectives . . . is a principal source of difficulty. . . . Political and social goals have continually demanded resources far greater than those which were in prospect."[15] Israel has frequently been ranked first in the world in government spending as a percentage of the gross national product.

The defense burden during much of Israel's history consumed a crushing 20 to 30 percent of the gross national product, an outlay unmatched by any contemporary state not engaged in full-scale war and several times the level of defense spending in any other democratic state. This heavy weight on the economy increased over time, growing from less than 10 percent of GDP before 1967 to a high of near 30 percent in the late 1970s, declining only in the 1980s after peace with Egypt.[16]

Because of small size, historical legacy, and a state of emergency, the Israel government formally has a very centralized structure, with authority concentrated on the national level and few institutional constraints on executive power (so long as supported by a majority in the Knesset).

As already indicated, the ideologies imported by early settlers were not unambiguously aligned with Western-style liberal democracy. Labor Zionism, especially among more leftist factions, flirted very seriously with democratic centralism and other doctrines of elite control then current in Eastern European revolutionary circles. Later the nationalistic right—Revisionist Zionists in particular—stressed the values of unity, military strength, and strong leadership, again reflecting the influence of contemporary antidemocratic ideas elsewhere. Furthermore, Israeli society has faced the challenge of all postrevolutionary societies: the challenge, in Shmuel Eisenstadt's words, of "the transformation of revolutionary groups from socio-political movements into rulers of states"—a process often attended by the collapse of democracy as ideals meet the pressures of reality.[17] One consequence of the influence of Eastern European revolutionary or postrevolutionary models of democracy has been, in the eyes of many close observers, that the emphasis in Israel has been on the formal and procedural aspects of democracy rather than on its content, especially in such areas as individual and minority rights.[18]

There are also elements in Jewish religion, as in any religion, that at the least create some tension with the demands of democracy. From the religious perspective, the dictates of God-given law must always take precedence over man-made rules and institutions. The biblical injunction that "thou shalt not follow a multitude to do evil" (Exodus 23:2) is often cited as an argument against majority rule. In any event, many in the religious (Orthodox) community refuse to recognize the legitimacy of democratically derived laws that they feel to be in conflict with the "higher law" as developed over the centuries by rabbinic Judaism.

Finally, after the 1967 war many Israelis asked how long democratic institutions could be maintained within Israel itself while the military administration of territories occupied in the war continued. These territories (except for East Jerusalem and the Golan Heights) were not made juridically a part of Israel but fell under the international law of belligerent occupation. This law was never designed for such a protracted period of control, and many feared that the reality of creeping de facto integration would erode democracy not only in the occupied territories but also in Israel itself. This issue will be the specific focus of chapter 10.

Concern over the strength of Israeli democracy increased considerably after the electoral upheaval of 1977, following which Menachem Begin's Likud bloc formed the first government not led by Labor in Israel's history (or in a sense, since the 1920s). Were Begin and his revisionist comrades, who had flirted with doctrines of the far right during the 1930s, truly dedicated to the democratic process? The increased visibility and political power of voters of African and Asian background and of religious nationalists— groups without strong ties to Western liberal values—added to the sense, among secular Westernized Israelis, of a rising tide of Jewish parochialism and religious obscurantism. The rise of the explicitly antidemocratic Meir Kahane, who won a Knesset seat in 1984 on a protofascist program calling for the expulsion of Arabs from Israel as well as the occupied territories and who according to polls would win several seats in 1988, brought these concerns to a head.

With all these influences to overcome, how does public support of democracy in Israel measure up? The bottom line is that there is strong support for democratic values generally among the Israeli public, but this support has some clearly identifiable soft spots.

Beginning in 1987, a systematic series of surveys was carried out by the Israel Democracy Institute (IDI; formerly the Israel Diaspora Institute) on similar issues. These surveys confirmed the Israeli public's low level of trust in political institutions, with the government, Knesset, and parties consistently falling much lower in prestige than the army, courts, and universities. Furthermore, over one-third of the respondents, time after time, stated that

Israel was "too democratic" or "far too democratic." Application of various demographic criteria showed that these opinions were not just conflict-related but also were a function of more traditional ways of life: those of African or Asian background, those professing a higher degree of religious observance, and those with lower levels of educational achievement were all more likely to express attitudes hostile to democracy.[19]

These surveys also demonstrated three particularly weak areas in public support of democracy—weaknesses that make some sense in light of the peculiarities of Jewish history and Israeli circumstances.

First, the Israeli public demonstrated a marked deference to authority on matters directly linked to security. As Yochanan Peres concludes, "a significant minority is prepared to curtail democracy when faced with the slightest threat to national security."[20] One aspect of this tendency was the marked support for strong leadership, even at the expense of democratic norms.

Second, there was a marked willingness to curb the media whenever the state's image or interests were threatened. This aversion to unfavorable publicity may reflect the traditional closure of the Jewish community and its obsession with the image projected to the outside world (what the goyim, or non-Jews, think), as well as security concerns related to the revealing of sensitive information.

Third, and most marked, there was a special weakness with regard to minority rights—that is, with regard to the non-Jewish minority in Israel. IDI studies and other surveys showed greater intolerance in Israel toward target groups on the left than toward those on the right end of the spectrum. The explanation, fairly clearly, is that the disliked groups on the left are either Arab groups or are perceived as pro-Arab.[21] Thus, while majorities of around 80 percent support democracy generally, only half of the population opposes discrimination between Jews who harm Arabs and Arabs who harm Jews. The ideal of equality before the law runs into considerable resistance when applied to Arabs; it is the "Achilles heel" of Israeli democracy.[22]

Survey results give us an important part of the picture regarding the overall strength of Israeli democracy and the threats it faces. Another important piece of the puzzle is the intense public discussion, within Israel, over these same issues. From its very inception, Israeli democracy has been barraged by complaints regarding its flaws and by lamentations heralding its imminent collapse. The character of this critical debate has, of course, evolved over time as the system itself evolved. In the pre-1977 critiques, focus was on the general dominance of parties in public life, the lack of internal democracy within parties, the long-standing hegemony of one party within the government, and the role of nongovernmental institutions (such as the Labor Federation) in what would elsewhere be governmental affairs.

After 1977, with the loss of coherence associated with the long period of Labor hegemony, the discussion of democracy shifted to other targets.

Government seemed unable to cope with the increasingly complex problems it faced. The vociferous debate over the future of the occupied territories seemed to threaten the very fabric of the system. The state of the economy reached crisis proportions. Scandals in public life multiplied, and faith in public institutions plummeted. Extremism seemed to flourish; extra-parliamentary groups such as Gush Emunim (Bloc of the Faithful, a group promoting Jewish settlement in the occupied territories) adopted postures that questioned parliamentary rule, if not democracy itself. Religious symbolism and pressures became more visible in public life, injecting new sources of tension and conflict. Elections became rowdier, and there appeared to be much more violence in public life. Many on the left feared what they saw as the demagoguery of the nationalistic right, which controlled the government and maintained close ties to more extreme groups that seemed to threaten the very basis of democratic rule.

In short, the particularistic side of Jewish life was resurgent after a long period during which the presumed universalism of Labor Zionist ideology had had the upper hand (at least on the surface). There was a human reality that had been obscured by the success of Labor Zionism. Those who came to Palestine or Israel were largely refugees motivated not by socialist ideology or Western liberalism but by desperation; they were far more closely wedded to tradition than were their Zionist mentors. They were not in revolt against Jewishness, as were many Zionist ideologues, and as ideology faded it was perhaps inevitable that Jewishness would make a comeback (though, as we shall see, it was never really absent). Along with a renewed emphasis on Jewish values came, also perhaps inevitably, objections to the universalistic pretensions of Western liberalism—including attacks on the primacy of democracy. One began to see statements such as the following, taken at random from numerous examples: "The perpetuation of the Jewish character of Israel is paramount to and transcends all other considerations, including the ideal of democracy. . . . Teaching and indoctrinating the young as to democratic values in the abstract and out of Jewish context is fraught with danger. . . . Assimilation, like Nazism, is anathema to Jewish survival and no less odious."[23]

A sustained, reasoned, intellectual challenge to democratic ideals was mounted in some nationalistic and religious circles, such as the pages of the right-wing intellectual journal *Nativ*. Accepting the argument of a conflict between Jewishness and democracy in Israel, these critics drew exactly the opposite conclusion to that drawn by their liberal opponents: democracy would have to be compromised, as preserving the Jewish character of the state was the first priority. Behind this was the assumption that Arab hostility to Israel was a given, and that consequently self-preservation meant some curtailing of Arab rights. Under such conditions, Israel could not afford pluralism; equality could be extended only to those fully accepting the state and their duties as citizens, and acts of hostility should be suppressed without apology. Any people, it was argued, has a distinct character that is inextricably linked to its statehood. The essence of nationhood was particularism, not a vague set of liberal principles that few states observed in practice anyway (especially when their survival was at stake).[24]

All of this adds up to a rather dismal view of Israeli democracy, or at least of trends that threaten to undermine it. But is the pessimism justified? Do the opinion surveys, the dire predictions, and the open attacks on democratic principles all reflect an actual decline in democratic practice, as the particularistic side of Jewish life reasserts itself? The answer is that the total picture is much more complex. To each claim or finding outlined above, there is generally an opposed counterclaim challenging the picture of erosion in democracy.

DEMOCRATIC REALITIES

What expectations do we bring to bear in evaluating democratic attitudes, in Israel or elsewhere? If political institutions are held in low repute everywhere, what is the significance of the Israeli data? Beginning with the assumption that Israel is to be judged as other countries are judged, the comparative perspective becomes necessary. Such problems as minority rights in a conflict situation, security pressures on civil liberties, the role of religion in politics, and overwhelming pressures on available resources can be fully evaluated only by comparing the Israeli case to others, similar and dissimilar.[25]

More fundamentally, one must begin with a recognition of the general tenuousness of democracy. Democracy is a relatively recent and still far-from-universal human achievement; if we posit universal suffrage, including women, as part of the minimal criteria, there were no democracies at all until the early twentieth century, and only twenty-three states have been continuously democratic since the immediate post-World War II period. All of these are relatively well-developed, prosperous nations; all but Israel, India, Costa Rica, and Japan are in Western Europe, North America, or the British Commonwealth.[26]

Looking at matters comparatively, it appears the Israeli public is not substantially more intolerant than the U.S. public, and that existing differences can be explained by differences in the nature and degree of threat to which the two societies are exposed. The major comparative study, published in 1983, concluded that "the two countries are quite similar, with Americans only slightly more tolerant." On the abstract level, there was no difference; for example, 85 percent of Americans and 83 percent of Israelis endorsed the principle of free speech.[27] Differences appeared when the principle was put in the context of the least-liked target group, with a result that support of free speech declined by 30 percent among Americans and by 45 percent among Israelis. This is explained by the fact that there was less agreement among Americans on the identity of the target group—a situation of "pluralistic intolerance"—while in the Israeli setting of "focused intolerance" the Arab minority is more clearly identified and linked with an external threat.[28]

Outside observers, employing presumably objective criteria regarding freeness of elections, competitiveness, and individual rights, have always ranked Israel among the democratic polities. The annual Freedom House series ranks Israel among the "free" nations while also putting it on the second rung regarding political rights, as a nation with a functioning electoral system but "particular problems."[29] Israel·made Dankwart Rustow's 1967 list of thirty-one democracies, Robert Dahl's 1971 roster of twenty-nine "polyarchies," and G. Bingham Powell's 1982 enumeration of twenty nations with continuous democratic regimes from 1958 to 1976 (as well as Arend Lijphart's similar list of twenty-one, mentioned earlier).[30] In short, those who approached the topic with empirical criteria, rather than semantic arguments, have had little difficulty recognizing the essentially democratic character of Israel's political system.

Israel also appears in general discussions as one of the major case studies of democracy in a deeply divided society. Ethnic and religious cleavages clearly make the achievement of democracy more difficult; analysts point to a strong correlation between homogeneity and political democracy.[31] Generally, only a handful of states with deep and numerically significant ethnic divisions have maintained stable democracies: Switzerland, Belgium, Canada, arguably India—and Israel. Thus it is not too surprising that one of the weaker aspects of Israeli democracy is minority rights, or that the style of democracy adopted by Israel is that considered by political scientists to be most suitable for deeply split societies.

WHAT KIND OF DEMOCRACY?

How has Israel preserved the essentially democratic character of its political institutions against such odds? In answering this question, it is important to understand just what kind of democracy Israel has managed to maintain and where the strength of its democratic habits lie. It is useful to begin with the distinction that Arend Lijphart makes between majoritarian democracy, on one hand, and consensus democracy or consociationalism on the other.

Majoritarian democracy—or the "Westminster model" in Lijphart's words—is based on the idea that majority rule is the essence of democracy and that this principle should not be diluted (by a minority veto, for example). The British style of parliamentarism, with bare-majority governments, fusion of executive and legislative power, and tendency to unicameralism, is an expression of the majoritarian ideal. It also can be characterized by a unidimensional two-party system with one-party governments, by nonproportional electoral systems, by centralized as opposed to federalized government, and by unentrenched (or even unwritten) constitutions that can be altered by ordinary acts of parliament, since all of these arrangements help to guarantee that the untrammeled will of the majority will prevail.[32]

Consensus democracy and the related concept of consociationalism embody the idea that the exclusion of losing groups or minorities from all decision-making is, in some basic sense, undemocratic. This model regards the diffusion and sharing of power according to some principle of proportionality as the ideal to be pursued. Lijphart identifies the eight characteristics of consensus democracy that stand in contrast to the majoritarian model. The following five characteristics fall along what could be called an "executive-parties" dimension:

1. Executive power-sharing. There is a tendency to share executive powers beyond a bare majority, making otherwise powerless minorities a part of the system.
2. Executive–legislative balance. The executive and legislative branches, instead of being fused, serve as a check on each other.
3. Multiparty system. The presence of many parties makes it unlikely that any one party will gain a majority, necessitating coalitions among smaller parties in which the interests of each is safeguarded.
4. Multidimensional party system. The formation of parties along many lines of cleavage—such as socioeconomic, ethnic, or religious—also enforces the pluralism of the system and the need to build coalitions protecting the position of smaller groups.
5. Proportional representation. Apart from providing the underpinning for a multiparty system, proportional electoral systems are the classic method of guaranteeing a voice to minorities and smaller groups in society.

The other three characteristics of consensus democracy comprise a "federal-unitary" dimension:

6. Federalism and decentralization. Different levels of government serve as a check on each other, and the reservation of powers to local jurisdictions is a means of providing autonomy to distinct groups.
7. Strong bicameralism. The second chamber in a two-house system usually serves as a check, representing territorial divisions or minorities to be protected from the tyranny of the majority.
8. Written and rigid constitutions. The final guarantee for minorities is the entrenchment of provisions that cannot be changed by a simple

majority, either by requiring an extraordinary majority for constitutional changes or by providing a formal or informal right of veto to minorities in matters affecting them.[33]

Consociationalism is a similar concept developed to describe nonmajoritarian power-sharing practices of democratic states. Lijphart identifies four such practices: grand coalition, segmental autonomy, proportionality, and mutual veto. Clearly these features largely overlap the two dimensions of consensus democracy, though consociationalism is a broader concept that covers informal practices as well as institutional structures.[34] Since informal arrangements are critically important in Israel, the broader idea of consociationalism is especially applicable.

With its multiparty system and uncompromising proportional representation, Israel clearly ranks among the more "consensual" regimes on the executive-parties dimension of consensual democracy. On the second consensual dimension, however, Israel is "majoritarian" in federal-unitary features (centralization, unicameralism, an unwritten constitution).[35] But this mixed picture exists primarily on the level of formal institutions; when viewed in terms of the broader concept of consociationalism (see chapters 3 and 4), informal power-sharing is much more evident.

A focus on the formal structure and powers of Israeli institutions is misleading. The Knesset may at first glance invite comparison to the Westminster model. But most important policy decisions have been the product of a bargaining process in which not only various branches of the government but also important quasi-governmental bodies and major social groups are all active participants in setting the political agenda, controlling the debate, and shaping the decisions that result. In practice, then, Israeli democracy has important power-sharing consociational features: grand coalitions, autonomy, proportionality, mutual veto, pluralism, and social bargaining.[36] It is a process that owes less to formal structures, of British or other provenance, than to the way Jews have traditionally conducted their political life and to the circumstances under which the Israeli system developed.

In building our portrait of Israeli democracy, the first strand of our analysis will be Jewish traditions. It is important to know how Jews conducted their political life before the appearance of Zionism and Israel. As Jews are a people who live by their traditions, even when rebelling against them, it should not be surprising to find continuity between Jewish political experience in the autonomous communities of the Diaspora and Israeli politics of today. In both cases, Jews have conducted their politics as an exercise in vigorous bargaining among the major groups in society, striving to include as many elements of the community as possible and sharing power among them, with uneasy lines of authority and a confrontational style but also a saving sense of the need for unity. Jewish political traditions help to explain the consistency of this behavior and to understand many of the unusual features of the Israeli scene.

There is a paradox here, as one of the aims of Zionism was, as noted, to "escape" from Jewish history. But as in other spheres of life, the Zionist movement and the State of Israel found themselves responding "Jewishly" to the challenges they faced. Even in organizing to promote their revolution in Jewish life, Zionist pioneers were consciously or unconsciously drawing on familiar political practices and habits. In any event, it would be difficult to explain the vigor of Israeli democratic institutions without reference to the values that sustained Jewish life for centuries under trying conditions. The "Jewishness" of Israel helps to explain both the successes and the shortcomings of Israeli democracy.

To this foundation we must then add a second strand that is clearly crucial to the molding of Israeli life—so crucial that it has often been regarded as the central factor. This is the influence of secular ideology—the prevalent ideas of the time that impinged on the thinking and behavior of Israel's founders and that continue to shape intellectual life in the country. These ideas, largely of non-Jewish origin, served to reinforce the universalistic elements of Jewish life, reducing differences with other nations by channeling Jewish endeavors along the lines of Western liberalism, or various socialist models, or the rising tide of nationalistic ideologies (though nationalism was, of course, a double-edged sword in this regard). Much of this ideological force, as expressed in Labor Zionism, Revisionism, or other variants, represented at least on the surface a revolution against the Jewish past. And while most immigrants came not as rebels against tradition but as refugees who had never questioned those traditions, the society they entered was to some degree shaped by the ideas that had preceded them.

A third strand that will then be added to the analysis is the plain and simple force of objective conditions. The Jewish community in Palestine, and the State of Israel after it, evolved under the pressure of unique circumstances and historical traumas for which there is no exact parallel elsewhere. The realities "on the ground" (as the Hebrew phrase puts it) were often more immediate than either traditions or ideologies, and required uncontemplated adjustments. Building a new society where none had existed before would have been daunting enough, but one overwhelming concern dominated from the outset: the search for security. If refugees in the earlier period found themselves forced by physical threats to put security ahead of other concerns, the coincidence of the Holocaust and the war for independence made it into an obsession for those who came later. Some of these pressures made Israel more "a nation like other nations," while others served to accentuate the sense of isolation and the cult of self-reliance.

The final strand to be delineated is what, for want of a better term, is called modernization. Israeli society and politics have in recent decades been subjected to the forces of Westernization, technological change, the rise of mass politics and mass communications, and all the other intrusions of a shrinking world. While these forces ought to make Israel more like other nations, they also contribute to the decline of ideology, once the main driving force behind universalist aspirations. In this vacuum, particularistic impulses and traditions that had never been far from the surface can reassert themselves. And as the influence of classic Labor Zionist ideology and other ideologies waned, traditional political habits—protest, civil religiosity, extraparliamentary politics—reemerged more strongly.

The interweaving of these four threads, then, will tell the story of Israeli democracy and help us understand both its strengths and its weaknesses.

TWO

Jewish Politics

Is there continuity in Jewish political habits? Certainly political life in the shtetl, the nineteenth-century Jewish community in the towns and villages of Eastern Europe, had elements that would seem familiar to students of contemporary Jewish politics, either in Israel or elsewhere. A anthropological portrait of shtetl politics, drawn from contemporary sources including Yiddish literature of the period, could almost stand as an account of proceedings in the Knesset:

> The actual mechanics of election vary widely, but a constant feature is the campaigning inseparable from all elections, the forming of factions, the influencing of the humble members by the city bosses. . . . The meetings are not notable for parliamentary procedure. On the contrary, there is little order and more talking than listening. . . . Majority rule is followed but not accepted. The minority may concede momentary victory but the issue is not considered settled. . . . There is no blind following of a leader on the theory that he is right and we will support him whatever he says. On the contrary, the leader's dictum is always subject to analysis and criticism. "Every Jew has his own Shulhan Aruch," they say, meaning his own interpretation of the Law.[1]

Since this was the immediate political legacy of most of those who shaped the political institutions of Zionism and of Israel, a certain similarity should not be surprising. Political patterns that developed over centuries of experience in self-government could hardly fail to leave an imprint. This chapter seeks to identify the political traditions resulting from that experience, with special attention to the immediate milieu in which the Zionist movement developed. Following this, chapter 3 will record the impact of the external ideologies of the "Zionist revolution"—liberal, socialist, and nationalist—on the way Jews had habitually practiced their politics and trace the interaction of these forces, as further shaped by concrete historical circumstances, through the early Zionist movement and the pre-state Jewish community in Palestine (the *yishuv*).

One of the great contributions of twentieth-century Jewish historians has been to challenge the notions that Jews have no political history and that Jewish history is a lamentable chronicle of persecution, suffering, and powerlessness. The noted Jewish historian Salo Baron in 1928 attacked the "lachrymose" depiction of the Jewish past; an important recent study argues that Jews were not powerless but exhibited "a wide spectrum of persistent and ongoing political activism."[2] Ironically, the view that Jews were apolitical and powerless was shared both by Zionists—who saw it as the feature of Jewish life most in need of change—and by opponents of Zionism, who regarded Jewish noninvolvement with power as the unique mark of Jewish virtue.[3] Yet to survive two millennia of hostility required not only spiritual strength but also a capacity for organization and for the assertion of collective interests: in other words, a capacity for politics. As David Biale contends, "without some modicum of political strength and the ability to use it, the Jewish people would certainly have vanished."[4]

The Jewish experience in self-government over the centuries has actually been a rich one; Jews have often managed their own self-contained political system. "The Jewish people," it has been argued, "is most probably the only people which has realized the principle of personal autonomy in its life, creating in different countries under different political regimes certain forms of national autonomy and national organizations recognized in public law as state institutions"; more concretely, the Encyclopedia Judaica lists over 120 cases of Jewish autonomy, in various forms, over the ages.[5] Wherever Jews lived, they held in common not only the heritage of Jewish law and other normative Jewish institutions but also patterns that arose from their universal position as a beleaguered minority: contention with a hostile environment, provision of needs that could be met only within the community, self-organization to minimize the intervention of outside authorities, and maintenance of relations with those authorities. In some places and periods (such as Europe in the Middle Ages) it was inconceivable for a Jew to live as a Jew except as part of a Jewish community. Long before the modern concept of a nation had been devised, Jews had acquired many of the attributes that nationhood is said to entail, including a sense of community and a felt need for collective expression.[6] Thus, despite substantial differences in other respects, Jewish political experience in its varying historic contexts was both extensive and, in a general way, similar.

THE POLISH-RUSSIAN KAHAL

The long Jewish experience with political forms is reflected in a rich classic political terminology, much of which remains in use in modern Hebrew. Apart from an extensive vocabulary in legal and judicial matters—as would be expected given the Jewish focus on law—there are terms for such concepts as community, citizenship, authority, factions or parties, and various ranks of officialdom (such as *nasi*, the title used for the head of the Sanhedrin in ancient times and for the president of Israel today). Classical Jewish usage also included the equivalent of a separation of powers by dividing authority among the three "crowns": Torah, kingly (civil) authority, and the priesthood.[7] The covenantal idea, central to Judaism, also has important political implications, since it implies that legitimate authority derives from voluntary contractual arrangements. As some observers note, this has been the universal pattern of Jewish congregations and communities across different ages and cultures.[8] The development of the synagogue as a center of communal life had political connotations; the term itself (in Hebrew or in Greek) means simply "house of assembly," and synagogues evolved into "the focal institutions of an ethnic-religious group living outside its own land."[9] But the primary institution of Jewish political expression, as it developed over time, was the community itself: the *kehilla* or the *kahal*, as it came to be known.

The origins of the *kehilla* as an organized response to the realities of Jewish dispersion apparently lie, together with the origins of the synagogue, in the last days of the Second Temple period. But the classic period of the *kehilla* was from the eleventh to the twentieth centuries, especially in Europe. The functions carried out by the *kehilla* varied according to the circumstances, as did the ways in which authority was organized. Generally all adult Jewish males were regarded as members of the community, but forms of government varied from autocratic to fairly egalitarian, with variants of oligarchy or aristocratic republicanism as dominant modes.[10] As it functioned throughout the Middle Ages, the *kehilla* usually had an established court system (whose roots went back to talmudic precedents), with the threat of *herem* (excommunication, a severe measure in a period where Jewish life outside the community was unthinkable) as a primary means of enforcement. The community also levied taxes, or apportioned among its members the tax burden imposed on the community as a whole, and carried out a system of tithes to provide for the needy. According to the custom of *herem hayishuv*, community consent was required before a newcomer could settle there (the equivalent of immigration control). One custom of note, in some locations, was that a community member could interrupt prayers in order to secure a public hearing of grievances.[11]

Over time, the *kehilla* developed a law-making authority in addition to the judicial institutions. These man-made laws or *takanot* (distinguished from laws of divine origin) covered all areas of life, from commerce and family life to criminal acts, civil disputes, and even the regulation of clothing to be worn. Various bodies were chosen to legislate these matters, sometimes with the approval of rabbinical authorities, who also served as courts of appeal. At least one noted authority—Rabbi Gershom—called for majority rule in communal affairs, citing talmudic sources.[12] During the sixteenth to the eighteenth centuries, however, as the size and complexity of the *kehilla* grew, the structure became more formalized and more hierarchical, and authority was concentrated in the hands of a limited number of people. This was especially the case in Poland, increasingly the demographic center of the Jewish world, where a series of royal charters (1551, 1576, 1592) enlarged the prerogatives of community institutions and reinforced the authority of the existing officers and rabbis.[13]

The same period was also marked by the development of super-*kehilla* organizations tying the various communities together. Functioning mainly in Poland, Lithuania, Moravia, and western Hungary, such an organization (known sometimes as a *medina*, the term used in modern Hebrew for "state") was composed of representatives sent by the various local communities, and it sometimes elected its own executive officials. These bodies, the best known of which was the Council of the Four Lands, carried out fewer direct governmental functions than the *kehilla* itself but dealt with matters of common interest to all the Jewish communities, such as relations with governments and other external authorities.[14]

The classic *kehilla*, or *kahal* as it became known, that flourished in the Jewish towns and villages of Poland and Lithuania during the sixteenth to the nineteenth centuries had most of the aspects of a political system. Jewish communities elected both secular leaders and rabbis, levied taxes, maintained courts with varying types of sanctions, established extensive welfare systems, passed laws regulating extensively all aspects of life in the community, and appointed agents (*shtadlanim*) as "diplomats" to represent the community in its relations with external authority. A distinctive and persistent political tradition grew out of the normative institutions of Judaism as shaped by the peculiarities of Diaspora existence in its Eastern European variant.[15]

At the end of the eighteenth century most of this population was incorporated into tsarist Russia, which thus became the homeland of over half the world's Jews. This is also the historical context of most importance to the subsequent history of the Zionist movement and of Israel.[16]

The noted anthropologist Margaret Mead once remarked upon her surprise in discovering that Eastern European Jewry constituted a distinct cultural unit "which was essentially all of a piece whether they paid their taxes and marketed in Polish or Ukrainian or Hungarian or were ruled by Czar or Emperor."[17] What Russia had inherited from Poland was, in the words of Salo Baron, "a strong and all-embracing communal organization" whose activities included the regulation of wages and prices, the survey of weights and measures, control over land acquisitions, and even such minutiae as the performances and fees of musicians at weddings.[18] Even as this Jewish population passed under Russian rule, however, the *kahal* governance was under pressure from various quarters. The political disintegration and economic impoverishment of eighteenth-century Poland had weakened Jewish institutions, while external authorities increasingly interfered in internal Jewish matters. Symptomatic of the decline in self-governing institutions was the dissolution of the Council of the Four Lands in 1765.[19]

A more subtle threat to Jewish autonomy was the growth of the secularized civic state as a model of political and social organization. Following the Enlightenment and the French Revolution, the idea of government dealing directly and neutrally with citizens of equal rights and duties spread from west to east in Europe. In this universalist ethic, the importance of religion or other particular identities was supposedly diminished. The corporatist or communal features of medieval and early modern societies, into which Jews could fit collectively, were replaced in theory by a direct and unmediated relationship between individuals and their government. This presumably made it possible for Jews to be accepted fully as individual citizens in the states to which they belonged. But would they be able to achieve real equality without sacrificing their identity as Jews? While the Emancipation of the late eighteenth and early nineteenth centuries did offer new latitude to Jews as individuals, it also put them in a somewhat anomalous position. The old order, with all its disabilities, left little room for a Jewish identity crisis: unless they converted, Jews remained Jews and had little place outside their own community. But in the new civic state, could Jews be fully accepted also as Germans or Poles? The anomaly sharpened in the course of the nineteenth century as nationalism swept across Europe and became more particularistic, emerging—as we will see—as a central impetus in the rise of Zionism.

In the meantime, Jewish communities were being forced to surrender their civil functions to the state, sometimes as part of a process of democratization but sometimes not. Tsarist authorities sought to curtail Jewish autonomy, though primarily because of the instincts of absolutism rather than the influence of new conceptions of governance. The tsarist regime formally abolished the *kahal* in 1844, transferring its functions to existing municipal bodies (in which Jews were a minority). But clearly Jewish self-government continued to function unofficially, as demonstrated by the continuing efforts of the Russian government to suppress such activity. In 1870 the Council of State declared that Jewish communities were "a secluded religious and civil case, or one might say, a state within a state," and called for a commission "to consider ways and means to weaken the communal cohesion among the Jews"; subsequently the commission received a report that the Jews "possess complete self-government in their *kahals*. . . . "[20]

The 1844 decree left some openings for the continued operation of Jewish communal institutions. Synagogues chose rabbis and other religious officials, and they also continued to elect deputies for other specified tasks (such as welfare). In Polish areas, where most Jews lived, other autonomous institutions were allowed to continue. In most places, the Jewish community continued to take care of its own needs, whether clandestinely or openly, and Jews continued to refer to these arrangements as a *kahal* even though it had no legal standing. As one historian of the period concludes, "it was a badly mutilated body . . . but what was left was sufficient to construe it as an organ of Jewish self-government possessing within the small limits of its jurisdiction power of compulsion."[21] When new political ideologies and movements appeared, therefore, the *kahal* offered a strong tradition of Jewish self-governance as a point of departure. Jewish experience with autonomy could be used; it simply needed to be extended and democratized. As a leader of the Bund (Jewish socialists) declared, "no matter how the communal institutions are crippled, they are still the organs of Jewish self-government, and the road to our autonomy leads to them . . . autonomy is the same community, but better organized, more democratic and possessing increased powers."[22]

In addition, as Eli Lederhendler argues, the tsarist assault on the powers of the *kahal* contributed to the rise of "modern" Jewish politics by fragmenting and diffusing the concentration of power in the traditional community and by further increasing the pluralism and blurred lines of authority. Splits within the community, between competing religious movements and rabbinic courts, or between proponents of the "Jewish Enlightenment" and the traditional leadership, helped lay the groundwork by the end of the century for a Jewish politics based on popular support rather than on authority derived from the (Gentile) state.[23]

To summarize: before the emergence of Zionism, before the spread of Western liberal, socialist, and nationalist ideologies, Jewish communities throughout the Diaspora had long experience with voluntaristic and representative political institutions. In Eastern Europe, in particular, Jewish self-government had achieved a strong hold in communal life and consciousness. While in most respects not democratic by contemporary standards, it contained within itself the seeds for democratic growth. As Shlomo Avineri concludes, "it is in those myriads of Jewish communities, struggling to survive in a hostile environment, carving out for themselves their rules and regulations and developing their institutions, that we have the origins of Israeli democracy."[24]

THE ELEMENTS OF JEWISH POLITICS

What, exactly, were the habits of governance with which Jews met the new realities of the late nineteenth century?

The basic fact of Jewish politics was the very tenuousness of the framework within which politics were conducted. The scope of political activity and sometimes even the simple physical security of the Jewish community itself were subject to the sufferance of the larger community of which it was a part. In the past, even the basic right of residence had been subject to petition and negotiation with local rulers. At all times, the possibility of outside intervention in the community's internal affairs—sometimes as the result of the actions of "informants" from within the community itself—set limits to the extent and definitiveness of political activity.

Given their insecure status in societies where they comprised the most obviously different group, Jews needed to deal with outside and often hostile authorities over matters that others took for granted. Jewish history generated a psychology characterized by "the hypervigilance of the haunted, the alert scanning of the insecure, and the continuous suspiciousness of the vulnerable."[25] Jews learned to dread events over which they had no control and perfected great skill in detecting the potentially disastrous side of seemingly benign developments internally and externally. This "*gevalt* syndrome," or doomsday mentality, expresses as well as anything the deep-seated pessimism and anxiety rooted in the vicissitudes of Jewish history.

Historically, Jewish communities reacted to threat by closing off from the outside world, building the best possible barriers to maintain separation and minimize outside intervention. In the traditional mindset, the outside was seen as "totally strange and alien, the terrestrial manifestation of the *sitra ahara* or forces of evil."[26] Religious practices such as dietary laws, and the deep-seated Jewish aversion to intermarriage with non-Jews, are often seen as expressions of the felt need to maintain the clearest possible separation from the non-Jewish world. In time, survival as a people was linked in Jewish thinking to the minimizing of external ties; separation became synonymous with Jewish survival itself.

The other side of closure was the forging of a strong sense of shared fate, and a remarkable cohesion, within Jewish communities. The protective embrace of one's own group was the primary defense against a hostile environment. This engendered among Jews what has been described as a "familial," "kinship," or "clan" relationship. Amos Oz, the Israeli novelist, portrays it as a "tribal feeling" that "creates a perpetual intimate warmth which is sometimes necessary and comforting"; in Boas Evron's words, "the Jewish God reassumed the traits of a tribal deity."[27] This is related to what Baruch Kimmerling calls the "primordial" definition of Israeli collective identity, and with what Charles Liebman calls the "communitarian" conception of the state, in which individuals see themselves as members of a community, rather than the modern Western "civic" conception that sees the state as an impersonal entity with interests of its own.[28]

The strong tradition of separation was apparent in the attitude to state laws and courts. Jewish norms dictated compliance with non-Jewish law where it presented no problems (under the doctrine of *dina demalchuta dina*—the law of the kingdom is law), but Jewish laws and courts were considered to have a higher validity. There was therefore no compunction in evading state laws in case of conflict between the two, or when they posed other problems. Jews tried to keep their disputes within Jewish courts (which often operated more efficiently and equitably anyway) whenever possible. It was also considered honorable, for example, to hide young men, especially religious students, from military conscription.[29] Expediency in relations to the outside world was also expressed in the frequency of bribery as a common method of dealing with government officials (not that this put Jews apart, as such venality was common practice in such settings as tsarist Russia and the Ottoman Empire). As noted, special agents, or *shtadlanim,* were often delegated as diplomats of a sort to represent the community's interests in dealing with officialdom.

Part of the separation from the outside involved a strong presumption against revelations likely to damage the Jewish community. Habits of secrecy, and of intimate and confidential modes of operation, helped the *kahal* to survive in Russia after its abolition. Special contempt is reserved in tradition for the informer (or *malshin*) who reveals damaging information to outside authorities; Jewish law provides for the trial and punishment of those guilty of this threatening act. In some "informer's trials" in Poland recourse to outside authority was reserved in the classic *kahal* for community officials only, and this right was in a sense the defining attribute of their superior authority within that community.[31]

Whatever the attitude toward the outside, however, did Jewish traditions favor democracy within the community? As far as the sources of Jewish law are concerned, there is considerable debate. Some stress the voluntary nature of the Covenant, the requirements in talmudic law regarding public consent to appointments and regulations, and the traditional resistance to centralized authority. Shmuel Eisenstadt refers to "the basic 'democratic' or rather egalitarian premises of the Jewish tradition, premises of basic equality and of equal participation and access of all Jews to the centers of the sacred realm. . . . "[32]

Others argue that traditional Jewish concepts put religious particularism above man-made legislation and cannot be made to encompass universalistic Western liberal versions of democracy and human rights. While the religious mandate of a "higher law" has the virtue of denying the legitimacy of arbitrary authority, it also is "contrary to the people's political sovereignty upon which every liberal democracy is based."[33]

It is difficult, however, to point to a fully developed "Jewish political theory." Jewish theorizing is legalistic rather than speculative in style and is usually derived from the discussion of actual cases; it constitutes "a massive, finely reasoned, intricately articulated portrait of public life at the level of practice."[34] Taking this more sociological perspective, it appears that Jewish communities were indeed governed oligarchically by and large but with some strong populist elements such as institutional pluralism, the absence of central ecclesiastical authority, and (at least in late nineteenth-century Eastern Europe) the presence of competing elites.[35]

In this regard, the voluntary character of Jewish self-government was of decisive importance. The *kahal* was backed by state enforcement in some cases—mainly the collection of taxes—and was sometimes granted other means of compulsion such as the seizure of property or the imposition of fines. But these means were limited, especially by the late nineteenth century. The organized Jewish community could also impose a *herem,* or excommunication, which was a very serious sanction in the pre-Emancipation period when there was no Jewish life outside the community: "communal elders could still force a rebellious member to his knees by refusing him certain religious services, such as circumcision, rabbinical wedding, or the religious burial in consecrated ground."[36] Even suppression of the *kahal* in 1844 did not end the effectiveness of this measure completely. In the past *kahal* officers could also deliver a community member to the state authorities if his crimes warranted or could sanction other informal acts of coercion (as in the 1649 Moravian decree giving community members permission "to issue forth against [a wrongdoer] with all vigor, to deprive him utterly of his capital and his home"[37]).

But even at the peak of *kahal* powers, enforcement did not depend in the end on formal sanctions as much as on the reputation of the rabbis issuing decrees, on public opinion and pressure, and on shared values and interests such as offering no pretexts for outside intervention. This sufficed to maintain a modicum of public order, but it rested on a large measure of voluntary consent. The fact was that there was no obligatory final authority within the Jewish community.[38] And in the circumstances of tsarist Russia, by the late nineteenth century, active participation and cooperation was highly dependent on the good will of community members. In a very real sense, it was government by consent of the governed.

Since it was voluntary, Jewish self-government also had to be inclusive. Disgruntled groups and individuals were not at the mercy of the will of the majority; they could opt out of active participation in the community. Given the need for unity against a hostile environment, there was a strong incentive to give all groups in the community a stake in the system. It was understood that benefits must be broadly shared among all members of the community, even when this meant overcoming deep social, ideological, and religious divisions that would ordinarily make cooperation difficult. The principle of proportionality in power and benefits was widely understood and applied before the term itself came into use, as the only conceivable approach in a community or movement that lacked governmental powers.

The best expression of the "participatory mode" in Jewish politics was the regular conduct of elections, in times and places where electoral politics was unknown in the surrounding societies. In the classic *kahal,* both lay leaders and rabbis were chosen by a group of electors (*mevorerim*), who were in turn elected by all eligible voters. Elections were regarded as events of great importance and were vigorously contested. Eligibility to vote rested on the payment of taxes, sometimes at a specified level, but scholarship could be substituted for wealth in some cases. Elections to important positions were for fixed terms, thus upholding the accountability of those elected and providing for rotation in office.[39]

Issues of human rights were also the subject of considerable attention in Jewish law and in traditional governance. One important difference, however, is that individual rights in Jewish law are not stated as rights but are inferred from the duties that are imposed. Jewish law enumerates a large number of obligations and prohibitions, many of which clearly imply recognition of the rights of others who are protected thereby. For example, the commandment "thou shalt not kill" assumes the right to life and led ultimately to a severe circumscribing of the death penalty in Jewish law. Similarly, other commandments and rabbinical rulings clearly protect the right to liberty and security of person, the right to property, freedom of speech and of movement, and even social and cultural rights (in modern terminology) such as the right to work, the right to an education, and the right to rest and leisure (embodied in the institution of the Sabbath, which passed from Jewish law to the world at large). Jewish law is especially strong on legal and judicial safeguards, with provisions that match or surpass those in modern liberal democratic states: there is a presumption of innocence with provision for defense of the accused as well as interrogation of the accuser, and confessions are not admissible even if made voluntarily.[40]

Given its voluntaristic and inclusive nature Jewish politics was inevitably pluralistic. In the first place, the coexistence of an overarching external system and a sphere of communal politics guaranteed that there would be competing laws, jurisdictions, and authorities. Second, each community chose "secular" officials as well as a rabbinic leadership, and the lines of authority between the two were often unclear and thus the cause of controversy. Part of the problem was that the very distinction between "religious" and "secular" is a case of modern terminology being imposed retrospectively; the term "secular" would have made little sense in the classic *kahal,* and consequently the term "religious" had limited relevance as its opposite. Rabbis are now referred to as religious authorities because of their credentials in traditional Jewish law, but in the past they also dealt with what would be regarded today as civil matters, while the so-called lay leaders, or nonrabbinical officials, likewise dealt with religious as well as secular questions.

Further divisions within the Jewish communities came in the eighteenth and nineteenth centuries as a result of new spiritual and intellectual currents. First was the appearance of Hasidism, a movement of religious renewal and mysticism, which established yet another center of activity and authority within the *kahal*. Later came the Haskala, or Jewish Enlightenment, which served as a vehicle for Western liberal ideas and inspired new forms and organs of political activity. The Haskala, whose influence among Russian Jews peaked after the middle of the nineteenth century, did not fit easily into the old leadership or the old *kahal* order, which in any event was in flux. Haskala proponents (or *maskilim*) formed new institutions and organizations that were not part of the *kahal* nor directly under state authority either. They created, in fact, a "public space" where none had existed before.[41] It served as a bridge between traditional politics and the modern political movements that emerged shortly thereafter; many of the early Zionists had been raised in a Haskala atmosphere.

The pluralism of late nineteenth-century Jewish life, in the Russian setting, was striking. Groups of all types proliferated: artisan guilds, mutual aid societies, cultural associations, political parties, educational groups, savings and loan associations, defense organizations, charitable associations, burial societies, and workers' groups. In the late tsarist period, according to one estimate, each Jewish community had on the average some twenty different associations, while the large city of Vilna, in 1916, had a total of 160.[42]

The presence of so many groups, many of them carrying out quasi-governmental functions, served to increase the diffusion of power and further blur the lines of authority. Essential unity was preserved through mutual recognition and accommodation and by an underlying understanding that the legitimacy of these divisions rested on the adherence of all to community norms and interests. But as a result formal structure deviated from the informal bargaining by which governmental functions were actually exercised. The existence of different centers of power also helped legitimize opposition; even rabbinical decisions could be impeached, since there were competing authorities who could be invoked against each other.[43]

The style of politics under such conditions is likely to be, and indeed was, contentious. As Avineri has pointed out, earlier habits help to explain not only the origins of Israeli democracy but also "some of the lack of elegance which accompanies it. . . . the Israeli Knesset sometimes resembles an unruly synagogue meeting more than the serene atmosphere of Westminster."[44] The tradition of opposition to power, or basic disrespect to authority, goes beyond matters of parliamentary procedure, however. Sam Lehman-Wilzig, in a study of Jewish "oppositionism," finds in the Bible more than fifty cases of resistance to authority; the Prophets existed as embodiments of protest, and nothing expresses the argumentative spirit better than the structure and content of the Talmud (where opposing viewpoints are both termed "words of the Living God.")[45] As noted, disobedience to temporal law is mandated when it conflicts with divine ordinances. Jewish law also put clear limits on majority rule, providing that the minority must be heard and even institutionalizing the role of dissent; it had a tendency toward "principled political anarchism."[46] The pluralism of institutions, plus a prevailing suspicion of all centralized power, gave rise to an attitude of expediency toward authority within the community as well as toward that outside.

As the excerpt at the beginning of this chapter indicates, leaders in the traditional shtetl were always subject to challenge, and no authority was final: "Every Jew has his own Shulhan Aruch." The informal arrangements, often more critical than the formal hierarchy, were also based more on personal relationships and mutual help—thus the importance of *protektsia* (connections), a term still central to modern Israeli life.

Furthermore, while the stress on law and the quality of legal institutions was always one of the hallmarks of Jewish life, the lack of clear jurisdictional lines encouraged evasion of the law. The laws of the state were considered inferior to Jewish law and were submitted to only out of necessity; whenever possible they were avoided. These attitudes carried over within the community, where the letter of the law was regarded as less than decisive, where lines of authority blurred, and where personal arrangements operated alongside formal procedures as a parallel method of handling relations between the individual and the state. This has been defined by Ehud Sprinzak as a pattern of "illegalism," or of expediency toward the law, growing out of the realities of ghetto life in Eastern Europe as reinforced by the "baksheesh" (bribery) culture of the Ottoman Empire and the "naive socialism" of the early Zionists.[47]

The communitarian frame of mind and the lack of a history of statecraft on the highest level contribute to what many observers have identified as a lack of state (or civic) consciousness among Jews, both before and after the actual achievement of statehood. The habits of discipline and sense of public duties, developed elsewhere through long endurance of authoritarian rule, are underdeveloped among the Jewish people (a curious instance in which the lack of autocratic precedents can be regarded as a deficiency). In certain respects, therefore, Jews were not well prepared for the task of state-building.[48]

A softening element in this contentious struggle, though, was a strong tradition of social justice and charity in Jewish life. The care of the poor, the disabled, and the elderly was considered to be a duty of the entire community. A number of institutions of long standing handled a variety of social services from birth to burial. In some ways, these services covered a broader range than the public services in most modern societies, laying the basis for a welfare state before such existed, as well as constituting a fertile ground for the socialist ideas that became current. A "collectivistic" or "cooperative" model of social organization had very strong roots in the Jewish tradition.[49] Like other aspects of Jewish communal politics, the philanthropic and charitable element, though essentially voluntary, was backed by a strong sense of obligation and by serious community pressure. At times, the charitable societies were "strong enough to defy the very *kahal*," and thus they offered additional checks and balances within the Jewish community.[50]

A final, and perhaps crucial, feature of traditional Jewish politics was that it seldom dealt with non-Jews within the community. Jewish law and Jewish politics within the community applied only to Jews. Relations between Jews and non-Jews were under the jurisdiction of the state and governed by non-Jewish law, but within the community Jewish law prevailed. Furthermore, this Jewish law was in many respects highly particularistic. Jacob Katz notes how surprised many Jews were to be reminded by the "scientific" antisemites, in the 1880s, of the discriminatory elements in Jewish tradition: "Even learned Jews sincerely maintained that Judaism had always taught universalistic ethics only."[51]

Jewish law in fact clearly distinguished Jewish rights from general human rights, as a consequence of the fact (noted above) that rights, in Jewish law, are inferred from obligations. Non-Jews have fewer obligations than Jews, basically the seven commandments of Noah, and thus they also have correspondingly fewer rights inferred from these obligations. Specifically, this means the rights to life and property, and security from injustice, lawlessness, and bloodshed.[52] There were, to be sure, numerous biblical injunctions regarding the humane treatment of foreigners: "Thou shalt neither vex a stranger, or oppress him: for you were strangers in the land of Egypt" (Exodus 22:20); "One law and one code shall there be for you, and for the stranger that sojourns with you" (Numbers 15:16). Injunctions in the Talmud also invoke the principles of "the interests of peace" and "avoidance of ill feelings" as grounds for kindness toward non-Jews, even if this involved a breaking of Jewish laws.[53] But talmudic law, by distinguishing among resident aliens between the *ger tsedek* (who has converted to Judaism) and the *ger toshav* (who has not), limits the demands of strict equality to the former. The *ger toshav*, on the other hand, is subject to a number of disabilities: they may not act as agent for a Jew, they are generally disqualified as a witness in civil matters, and even their right of refuge is circumscribed. According to Maimonides, no non-Jew (a category he extends to include converts "even after many generations") may be put in any position of power (*serara*) within the Jewish community.[54]

The essence of Jewish law toward "strangers" was, therefore, humanity; the idea of civic equality of Jews and non-Jews in a Jewish society was as unthinkable as the idea of equal status for Jews in non-Jewish society was at that time. Furthermore, the injunction of humane treatment was geared solely to the individual, not to non-Jewish groups who might claim recognition of their collective identity. Recognition of the rights of individual aliens to humane treatment did not provide for any collective legal or political expression of non-Jewish identity, and the matter was never seriously tested under Diaspora conditions. There the Jewish law of the *ger toshav* was adequate to deal with those non-Jews who chose to live, as individuals, in a Jewish community. Jewish communities never had under their jurisdiction large non-Jewish populations seeking to maintain their own collective identity, and thus Jewish political traditions were singularly unequipped to deal with such a situation. These traditions were not racist in the modern sense; they simply had nothing to say about minorities as such.

One should recall that the idea of a dual system of law and governance was normal in the period before the idea of a civic state, neutral on matters of ethnicity, religion, and nationality, became well established. As Katz says, "The concept of a uniform code of law, regulating human affairs regardless of race and creed, never entered the picture. The double legal and moral standard was not merely a mental reservation but was the accepted practice in all sections of society. The respective Jewish and non-Jewish sections of society were governed by their own mutually exclusive laws."[55]

Jewish law also meshed with social reality; while litigation among Jews was normally handled within the community, matters involving Jews and non-Jews were handled by the non-Jewish (state) courts and authorities. The idea that such distinctions were in their very nature invidious or illegitimate had not yet taken root on either side.

In summary, Jewish history, especially in Eastern Europe but also elsewhere, included a striking exposure to a certain kind of political experience. The main elements of this experience were as follows: (1) struggle for survival on both community and individual levels in a hostile environment; (2) self-regulation through well-developed legal and judicial institutions, and the development of legislative mechanisms as well;(3) processes for selecting the community's own leadership, with at least some input from the larger public; (4) provision of a broad range of community services without reliance on the outside; (5) a resulting tendency to a collectivist or cooperative model of social organization: (6) enforcement without recourse, in most cases, to the most direct forms of coercion; and (7) typically, a gap between the formal structure of power and the actual influence patterns within the community.

Though not "democratic" by modern standards, these governing practices did provide a foundation for the growth of democratic institutions. They did this by providing modes of participation that reflected the essentially voluntary nature of community membership, by fostering (before the appearance of modern liberal political theory) an attitude of skepticism toward all authority, and by developing a body of law that de facto mandated important basic human rights. Though Jewish tradition, like all traditions, was basically the legacy of a particular people, it incorporated a number of elements that would eventually be regarded as having universal validity as part of modern democratic theory.

Clearly Jewish political traditions strongly inclined toward consociational, rather than majoritarian, democracy (see chapter 1). Competition between different centers of authority, the lack of defined hierarchy, proliferation and influence of organized groups, and the reality of bargaining and power-sharing, rather than the undiluted rule of the majority, marked Jewish political experience. By the late nineteenth century, moreover, the Eastern European Jewish community was divided into a multidimensional political and social system, with splits along socioeconomic, religious, and ideological lines as well as among traditional elites. Even before theorists had identified the essence of consensus or consociational democracy, Jewish communities exemplified many of its characteristic patterns.

Traditional Jewish politics also illustrated the primordial or communitarian conception of a political body, more than the civic conception of an ethnically neutral state. Jewish experience put a premium on solidarity, on group cohesion, rather than on abstract notions of political relationships. This was entirely predictable for a people whose identity as a nation had been strongly forged by circumstances even before modern nationalism had given a name to such forms of group identity.

However, traditional Jewish politics also contained serious sources of weakness, in terms of democratic potential. One was the long habit of secrecy, of concealment and closing off from the outside. A second was the absence of civic habits as they developed elsewhere, as well as the development of an attitude of expediency toward the law. Tied to this was a contentious and even unruly style of politics; sometimes even the basic element of simple civility seemed lacking in public life. But perhaps the most glaring weakness of traditional Jewish politics derived from the very strength of its sense of community; there was little guidance or experience in encompassing groups who were not a part of this community.

THREE

The Zionist Revolution

Whatever the weight of tradition, the fact remains that Israel, more than almost any other state, is the result of an idea imposed on reality. Most nations represent an evolution of geographic and ethnic circumstances. But—like the United States in certain respects—Israel would not have come into existence without the strength of beliefs that moved their adherents to create new political realities.

Just as the ideas of the American Revolution must be understood in the context of the republicanism and rationalism of the late eighteenth-century Enlightenment, so political Zionism—the drive to normalize the status of the Jewish people by achieving political sovereignty—reflected late nineteenth-century European ideologies of nationalism, socialism, and liberal democracy. Of course the aim of returning to Zion had always been central to Jewish thought and ritual, affirmed in daily prayer and by the continuing presence in Palestine of a small Jewish community. But it was the ideological ferment of nineteenth-century Europe that transformed what had been a vague religious aspiration into a largely secularized political movement with an active program for Jewish settlement and sovereignty in Palestine. The Zionist revolution was to affirm a secular self-identity as a nation along with, or even in place of, traditional religious and communal self-identity.

The center of the Jewish world at the time was tsarist Russia, which then included the Baltic states and Poland. In the early 1880s some four million Jews—well over half of world Jewry—lived under tsarist rule.[1] From the time of the assassination of Tsar Alexander II in 1881, this population was subjected to a wave of officially inspired persecution that was part of the regime's response to the impact of revolutionary and nationalistic ideas within Russia.

The historic Jewish response to such repression was flight to more hospitable locales, and there was little difference this time. Between 1881 and 1914 about two and a half million Jews left Russia, most of them for the United States and other Western countries. But a small number, roughly 3 percent, chose to return to the ancient homeland instead.

Why did this tiny proportion choose such a novel response to such an age-old problem? Antisemitism was a major thread of Jewish history, but it had never sparked a significant movement for a return to *Eretz Yisrael* (the Land of Israel, as geographic Palestine was known in Hebrew). Zion had always appeared more bleak and inhospitable than the alternatives, and this was no less true in the declining years of Turkish rule there. Furthermore, the previous century had been the century of Emancipation: ghetto walls were torn down across Europe as secularization removed ancient barriers to Jewish participation in public life. Why, in such an improving climate, should a part of the Jewish community suddenly reject patterns of minority existence that had persisted for two millennia?

One reason was that Emancipation posed new dilemmas to which traditional solutions were irrelevant.[2] In a society sharply divided along religious lines, Jews suffered many disabilities, but the very sharpness of the division left them with a clear sense of their own identity. When nationality replaced religion as the main point of reference, Jews were in a more problematic position. The relationship of Judaism to Christianity was clear, but the identity of Jews as Frenchmen, Germans, or Russians was ambiguous. Presumably the path to integration was open, but could it ever be totally successful? And would such success mean the complete loss of any meaningful identity as Jews? The problem was particularly acute in Eastern Europe; while there was some room in the Western European conception for a citizenship defined simply by membership in a common state, the exclusive identification of a state with a single nationality was much stronger in Eastern Europe.

One possible response was, nevertheless, total assimilation, and a large part of the Jewish community chose this path. Another answer was to embrace an ideology that denied ethnicity itself. Thus the appeal, to large numbers of Jews, of revolutionary socialist doctrines that put class interests above national and ethnic divisions or of Western liberal democratic ideals that put all individuals on a setting of civic equality.

Others responded, however, by embracing the idea of nationality and extending it to include the Jewish people. In an age when Greeks, Italians, Serbs, Romanians, and Albanians were rediscovering their own national identities, it should be no surprise that Jews reacted with a reaffirmation of *their* identity. By virtue of their 3,500-year history as a people, with distinctive cultural patterns, languages, religion, and a strong self-identity enforced by external hostility—by any test, in fact, but that of geographic concentration—most Jews felt their claim to recognition as a nation was as valid as that of other emerging nationalities of the period.

Jews thus sought answers to new external realities in new ideologies, which were also of external origin. What were these ideologies, and why were Jews so susceptible to their influence at this point in their history?

THE IMPACT OF IDEOLOGY:
NATIONALISM, SOCIALISM, LIBERALISM

Nationalism is the main thrust of political Zionism; however Zionists differed in other respects, the common core was application of the principle of the nation-state to the Jewish people. Where it clashed with other ideologies "the fact is undeniable that both emotionally and practically nationalism prevailed."[3] Nationalism was of course one of the great forces of the time, and by the end of the nineteenth century it was generally accepted in the Western world that political sovereignty should correspond to ethnic ("national") divisions; that is, that the nation-state, rather than the dynastic state or the multinational empire, should be the basic unit of world politics. This principle was to achieve its climactic vindication, at least in theory, in the results of World War I. That Jews should also choose the nation-state as the best vehicle of national survival should not be surprising, therefore. David Biale remarks that Jews "have always demonstrated a shrewd understanding of the political forms of each age," and that adopting modern nationalism was therefore not essentially different from the "tradition of political imitation and accommodation" that was a legacy of Jewish history.[4]

In choosing nationalism as a framework, Jews were moving from a more particularistic, if not unique, place in the world to a more universal and common model. With their own nation-state, Jews would join a world community of kindred peoples, each exercising its right of self-determination in its own sovereign space. Even in this liberal and moderate version of nationalism, of course, there is some ambiguity, since one is universalizing a principle of particularism: the right of each people to its particular identity, its particular character, and its particular political choices. If this is taken to imply the goal of homogeneity within a nation, then the position of minorities (such as the Jews) does become problematic. But as long as each nation respects the reciprocal claims of other nations to their own self-determination, then in theory the nation-state could be universalized as the basis of a stable world order. We tend to forget that in the mid-nineteenth century—the period of the unification of Italy and Germany—nationalism was a liberal principle allied to the struggle for democracy and self-determination for all peoples.

By the time Zionism emerged, however, nationalism was slipping from this liberal and universalizable form to more particularistic expressions. Far from accommodating the rights of other peoples on an equal basis, this more assertive nationalism focused on the presumed virtues or rights of a particular people. Taken to the extreme (with Italy and Germany again as illustrations), in its twentieth-century manifestations it preached not only racial or ethnic homogeneity but also denial of self-determination to others.

Historically, Zionism was an emulation of the first nationalism and a defense against the excesses of the second. In its earlier guise, liberal nationalism in league with democratization had indeed improved the situation of Jews throughout Europe. But in its later manifestation as "exclusive" nationalism, the position of Jews in new nation-states became increasingly precarious. The drive for a Jewish state therefore had behind it both a powerful positive pull, in the desire for Jewish self-determination and self-expression, and a strong negative push, in the simple need for escape from this second strain of nationalism.

Exclusive nationalism gave rise to a new and more vicious ethnic anti-semitism, which for many nullified assimilation as a solution to the problematic position of Jews. When religion was the criterion, Jews at least had the option of conversion. But one could not convert to a new ancestry; consequently even the most thoroughly assimilated Jews were not totally accepted in the new hypernationalist European societies. This was driven home by events like the Dreyfus trial—in liberal France yet—where a Jewish army officer, totally French in culture and loyalty, was falsely convicted of treason in a conspiracy involving the high military command. The final proof, some decades later, was the fate of German Jews, perhaps the most assimilated community in Europe. Many early Zionists, including Theodor Herzl himself, began as assimilationists but became convinced by events that integration would not end the persecution of Jews as a minority. Thus the achievement of political sovereignty was seen not only as an inherent right but also as a necessary response to the position of Jews as an exposed minority in Europe and elsewhere.

Eventually some within the Zionist movement also moved from the first form of nationalism to a more assertive and particularistic version. Like their counterparts in Europe, the "nationalist right" among Zionists asserted the exclusive right of the Jewish people to all of Eretz Yisrael, condemned any "compromise" of this right, and stressed the values of order, discipline, and authority above individual rights and democracy.[5] Organized as the Revisionist movement in the 1920s, under the leadership of Vladimir Ze'ev Jabotinsky, this viewpoint was taken to extremes by others (some even copied elements of European fascism at its peak in the 1930s). Revisionists sought to realize their goals through a political-military strategy, rather than by the slow buildup of a Jewish presence through grassroots settlement activity—Zionism from the top rather than from the bottom.

If nationalism was an ideology with both universalist and particularist potential, the role of socialism should be less ambiguous. Based on a materialist and "objective" view of history, socialism presumes to transcend national differences and provide a class-based analysis of universal applicability. It must be noted at the outset, however, that socialism appealed to Jews in part because of clear points of convergence with Jewish traditions. Among the compatible elements were emphasis on collective identity and interest, concern with social justice, a conception of ultimate deliverance (messianism), perception of a basically hostile environment, and justification of revolt against established authority. The case should not be overstated; clearly other elements in socialism were foreign to Jewish thinking: the primacy of economic factors, historical determinism, the cosmopolitan focus on class rather than nation, the denigration of religion, the argument for centralizing power, and belief in impersonal forces (rather than personal connections). But still many Jews saw secular socialism as "old wine in new bottles," and some non-Zionist Jewish socialists saw the revival of traditional Jewish autonomy (the *kahal*) as a logical means of achieving their ends.[6]

The Haskala had also prepared the ground for socialism by exposing many Eastern European Jews to major currents of Western thought and secularizing their outlook. Changes in Russia also had a major impact: education had advanced sufficiently to create an intellectual class (of both Russians and Jews), but opportunities for integration into the system were blocked. This creation of an alienated group of "rootless intellectuals" is the classic recipe for producing professional revolutionaries, and nineteenth-century Russia is a classic example. And since Jewish intellectuals were even more marginal than their Russian counterparts, they were also heavily overrepresented in this "school of dissent."[7]

The structure of Jewish life also enhanced the appeal of Marxist socialism, in particular. By the late nineteenth century, the Jewish population of Eastern Europe had to a great extent been urbanized, pauperized, and proletarianized (with perhaps 40 percent of Jewish workers, by one estimate, employed as cheap industrial labor). This came on top of a strong resentment of the rich by the poor in the traditional *kahal,* which had earlier been an ingredient in the appearance of Hasidism as a movement. The convergence of all these circumstances created a state of ferment "that stamped the tradition of radicalism irrefragably upon the souls of untold thousands of Russian-Jewish young people."[8]

The first wave of Jewish socialists were indeed universalistic in outlook; they rejected specifically Jewish concerns and outlooks in the belief that all problems would be solved by eliminating class-based oppression. As one orator proclaimed in 1892: "We Jews repudiate all our national holidays and fantasies which are useless for human society. We link ourselves up with armies of Socialism and adopt their holidays."[9] The Jewish participants in the Vai Narod (Movement to the People) tried to take the case for socialism to the Russian peasantry, with even less success than their Russian comrades. Jewish socialists turned to their fellow Jews, in the end, largely for tactical rather than ideological reasons: it was only among Jews that they had any success. But their program still had no Jewish content; when it was decided to establish Jewish agricultural colonies, there was no inclination to favor Palestine over other locations, and colonists were sent to South Dakota, Louisiana, and Oregon.[10] With the establishment of the Bund a brand of Jewish socialism was devised, but along non-Zionist lines. The Bund sought to achieve Jewish autonomy in existing places of residence, largely through the revival and democratization of the classic *kahal*.

The next step beyond the program of the Bund, combining socialism with full-blown Jewish nationalism, had actually been taken earlier by one of the founding figures of socialism. Moses Hess, a German Jew and collaborator with Karl Marx, in 1862 published *Rome and Jerusalem,* calling for the establishment of a Jewish socialist commonwealth in Palestine. The idea attracted no support at the time but was picked up and elaborated fifteen years later by Aaron Liberman, a Russian Jew, who adapted it to Russian circumstances. Then in 1898, only two years after Herzl published *Der Judenstaat,* Nachman Syrkin published an influential pamphlet that approached Zionism systematically from a socialist context. The final synthesis of Marxism and Zionism was carried out by Ber Borochov, whose first important writing appeared in 1905.[11]

Even then, Zionistically inclined socialists did not rush to embrace Jewish nationalism wholeheartedly. The strongest group in early Labor Zionism, the Zionist Socialists, were actually supporters of "territorialism," the idea that a Jewish state could and should be built in any suitable location. Fixation on the historical attachment to Palestine was, in their eyes, romantic nationalism. The important justification for building a new state was to correct what was considered to be the abnormal, distorted structure of Jewish society, and this could be done in any territory in which Jews were free to build their own "normal" society.

Whether attached to Palestine or not, Labor Zionists all shared this preoccupation with the total restructuring of Jewish life. Labor Zionism targeted the "unnatural" economic role that had been forced on Jews in the Diaspora. It urged Jews to move out of such accustomed trades as commerce, finance, and the professions, and to create a Jewish proletariat based on manual labor, a return to the soil, and self-reliance in all spheres of production. In contrast to most other nationalisms, Labor Zionism strongly stressed self-transformation as well as the achievement of external political aims. In the words of the Zionist slogan, Jewish pioneers came to Eretz Yisrael "in order to build and to be built in it." The establishment of the kibbutz, or rural communal settlement, was a perfect expression of these ideals.[12]

Labor Zionism represented a clear break with the Jewish past and a clear call for a program that would make the Jewish people "a nation like other nations." And while its success may have rested in part on its compatibility with some Jewish traditions, it also contributed important novel elements to the Zionist enterprise. The socialist method of building "from the bottom up," by the slow and patient construction of settlements designed to restructure Jewish life, became the dominant model in the Zionist self-image (even though most settlers came to cities, hardly a novel departure). Socialist ideology provided the rationale—and the manpower—for the mobilization of human resources under prevailing conditions, without waiting for deliverance by the powers-that-be.[13] But perhaps most importantly, socialism (like nationalism to a lesser degree) put Jewish politics into a conceptual framework and vocabulary of general relevance. It helped to provide the link to secular, Western ideas and influences by which its own progress could be guided and judged.

The direct influence of Western liberalism, as opposed to Eastern European socialism, was more attenuated but still a factor. Even in tsarist Russia, Lockean ideals of limited government and individual rights were not unknown (if socialism could penetrate the walls of absolutism, so could other ideas). The concepts of democracy, if not its practice, had by this time acquired general currency. The early Zionist leaders from Central Europe lived in an intellectual milieu where liberalism was prevalent. A number of "Western" Jews (including, by virtue of his long residence in England, Chaim Weizmann) occupied important posts over the years in the Zionist movement. The British and U.S. branches of that movement were important and vocal in supporting their own political ideals. Finally, the British government presided for thirty years over the development of the Jewish national home, as the Mandatory power.[14]

While some Western conceptions of unfettered individualism and uncompromising secularism ran against the grain of nationalist, socialist, or religious influences, democratic ideas were also reinforced—it should be recalled—by both traditions and circumstances. Even when democracy was not practiced as a matter of intellectual conviction, some sharing of power had often been necessary because of the voluntary basis of Jewish self-governance.

Western liberalism has been especially visible in two areas. First is the legal and judicial system with its strong borrowings from British and other Western sources.[15] Second is the economic sphere, where the opponents of socialism (organized historically as the General Zionists) adopted liberal economic doctrines as a platform. The General Zionists originally were simply those Zionists who were not socialist, religious, or revisionist; they occupied a centrist position by virtue of their opposition to both left and right. When they were organized as a party, in the 1930s, a large influx of immigrants from Central Europe reinforced the party's liberal image. General Zionists became the movement most clearly identified with Western liberalism, especially in economic policy but also to some extent in political matters.

The fourth strand of the Zionist movement, after Labor, Revisionist, and General Zionists, was religious Zionism. Religious Zionists accepted the aim of rebuilding a Jewish state in Palestine but sought to do so in strict accordance with traditional Jewish law. Clearly this was the least revolutionary and least universalistic version of Zionism; it remained a small minority within the Zionist movement and, for a considerable period, within the Jewish Orthodox community as well. Perhaps nothing else indicates as well how Zionism was seen as a revolutionary threat to traditional values and hierarchies in the Jewish world. In the eyes of rabbinical authorities, the Zionist movement was regarded as a secular nationalist movement that threatened traditional Judaism. They correctly associated it with the secularizing Haskala movement, which had posed the same threat, and which they had also opposed. The vast majority of them "knew danger when they saw it" and took a hard anti-Zionist line.[16] This left only a small number in the religious Zionist camp—the forerunners of today's National Religious Party—who were able, in the early days of Zionism, to reconcile its basically secular and revolutionary ideological thrust with religious Orthodoxy.

ZIONISM: CHANGE AND CONTINUITY

The conflict between change and continuity was basic to Zionism, which might be described as a set of ideologies laid over a substratum of habits and traditions. These ideologies conflicted, in varying degrees, with the traditions. But whether subscribing to nationalist, socialist, or liberal ideologies—or, like Labor Zionists, to some combination of these—Jews of Central and Eastern Europe in the late nineteenth century were indeed, in large numbers, seeking a break with the past. They filled the ranks of non-Jewish revolutionary movements in disproportionate numbers, and those who rallied to the Zionist call also saw themselves as being in "revolt" against past patterns of Jewish history. Zionists sought to escape from the particularism of the Jewish past and to rejoin history by recasting Jewish life into new universal molds provided by modern ideology. In David Vital's apt phrase, they wished "to extricate the Jews from a rhythm of national history such that the quality of their life at all levels was determined in the first instance by the treatment meted out to them by others. . . . to cease to be object and become subject." They felt that "the course of Jewish history must be reversed"; the significance of Zionism was nothing less than "the re-entry of the Jewish people into the world political arena."[17]

Traditional Jewish life was seen (with some exaggeration) as politically impotent, as a manifestation of weakness inseparable from the condition of exile. In some cases, the dissociation with the Jewish past reached extreme proportions. Herzl himself largely accepted the antisemitic portrait of Jews as avaricious, unprincipled, parasitic, and vulgar, while arguing that it was Christian oppression that had so deformed the Jewish character.[18] In one of the well-known stories of Yosef Haim Brenner, a leading literary figure of early Labor Zionism, the protagonist attacks the particularities of Jewish life in harsh language: "With a burning and passionate pleasure I would blot out from the prayer book of the Jews of our day 'Thou has chosen us' in every shape and form."[19] The basic logic of this orientation is best demonstrated, perhaps, by those who took it to the very limit. The Canaanite movement, active in the *yishuv* during the 1940s, rejected any connection with Jews or Judaism and sought to assimilate with the indigenous Arabs as a new Hebrew nation. On the other hand, one of the most common themes of Israeli literature has been an attack on Zionism for having detached Jews from their roots; a well-known example is Yudkeh's long and anguished sermon against Zionism's failings in the famous short story by Haim Hazaz.[20]

Yet despite the endeavors of its disciples and the allegations of its enemies, Zionism was never wholly at odds with tradition. For one thing, Zionism was itself a reaction against the claim that the spread of modern Western ideologies would solve the Jewish problem. Zionism could even be seen as a repudiation of the civic liberal ideal; it "appeared as a criticism of the Jewish problem based on civic emancipation alone; and it was an effort to reestablish continuity with those traditional conceptions of the nature and goal of Jewish history that had been discarded by Jewish disciples of the Enlightenment."[21] One traditional conception of Jewish history with which Zionism was closely associated was messianism. Zionism was in a sense a transformed messianism, drawing its strength from age-old aspirations deep in the Jewish spirit; even a socialist such as Nachman Syrkin could proclaim that "the messianic hope, which was always the greatest dream of exiled Jewry, will be transformed by political action. . . . Israel will once again become the chosen people of the peoples."[22]

Furthermore, while Herzl and some of the more Westernized Zionists may have had little feel or regard for Jewish tradition, their followers in Eastern Europe were closer to it. They did not reject the past outright but combed it for what might be useful in building the future; "continuity was crucial: the Jewish society at which they aimed . . . had to contain within it the major elements of the Jewish heritage."[23] The past was invoked and reinterpreted in order to restore Jewish dignity (as in the cults of the Maccabees, Masada, or Bar-Kochba); precedents for "new" Zionist departures were sought in the historical sources. The relationship to history might be selective, and there was a marked tendency to revere antiquity while reviling Diaspora life, but on the whole few Zionists rejected all connection with

Jewish history. As the leading study of the subject concludes, "between the two poles of continuity and rejection, Zionism established itself on a broad common base best described as dialectical continuity with the past."[24]

It was unrealistic to believe that a Jewish state could be established without reference to four millennia of Jewish history. Tradition supplied Zion itself as the focus of Zionism; even for the most secular of Jews, only Palestine had the power to mobilize the imagination of would-be settlers. Holidays and national symbols were inevitably drawn from the past, even if attempts were made to alter their content and significance. The very legitimacy of the entire enterprise rested, in the end, on Jewish history and religion, a factor that grew in importance as conflict with the Arab population developed. And if this was the case for the secular Eastern European Zionists who settled in Palestine during the early days, it was that much more the case for religious and non-European Jews who were already settled there, or who came later; among these populations, the primordial tie to Judaism was strong and the impact of revolutionary ideologies, including the model of the civic state, was very faint.

The "dialectical continuity" with the past was often obscured by the rhetoric of revolution and universalism. But even Herzl himself was capable of relapsing "into the set and mode of thought in which particularity and specificity are celebrated as a matter of course" (with the dialectical process also reflected in Herzl's depiction of his utopian state of the future as an "old-new" land).[25] Cultural Zionists, following Ahad Ha'am, also sought to revolutionize Jewish life, but by drawing explicitly on Jewish sources of spiritual renewal and thus founding "not merely a state of Jews but truly a Jewish state."[26] Even the most radical Zionist revolutionaries demonstrated links to tradition in subtle ways: in focusing on a redemptive process (albeit a secular one), in showing little interest in political programs not centered on Jewish interests, and in their "mildness" as revolutionaries in the Jewish context (where the emphasis was on building rather than destroying).[27]

The revolutionary content of Zionism was further attenuated in the new settlements of Eretz Yisrael, where ideology struggled not only with the habits and traditions that new immigrants brought with them but also with new realities about which doctrine was ambivalent or even irrelevant. Indeed, the very fact of Jewish settlement in Palestine was more a product of circumstance than of ideological appeal. As Jacob Katz notes, the aim of uprooting a people and replanting them elsewhere "was beyond the strength of the National idea in itself."[28] It took place only when persecutions and pogroms in Eastern Europe accomplished the uprooting. Even then, very little of the "replanting" was shaped by the national idea; of the two and a half million Jews forced out of Russia between 1880 and 1914, only about 70,000 arrived in Palestine, and many of these did not remain.

This process of self-selection had crucial implications. So long as other destinations were available to the vast majority of uprooted Jews who were not devout Zionists, then the new *yishuv* would represent a high concentration of the most ideologically committed. Thus the more revolutionary elements of the Jewish intelligentsia were able to establish the conceptual and institutional framework that prevailed for decades and absorbed later mass immigrations of nonideologized Jews who arrived simply because they had nowhere else to go.

EARLY ZIONIST INSTITUTIONS

Settlers of the first *aliya,* or wave of Jewish immigration to Palestine,[29] in the period from 1881 to 1905, were imperfect rebels against Jewish tradition. Untouched as yet by the secularism of the second and third *aliyot,* these members of Hibbat Zion (Love of Zion) build synagogues in their settlements and consulted the rabbinate on matters of Jewish law. In designing their governing institutions, they also drew on political legacies they knew, devising written charters ("covenants") whose style and terminology were distinctly reminiscent of the traditional *kahal.* In fact, Vital characterizes these arrangements as "far too smooth a carry-over into the new Hibbat Zion societies of the mental and organizational habits of the properly philanthropic institutions of the community—which often represented everything Hibbat Zion was in rebellion against."[30]

Apart from any conscious copying of past models, however, the conditions of the *yishuv* replicated in important respects conditions with which Jews had contended in the past, and not surprisingly they responded along familiar lines. There was no enforceable central authority in Zionism, even after the movement was formally launched (as the World Zionist Organization) in 1897. Early settlers were few in number, in a hostile setting, and relied on each other for mutual support. Being self-selected, they also had a high level of political consciousness and commitment and a strong sense of initiative. Voluntarism and partnership were, of necessity, the only means to establish and maintain a coherent political Jewish entity under these conditions. This meant, of necessity, the toleration of differences, since only by compromise would a common framework among the different settlements work. The framework was even looser, of course, than the *kahal:* it was built from the bottom up, pulling democratically established settlements together in a loose federation at the national level and laying the first groundwork for the "state within a state."[31]

The combination of revolt and continuity that this represented is portrayed by Shlomo Avineri:

> When a few members of a pioneering group decided to establish what eventually became the first kibbutz, the only way known to them to do this was

to have a meeting, vote on the structure proposed, elect a secretary and a committee. Those people were revolutionaries and socialists, rebelling against the ossified rabbinical and kehilla structure of the European shtetl; but the modes of their behavior were deeply grounded in the societal behavior patterns of the shtetl, the force of dialectics. . . . It was out of these traditions that the Zionist Organization knew how to hold Congresses and elections. . . .[32]

It was this reality, more than Theodor Herzl's exposure to Western liberalism, that shaped the democracy of the Zionist movement. In fact, had it been up to Herzl, Zionism would have been far less democratic. Herzl was an "old-fashioned conservative" who, a few months before publishing *Der Judenstaat,* had recorded in his diary that "democracy is political nonsense."[33] After entering the Zionist scene, he was repelled by the infighting among various factions: "We haven't a country yet, and already they are tearing it apart."[34] Herzl's plan was to settle the problem from above by dealing with monarchs, statesmen, and powerbrokers; only when rejected by the aristocrats did he threaten (and eventually act) to lead a mass movement. Even then, he remained "strongly committed to authoritarian leadership from above . . . even though circumstances forced him to modify it in practice."[35]

When Herzl convened the First Zionist Congress in 1897, the model of parliamentary democracy was taken as a matter of course. The Zionist movement lacked even that small measure of coercive authority that Jewish community officials had possessed and had to proceed entirely on the basis of voluntary participation. Given the fact that Herzl dominated the proceedings and wrote the standing orders that governed this and subsequent congresses (based in part on his four years spent observing the French Parliament), he is often credited with laying the basis for the Israeli Knesset. This may be true regarding much of the parliamentary procedure; some of the rules written in 1897 are still operative in the Knesset.[36] But in a larger sense Herzl was not the founder of Israeli democracy; he was only coming to terms with a reality that he could not have changed anyway.

One important element of this reality was the appearance of political parties, which within a few years became the main actors on the Zionist stage. The role of parties was an important element in building a Jewish state from the bottom, Israel being one of the instances where parties came before the state rather than the reverse. It was also important in the development of the electoral system. The First Zionist Congress adopted, as a matter of course, a system of proportional representation in which local Zionist organizations were represented on the basis of one delegate for every hundred members. With the growth of parties within the movement, proportional representation of ideological groupings was added at the Fifth Zionist Congress (in 1901). It should be noted that the principle of proportionality was followed by the Zionist movement well before proportional representation was established in national electoral systems.[37]

The capacity of the Zionist movement to encompass diversity, by virtue of its voluntaristic and power-sharing structure, was astounding. The movement included antithetical worldviews that would have split most movements many times: socialist and nonsocialist; traditional and revolutionary; religious and secular; political Zionists determined on statehood and culturalists who abjured political goals. Nothing better demonstrates how the logic of inclusion worked than the case of religious Zionists. This logic was expressed by Max Nordau at the Third Zionist Congress, in 1899, when he appealed to religious Jews to join the movement: "Within Zionism everyone is guaranteed full freedom to live according to his religious convictions. . . . For we do not have the possibility of imposing our will on you if it happens to be different from yours!"[38] One of the most vigorous debates in early years was over the push of cultural Zionists, led by Ahad Ha'am, to institute a program of Jewish national education, which was seen by religious Zionists as a threat to their traditional role in education. This led to the recognition, in the Fifth Congress, of "two streams with equal rights—the traditional and the progressive," and to setting up two committees to correspond to the two views.[39]

In a pattern that was to continue, religious Zionists formed coalitions with other groups to protect their own interests. Herzl obtained their support—most notably in the emotional 1903 "Uganda" debate over the idea of Jewish colonization in British East Africa—in return for holding the line on the educational demands of the Ahad Ha'amists.[40] Power-sharing, decentralization, mutual veto, coalition-building, multidimensional politics—features of consociational democracy that had their counterparts in traditional Jewish politics—flourished in this setting.

THE ARAB ISSUE

Relations between Jews and Arabs in Palestine "are totally different from those of the Jewish people with any other throughout its lengthy history."[41] Jewish political traditions were of little use in dealing with non-Jewish nationalities within its own sphere. Jewish politics dealt with the non-Jewish world as a separate and hostile external environment, to be kept at bay as far as possible. Early Zionists thus had no precedents upon which to rely regarding the place of an Arab population in a Jewish state, as the very confusion of their responses would indicate.

The Zionist response to the Arab presence represents the usual spectrum of human adjustment to uncongenial realities: avoidance, denial, wishful thinking, hostility (and sometimes some or all of these responses simultaneously). And while the very profusion and confusion of the responses are testimony to lack of clear guidelines in tradition, most were consonant with one aspect or another of this tradition.

Avoidance is a normal response to a problem that did not exist in the past. For the Zionist pioneers, Palestine was effectively empty because "they did not expect to model the society they intended to build upon anything provided by the indigenous population."[42] Theodor Herzl, when he passed through a large number of Arab villages during his visit to Palestine, made no references to Arabs in his diary or his written reports afterward: "the natives seemed to have vanished before his eyes. . . ."[43] Apart from the inconvenience of their presence, the invisibility of the inhabitants was probably reinforced by the assumption in European nationalism—also basic to Zionism—that a people without a state did not, in fact, have a national identity. In any event, such myopia was common among Zionist leaders, especially those outside Palestine (inside Palestine it was harder to ignore the issue), in the period before the Young Turkish Revolution of 1908 pushed national questions to the fore. Furthermore, it has persisted as a recurring phenomenon throughout the history of the conflict, often in the form of a tendency to minimize the importance or reality of Israeli Arab issues (as in David Ben-Gurion writing, in 1952, that Israel "was virtually emptied of its former owners" even though Arabs still constituted 12.5 percent of its population).[44]

One form that avoidance took among early Zionists was to place an undue weight on the achievement of a Jewish majority. Once Jews could simply outvote the Arab population in Palestine, it was felt, all would be settled in congruence with democratic procedures and the "minority problem" would fall into place. Even Ahad Ha'am, whose famous 1891 article on the Arab issue was the first to challenge the prevailing avoidance of the issue, came eventually to the conclusion that a Jewish majority would make it possible to respect Arab rights as individuals while achieving Jewish national rights in Palestine.[45] But as Jewish history demonstrates, establishing the right of a majority to rule does not, in itself, resolve the issue of minority rights.

Most Zionists, however, found it impossible simply to ignore the Arab problem. As time went on, especially among those settled in Palestine, better answers were required. The publication of Yitzhak Epstein's article "The Hidden Question" in *Hashiloah*, in 1907, inaugurated a vigorous debate over attitudes toward the Arabs, which Epstein defined as a question "which outweighs all others."[46] This debate did not, however, provide any resolution but reflected the confusion on the issue. The very proliferation of ways of viewing Arabs—as Semitic cousins, as natives, as Gentiles, as Canaanites, as an oppressed class, as a second national movement alongside the Jewish one—indicated the lack of a clear dominant view.

Naive assimilationism was a response favored by some early settlers, who recognized that the Arab presence could not be ignored but who sought to deny the reality of any underlying conflict. The established population could be viewed as kinsmen, as direct descendants of the ancient Hebrews who would willingly cooperate in the reestablishment of the ancient homeland. Even if they did not convert to Judaism, an appeal on the grounds of common ancestry and ethnic kinship might serve to reconcile Arabs to the Zionist enterprise.[47] Such ideas did not strike a chord among either Jews or Arabs, however, and withered over time. Nevertheless, they did not die out completely; in the 1930s, Rabbi Benjamin (Yehoshua Radler-Feldmann, founder of Brit Shalom, a movement that advocated a binational Arab-Jewish state) was still promoting his own version of pan-Semitism.[48]

Paternalism was another variant of the approaches that sought to transcend Arab-Jewish conflict by stressing common interests. The Westernized Jews who led the Zionist movement saw the native population of Palestine as a backward people who could only benefit from the blessings of modern civilization that Jewish settlers would bring. When Herzl finally dealt with the Arab problem, in *Altneuland,* he portrayed an Arab notable deeply grateful for the economic prosperity and modernization brought by Jewish skills; Max Nordau, in defending Herzl from Ahad Ha'am's accusations of insensitivity on the issue, argued that Jews would bring progress and civilization to Palestine just as the English had to India. Chaim Weizmann later explained to Lord Balfour that the Arab problem was economic rather than political and that Zionism would coexist peacefully with the Arabs of Palestine by insuring economic development.[49] Of course all of this was being argued at a time when the superiority of European culture and the advantages of its diffusion were articles of faith and "colonialism" was still considered a progressive concept in the West.

Class solidarity was a more sophisticated path for denying the reality of a national conflict. Labor Zionists argued that the common class interests of Jewish workers and the masses of impoverished Arab peasants created the basis for joint action against the (Arab) effendi, or landowning class. Despite the lack of response from the Arab "proletariat," this conception had at least two practical advantages that guaranteed it a long lease on life. First, Arab hostility to Zionism could in this view be attributed to the reactionary interests of the effendi rather than to the bulk of the Arab population, with which Zionism was said to have no quarrel. Second, analysis on a class basis made it possible to skirt the issue of whether the Arabs of Palestine constituted a nation or a people, equal in status (and rights) with the Jewish people.

In reality, both paternalistic and class solidarity perspectives, like the naive kinship theories, saw assimilation as the answer to the Arab problem.

The basis and form of assimilation had simply become more sophisticated. All three assimilationist approaches had in common the denial of an objective conflict between the Arab and Jewish populations in Palestine, or at least a stress on common interests that would override conflicts. They stressed the material benefits that would accrue to the Arab population, whose interests are defined as economic or social rather than political or national. As Herzl wrote in an oft-quoted letter to Ziah El-Khaldi in 1899, "[Arab] well-being and individual wealth will increase through the importation of ours. Do you believe that an Arab who owns land in Palestine . . . will be sorry to see [its] value rise five- and ten-fold? But this would most certainly happen with the coming of the Jews."[50]

Behind the stress on material benefits lay the even more important tendency to recognize Arab rights on the individual level, and not as a national group. This was of course entirely consonant with the traditional Jewish view of non-Jews, who were accorded humane treatment as individuals but were not recognized as a collectivity. Needless to say, it also fit perfectly into the political arguments being made by the Zionist movement. The demographic realities of Palestine at the time lent some credence to this view; Arab nationalism was in its infancy, a strong Palestinian Arab identity had yet to take shape, and both Jewish and non-Jewish observers tended to describe the population in segmented terms as "Muslims," "Christians," or according to tribal or clan affiliations.[51]

This distinction between individual and national rights made it possible for Zionist leaders to affirm full support for the civil rights of the non-Jewish "residents" or "inhabitants" of Palestine, while pressing the Jewish national claim to Palestine as a whole. David Ben-Gurion, for example, could argue that "we have no right whatsoever to deprive a single Arab child . . . " while also making the claim that in a "historical and moral sense" Palestine was a country "without inhabitants."[52] Even those who did recognize the Arabs as a nationality or as a parallel national movement—a number that grew over time—still tended to deny that they possessed the same kind of national rights in Palestine that Jews did. At best, they might be accorded the status of a recognized and protected but subordinated minority.

Separatism was the natural response of those who found the various assimilationist models untenable or undesirable. While the label covers a spectrum of responses, what they had in common was belief that Zionist goals, even in the minimalist version, were bound to be unacceptable to the Arab population of Palestine and that a clash of interests was inevitable. While some thought that this clash might be worked out in nonviolent ways, all saw a strongly competitive element in the relationship and felt that the integrity and security of the Zionist undertaking dictated a course of self-reliance rather than pursuing the chimera of Jewish-Arab collaboration.

In some ways, those skeptical about assimilation found it easier to recognize and deal with Arabs as a collectivity. Since they did not expect Arabs to forego their national identity in pursuit of individual or material gain, Arab nationhood could be viewed as a simple fact of life. This did not necessarily mean recognition of equal national rights, but at least as recognized rivals Arabs were visible as a group.

In later years, separatism was increasingly a defense against Arab hostility. Among the followers of Ze'ev Jabotinsky it took the form of preparation for the armed conflict that was regarded as inevitable. But streaks of separatism appeared among nearly all Zionist groups, as a natural (and Jewish) response to an environment perceived as basically hostile. Jews had been unremittedly conditioned over long historical periods to regard the external environment as hostile; in traditional terms, the Arabs were simply the latest group of Gentiles to whose hatred Jews were exposed. This seemed to be readily confirmed in the Palestinian context: Arabs refused to recognize Jews as a people or nation with rights in Palestine; they engaged in frequent acts of anti-Jewish violence that were seen as a continuation of traditional anti-Semitic persecution; and they displayed no interest in the various visions of integration or cooperation that more idealistic Zionists put forward.

Zionist approaches to the Arab question thus moved between integrative and separatist strategies.[53] While particular leaders and parties could and did mix elements from different strategies, there were often conflicts and inconsistencies as a result: Arabs could not benefit fully from the Jewish enterprise without being a part of it nor could security considerations take precedence without impinging on Jewish-Arab interaction. Both tradition and the immediate environment gave mixed signals on how to resolve these dilemmas, and many were left unresolved then as well as after the founding of the state. But at the same time, it must be said that both tradition and the immediate environment gave an advantage to separatist tendencies over the integrative visions.

For example, Labor Zionists, who might have been in the forefront in developing institutions of class solidarity with Arab workers, opted instead for "socialist separatism." This was extended to the principle of *avoda ivrit*, the employment of Jewish labor in all Jewish enterprises in the *yishuv*. It was simply assumed, with little explicit thought of exclusion, that the institutions of Zionism were established by and for Jews. Arab participation in them was not a major issue, even if it did cause ideological difficulty for a few. While such practices appear as illiberal discrimination to later generations, at the time they had the progressive connotations of self-reliance, the rebuilding of a normal Jewish occupational structure, and the avoidance of colonial practices based on exploitation of cheap native labor.

UNDER THE MANDATE

Under the *millet* system of government in the Ottoman Empire, each ethnoreligious community enjoyed a wide degree of autonomy in its own internal affairs. The Jewish community in Palestine, including the new Zionist settlements, had exploited this to establish its own institutions covering a broad range of religious, educational, cultural, economic, legal, and even political matters. The customary British style of indirect rule, as practiced in the new Palestine Mandate after World War I, gave even more latitude to the growing *yishuv* (which increased from 60,000 to 650,000 during the Mandatory period). But in contrast to most colonial situations, institutions were not copied from the colonial power. There is some debate about the influence of the British model on the development of the Jewish (later Israeli) political system, but in summary it appears that the major British contribution—apart from the idea of a cabinet with collective responsibility and some parliamentary trappings—lay in the realm of legal and judicial practices. The British established English (along with Arabic and Hebrew) as an official language in the courts, appointed British judges to the senior positions, and established the legal education system used throughout the Mandatory period. Ottoman law remained in effect where not supplanted, but most of it was replaced by Mandate legislation (on the British model) by 1948, while English common law was used to cover gaps in existing law. Thus legal and judicial institutions and practice were the main legacy directly inherited by the Jewish state from the Mandatory power (or from any Western source).[54]

For the rest, the Jewish community drew on its own experience in communal politics and on already existing Zionist institutions, including those established in the *yishuv* before the British came on the scene. There is striking institutional continuity from the earliest Zionist bodies, through the period of the British presence, to the State of Israel. The Jewish community succeeded during the Mandate in establishing its own state-within-a-state, complete with institutions that in some cases—political parties, educational and cultural groups, charitable and welfare bodies, burial societies, religious organizations, economic guilds, workers' groups, and even private companies—were hardly more than a transplant from the Diaspora. Whatever the importance of previous experience in this community-building enterprise, by the end of the Mandatory period the Jewish community had far outstripped Palestinian Arabs in establishing communal self-government, providing a solid foundation for Jewish statehood.

The central Mandate structures established by the British lacked legitimacy in the eyes of both Jews and Arabs, and had little impact on either. Palestine consisted of two communities with little in common: each had its own political system, educational and cultural bodies, and military forces. The two communities lived apart; there was almost no social interaction, and even economic relations were limited. Efforts to establish overarching common bodies almost always failed, and relations between Arabs and Jews were closer to the model of an international system than to coexistence within a shared political framework.[55]

Within the Jewish community matters were quite different. The terms of the Mandate called for the creation of a Jewish body to advise the British on matters related to the Jewish national home, and the Jewish Agency (effectively an extension of the World Zionist Organization) was set up for that purpose. At the same time the British authorities also officially recognized the Jewish community in Palestine as a legal entity (Knesset Yisrael, the Assembly of Israel), and allowed it to select governing bodies. These bodies were set up as a three-tiered structure—Assembly of Delegates, National Council, Executive Council—modeled on the structure of the World Zionist Organization.[56] Membership in Knesset Yisrael was still voluntary, as individuals could withdraw if they chose (and many of the anti-Zionist Orthodox did so). Otherwise voting was universal (including women) and secret, with seats awarded to party lists on a proportional basis (the same system used before and since). The existence of two parallel structures—the Jewish Agency and Knesset Yisrael—also perpetuated the tradition of competing centers of authority.

The leadership of the *yishuv* still faced the problem of the *kahal*: how to make decisions binding on all groups within the Jewish community. Since the cost of being outside the communal arrangements was relatively low, minorities possessed almost a veto power. The leadership focused on the building of coalitions that were as inclusive as possible and on a political system described as an "open-ended, informal set of federative arrangements."[57]

Even during the period of greatest crisis, the *yishuv* remained largely united and politically stable, in part because of the "autonomism" of the constituent bodies.[58] The acid test came in relations with the Revisionists, who eventually split with the Labor-dominated center and attempted to form their own rival bodies. But the strategy of separation proved to be self-defeating, helping Labor Zionists (primarily Mapai at the time) to delegitimize their opponents as the subverters of Jewish unity during a time of troubles.[59]

The *yishuv* organized itself as a "quasi-state" within the Mandate framework and established the institutions that were to dominate Israeli life. The Histadrut, or Labor Federation, grew to play a role in the economy far beyond that of an ordinary labor union. The Jewish Agency, as an organ of the World Zionist Organization, handled relations with Jewish communities abroad, represented the interests of the *yishuv* diplomatically, and coordinated immigration and settlement within Palestine. The bodies elected by

Knesset Yisrael levied taxes and supported religious and other institutions. At the center were the political parties, which were actually ideological movements. Together with the Histadrut, the parties provided a set of institutions and services substituting for the governmental and societal infrastructure that did not exist: schools, newspapers, banks and loan funds, health-care plans, youth movements, sport clubs, housing companies, and various welfare services. Most of the new settlements were established by particular movements. The centrality of the parties in Israeli politics is not just a result of the electoral system; rather, it was the dominance of parties that shaped the electoral system.

Observers have noted the similarity of pre-state Jewish politics to consociationalism, or to similar concepts of "compound polity" or "segmented pluralism."[60] Society is organized into separate camps, each with its own institutions, that share power and distribute benefits proportionately by a process of bargaining and coalition-building. In the *yishuv*, Labor Zionists were forced to share power despite their central position; grand coalitions (or more than minimal winning coalitions) rather than simple majority rule was the practice; the political system was multidimensional, being split along several axes; there was separation of power between competing authorities; and representation was proportional.

Again, the classic expression was in relations with the religious Zionists. The patterns of power-sharing initiated in the World Zionist Organization carried over into the *yishuv*. Beginning in the 1930s, the secular leadership of the *yishuv* made explicit arrangements with the religious Zionist parties (Hapo'el Hamizrahi and Mizrahi) on the proportionate division of jobs and other benefits, beginning a forty-year period of partnership between Labor Zionists and religious Zionists. Efforts were also made to bring Agudat Yisrael, representing the *haredi* (ultra-Orthodox) non-Zionists or anti-Zionists (the "old *yishuv*") within the purview of the new communal institutions. Chaim Weizmann sought throughout the 1920s to bring Agudat Yisrael into the National Council, which had the advantage of controlling most of the funds available. In the first stage, this led to Zionist funding of Agudat Yisrael educational institutions, and later, in 1934, to formal cooperation between Agudat Yisrael and the World Zionist Organization. Finally, following World War II, the Agudat Yisrael leadership supported the establishment of a Jewish state, and in return David Ben-Gurion, the chairman of the Jewish Agency, pledged public adherence to certain basic religious laws.

The system of proportional representation adopted was (and remains) the purest form possible. Parties submitted rank-ordered lists of candidates, but voters chose a party rather than individual candidates. Each party then received a proportion of seats matching its proportion of the vote (if there were one hundred seats, a party with 10 percent of the vote would be awarded ten seats, which would go to the first ten candidates on its list). Proportional representation was maintained as the only method of drawing in all parties on a voluntary basis, and the principle of proportionality was extended to all appointive positions, to the allocation of funds, and even to the distribution of immigration certificates.[61] This method of allotting benefits according to "party key"—that is, in strict proportion to electoral success—was also, obviously, one of the incentives for voluntary cooperation and one of the coercive tools available to those at the center, who could (and did) withhold funds or immigration certificates from those who broke ranks.

This reality was quite different from what socialist ideologues originally had in mind. In the early 1920s, with the Soviet experiment just underway, they had envisioned building a society along entirely new lines; when the Histadrut was founded in 1921, Ben-Gurion advocated organizing it as a country-wide commune with military discipline.[62] Despite the dominance of agrarian socialist ideology as the governing paradigm of the new society, the gap between it and reality became enormous. The dominance of Labor Zionism, for about half a century beginning in the late 1920s, is in many respects a puzzle. Neither the pre-Zionist Palestinian Jewish community (the "old *yishuv*") nor the pioneers of the first *aliya* were disposed to secular socialism. The second *aliya* (1905–1914) is generally regarded as the generation that established Labor's hegemony, but the prevailing image of this group has been challenged. Daniel Elazar concludes that among the 35,000 to 40,000 who immigrated during these years "relatively few of those thousands fit what was to become the mythic mold of the young Eastern European Zionist socialist revolutionaries who come to the land to fulfill the ideals of Russian-style Marxism, Zionist version."[63] At the end of World War I the number of "pioneers"—rural and urban laborers with Zionist commitments—was in the low thousands, and of these only an estimated 44 percent identified with the socialist parties.[64]

The third *aliya*, in the years immediately following World War I, presents a somewhat different picture. This group, mostly from revolutionary Russia, was significantly more radical than its predecessors.[65] Yet, given the still modest numbers involved, this did not radically alter the demography of the *yishuv*. Furthermore, beginning in 1924, immigration was no longer limited to self-selected volunteers imbued with strong Zionist motives. As the gates of entry closed in the United States and other traditional places of refuge, Palestine became the destination of entire communities of persecuted Jews who simply had nowhere else to turn. The fourth *aliya*, in the mid-1920s, brought in a number of middle-class Polish Jews fleeing antisemitic economic measures. The fifth *aliya*, in the 1930s, was triggered by persecution in Germany, Austria, Poland, and Romania, which forced many urbanized, professional Jews to seek refuge in Palestine. Another 100,000 refugees from the Holocaust arrived, legally or illegally, during the 1940–1947 period. Later came the "displaced persons" from World War II. After the establishment of the State of Israel in 1948, there was a mass influx of entire Jewish communities from the Arab world. Altogether, about two million Jewish refugees reached Palestine or Israel during these years. These refugees and their descendants constitute a vast majority of the present population of Israel. Any explanation of Israeli political attitudes that does not begin with this reality—that Israel is a nation of refugees—is inadequate.

The agrarian image of a return to the soil, as fostered by kibbutz ideology, was always exaggerated. A majority of new immigrants settled in cities; at its peak, in the 1930s, the agricultural sector accounted for less than a third of the Jewish population. The gap between ideology and reality was reflected in a 1945 survey of Jewish schoolchildren in which 75 percent declared that agriculture was the most important career for building the country—but only 12 percent planned to become farmers.[66]

The puzzle, then, is not the eventual decline of Labor Zionism but rather its long hold on power. During this period, the bulk of the population came holding no strong prior commitment to socialism, the dignity of manual labor, a return to the soil, a change in the traditional Jewish occupational structure, the secularization of Jewish life, a pragmatic approach to territorial issues, or other features of an ideology rooted in the ferment of late nineteenth-century Eastern European revolutionary movements. They did not come to Eretz Yisrael in order to wage a "revolution against Jewish history."

How did Labor Zionists achieve their hegemony? First, while beginning as a minority even in the earlier *aliyot*, the socialists were intensely committed and tireless organizers. By the time that massive immigration began, they had built an infrastructure (the Histadrut, for example) to absorb and socialize (in both senses) the newcomers. Second, at least some of the new immigrants, having passed through the wrenching experience of persecution and flight, were more open to radical Zionist perspectives than they had been previously (and the Holocaust demonstrated what their probable fate would have been had the Zionists not provided, exactly in line with Herzl's original vision, a haven from the tempest). Third, the fact that they were building a "new society" made it easier for the Zionist pioneers to apply their ideological precepts. They began with a clean slate, freed of the need to deal with established institutions. The "old rulemakers," those who might have resisted the new doctrines, were underrepresented and outgunned.[67] Fourth, the decision of Labor Zionists to focus on "practical" Zionism, on the patient construction of a base in Palestine itself, translated over time into an enormous advantage over those (such as the Revisionists) who continued to focus on the world stage or on Zionist politics outside Palestine. Finally, once

Labor Zionists actually did control the center in Palestine, they were able to use their leverage effectively to legitimize and propagate their version of Zionism as the standard brand.[68]

Moving into leadership of the *yishuv* meant, of course, further compromise with realities, and a wider gap between ideological premises and practical policies. This is pointed out most acutely by Mitchell Cohen, who argues that Labor Zionists achieved dominance by shifting to a policy of "revolutionary constructivism" that separated the concepts of class and nation, stressing the development of the *yishuv* as a whole rather than classical socialist goals. This strategy isolated and overwhelmed the Revisionist opposition of the time, but at the cost—in Cohen's view—of subverting Labor Zionism's own future. This move from "class" to "nation" can indeed be seen as an abandonment of socialist ideology, at least in its purest form, but it can also be seen as a move toward a more "civic" conception of the political order, even in the context of communitarian Jewish political practices. The culmination of this came after statehood with Ben-Gurion's efforts to instill a "civic culture" (*mamlachtiut*) into Israeli political life (see chapter 4).

Another reinforcement of the move to greater pragmatism was the fact that by the late 1930s security had become a major obsession. At the outset Labor Zionists had believed that their goals could be achieved without displacing the Arab population in Palestine or injuring its basic interests. This was perhaps somewhat utopian, since the minimal Zionist aim—a Jewish state in at least part of Palestine—was never likely to be acceptable, in an age of rising Arab nationalism, to an Arab population that regarded its claims to Palestine as exclusive.

In any event, each new wave of Jewish immigration evoked a new round of violence; there were widespread Arab assaults on Jews in 1920 to 1921 and in 1929, while in 1936 to 1939 there was a general uprising that approached the dimensions of a civil war. In addition, leadership of Palestine Arabs passed into the hands of more fanatical elements, and in particular those of Haj Amin Al-Husseini, the mufti of Jerusalem. The mufti, whose forces liquidated many of the more moderate Arab leaders during the 1936–1939 period, preached the destruction of the Jewish community in Palestine and later fled to Nazi Germany where he gained notoriety by endorsing the Nazi solution to the Jewish problem.

The impact of this on the *yishuv* was to discredit efforts to achieve a negotiated settlement of Arab-Jewish issues. Those who promoted such an effort—in particular, Chaim Weizmann, president of the World Zionist Organization during much of this time—were gradually pushed aside by those within the Labor Zionist movement who stressed the need for self-defense and for creating facts on the ground. Foremost among the latter was Ben-Gurion, who by the early 1930s had become the most prominent leader in the *yishuv*.

But while Ben-Gurion represented a "realist" perspective on the question of diplomacy versus practical measures, he also represented a pragmatic approach to territorial issues, in contrast to the Revisionists. The leadership of the *yishuv* had reluctantly come to terms with the British partition of the Palestine Mandate, in 1922, by which 77 percent of the original Mandate—everything east of the Jordan River—was established as the Emirate of Transjordan under the rule of Abdallah, Faisal's brother, and closed to Jewish settlement. Under Ben-Gurion's leadership, they also accepted in principle British proposals, in the late 1930s, to partition what remained into Jewish and Arab states, though there was considerable criticism of the specific borders proposed.[69] Finally, a majority under Ben-Gurion also accepted the UN partition plan of 1947, which from a Jewish perspective was an improvement on the 1930s proposals but which still left Jerusalem outside the proposed Jewish state (see Map 1).

The Revisionists opposed all of these measures, beginning with the creation of Transjordan, and split with the existing leadership over its acceptance of the principle of partition. As noted, they continued to insist on the priority of Jewish national rights in all of historic Palestine (including Transjordan).

There was still a tendency to avoid hard thinking about the future position of Arabs in a Jewish state by focusing on the simple push for a Jewish majority. Except for the few supporters of binationalism clustered around Brit Shalom, majority rule was the spoken or unspoken aim that unified all Zionists from left to right. The shared assumption seemed to be that the very act of achieving majority status would reduce the Arab issue to a "mere" question of minority rights, which could be resolved with a modicum of good will. Ben-Gurion referred to Canada and Finland as examples of states where a dominant majority determined the character of the state but ethnic minorities lived peacefully; he indicated, however, no understanding of the guarantees and compromises, including dilution of the state's dominant ethnic image, often required to make such systems work.[70] There seemed to be an unquestioned confidence—one that could find little support in the contemporary history of majority-minority relations elsewhere—that the simple act of outvoting a national minority would resolve the problematic relationship. Even Jabotinsky, whose followers later minimized the importance of numbers, paid homage to the principle of a Jewish majority as the solution to existing contradictions.[71]

Only Brit Shalom, following the assimilationist logic to its conclusion, pursued a solution that was not dependent on relative numbers but gave explicit and equal recognition to the two nations in Palestine. Binationalism, however, was not what the Zionist movement was about, and such ideas remained the province of a small number of intellectuals outside the mainstream. Even the advocates of binationalism, however, assumed that Arab national aspirations, which they were ready to recognize, could be limited and accommodated within a partly non-Arab framework, and in this they also seem to have misread Arab thinking. The lack of Arab interest and response, no less than the lack of Jewish support, led to the demise of Brit Shalom.

The advocates of paternalistic cooperation and class solidarity were also weakened by lack of response and the unfavorable turn of events. Those who put their trust in the blessings of Western civilization turned naturally to Great Britain, the Mandatory power, as intermediary in the civilizing mission. Chaim Weizmann, among others, saw the British presence as obviating the need to negotiate directly with the Arabs; in time this clearly became a weak reed. Labor Zionists acted intermittently on the basis of presumed common interests with Arab workers, as when they urged restraint in response to the Arab riots of 1929 on the grounds that there was no "real" conflict between the two peoples.[72] At least as late as 1936, mainstream leaders in Labor Zionism still professed to believe in collaboration on a class basis; in a book published that year, Ben-Gurion states, in a typical passage: "The majority of the Arab population know that the Jewish immigration and colonization are bringing prosperity to the land. Only the narrow circles of the Arab ruling strata have egotistical reasons to fear the Jewish immigration, and the social and economic changes caused by it. The self-interest of the majority of the Arab inhabitants is not in conflict with Jewish immigration and colonization, but on the contrary is in perfect harmony with it."[73]

How far Ben-Gurion actually believed this, by 1936, is open to question, but the dogma of class solidarity remained in the public rhetoric of Labor Zionist leaders even after the 1936–1939 Arab uprising. After World War II, when leftist Labor Zionist groups merged into the United Workers Party (Mapam), they continued to advocate "cooperation and equality between the Jewish people returning to their land, and the masses of the Arab people residing in the country."[74]

But the stance of Labor Zionist groups was contradictory, since they continued to promote *avoda ivrit* and to maintain the Histadrut and other labor organizations as purely Jewish institutions. A consistent policy of class solidarity would have necessitated the development of frameworks for joint action, but even Hashomer Hatsa'ir (the most doctrinaire party) chose to postpone discussion of a joint Jewish-Arab workers' association (the other parties rejected it outright).[75] Furthermore, Labor Zionists, as other Zionists, continued to differentiate between the national rights of the Jews in Palestine and the rights of Arabs to continue living there as inhabitants or residents, that is, as individuals. Ben-Gurion tended to refer to a Jewish "people" and an Arab "community." Even when the existence of an Arab people or nation was conceded, it was usually described as part of a larger Arab nation rather than as a group with distinct national ties or claims to Palestine.[76]

The Arab uprising of 1936 to 1939 had a double impact on Zionist attitudes. In its wake, it became harder to deny the existence of an Arab national movement in Palestine, encompassing not simply an unrepresentative landowning class but a broad spectrum of the Arab population. Still, recognition of Arab nationality did not necessarily imply recognition of equal national rights in Palestine. A second result was to make many advocates of cooperation into advocates of separatism. These two developments were related: those who had advocated assimilation in various forms, and were now forced to recognize the strength of Arab particularism, came to separation as the next logical course. The practical expression of this was support for the idea of partition, which drew its strength largely from those in the middle of the spectrum who had supported cooperation.

The partition plans floated in the late 1930s created, not for the first time, some strange alignments and bedfellows within the *yishuv*. Groups on the left opposed partition and clung to visions of Jewish-Arab cooperation in an undivided Palestine. Other opponents were the Mizrahi (religious Zionists), who opposed partition on biblical grounds, and of course Jabotinsky's Revisionists on the right. Even some of Ben-Gurion's own party members deserted him on the issue, but on the other hand he gained many partition supporters from among the liberal and centrist, nonsocialist parties.

One of the ironies of the partition debate was that some of the new supporters of partition were now more committed to separatism in principle than were the Revisionists. While the Revisionists had no plans to assimilate with Arab society, they preferred living with a large Arab minority to dividing Palestine. As noted, Jabotinsky had less trouble recognizing the Arab national movement than did his more liberal opponents. In fact, taking Arab nationalism seriously was a cornerstone of his thought. He simply recognized it as a rival nationalism and planned to defeat it by massive Jewish immigration and (if necessary) military force.

For some advocates of partition, however, the idea of a "transfer" appeared as a logical and just corollary of the division of Palestine: if Jews were to accept a state in only part of the homeland, then at least they should be relieved of a hostile population that would best be relocated to the Arab state to be created. The concept of "population transfer" did not then carry the negative connotation that it acquired later; following World War I, a large number of transfers had been carried out more or less peacefully. As it happened, the idea was never taken seriously.[77] But the fact that it was mentioned does suggest that at least some *yishuv* leaders no longer believed that the achievement of majority status would automatically resolve minority issues.

The debate on the "Arab problem" during the Mandatory period is very instructive. The strange and fluid configurations that developed when practical decisions on Arab relations had to be made clearly illustrate the inadequacy, confusion, and arbitrariness of the guidelines furnished by historical experience and prevailing ideologies. The debate over partition was but one case; similar kaleidoscopic variations could be observed regarding debates over British proposals for legislative councils and important debates within the Zionist movement (for example, over such issues as publishing an Arabic-language newspaper or admitting Arab members to *yishuv* institutions). Nor were the positions of individual leaders much more predictable than those of the shifting party and organizational alignments. Ben-Gurion went through five or six different stages in his approach to Arab issues, according to close observers.[78] Clearly this was one area in which consensus did not exist.

Nevertheless, by the end of World War II the Jewish community of Palestine had achieved tremendous cohesion, unity, and determination in the face of adversity. Despite internal divisions that sometimes led even to bloodshed, the *yishuv* was able to maintain a level of organization and self-defense extraordinary for a community without formal governmental powers: it levied and collected taxes, established an army, represented its own interests internationally, administered welfare and educational services, and set its own economic and social policies—all on a voluntary basis. The strength of this social cohesion was apparent in the 1948 war, in which Jewish fighting forces managed not only to retain control of the territory allotted to a Jewish state but also to capture additional territory, including most of Jewish Jerusalem and a corridor linking it with the rest of Israel (see Map 2).

FOUR

Building a Civic State

In 1948 the first sovereign Jewish state in almost two millennia was launched. During the first two decades of statehood the basic patterns of Israeli politics were set, internal stability was secured, and the government established its legitimacy and its capacity to provide effective direction. Under the circumstances, this was no small achievement. The remarkable coherence and continuity attained in the early days of statehood has been a common theme in studies of the period.[1]

The imposition of binding authority stands in sharp contrast to the weak and contested institutions of the *yishuv*. Yet it was the existence of the *yishuv* framework that made a smooth transition possible, and it was through established principles of inclusion, compromise, and (with one or two notable exceptions) voluntarism that the passage was negotiated peacefully. The bargaining to bring in the non-Zionist ultra-Orthodox (Agudat Yisrael) has been described in the previous chapter. A month before the British exit from Palestine in May 1948, *yishuv* leaders combined the executive bodies of the National Council and the Jewish Agency, and added representatives from groups not included in these bodies (because they had boycotted the previous elections): Agudat Yisrael, the Revisionists, the Sephardim (representing non-European Jews; on the meaning of "Sephardi" in Israel see chapter 7), and the Communists. This People's Council of thirty-seven members, proportionally representing the significant groups within the Jewish community, became the legislative body of the new state, and from it was chosen a smaller body (People's Administration) that became the executive branch (the cabinet or government in Israeli parlance). Only the Communists and (after some debate) the Revisionists were excluded from the cabinet.

During the early statehood period there was a push toward universalistic civic models, including the majoritarian model of democracy rather than more traditional consociational practices. Majoritarianism appealed to Mapai, the dominant party in the Labor camp and the central party in the system, since it stood to gain from changes that reduced the need for power-sharing.[2] Mapai remained the largest party throughout this period, despite the existing gap between the ideology of the Labor elite and the more traditional moorings of the general public, and despite a huge influx of non-ideologized immigrants that widened this gap yet further.

Mapai's success was due in part to the effective leadership of David Ben-Gurion, who dominated the scene from the early 1930s until his resignation from the prime ministership in 1963. Central to the "Ben-Gurion system" was the concept of *mamlachtiut*, a term of his own devising that is usually translated as "statism." But "statism" is misleading because Ben-Gurion did not consider the state as an end in itself. Ben-Gurion sought to instill respect for what Peter Medding terms "legitimate state public authority," or in Ben-Gurion's own words, "a sense of public responsibility."[3] This is clearly related to the universalist ethic of the civic state, and in fact the term "civic-mindedness" may come closest to conveying the broader nuances of what Ben-Gurion meant by *mamlachtiut*.

THE BEN-GURION SYSTEM

As Ben-Gurion saw it, Jewish history left a legacy that was inimical to statehood: "We brought with us from the diaspora customs of disintegration, anarchy, lack of national responsibility and unity. . . . "[4] He also condemned the pre-state communal politics of the *yishuv* for its destructive splits and challenges to the collective framework. In response he sought to establish the universally binding character of the new state, not as an end in itself but as an instrument for achieving the common goals of Zionism in restoring the Jewish people to normality among the family of nations.[5]

But while *mamlachtiut* was revolutionary as policy, it also had a dialectic relationship with the Jewish past. Unlike those who thought tradition and civic statehood to be irreconcilable, Ben-Gurion sought to redefine tradition so as to make the two compatible. This was accomplished, as with much in Zionism, by the selective use of the past and by filling traditional concepts and symbols with new content (giving religious holidays, for example, a much more national connotation). Like many others, Ben-Gurion turned to the Bible and to the ancient period—the time of Jewish statehood—rather than to the long intervening history of exile and passivity. Even the term he employed (derived from *mamlacha*, or "kingdom") reflected a preference for the heroic models of antiquity.[6]

Ben-Gurion was thus not working strictly according to the Western civic conception of the state but with a synthesis in which the state has positive functions in Jewish terms. Foremost among these functions was to preserve and promote Jewish unity, the lack of which was, for Ben-Gurion, the bane of Jewish history. He was therefore willing to build into the state structure a high tolerance for pluralism, as in his accommodation with religious interests (including the anti-Zionists who had opposed him at every step). This ran counter to Ben-Gurion's strong bias for majoritarian rather than consociational democracy, especially with regard to the electoral system; he viewed proportional representation and the proliferation of parties as pernicious arrangements that put partisan interests ahead of the general welfare.

But if *mamlachtiut* was not strictly based on the civic model, it was even further from the socialist faith that saw the state as an instrument for achieving the goals of the working class. Was Labor Zionism, at least in the Mapai version, moving closer to Western liberalism than to classic Marxism? Ben-Gurion expressed increasing ambivalence on some ideological points, such as the primacy of the kibbutz model. He criticized the kibbutz movement for its sluggish response to the national task of absorbing new immigrants: "Only pioneering that is prepared to serve the state faithfully in all its revolutionary tasks in their new form will from now on be worthy of the name."[7] On many issues, he found greater support from the "civic" parties in the center of the spectrum (Progressives and General Zionists) than from his colleagues on the left, who were threatened both ideologically and institutionally by some of his projected reforms.

The first task of *mamlachtiut*, to bring all elements of the Jewish community under government authority, was accomplished with relative success. The arrangements with the ultra-Orthodox community have already been mentioned. The military arm of the Revisionist movement—Etsel (also known as Irgun), led by Menachem Begin—discussed various options including establishing its own government, but in the end was integrated into the new Israeli army. This process was marred by only one major incident, the *Altalena* affair of June 1948, when Ben-Gurion ordered the use of force to prevent the unloading of a ship's cargo of weapons sent by Etsel from Europe. Herut, the political successor to Etsel, was the first party to be founded after independence and quickly integrated into parliamentary life.

The second line of attack was to reduce sectarianism in public life. Ben-Gurion moved to dismantle the Palmach, the elite "striking force" that had its own command structure, because of its close links with the left-wing socialist party Mapam and its affiliated kibbutz movement. Regarding the use of the party key to distribute governmental jobs, after ten years of debate the Knesset finally passed three laws in 1959 designed to ensure appointment by merit, rather than by political considerations, at all but the highest ranks of the civil service.

Ben-Gurion also moved, where possible, to put public services on a civic, nonpartisan basis. After a lengthy fight, the four independent educational networks were reduced to two state systems (one secular, one religious) and one state-supervised and state-supported independent system (in the ultra-Orthodox community). Independent labor exchanges were also eventually taken over by the state. However, Ben-Gurion abandoned efforts to nationalize health services—provided mostly by the Histadrut—because of fierce resistance from his own political camp.[8]

These efforts were backed up by programs to regularize and professionalize government operations. The Declaration of Independence, like its U.S. counterpart, is a repository of liberal universalism. According to its words, the State of Israel "will promote the development of the country for the benefit of all its inhabitants . . . will uphold the full social and political equality of all its citizens, without distinction of race, creed or sex; will guarantee full freedom of conscience, worship, education and culture . . . and will dedicate itself to the principles of the Charter of the United Nations." There is argument over whether these provisions have constitutional status in Israeli law; the Israeli Supreme Court has ruled they are not constitutional, but they may nevertheless have constitutional significance in ruling between two interpretations of a law where the intent of the founders of the state is an issue.[9] Also, in a 1994 amendment to the Basic Law: Freedom of Occupation, it is stipulated that interpretation of that basic law, as well as the Basic Law: Human Freedom and Dignity, was to be in accord with the spirit of the Declaration of Independence.

The Declaration of Independence, and the formation of a provisional government, were to have been followed by a formal written constitution. The writing of a constitution was, however, stymied by basic disagreement (especially between secular and religious parties) over the basic character of a Jewish state—a question that could hardly be avoided or circumvented in a written constitution. Instead, a compromise was reached whereby certain "Basic Laws" would be adopted one by one, thus assembling over time the building blocks of a finished constitution.

The basic structure and prerogatives of the legislative and executive branches were set in the Transition Law adopted by the newly elected Constituent Assembly (which declared itself to be the First Knesset) in February 1949. Known as the "Small Constitution," this was the foundation for later Basic Laws on these matters and thus determined the basic operations of government that still exist.[10]

The area in which Western liberal norms penetrated most deeply was the legal and judicial system. This involved the continuing construction of a system of civil courts alongside the traditional Jewish courts. The superiority of rabbinic law was no longer assumed; Israel now had a body of civil law, much of it derived from or influenced by Western sources, that took precedence. The coercive authority of religious leaders was limited to a very small sphere, apart from those who voluntarily accept rabbinical rulings (on the other hand, in the area in which they did wield authority—basically family law—rabbinical courts were now backed by the police power of the state).

Why should foreign influence be stronger precisely in law and judiciary, the greatest strength of traditional Jewish governance? This was due in part to the development of a dual court system during the Mandatory period, as the British established civil courts in place of the previous Ottoman institutions. The rabbinic courts continued to function as they had before, within their own community and parallel to similar courts in other communities. The secular courts drew upon both Ottoman and British law (with Ottoman law also being strongly Western-influenced because of its borrowing from the French code). The Jewish aptitude for law is demonstrated in this case by the quick adaptation to, and adoption of, the Mandatory legal system and its continuation as the basis for an Israeli civil system. Thus the traditional strength of the judicial framework was respected and maintained, while the substantive content shifted to Western secular legal principles.

There was some overlap with Jewish law, and Jewish law was specified as one of the sources for Israeli law. But the role of Jewish law in civil courts has been minor, for a number of reasons: the complexity of Jewish law itself, its lack of answers on many contemporary issues, unfamiliarity with it on the part of secular judges, and the existence of a large body of law and precedent designed precisely for the issues faced in civil courts. The greatest contribution of Jewish law, as it turned out, was in the area of terminology, where the traditions of the centuries had developed Hebrew nomenclature for almost any legal concept. But even here, traditional terms were often given new meanings in the new context; even the legal definition of "Jew" became a matter of contention between religious and civil authorities.[11]

The process of anglicizing Israeli law, mainly through the continuing infusion of English common law, continued in the first twenty years of statehood. After that, the increased role of Israeli legislation reversed the process. But general legal procedures, reasoning, and precedents remain similar to those of countries in the common law tradition. Also, a number of key jurists in the formative period were from what in Israel is termed an "Anglo-Saxon" (English-speaking) background; of the fifteen justices appointed to the Supreme Court from 1948 to 1963, nine had received at least part of their legal education in English-speaking countries.[12]

The independence and professionalism of the judiciary are protected by a nonpolitical appointment process. Supreme Court justices, for example, are selected by a commission that includes three justices, two cabinet ministers, two members of the Knesset chosen by secret ballot, and two members of the Israeli Bar Association. Attempts to bring political pressure to bear have usually met a sharp response.[13] At the same time, judges have shown

caution in dealing with controversial political issues and have generally refused to substitute their judgment for that of the executive branch on matters other than legal interpretation. But the Supreme Court has asserted the
right to nullify both legislation that contravenes entrenched provisions of a
Basic Law and administrative actions judged to be contrary to the basic values of a free society. The successful depoliticization and high prestige of the
judiciary provides one of the "paradoxes" of Israeli civil life: "These characteristics make the Israeli judicial system very un-Israeli and hence important
as a bastion of Israeli democracy in a sea of forces that would hasten the erosion of its foundations."[14]

The penumbra of impartiality extends to a number of quasi-judicial elements in the Israeli government. The attorney general, though appointed
by the cabinet, enjoys a wide degree of independence, including the power
to prosecute members of the government. The state controller, responsible
only to the Knesset, issues yearly reports on government operations, notable
for their critical impartiality, that receive great publicity and are taken seriously. In recent years the controller has also functioned as a public ombudsman, receiving and acting upon grievances of individual citizens in
their dealings with bureaucracy. A law in 1968 also made provision for the
appointment of independent commissions of inquiry, with full investiga-
tive powers and the right to make specific recommendations (Ben-Gurion's
long campaign for a judicial investigation into the notorious Lavon affair
may have helped in the passage of this law).[15] The development of "consti-
tutionalism" and civic culture through the judicial system and analogous
bodies will be explored further in chapter 6.

Another area of progress in civic-mindedness, less mentioned perhaps
because it was so obvious, was foreign affairs and diplomacy. That these
realms belong to the prerogatives of a sovereign government is not disputed, and the pressures of the situation ensured that Israel's interests as a
state remained at the core of policy. Nevertheless, even here some particular traditions shaped at least the style of Israeli diplomacy: the assumption
of a hostile world was reflected in anger toward external criticism (in the
United Nations, for example), the legacy of *shtadlanim* was seen in the use of
special emissaries and tendencies to practice diplomacy secretly or through
back channels, and the fate of Jewish communities throughout the world
was a consistent concern in foreign policy.[16]

However, the Holocaust had already made the *yishuv* more independent
by eliminating its Eastern European base of support. On the question of
the role of other communities, Ben-Gurion again took the *mamlachtiut* position, refusing to compromise Israeli sovereignty by formalizing a role for
Jews who were not citizens of the state. On the other hand, as a matter
of practical compromise with the World Zionist Organization, the Jewish

Agency continued to function and to share responsibility with the government on immigration and settlement.[17]

Apart from foreign and defense policies, where both necessity and tradition supported the need for clear authority, policy was also centralized in some other areas. In economic policy, Mapai's central role in both the government and the Histadrut ensured a high level of coordination and control. In local government, inheritance of the Mandate structure meant a high degree of centralization, in contrast to the pre-Mandate *yishuv* structure where authority flowed from the local settlements to the top.[18]

But the key to centralization of authority in the Ben-Gurion system, and perhaps the greatest break with traditional patterns, was the way Ben-Gurion combined the parliamentary model with strong parties and coalition politics to produce a government with not only a strong civic aspect but also with many elements of majoritarianism. Strong parties had been at the center of *yishuv* politics; after statehood, they lost some of their functions as ideological movements providing a broad array of services directly to their members. On the other hand, most of them gained a share in running the new government and thus extended their power indirectly, over a broader area and through neutral and more effective machinery.[19]

Since no party ever captured a majority in an election, control was achieved by assembling a workable majority coalition and imposing the principle of collective responsibility. This tenet, taken from the British, meant that all ministers were bound by cabinet decisions. Parties thus could refuse to go along with a cabinet majority only if they were willing to sacrifice their share of power by leaving the coalition. Furthermore, Ben-Gurion constructed his coalitions in such a way that no single party could make the obvious counterthreat to bring down the government by leaving. This greatly reduced the actual power-sharing required for the central party (Mapai) to put together a government.[20]

The result, as in other parliamentary systems, is to eclipse the parliament. Although the legislative branch theoretically controls the government, the reality is executive dominance. Arian puts it most tersely: "One of the important myths of Israeli political life is that checks and balances exist within the system. This is simply not so."[21] So long as a government coalition, working through disciplined political parties, commands a stable majority in the Knesset, then it—and not the Knesset—is the locus of important decision-making. This is one of the hallmarks of the Westminster model of majoritarian democracy, and the most majoritarian aspect of the Israeli system (so long as the above assumptions hold). It is also, perhaps, Ben-Gurion's greatest accomplishment in pulling the Israeli government away from the hold of Jewish politics.

Needless to say, this leaves the Knesset with limited functions. The Knesset serves to register the results of an election, and thus the bargaining strength of each party, until the next election is held. It is also where the bargains and decisions reached are formally validated by legislative approval, serving, in other words, a "legitimizing function" primarily. But it is a weak institution, dependent on the government rather than the reverse.

Ben-Gurion's success in establishing effective cabinet rule led of course to criticism that there was too much concentration of state power. As already noted in chapter 1, fears for Israeli democracy were widely expressed and focused particularly on the majoritarian aspects of the Ben-Gurion system:

1. The lack of effective oversight by a Knesset dependent on the government.
2. The dominance of parties within the system, with few counterweights.
3. The dominance of one party; little chance for a government without Mapai.
4. The lack of democracy *within* parties, which tended to oligarchy.
5. The role of interlocking institutions (the Histadrut) tied to the power center.
6. The tendency of a dominant elite to heavy-handed paternalism.

The last point may merit additional comment. Rooted in the elitist traditions of Eastern European socialism and long accustomed to making the important decisions in the molding of a new society, many of the aging generation of Labor Zionists slipped easily into an attitude of benevolent despotism. To take just one illustration: in 1953 the cabinet, facing a growing exodus because of economic hardships, debated a proposal to withdraw from Israeli citizens the right to leave their country. Moshe Sharett, one of the more liberal and Western-oriented Mapai leaders, supported the proposal and even wrote in his diary that "the State should save them and their offspring—if necessary against their will—from the eternal gypsy curse with which they seek relief from absorption pains in their sole home in all the world."[22]

Intense ideological differences still prevailed during this period, leading to questions about the legitimacy of those on either end of the spectrum. At one point, security services implanted listening devices in the offices of Mapam—a party that was at various times a member of government coalitions. On the right, Herut was sometimes condemned as a "fascist" movement and was excluded not only as a potential coalition partner but also in the sharing of benefits. Although the first twenty years represented a high point in applying civic ideology to Israeli political life, it was also in some ways the least democratic period in the nation's politics. Many democratic trends—greater political competition, more autonomous social groups, less control of media, a judiciary more active in protecting rights, repeal of emer-

TABLE 1   Knesset Seats by Bloc and Party, 1949–1969

	Year of Election						
	1949	1951	1955	1959	1961	1965	1969
Labor Zionists	65	60	59	63	59	63	60
Mapai, Labor[a]	46	45	40	47	42	45	56
Others	19	15	19	16	17	18	4
Center-Right	33	35	33	31	34	31	32
Herut	14	8	15	17	17	26	26
General Zionists[b]	7	20	13	8	17		
Others	12	7	5	6	0	5	6
Religious	16	15	17	18	18	17	18
NRP	16	10	11	12	12	11	12
Haredi		5	6	6	6	6	6
Others	6	10	11	8	9	9	10
Non-Zionist left	4	5	6	3	5	5	6
Arab lists	2	5	5	5	4	4	4

SOURCE: Compiled by the author.

[a]In 1968, Mapai merged with two smaller parties to form the Israel Labor Party. From 1969 to 1984, the Labor Party and Mapam appeared in elections on a joint list (the Alignment).

[b]The General Zionists and the Progressive Party merged into the Liberal Party in 1961, and the Liberals (without most of the former Progressives) formed an electoral bloc with Herut from 1965.

gency regulations, less politicization in the civil service—became important factors only later in this period.

The long dominance of Labor Zionists was the central political fact of the first thirty years of statehood. This dominance was the result of a combination of external and internal circumstances that seemed to mold a national consensus around Labor leadership while disguising the developments that were slowly eroding it.

The remarkable political stability during this period is expressed in the consistency of voting behavior. As Table 1 shows, in the seven elections between 1949 and 1969, Labor Zionist parties as a bloc consistently gained at least half of the 120 available seats (from 59 to 65 seats, or 49 to 54 percent, to be precise).The Center-Right parties (a category that combines General Zionists and Revisionists) consistently received a little less than a third of the seats (from 31 to 35 seats, or 26 to 29 percent). Religious parties varied between 12.5 and 15 percent.

This striking regularity took place during a period of mass immigration and enormous social and political upheaval. A number of explanations are usually offered: (1) Given the consensus produced by the concern for survival, there was a tendency to stick to existing leadership; (2) in the circumstances of mass immigration, parties were able to recruit new members in rough proportion to their existing strength; (3) newcomers were more interested in concrete benefits than in ideology, and this instrumental dependence again worked in favor of the existing establishment, which had control of the benefits; (4) Ben-Gurion and Mapai were identified with the state, as the aura of the founding period had not yet faded; (5) the tendency to defer to official leadership in certain policy areas carried over into passive support at the polls.[23]

The capacity of parties to recruit new members in proportion to their existing strength was even institutionalized in the arrangements for absorption of new immigrants, which were governed by the omnipresent party key. The various camps and settlements were actually allocated to parties according to their electoral strength in the Jewish Agency, Histadrut, and Knesset. Mapai initially received over 50 percent of these allocations, meaning that over half of the new immigrants were dependent on services and instruction provided by Mapai personnel. In addition, new immigrants were funneled into the Histadrut Sick Fund (Kupat Holim Klalit) for health services, where they received three months of free membership and another year of services at a reduced rate—but in order to take advantage of this arrangement they had to become members of the Histadrut, where they were once again exposed to the dominant influence of Mapai.

The remarkable stability of voting patterns also reflected consensus on the tasks facing the nation and the basic strategies for dealing with them. The ruling Labor elite was able to align itself with this consensus not because of mass ideological conversion to its worldview, but because of accumulated institutional advantages, because of the need to focus on practical developmental problems (Labor Zionism's historic forte), and because it profited from a tendency to defer to existing leadership that was reinforced both by the threats to the state's existence and by the traditional Jewish habit of unification and closure against the outside.

In addition, different issues cut in different ways; Mapai and the National Religious Party disagreed on religious issues but found common ground on economic policy, while the relationship between Mapai and Mapam was sometimes the other way around. In this situation of cross-cutting alliances, no party was in total opposition to any other party; all would find some grounds for cooperation on at least one set of issues. There were at least three axes, or sets of issues, that cut in different ways in Israeli politics during this period.

First, on the normal left-right socioeconomic dimension, Labor Zionist parties were leftist and General Zionists (the chief ideological supporters of a free market) were rightist. Conflict on this dimension was somewhat muted, however, by the fact that the "far right"—Herut—favored a strong state role in the economy, partly in order to reduce the role of Mapai-dominated institutions such as the Histadrut but also as an expression of its general statist orientation and a certain populist streak.[24] In fact, because of the general acceptance of collective responsibility for social justice (translated in a modern setting into welfare statism), as well as the preoccupation with security, the left-right dimension never achieved in Israel the centrality it holds elsewhere. In fact, it has been obscured even more by a reverse correlation between income levels and party identification; see chapter 6.

Second was the axis of Arab-Israeli relations, which overlapped but was not identical to the first dimension.[25] There was, for example, a party to the left of Mapai on economic issues—Ahdut Ha'avoda—that took a more hard-line position on defense and territories. Conversely, the Progressives, a non-socialist party, took a fairly dovish position in foreign policy.

Third was the religious-secular axis, at this time not yet correlated with issues such as settlements in the occupied territories. Religious parties were not deeply involved in economic or foreign policy, beyond the prevailing consensus, but focused on religious matters. As late as 1968, Arian could note that "religious issues in Israel are largely independent of the left-right split."[26] This meant that the religious parties enjoyed a key position in the bargaining to establish a governing coalition. Though controlling only 10 to 15 percent of the seats, their flexibility on most economic and foreign policy issues made a bargain with them irresistible to Mapai. In return for concessions on issues on interest mainly to the religious community, the government would gain the consistent support of 10 to 15 percent of the Knesset, which greatly increased its leverage with parties making serious demands on mainstream issues. Consequently, the religious parties—the National Religious Party in particular—became the "balancers" of the system; with only brief interludes, the NRP was a member of every governing coalition until 1992.

The appearance of consensus was also strengthened in the early period by the weakness or absence of autonomous groups outside the party system. Most institutions and organizations in public life, including even most interest groups and most media, were tied to political parties, if not to the government itself or quasi-governmental bodies such as the Histadrut or the Jewish Agency. Only a part of the press was truly independent. There were relatively few political protest movements, and most of these were short lived. There was a low level of political activity and protest outside the system generally during these years; as late as 1972, a poll of secondary school students would show that fully 85 percent across the board—religious, traditional, or secular—believed in pursuing their political goals through the existing institutional framework.[27] It would seem, at first glance, that *mamlachtiut* had succeeded in creating an unmediated political system swept clear of significant autonomous centers of power.

Despite ferocious ideological warfare among the parties, many of the basic issues and decisions that faced the new state were either settled, or dormant, by the end of the first decade. On socioeconomic policy, the respective roles of the public and private sectors were basically settled, with considerable latitude for the latter but strong government direction and support for social welfare. The status quo that was reached on religious questions matched no one's ideological preferences but served as a reasonable point of reference that avoided major clashes (see chapter 8). The question of Israel's diplomatic orientation was settled by developments that left a pro-Western stance as the only choice. On security issues, there was general agreement on a policy of self-reliance, active defense, and de facto acceptance of existing borders. Territorial claims beyond the armistice lines of 1949 seemed increasingly unrealistic as time passed; Herut continued to insist on the Jewish right to all of Palestine as an article of faith in its creed, but the issue was dormant in Israeli politics. Nor did religious parties, at this point, challenge the territorial status quo.

This consensus did not, however, include non-Jewish citizens of Israel. Though members of the civic state by universalist criteria, the Arab minority in Israel was not in fact an actor in the political system in any meaningful way, nor did it have an equitable share of the benefits.[28] The case of Israeli Arabs is the acid test of civic-mindedness, since it poses the problem of an "enemy" minority; it demonstrates the character and limits of traditional communitarian politics in dealing with those outside the community (see chapter 9).

Even within the Jewish community the extent of the prevailing consensus, and the hold of Labor dominance, was limited. Some of the more divisive issues were merely dormant during these years, not resolved. Many of the factors that had given Labor an edge in mobilizing support were temporary in nature. There was a large and measurable gap between the political beliefs of the Labor Zionist elite and the general public; the electorate was voting to the left of its opinions, a situation unlikely to continue indefinitely.[29] Furthermore, the very longevity of Labor dominance produced bureaucratic ossification over time. By the late 1960s Israel was guided by a traditional political elite noted for its stability, longevity, and homogeneity, despite the growing pluralism of Israeli society. The longevity of this elite's tenure in power delayed the process of generation change, to an Israel-born leadership, that might have been expected sooner.[30] As a result, the change never fully took place, since it was soon superseded by a more fundamental revolution in Israeli politics.

In light of these facts, then, how much did *mamlachtiut* really change Jewish political life below the surface? Many of the "successes" in building a civic state were only minimal features of any sovereign state: a monopoly of legitimate authority in its own territory, control of defense and diplomacy. Ben-Gurion could also begin with a clean slate in structuring an army and a foreign service. In other areas, *mamlachtiut* was so intertwined with partisan advantages for Mapai that a judgment is difficult: this would apply to the dissolution of the Palmach, the attack on Etsel forces in the *Altalena* affair, and even the establishment of state-run labor exchanges (under the control of a Mapai minister of labor). In fact, anything that enlarged the scope of government during this period could be seen as an extension of Mapai's power.

Some argue that the enlargement of the state at the expense of the party was precisely what led to the eventual fall of Labor Zionism; Labor in essence disarmed itself, by allowing such critical functions as education to pass from a framework imbued with socialist values to a sanitized state network.[31] This greatly overstates, however, the actual impact of *mamlachtiut*. Mapai actually gave up little in the education reform, as it had only partial control of the Histadrut educational system, and gained in its place direction of the Ministry of Education.[32] As elsewhere, Labor Zionists moved from direct party rule in a sector of society to broader influence with more effective if "neutral" machinery.

Furthermore, in most of the new government machinery, even after the finalization of the civil service legislation in 1959, political appointments and the party key continued to be important. The legislation left a number of loopholes through which political appointments could be made, so that it is sometimes described as a compromise between a merit system and traditional patronage politics. While the scope of political appointments did narrow gradually over the years, only the most naive could avoid noticing a correlation between a minister's party affiliation and the political cast of his ministry. One should also add to the scorecard the areas in which *mamlachtiut* made no progress whatsoever, such as health services and electoral reform.

All in all, there was reason for the advocates of the Western model of a civic state to be disappointed in the final result. As Ben-Gurion himself expressed it in an interview at the end of his career, "Jews never understood *mamlachtiut*."[33]

THE PERSISTENCE OF JEWISH POLITICS

While Ben-Gurion's achievements in establishing effective executive power are impressive, it would be misleading to focus only on the structure and powers of Israeli institutions. As in traditional Jewish politics, there was often a mismatch between the formal procedures of government and the way in which decisions were actually made.

In this regard, the failure to adopt a written constitution is instructive. While absence of a constitution is usually regarded as a hallmark of majoritarianism, in the Israeli case it is more an expression of the traditional consociational style of Jewish politics. Religious party leaders were opposed in principle to the idea of a constitution, so the issue was averted through a compromise that made an eventual constitution possible but put the unbridgeable issue of principle aside for the moment. Unable to adopt a written constitution because of unbridgeable gaps of principle, the political elite devised a system whose stability rested on the sharing of power within the government and between the government and other institutions.

The government itself sometimes resembled a federation of competing bureaucracies. Ministries with different institutional histories (some of them predating the state), and with different constituencies, interacted like independent fiefdoms. There was a proliferation of government bodies or government-sponsored bodies with authority in specific areas; many decisions in Israeli public policy are made by such bodies as the State-Owned Companies Authority, the Council of Higher Education, the Israel Lands Authority, the Local Authorities Center, and even such bodies as the Vegetable Marketing Council and the Citrus Marketing Council. There was a fragmentation of functions among autonomous and overlapping authorities. Tax collection agencies, for example, included separate bodies for income tax, customs and excise taxes, value added tax, national insurance, property tax, television and radio taxes, and consolidated tax, as well as local tax agencies. Five different administrative agencies served the disabled community in Israel, while state planning was divided among at least five separate bodies (which set up some 200 companies). The proliferation of institutions, each jealously guarding its own territory, has reminded some observers of a classic feudal order.[34] Even in the area of local government there was less centralization among the more than 200 local autonomous authorities than would appear at first, as will be seen in chapter 6.

The Chief Rabbinate represents another autonomous institution carrying out public functions and providing what would normally be considered government services. This extends to an elaborate interlocking network that includes the Ministry for Religious Affairs, religious courts, local religious councils, religious state schools, and other state-supported institutions, all of it together constituting an institutional base from which Orthodox leaders negotiate with the central organs of power. Since ultra-Orthodox groups were independent of this official religious establishment, maintaining their own rabbinical authorities, court systems, schools, and other institutions, power was further diffused.

Another dimension of the diffusion of power was the prominence in Israeli public life of quasi-governmental institutions performing what would ordinarily be considered governmental functions. The Histadrut determined much public policy in such areas as health care, welfare, pensions, and wage policies, and remains a key participant—not just a source of influence, but an actor in the system—in broad economic decision-making. The Jewish Agency remained active in immigration, settlement, economic development, and relations with Jewish communities abroad. The Jewish National Fund continued to handle the purchase and management of public lands.

Among these various bodies bargaining has been the typical mode of operation, even when, as in the early statehood period, it might have appeared otherwise. Major decisions were usually preceded by negotiation not only within the dominant party and within the governing coalition, but also among government ministries and other official bodies, between the government and various quasi-governmental institutions, and even with private organizations and interests. Typical is the triangular bargaining process among the Ministry of Finance, the Histadrut, and the Manufacturers' Association that precedes any major change in economic policy. This reflects the division of the Israeli economy into three major sectors: governmental, Histadrut, and private. The economic divisions among these three sectors, and among the parties, were blurred considerably during the period of Labor dominance by the policy of extending state subsidies to keep down the cost of basic foodstuffs and to help nascent industries.

The reality of this pattern was also obscured for a considerable time by the dominance of one party. So long as Mapai controlled the government and the most important ministries within it, as well as the Histadrut and the Jewish Agency, then much of the bargaining took place within the party. But over time the role of parties as brokers declined as other bodies became more independent and more assertive. Finally, when control of the key institutions was no longer in the hands of a single party (after 1977), confrontations and bargaining became more intense and more public.

The role of parties is always critical, however, since they are still primary actors in the drama, and the crucial "governmental" decisions themselves are, as often as not, actually made in party councils, whether by the dominant party alone or in bargaining among the parties. The most important governing document in Israeli politics may be the coalition agreement among the parties following each election, which sets the agenda until the next election. Since parties often represent basic social divisions—particularly the religious parties—this is the stage at which some key minority interests are registered and taken into account.

Parties are also critical as the path for success in a political career. Normally it is only through a party that a political activist can advance. According to Gregory Mahler, 80.5 percent of the eighty-six Knesset members interviewed in 1974 and 1975 cited a history of party activity as the reason for their nomination to office.[35] The key to this process is, of course, the party list, since position on the list determines a candidate's chances of success. This was in the past centralized in the hands of the party leadership, an arrangement described as a major weakness of Israeli democracy and a prime illustration of the "iron law of oligarchy."[36] In fact, the entire party structure was highly oligarchic, based on the Eastern European model of layers of elected bodies, theoretically responsible to the rank and file but with power—including the all-important decisions on ranking candidates on the party list—actually flowing from the top. However, this process was less centralized than would appear. The ranking was in fact the product of intense intraparty bargaining, with a rough informal proportional representation operating to ensure the inclusion of important blocs and constituencies within the party. As a result, ironically, as the process became more democratic there were more problems in maintaining "balance" and minority representation on the lists.[37]

During the first two decades, Mapai was the center of every government, but it also had to share power with other parties. Mapai was the largest single party and was located in the middle of the political spectrum; it was inconceivable that any combination of parties on the two ends of the spectrum could organize a majority without Mapai. On the other hand, since Mapai never controlled a majority by itself, it was forced to seek coalition partners both from the left and from the right. The strength of the prevailing consensus is shown by the fact that only the Communists on the far left, and (until 1967) Herut on the far right, were ruled out as potential coalition partners. All other parties could conceivably become part of the government, and nearly all of them did at one time or another.

More-than-minimal governing coalitions that include most of the major groups of society are regarded as a feature of consociational democracy, as opposed to the majoritarian practice of rule with a bare majority. Since independence Israel has been governed about three-quarters of the time by more-than-minimal coalitions; that is, parties have been added to the government even though their votes were not needed for a majority in the Knesset.[38] On three occasions (1967–1970, 1984–1988, and 1988–1990), this even brought the two major blocs together in a Government of National Unity, a development which has only occasionally been matched by democratic regimes elsewhere. This kind of a "grand coalition" has not been the rule in the Israeli government either, though it has been routinely applied in other institutions such as the Jewish Agency and the World Zionist Organization. But overall the coalition-building has expressed the centrality of compromise and accommodation, trying to bring as many as possible inside the tent rather than leaving them in opposition. In this connection, the conventional wisdom that the religious parties have been the "balancers" in the system is exaggerated, especially for the earlier period. Religious parties (principally the National Religious Party) have been a part of almost every coalition, but up to 1992, only in ten of twenty-four coalitions was the government actually dependent on religious votes to keep a majority.[39]

There are also good political reasons to put together a more-than-minimal coalition. The prospective prime minister may simply be trying to domesticate pivotal groups and keep them out of the opposition, or show loyalty to faithful partners of the past, or simply build an extra margin for safety. But above all, Ben-Gurion's coalition strategy avoided dependence on one party, adding partners on both sides of the spectrum to neutralize each other and give himself greater leverage. This strategy outlasted Ben-Gurion: in the period from 1977 to 1992 there was at least one expendable party in the government at all times except for two brief periods in 1977 and 1990–1991. All in all, the tendency to broaden governing coalitions goes beyond the dominant-party period, and beyond what can be explained on tactical grounds alone, and has managed to encompass within one government parties with broadly different philosophical outlooks (dovish and hawkish, religious and secular, modernist and traditional).

The major expression of inclusiveness, however, was the dominance of proportionality. Cursory consideration was given at the outset to other electoral systems, but it was quickly decided to retain proportional representation. This would avoid any argument that might delay the early holding of the first state elections, reflecting the widespread acceptance of the principle of proportionality as well as the half-century precedent of its use. In 1958, the principle of proportionality was entrenched in the Basic Law establishing the Knesset, which was made subject to amendment only by an absolute majority of Knesset members rather than a majority of those present, as is the case with ordinary legislation.

In a wider sense, this was not just a matter of an electoral system but part of the entire system of power-sharing. In the Knesset, proportionality was extended to the deputy speakerships and to committee chairmanships and seats. Government-wide, the party key was the criterion by which offices, budgets, and ultimately the full range of institutional resources were divided among parties according to their electoral strength. This was of course already the case in the quasi-governmental institutions, such as the Histadrut, which continued to operate in accustomed fashion. The World Zionist Organization elected a total of eight vice presidents so that each party could sit on the Presidium. Within the government, this "spoils system" co-existed with the civil service legislation since it was not always easy to disentangle party interests from the merits of the case. Though the Likud was at first slow to exploit this system after coming to power, by its second term in office there was little hesitation; a government minister could even brag, in

1986, that stories on political appointments in his ministry actually helped him within his own party, and consequently he did not deny them even if there were false.[40]

Proportional representation guarantees a proliferation of parties, especially in Israel where the threshold for entry into the Knesset is set at the remarkably low level of 1.5 percent (before 1991 it was 1 percent). Generally twenty to thirty parties have run in the elections and ten to fifteen of them have passed the threshold. The proliferation of small parties has drawn much critical attention, and indeed the sheer number of bargaining partners has made coalition negotiation much more complex and has led to disproportionate material rewards (control of a government ministry by a two- or three-person faction, for example). But by their presence, small parties also serve several purposes in the system. During the earlier period, they served as a check on domination by Mapai. The easy access of small parties also checked oligarchic trends within parties, since dissatisfied factions always had (and often used) the option of seceding and running as a separate list, with reasonable chances for success. Small parties also serve to test the appeal of new ideas and the measure of dissatisfaction with the major parties. Finally, it is only through the low threshold for representation that minorities not close to the mainstream—particularly the ultra-Orthodox and the Arabs—gain direct representation in the Knesset.

The weakness of the Knesset also appears somewhat differently in this context. It is then seen not simply as a legislative body dominated by the executive but as one of the numerous arenas of bargaining and power-sharing brokered by the parties. As a legislative body, it is an easy target of ridicule. Seldom do Knesset deliberations change the thrust of government decisions. Nearly all government-initiated bills are enacted into law, and they account for the vastly greater part of the legislation adopted.[41] Only twice has the Knesset passed a no-confidence vote in the government. Parties not only control the votes of their members (except on minor matters or, occasionally, by prior agreement on particularly controversial issues), but they also control the time allotted for speaking in plenary sessions and the right to propose a private bill (a quota is issued to each party). Even the right to ask questions is limited: questions must be in writing, those from members of government parties are screened by party leaders, and there is no guarantee that the minister will respond with a serious answer. It is, therefore, not too surprising that the level of dissatisfaction and frustration among rank and file legislators is extremely high.[42]

Yet the Knesset is an integral part of the bargaining process and a mirror of the political culture in which it is embedded. It does more than merely process government decisions; though most legislation comes from the government, hardly any of it emerges in exactly the form it was introduced. And while the government rarely loses a no-confidence vote, it has often been defeated on other votes where the expression of contrariness is less heavily penalized. Debate is lively and provocative; the opposition has and uses the chance to dramatize its dissent. Furthermore, the sessions are totally open to the media, with television coverage usually focusing precisely on the most vociferous and unruly moments of parliamentary wrangling. As a result the Knesset's lack of decorum has become a standing joke; a frequent plea used to quiet a gathering is "Order, please! This is not the Knesset here!"

Knesset members also, surprisingly, play a role as representatives of specific constituencies. This is surprising because they are not formally elected from any constituency and because the lack of such ties is supposedly one of the weakest aspects of proportional representation. Yet in fact party lists are drawn up to include representatives of key groups both inside and outside the party: major city party branches, the kibbutz and moshav (cooperative) movements, the Histadrut, those from various communal or occupational groups, women, or minorities. The matter is even simpler for the smaller parties, whose supporters can clearly identify the one or two representatives who speak for them. As a result, many citizens actually do have their "functional" representative to whom they turn. In this way the intimacy of the system counters the distance presumably created by proportional representation.

Ironically, Knesset members say that they spend most of their time, and derive most of their satisfaction, from constituent services. Some admit spending little time in Knesset sessions, using it instead to respond to those who have turned to them for assistance. This often involves acting as an intermediary between private citizens and groups on one side, and government agencies on the other (a kind of informal ombudsman). Knesset members can and do, however, go directly to the minister responsible rather than dealing with lower levels of the civil service. These kinds of personalized channels do not differ greatly from traditional patterns, and therefore it is no surprise that "the Israeli bureaucracy is geared to this clientele style of problem solving."[43]

Interest groups in Israel also reflect this state of affairs. There is relatively little legislative lobbying of the traditional sort, since the important decisions are not made in the Knesset. There was also a relatively low level of truly autonomous bodies in the earlier period. Interest groups were organized to bargain with, or to pressure, the governmental ministries, parties, and other bodies that together made the important decisions. For this purpose, they not only approached decision-makers directly, as they would in most pluralist democratic systems, but sometimes become an integral part of the process. The kibbutz and moshav movements have been closely tied to the Ministry of Agriculture; the Israeli Manufacturers' Association works closely with the Ministry of Commerce and Industry. To an unusual extent, in comparison to like situations elsewhere, doctors are consulted on the policies of the Ministry of Health, bus drivers on those of the Ministry of Transport, and teachers on those of the Ministry of Education. In some cases, especially on economic issues, the interest group goes beyond the role of bargaining for its own interests, and itself becomes a participant in the decision-making. At a minimum, many such groups are able to informally veto proposals that they consider inimical to their interests.[44]

Even at its peak, therefore, centralized authority was offset by a bargaining style that permeated Israeli public life. What has been called a sense of "federative kinship" enables Israelis to regard official acts as points of reference, rather than as self-evident obligations. There is always room for argument; any decision can be (and usually is) contested both before it is made and after it has supposedly been finalized. Characteristically, therefore, there is a search for consensus before a decision is made, and strong disagreement usually leads to postponement of the matter pending further negotiations. Daniel Elazar argues that the pervasiveness of this consensual style of operation has made hierarchical organizations in Israel less efficient than those that respect and accommodate the traditional ways of doing business.[45]

Another dimension of this pattern is the tendency to deal with outside challenges by trying to bring them within the system. Such efforts of co-optation were partly successful in the pre-state period, as we have seen, and were pursued more energetically after statehood. The history of the gradual step-by-step inclusion of the ultra-Orthodox community has, in a sense, been an essay in co-optation of a potentially alienated and disruptive force. Discontent among Jews from Asia and Africa has typically been met by co-optation of leaders of those communities, at first on a symbolic scale and eventually on a broad—if not quite proportional—basis (see chapter 7). The few incidents of extraparliamentary protest that arose in the early period on this communal background led to co-optation of the leaders directly involved. This perhaps helps explain the relatively low level of protest and extraparliamentary political activity during these years, when the political system was still able to cope with the relatively few challenges that it faced by resorting to this traditional tool.[46]

While traditional protest and direct action may have been at a low ebb during the first two or three decades after 1948, the level of political awareness and knowledge was high. The Israeli public, as Jewish publics generally, was highly politicized and sensitive to developments likely to impinge on it. In a study done to compare Israeli "civic culture" with that of the five nations studied in Gabriel Almond and Sydney Verba's classic 1963 study, 79 percent of the Israeli respondents reported reading a newspaper at least once a week (the highest figure in Almond and Verba's study was 53 percent in Western Germany). Also, 76 percent of the Israeli sample followed political news on radio or television at least once a week (the highest elsewhere was

58 percent in the United States). In terms of political knowledge, 74 percent of the Israelis could name at least four government ministries and party leaders, as against 40 percent of the Germans, 34 percent of the Americans and the British, 23 percent of the Italians, and 21 percent of the Mexicans. Other studies have confirmed the general finding of a remarkably high (by comparative standards) level of political interest and awareness in Israel.[47]

This is matched by a fairly high level of participation in elections, with about 80 percent turning out regularly. Access to the system for new parties is relatively easy, as seen in the large number of parties contending. Only two parties that met the minimal requirements have ever been excluded from the election: the Arab nationalist party El Ard in 1964, on grounds that .it challenged the existence of Israel, and Rabbi Meir Kahane's party, Kach, after 1988 because its platform was judged to be racist.

Access to the media was more limited in the early period, since radio (and television, which began in the late 1960s) were under state control, and most of the press was party affiliated. This became more pluralistic and more flexible over time, however. In 1965 the establishment of the Israel Broadcasting Authority brought more autonomy to the electronic media, though a degree of political influence remained and the issue became even more controversial after the Likud takeover in 1977. Nevertheless, a variety of viewpoints are heard, especially during election campaigns when each party is given free broadcast time (again, in proportion to its electoral strength). The press over the years became increasingly variegated and critical, with much of the party press disappearing. Access to the foreign press, which is unrestricted, has undercut occasional government efforts to keep sensitive issues out of the media; once printed in a foreign publication, a story can be circulated freely in Israel and (usually) even reprinted in Hebrew translation by Israeli periodicals.

The intimate scale of Israeli politics should also be taken into account. The exposure of Israeli leaders to their own public is extensive: a prominent Israeli party leader, in or out of government, will spend a large number of hours every week in direct and unrehearsed contact with the public in various forums, all open to media coverage. Those at the very top appear almost nightly on Israeli news programs (watched by a vast majority of the nation), either in live interviews or in films of appearances elsewhere. The average educated Israeli has seen the prominent political figures so often on the screen and in flesh that they see them as acquaintances, if not as members of the family. Certainly the aura of office is eroded to a great extent by this close contact. Members of the public are not inhibited by any sense of awe in dealing with their own leaders; the mystery has been dissipated.

But while political awareness and knowledge were at high levels, participation in the early years was usually limited to verbal expression, as opposed to direct action. There were only a few instances in which a wave of public discontent was strong enough to force the hand of the government, notably in forcing the formation of the National Unity Government on the eve of the 1967 war, and in establishing a commission of inquiry to probe the government's failings in the Yom Kippur War of 1973. On the whole, however, during the 1948–1977 period Israel ranked about average compared to other nations on indicators of political protest and well below average on indicators of political violence.[48]

This lack of direct political activity can be attributed to the lack of nonpartisan civic organizations standing outside the system, to the seemingly unchallengeable centralization in Ben-Gurion's party government, and to the general aura of paternalistic control. Public reaction remained largely verbal because other channels seemed to be of little use. There were danger signals that the Israeli Establishment failed to note or to act upon. Despite (or because of) the high level of political awareness and knowledge, public appraisal of the government's performance and of the average citizen's ability to influence it (what political scientists call the "sense of political efficacy") were both remarkably low. In the comparison to the five nations studied by Almond and Verba in the 1960s, only 5 percent of Israelis thought that the government generally improved conditions, as against 58 to 71 percent in the other cases. Only 27 percent expected equal treatment from the government, fewer than the 32 percent in Mexico and well below the 56 to 89 percent in the other four democratic nations.[49] In answer to the question "Do people like yourself have an influence on the government?" only 25 percent responded positively in 1960, and only 15 percent in a 1969 survey. In a series of surveys in 1973, the affirmative answers ranged from about a third to less than one-half. Again, the figures were notably higher in other democratic countries.[50]

Most Israelis still felt that the best way to influence the government was through family or personal connections. The traditional Jewish reliance on connections was entirely consonant with prevailing Middle Eastern practices and with the pragmatic view of officialdom adopted by early settlers; only the fleeting British presence during the Mandatory period presented a model of objective and impartial bureaucracy. It is not surprising, then, to find that Israelis developed a low regard for civil servants as "relatively dishonest, unpleasant, inefficient, passive, slow, and unstable . . . Israelis find their national bureaucracy and its employees to be undesirable features of the political community."[51]

Underneath the seeming stability, there were signs of a basically confrontational view of politics that was only temporarily submerged. There was a widespread assumption that only direct action, outside the system and in defiance both of established procedures and the law, could actually achieve anything. One of the leaders of the dissident Black Panthers, a group active in the early 1970s, later reported that he had been urged by Establishment figures themselves to act disruptively in order to get attention and "to move things." Another Black Panther leader, emphasizing the need for street action for lack of a viable option, declared that "we must do things which are illegal but legitimate."[52] Contemporary Israeli Hebrew is rich with phrases that suggest the need and utility of bypassing established procedures and acting directly: "to move things," "to get by" (*l'histader*), "to create facts," "to whistle at (defy) all of them," "to take matters in hand," "to get what one has coming," "to pound on the table," "to turn tables upside down," "to make noise," "to take to the streets." Even when appearances seemed to indicate otherwise, the traditional attitude of expediency and disrespect toward established authority and procedures remained as a strong undercurrent in Israeli political culture.

This is linked to the long-standing pattern of "illegalism" identified by Ehud Sprinzak. Sprinzak defines this pattern as "an orientation that regards respect for the law and respect for the rule of law not as a basic value, but as a specific mode of behavior that one may or may not follow according to considerations of expediency."[53] Such behavior can be traced back to the Eastern European shtetl but was buttressed by the corrupt practices of the Ottoman system and by the premium put on circumventing British opposition during the Mandatory period. Its expressions include corruption, both personal and political; clientalism (*protektsia*) and patronage (including the traditional role of the *macher,* or man of influence, in Jewish life); a general contempt for civil law or other universal norms; ideologies that justify skirting the law (in the name of higher principle, or for "the good of the movement"); and extraparliamentary political methods, including violence.[54]

Some of these tendencies were curbed or submerged in the Ben-Gurion system; personal corruption was not so visible, and extraparliamentary activity was in temporary eclipse. But as Sprinzak notes, the push for *mamlachtiut* did not focus on the rule of law and in fact did not even include a legal theory as one of its elements.[55] There were in fact considerable abuses of power, bordering on corruption, by the parties in power—all in the name of "the good of the movement." The prevailing ethos was reflected in a letter that Levi Eshkol, then treasurer of the Jewish Agency, wrote to the controller of that agency regarding a case of petty corruption among some of its foreign representatives. Quoting from the Bible (Deuteronomy 25:4), Eshkol admonished the controller that "you shall not muzzle the ox when it treads the grain"—in other words, those working hard for the cause are entitled to some benefits under the table.

Thus the drive for "civicness" did not alter many habits of Jewish political behavior. It did achieve some coherence in government authority and pushed the system, at least temporarily, toward greater centralization and unqualified majority rule. A working parliamentary system was established, dominated by the executive and without separation of powers, and with no written constitution or other limits on parliamentary sovereignty. Local government was subordinated to central control, a dominant party assured coordination of the whole, collective responsibility prevailed in the cabinet, nonparty groups remained relatively weak, and governing coalitions fell short of the kind of "grand coalition" associated with a broad social contract. Thus, despite the elements of consociational democracy that remained, Lijphart classified the Israeli government as only semi-consociational, while Medding maintains that the majoritarian elements were at least temporarily dominant.[56]

Yet many elements of consociationalism, in the Jewish style, remained in the new state. Proportional representation, with the ubiquitous party key, and mutual veto, especially in religious matters, were central. But above all, there was power-sharing among different centers, obscured for the time being by the dominant role of the same party in these centers. Politics was still pervaded by a bargaining and negotiating style on most key issues.

Thus, even at the peak of *mamlachtiut,* the intense dialectic between universalist impulses and traditional patterns continued. Particularistic dimensions were submerged but not subdued. Furthermore, with the passage of time came increasing signs of the weakening of both Labor dominance and the civic and majoritarian elements Labor had imposed on the system. "The very establishment of a sovereign state created the potential for [basic themes and orientations latent in earlier periods of Jewish history] to erupt anew, to break through the existing institutional hold, thus generating continual challenges for Israeli society and the political system."[57]

However, this struggle was submerged in turn by an even more forceful reality: preoccupation with security. This overwhelming concern cut across the universalist-particularist tension in various and unexpected ways.

FIVE

The Filter of Security

The drift away from the civic model, analyzed in the previous chapter, also threatened to erode civilian control over the military. The potential for such a development existed in the system: just as the "interpenetration" of army and society involved civilianization of military life, it also opened the door to military influence on political decisions. The end of Labor dominance, in 1977, opened the door further. The loss of consensus and the polarization of opinions gave top commanders greater room to maneuver; the political orientation of the chief of staff acquired an importance it had not previously had. In addition, the big jump in defense budgets after the 1973 war also increased the importance of the military establishment and enlarged the infrastructure from which it drew support (Israel now had a "military-industrial complex" worth mentioning on an international scale).[1]

To many it appeared that this threat materialized in the 1980s. In his second government, formed in August 1981, Menachem Begin appointed Ariel Sharon, a reserve army general, as minister of defense. Though Sharon was not the first former military commander to serve in this civilian post— he was preceded by Moshe Dayan and Ezer Weizman—his appointment provoked apprehension because of the widespread perception that he had little regard for legal and political constraints (unconfirmed reports claimed that Begin himself worried aloud that Sharon's first act would be to surround the Knesset with tanks).[2] In carrying out the invasion of Lebanon in 1982, Sharon went far beyond the official aim of expelling Palestine Liberation Organization (PLO) forces from southern Lebanon, in effect carrying out his own undeclared agenda of driving both the PLO and Syria out of Lebanon entirely, overseeing the emergence of a Lebanese government friendly to Israel, and creating a situation in which Palestinians would have to pursue their political aspirations in Jordan rather than the West Bank.[3]

In order to pursue this design, Sharon misled the Israeli cabinet at various stages of the campaign, which eventually brought him into direct conflict with Begin. Ultimately the design failed of its own impracticality, but only the massacre of Palestinian civilians at Sabra and Shatila by Lebanese Christian forces, leading to the government inquiry under the Kahan Commission, brought about Sharon's resignation as minister of defense.[4] It might be pointed out, however, that some of the stiffest opposition to Sharon's moves came from within the army itself, where dovish military commanders spoke up both within and outside of channels—indicating that the close intertwining of civilian and military can work in both directions.

Ironically, the state founded to solve the perennial problem of Jewish security has itself been plagued by constant insecurity. Israelis cite security—"the refuge and protection which Israel gives each Jew"—more often than any other reason as a basis for Jewish rights in Israel.[5] As insecure as life in Israel might appear, its role as a means for Jews to provide for their own security, rather than being subject to what the fates decreed, was basic to Zionism's very purpose.

But viewed coldly and objectively, the realities of the threat to Israel's existence were overwhelming. The State of Israel was closed off by a wall of hostile Arab states committed to reversing the results of the 1948 war. Until 1967 the bulk of the population was within artillery range of hostile armies, and through the 1991 Persian Gulf War the Israeli public was never more than about five years from either the last conflict or the next one. The six neighboring Arab states enjoyed a population advantage over Israel that varied between 50 to 1 and 20 to 1. Egypt, Syria, Jordan, and Iraq together still have an advantage of about 8 to 1 in regular armed forces, 5 to 1 with all reserves mobilized, and 3 to 1 in major battle tanks and in combat aircraft.[6] Israel also faced a number of active terrorist organizations whose international support and sources of finance were without precedent. In addition, international isolation left the country increasingly dependent on a single major power for both vital military equipment and economic viability.

The economic pressures were enormous. Not only did Israel bear a crushing defense burden by any standard, but in the first years of statehood it also faced economic warfare (the Arab boycott) and a massive influx of new immigrants. In the first three and a half years under independence the population doubled, and by the end of the first decade it had tripled. In the 1970s defense spending as a proportion of GDP (gross domestic product) hovered in the 20 to 30 percent range, against the 3 to 6 percent common in Western countries or the peak figure of 12 to 17 percent in the former Soviet Union. But with the highest per capita national debt in the world, debt service topped even defense in the national budget, leading to an almost unbelievable level of total government spending: 60 to 80 percent of the GDP, depending on how it is measured.

Nor could Israel rely on international support to redress this imbalance. The circumstances that led to a convergence of U.S. and Soviet support for Israeli statehood in 1948 changed, and from the early 1950s the Soviet Union was increasingly the ally and armorer of Israel's enemies. Most Western countries would not sell arms to Israel, though many sold arms to Arab states. The international climate became yet more hostile with the rise of the Third World, which tended to regard Israel as part of the colonial West and the Palestinian Arabs as victims of Western imperialism.

Consequently security considerations became the central constraint of Israeli politics, the filter through which all other issues and debates were forced to pass.[7]

THE *DIKTAT* OF DEFENSE

Analysts sometimes define Israel's security as its ability to defeat any likely coalition of belligerents in all-out war. This would be difficult enough to guarantee under all circumstances. But Israelis, with their personal experiences as refugees, tend to interpret security more broadly as freedom from threat to their personal safety and the ability to live without fear of politically motivated violence. This is an infinitely more difficult level of security for any government to guarantee its citizens when daily existence is threatened by violence short of war: artillery bombardments, armed incursions, street violence, random terrorism, long-range missile strikes on civilian centers. We must distinguish between basic security (war-fighting capability) and current or personal security (control of lesser threats), and no account of the impact of security concerns on Israeli life can afford to focus exclusively on the former. In a 1993 survey, 85 percent of Israelis expressed fear of being attacked by an Arab during their daily activities.[8]

Security cannot be measured simply by the objective threats that a nation faces. In the end, it is a matter of a subjective feeling of safety in the minds of individuals, which is more difficult to achieve among a Jewish generation that passed through successive waves of twentieth-century antisemitism culminating in the Holocaust. The Jewish worldview is in any event the product of twenty centuries of religious and ethnic persecution; no minority in history has been so unremittingly conditioned to regard the world as an essentially vicious place. The Holocaust was merely the latest and most brutal chapter in a long history. Nevertheless, Jews throughout the world were stunned by the world's lack of response to Nazi genocide. They noted the lack of any international effort to save Jewish lives in Europe and the general closing of doors to would-be refugees. Even after the war, the Palestinian Jewish community, most of whom lost family and friends in the Holocaust, were not allowed to receive the survivors. In the words of a leading Israeli literary figure, the Holocaust left a "latent hysteria" in Israeli life.[9]

A mood of despair and outrage, born of the Mandate experience and the Holocaust, intensified during the period of the Israeli War of Independence. Though the United Nations recommended establishment of a Jewish and an Arab state in Palestine, no effort was made to enforce this decision against Arab opposition. The Jewish community was left to face the regular armies of five Arab states, some of them armed by Western states while Israel contended with a general arms embargo (broken only, to some extent, by Soviet-bloc countries). Despite the widespread perception that another Holocaust was in the making, the world seemed as indifferent or as passive as it had the first time.

This sense of isolation in a hostile world was further strengthened by the events of 1956–1957 and 1967. In the first case, Israel faced universal condemnation for what most Israelis regarded as a necessary act of self-defense to stop attacks along the Egyptian border and to end an illegal blocking of access to Israel's southern port, Eilat. Israel was then forced to withdraw from Sinai in return for international assurances of free passage to Eilat that turned out to be valueless when tested ten years later. When these guarantees collapsed, in 1967, Israel again stood alone. Once more, as Israelis saw it, only the strength of their own armed forces prevented national destruction.

In some ways the constraints of security favored universalistic and civic ideas, and in other ways they reinforced particularistic and traditional leanings. In either case, security concerns meant greater pressure on democracy, encouraging either greater centralization of authority or greater clannishness in dealing with the outside.

The centrality of foreign affairs and defense ought to promote *mamlachtiut* (civic-mindedness), since the need for national unity under crisis conditions was obvious. Some maintain that it is only the external threat that has held Israel together. The army and the foreign service operated basically outside the "bargaining" framework and could be built along rational civic and statist lines. In foreign policy, there was little bargaining over a compromise policy; one approach was dominant before 1977 and from 1992 to 1996, and another has been dominant whenever the Likud was in a position to set or veto policy.

The need for unity translated into a strong tendency to defer to the existing leadership, despite the strong Jewish tradition of skepticism toward authority. The question then became: is there too much deference to authority? Whatever happened to the traditional Jewish opposition to the concentration of power? The truth is that obsession with security actually meshes very well with proclivities rooted in the Jewish past. The threat of danger from the outside was to a great extent what made consensus and voluntarism work in the *kahal* and in the *yishuv*. Increased threat usually forced Jews to bond more closely together, with tradition as the glue that held them together and ensured their survival. Finding themselves surrounded by enemies who swore to destroy them did not strike Israelis as a novel occurrence calling for new departures; to the contrary, it evoked a long collective memory of similar threats (or threats seen as similar) of which this was merely the latest instance. Four of the major holidays on the Jewish calendar (Passover, Purim, Hanukkah, and Tishah b'Av) commemorate a threat to Jewish existence in one form or another. The main difference this time was that Jews were organized to fight back.

Wars with Arab states were not seen as events in international politics rooted in a territorial dispute, but as acts of primordial hostility that evoked images of the Holocaust and other historical attempts simply to kill Jews. Acts of terror against Israeli civilians were seen not as political actions designed (however brutally) to achieve Palestinian national aims but as plain and simple acts of antisemitism. A deep sense of "familism" has always pervaded the Israeli reaction to these events; the death of a single Israeli "on a national background" (that is, by an Arab, for political reasons) is seen by most Israelis as an attack on a family member and as a personal threat, evoking a degree of horror and rage far beyond that triggered by an ordinary "nonpolitical" murder. Finally, traditional Jewish politics included a tendency to secrecy and closure to the outside, and a problematic approach to non-Jewish minorities. The first of these will be examined in the following section, and the second in chapter 9.

The consensus was that Arab threats should be taken seriously—that they were not just words—and that the security of Israel was always in jeopardy, since a single defeat would mean national destruction.[10] Demonstrations of Arab moderation were regarded with suspicion, as they were likely to be tactical maneuvers rather than abandonment of the basic design of destroying Israel. This primordial "us–them" view of this conflict clings to the assumption of unyielding hostility as an explanation that makes sense of a threatening world and reinforces the Jewish self-image as the perpetual victim of unreasoning hatred, rather than simply as the party to a conflict.

In this view there was no choice but self-reliance. International support or guarantees could not be trusted as a reliable basis for national security. The only reliable outside allies were the Jewish communities of the world. Apart from other forms of support, the Jewish Diaspora was also important as a source of immigration, the raison d'etre of the state. Israel was concerned with the well-being of Jewish communities elsewhere, and its relations with other nations have often been affected by the interests of local Jewish communities.

Given perceived vulnerability and self-reliance, Israelis adopted an active defense. They stressed the need to anticipate, to seize the initiative, and to take the war to the other's territory. The preemptive attacks of 1956 and 1967 are cases in point. In terms of concrete defense doctrines, this was expressed in the focus on mobility, forward deployment, and threats of punitive counterblows that in some ways resembled strategies of nuclear deterrence.[11] But if Israel tended to active defense on a military level, it showed an aversion to risk taking in politics or diplomacy. Israeli diplomacy tended to be reactive, responding to events and shunning bold initiatives. There was a distinct distaste for diplomatic methods in general, given the meager resources that Israel possessed for playing the diplomatic game and natural suspicion of a process in which Jews had little experience and for which history had not taught them to have high regard.[12]

Another element in the consensus was a pro-Western orientation. There were, in the beginning, neutralist tendencies in the Israeli leadership, given their East European ties, socialist sympathies, and hopes of continuing support from both sides of the Cold War. But the behavior of the Soviet Union from the early 1950s, toward Jews within its borders and Zionism generally, soon led to a revision of this attitude. Even before the Soviet Union adopted a pro-Arab stance and moved to arm Israel's enemies, it had for ideological reasons tried to discredit the idea of Israel as a homeland for all Jews, especially Soviet Jews. In the Soviet version of socialism there was little room for recognition of Jewish nationality.

Israel thus found itself pushed into closer cooperation with those who opposed the Soviets. This was reinforced by a natural affinity of values with democratic Western countries, as well as the importance of Jewish communities in the West and especially in the United States. Economic realities also played a role, as the Israeli economy quickly developed close linkages with the West. Pro-Soviet views, which had once been frequently heard in Labor Zionist circles (especially in Mapam), practically disappeared from Israeli public debate within a decade.

On specific issues, there was a consensus that Arab refugees from the 1948 war should be dealt with only in the framework of final peace treaties with the Arab states, and that most of them would have to be resettled in Arab countries, as Jewish refugees from Arab countries had been resettled in Israel. There was also general acceptance of the 1949 armistice lines as a basis for final borders; those who still sought the whole of Palestine were stymied by the seeming impossibility of the goal. By 1965 even Herut, in adopting a common electoral platform with the Liberals, had dropped specific territorial claims beyond the existing lines. The dominant view was that the key to an Israeli-Arab peace was negotiation with Jordan, which by annexing the West Bank held most of what was to have been the Arab state in Palestine. In fact, negotiations with Jordan's King Abdallah were carried out immediately after the 1948 war and ended only when the king was assassinated in 1951.

Events seemed to support the traditional Labor attitude that a compact but clearly Jewish state in part of Palestine was preferable to the assertion of sovereignty over all of Palestine, which would always have a large Arab population even if Jews did come to constitute a majority. In the 1950s and 1960s Ben-Gurion was the key representative of this "low territorial profile" that combined minimal rule over Arabs with an active defense.[13] The molding of a consensus was furthered by Ben-Gurion's strong personality and by the fact that many Israelis, especially new immigrants, tended to identify him with the state itself because of his historic role in Israel's founding.

The tension between security demands and democracy was greatest precisely at those points where democracy was weakest in tradition. The dictates of security fit in only too well with the passion for secrecy and the lack of provision for the collective rights of non-Jewish minorities. There were other manifestations of security mania that may be linked to the past. The penchant for activism can be seen as overcompensation for the passivity and weakness of the past, leading to such heady gestures as the challenging of Soviet anti-aircraft crews, and even Soviet pilots, during the 1969–1970 war of attrition on the Suez Canal. Many observers noted a "cult of toughness" among Israeli youth, symbolized by popular figures such as Meir Har-Tsion, a soldier whose exploits became legendary.[14]

None of this is very surprising; mobilization against external threats is generally thought to be inimical to democracy. In 1941 the noted social scientist Harold Lasswell projected as "probable" a state of the future in which the specialists in violence would dominate and in which the entire population would be mobilized on behalf of the national military effort. This "garrison state," as he later elaborated, would be characterized by constant increases in defense spending, the expansion and centralization of government, the withholding of information, the weakening of political parties and the legislature, loss of civil liberties, and the decline of courts as limits on the government.[15] Such a course of development seemed quite possible in the Israel of the 1950s, and indeed some of these developments (such as higher defense spending and weaker political parties) came to pass. Yet overall Israel did not become a garrison state by Lasswell's definition.

Why has Israel not behaved like a society under siege? Why hasn't the army become the dominant institution in the country?

One answer to this question, often overlooked, is that a crisis that extends for half a century is no longer a crisis but a normal state of affairs. The high state of tension and the high degree of mobilization become routinized; it is impossible to keep an entire society forever living at the highest pitch of anxiety. Normality sets in; ordinary patterns of life develop even under the most unpropitious conditions. As will be seen, the "emergency regulations" under which Israelis live become less emergency-like, and more regularized and routinized, as time passes. A better image for the cycle of war and normality in Israel may be the concept of the "interrupted society" as developed by Baruch Kimmerling. Israelis pull together in time of genuine crisis (wartime), but revert to more disorderly and individualistic behavior when tensions are "merely" normal.[16] This, also, is hardly a new pattern in Jewish life, but reflects in a general way the rhythm of intermittent threat and quiescence that characterized much of Diaspora life.

The absence of a strictly military tradition also helps account for Israel's relatively nonpolitical army. There was no history of a military role in politics, and in fact it was the political leadership (in the *yishuv*) that invented the military. The fighting forces—Hagana and Etsel—began as extensions of civilian organizations. Ben-Gurion made sure of civilian supremacy before and after statehood, while moving to professionalize the military force being created. To keep the army out of politics, he took over its direction personally, serving as minister of defense as well as prime minister. Ultimate control of the military was vested in the cabinet, through the minister of defense, with the chief of staff (the highest-ranking military professional) appointed by the cabinet on the recommendation of the minister of defense. These arrangements were formalized in the Basic Law: Israel Defense Forces, adopted in 1976.

There are imperfections in civilian control as the system actually operates. Much depends on the minister of defense, who is the link between military professionals and the civilian government. So long as the minister is a strong representative of the cabinet, and at the same time holds the respect of the top military leadership, the structure can work as designed. But this is a highly personalized arrangement, like so much in Israeli politics. In essence, civilian control is not really institutionalized in a civilianized Ministry of Defense but rests on one person. There is no assurance that the cabinet will control the minister of defense, and any outside oversight (by the Knesset, for example) is usually weak and after the fact.

So long as Ben-Gurion held both positions, until 1963, his personal stature was a guarantee that military officers would not exceed their role. But when the two positions were divided, and when former military professionals became ministers of defense, the lines of authority became murky and an avenue for military influence on policymaking was opened up. This peaked in the Lebanese War in 1982, when Minister of Defense Ariel Sharon conducted his own policy rather than that of the cabinet and (as a former commander himself) also took over some of the operational responsibility in the field.

However, when military officers did cross the line into political matters, their views were not uniform but ran the same gamut as their civilian counterparts. In fact, much of the dovish opposition to the Lebanese War came from within the army itself, as did many of the more moderate views on dealing with the Palestinian *intifada* (uprising) that began in 1987. The universality of military service and the ad hoc way in which the military was built limit the development of a military ethos and careerism separate from the society at large. Nearly all Israeli males, and a high proportion of young women as well, pass through a required period of service. But the regular army remains relatively small; most of the forces mobilized in wartime are reservists drawn from all walks of life. The small core of career army officers is also rotated out for early retirement by the time they are in their forties, thus limiting the development of a senior class of professional officers who might gain institutional status in the Israeli bargaining network. Given the scale of the country, there is little "garrison life"—most soldiers go home on weekends and some even commute on a daily basis. The social democracy in the Israeli army—its informality, lack of attention to rank, and absence of spit and polish—has long been notorious.[17]

Thus no separate military caste has developed in Israel; the army reflects the society, with a spectrum of views that differs very little (the slight difference in voting patterns seems to be a function of age rather than military service). Left-wing positions are as well represented in the army as elsewhere; many dovish political parties and movements have featured former top military commanders in their leadership. Left-wing kibbutzim have traditionally supplied officers and men for the most prestigious elite fighting units.[18] Where army and society are so intertwined and interpenetrated, civilianization of the army is as apparent as militarization of society. The blurring of lines between the two works in both directions. The leading military sociologists in Israel summarize the situation in these words: "Although Israel has been immersed in a prolonged violent conflict, it does not behave like a society under siege. Its democratic government and routine civilian life are a far cry from the type of 'siege mentality' bred by living under a constant state of emergency. Israel has not turned into a garrison state, a modern Sparta ruled by specialists in violence whose entire way of life is subordinated to meeting the challenge of an external threat."[19]

The problem is not an institutionalized army against civilians, then, but rather the way in which the constant preoccupation with defense has affected attributes of the whole society. Militarism can exist in a political culture even when civilian supremacy in the government is secured.[20] In the Israeli case, army and society share the view that military considerations have priority and that the conflict should be interpreted predominantly in military terms; military values penetrate areas of life from economic planning to gender relations. With security as the dominant standard and a high priority assigned to defense in the allocation of resources, the impact is felt everywhere. Decisions on industrial policy, on the transportation infrastructure, on educational priorities—on almost any policy issue—are run through the security filter. The bigger question is whether this has caused an erosion of humanitarian values of Western liberalism or of traditional

Judaism. How has democracy survived these pressures, and what has been their impact on the tension between modernism and tradition?

CIVIL LIBERTIES UNDER PRESSURE

Even the most democratic and civic-minded of countries has found that the conflict between war and human liberties is profound. Writing in 1917, J. A. Hobson recounted the vast invasions of liberty that took place during World War I in Great Britain and warned his fellow citizens that the termination of actual hostilities would not bring about a quick restoration of previous norms.[21] In Israel there are even fewer safeguards than in other democratic nations: there is no written constitution and no bill of rights, and in the prevailing conception civil liberties "are *granted* to the individual by authorities rather than *assured* the individual."[22]

Despite all this Israel has been relatively free of restrictions on freedom of expression. As the annual human rights report of the U.S. Department of State summarizes the matter, "Israeli society is characterized by its openness and by the wide-ranging and lively public debate of all issues of popular concern."[23] To take one striking example, during the 1973 Yom Kippur War an Arab member of the Israeli Knesset published a poem eulogizing the Egyptian soldiers who had launched an attack on Israeli forces across the Suez Canal. Clearly security concerns have not had the impact on human liberties that could have been projected from the general experience of democratic regimes in wartime.

If Israel's record is generally good, especially in a comparative perspective, it clearly has its weak points. The major weaknesses in Israeli civil liberties are in the area of religious laws, many of which conflict with secular democratic standards, and in the role of emergency regulations in the country's governance.[24] The issue of religion and politics will be covered in chapter 8; here we will focus primarily on the tension between civil liberties and the use of "emergency" measures to protect national security.

On May 19, 1948, four days after the declaration of Israeli independence, the provisional government of the new state proclaimed a state of emergency. This state of emergency has been in force continuously ever since.

When the emergency was first declared, the 650,000 Jews of Mandatory Palestine had already been engaged for almost six months in a civil war with 1.5 million Palestinian Arabs, and they faced an invasion by the regular armies of five Arab states with a total population of about 30 million. The new state survived by an effort of total mobilization, but about 1 percent of the population was killed—almost fifty times the American casualty rate in Vietnam. After 1948 Israel remained on a permanent war footing. A protracted official state of emergency may be more understandable for

Israel than for almost any other contemporary state. But it is difficult to maintain the same sense of urgency for such an extended period of time. The protraction of the crisis leads, inevitably, to a routinization of crisis procedures, to a normalization of what were originally extraordinary measures. The crisis becomes devalued over time.

The most drastic and controversial emergency provisions are the Defense (Emergency) Regulations promulgated by the British Mandatory government in 1945, which remain in effect except where explicitly annulled or superseded by either actions of the cabinet (under Section 9 of the Law and Administration Ordinance) or by Knesset legislation.[25] The 1945 Defense (Emergency) Regulations were a compilation of old and new Mandatory orders issued in response to the double threat of internal rebellion and world war. Following the Arab "revolt" in Palestine in 1936, the Privy Council in London adopted the Palestine (Defense) Order in Council 1937, authorizing the British high commissioner in Palestine to enact such defense regulations "as appear to him in his unfettered discretion to be necessary or expedient for securing public safety, the defence of Palestine, the maintenance of public order and the suppression of mutiny, rebellion, and riot and for maintaining supplies and services essential to the life of the community."[26] The subsequent regulations reflected the preoccupations of a colonial power facing widespread unrest and the threat of war; according to one British expert, they were "the type of regulations that came from the Boer War."[27]

In September 1945, facing now the prospect of Jewish rebellion, the Mandate authorities published the collected set of regulations, including new measures on such subjects as illegal immigration.[28] The 147 regulations, covering forty-one pages, establish a virtual regime of martial law. They include a military court system empowered to try all offenses against the regulations, with no writ of habeas corpus and no appeal. Broad powers of search and seizure were given to British soldiers. Other sections of the regulations severely circumscribe "unlawful" groups and permit long-term detention without trial—a provision under which thousands of Jews were held, some for up to five or six years. The regulations permit deportation of even native-born citizens and establish prior censorship requiring a permit for any material of "political significance." Any area can be closed, with suspension of civil courts there, property can be requisitioned or destroyed, movement limited, mail opened, services suspended, or businesses closed—all by virtue of incontestable military orders. Furthermore, the military is not even required to publish orders that it intends to enforce.

The Defense Regulations aroused a storm of protest from the Jewish population in Palestine. Richard Crossman, after hearing Jewish complaints as a visiting member of the Anglo-American Committee of Inquiry in early 1946, recorded in his diary that "I certainly had no idea of the severity of the Emergency Regulations. . . . there can be no doubt that Palestine today is a police state."[29] This opinion was shared by Bernard (Dov) Joseph, later Israeli minister of justice, who in 1948 published a critique of British rule in Palestine that also used the term "police state" in describing the Defense Regulations.[30]

The State of Israel inherited all Mandate legislation, unless explicitly annulled. The new government thus found itself effortlessly in possession of a formidable apparatus of emergency powers that could be attributed to the law-abiding British. Only the section restricting immigration was canceled; the rest, despite previous criticism, remained on the books.

There were some efforts to jettison this dubious colonial legacy, especially from Israeli leaders who had themselves been detained under the Defense Regulations. Opposition leader Menachem Begin, who with his comrades in Etsel had been a prime target of the regulations, declared during a 1951 debate: "The law that you used is Nazi, it is tyrannical, it is immoral; and an immoral law is also an illegal law. . . . If these laws, terror laws of a repressive regime, remain in the State of Israel—the day will come when no group will remain unharmed by them. . . ."[31]

But in time it became clear that there was no overwhelming impulse to revoke or replace the 1945 regulations. The continuing threat to national existence made retention of some extraordinary powers, beyond normal civil and judicial procedures, seem the better part of wisdom. And it was unlikely that any subsequent Knesset legislation would provide the full range of measures fortuitously made available by the British.

With such wide powers available, the use of the Defense Regulations has been relatively limited. Whole sections of the regulations have hardly been utilized. Such measures as the death penalty and corporal punishment have never been invoked. The major use—and most controversy—involve a small number of the regulations: Regulations 86–101 on censorship; Regulations 109–112 on restriction, detention, and deportation; and Regulation 125 on closed areas.

The most broadly applied have been the censorship provisions, which still form the legal basis for control of the media. The regulations require the licensing of all media and put the decision in the hands of Interior Ministry officials, who need not justify their refusal to grant a license. An earlier 1933 Press Ordinance also gives the minister of interior power to stop the publication of any newspaper for any period of time. The Defense Regulations permit the censorship of any material "prejudicial to the defence of Palestine [Israel] or to the public safety or to public order."

For Israelis, control of the media is not just a question of genuine threats to security but also evokes the traditional sensitivity to how the community is seen on the outside. Amos Elon calls this "a provincial determination not to let the skeletons out," reminiscent of the biblical injunction "to tell it not in Gath and publish it not on the streets of Ashkelon."[32] A striking parallel to this verse was expressed by an Israeli chief of staff, Rafael Eytan, who declared that "nothing which might give satisfaction to an Arab, should be allowed to be published by the Israeli news media."[33] This may be an extreme view, but in fact the "right to know" is not officially recognized in Israel. On the contrary, the Defense Regulations dealing with censorship have been backed up by other statutes designed to reinforce secrecy.

In practice, restrictions are usually limited to sensitive security information. In the case of the press, censorship is softened by a voluntary arrangement, renegotiated in 1996, under which newspapers submit military and political material for review, and excisions can be appealed to a committee representing the press, military, and the general public. The clubbiness of this system certainly suggests a pragmatic Jewish approach to keeping secrets within the family, while circumventing the harsh potential of the British regulations. However, the arrangement covers only the press; books are submitted directly to the censor for review if they "relate to state security," and some have been withheld from publication or censored, usually because of revelation of secrets. Censorship of movies and theater has usually, though not always, been limited to material that is offensive to religious or social mores—such as pornography—and a narrow appeal process is available.[34]

Early attempts to censure extreme views in the press by suspending publication outright, through the emergency regulations, led to the *Kol Ha'am* case before the Israeli Supreme Court in 1953. In this case the high court struck down a government suspension of the Communist Party newspaper, invalidating censorship carried out on political rather than narrowly defined security grounds. But secrecy on security grounds has also been stripped away considerably by the general informal leakiness of the system. Cabinet meetings have often been leaked to the press, complete with direct quotations. The ubiquity of leaks may go some way to meet the public's right or need to know: "the news media are in a position to circulate sufficient amounts of information to enable the Israeli political system to function according to the democratic model."[35] Thus, in the end, the balance between security requirements and the need to know is shaped by the convergence of three traditional patterns: an urge to shield sensitive matters from outside scrutiny, an institutionalized bargaining relationship among the important players, and the usual informal flow of unvarnished opinion and information. Somehow the more sensitive information does not generally get out while the merely embarrassing facts usually do. But the arrangements governing this have little to do with formal rules, whether in emergency regulations or otherwise.

All of this applies, however, within the Jewish community and does not extend across the ethnic divide to the Arab minority in Israel. The Arabic-language press is concentrated in East Jerusalem, thus falling under Israeli law rather than the military occupation regime, though it serves the West Bank and Gaza population as well as Israeli Arabs. But permits to publish a newspaper have been denied because of suspicion of links to hostile organizations, and there is little chance for an appellant to disprove the "security risk" label.[36] Before 1996 Arab newspapers did not benefit from the voluntary arrangement described above but were required to submit all material for review, with no appeal process. Consequently even translated articles from the Hebrew press were sometimes disallowed.

Even more than the censorship provisions, other Defense Regulations have been applied almost exclusively to the Arab minority. From 1948 to 1966, many border areas, not coincidentally corresponding to Arab-populated areas, were placed under a military government whose legal basis was the 1945 Defense Regulations. The de facto result was that Jews and Arabs lived under different sets of rules despite the formal civic equality. Though restrictions on movement were applied elsewhere as well, their main use was in the military government area. Under Regulation 125, these areas were declared "closed," and all entrance and exit required a permit, though in practice this was seldom required of Jews passing through such areas. Under Regulations 109 and 110, persons under special suspicion could be further restricted in their movements, to a particular town or even house arrest.[37]

Most serious, perhaps, was the way in which Regulation 125 could be used to create "uncultivated" or "abandoned" land that, in accord with Israeli legislation, became subject to expropriation by the state. Villagers who happened to be elsewhere could be kept there or prevented from entering their home village. In some cases—in at least eleven villages in the 1949–1950 period—Regulation 125 was used to evacuate entire villages of their existing populations, on security grounds. The courts interfered in these cases only on technical grounds, or when it seemed clear that the motivation was not security.[38]

Most of the land expropriations occurred in the early 1950s, and the military government in Arab areas ended in 1966. From that point, at least formally, emergency measures under the British regulations applied equally to all areas of the country and all sectors of the population. The most serious continuing controversy regarding the use of the Defense Regulations has been the matter of administrative detention.

Regulation 111 empowered "a military commander" to detain any person in any place of the commander's choosing, for renewable periods of one year. In essence, this authority could mean indefinite imprisonment without trial, with no restrictions on the discretion of the commander, loose rules of evidence, and no judicial review apart from an "advisory committee" to make recommendations to the officer. As noted, this measure was used extensively by the British in the 1945–1948 period. It is argued that preventive detention may be the lesser of evils in dealing with the kinds of threats presented by terrorist organizations. The evidence available in such cases often cannot be used in a court of law: it is based on hearsay, or on intelligence sources that cannot be revealed, or on the testimony of informers whose identification would put them in jeopardy. Rather than changing the rules of the courtroom in order to obtain criminal convictions, it is preferable to adopt lesser measures, still subject to some form of review, that make it possible to act when a reasonable certainty of danger to society exists.[39]

There is, inevitably, controversy about whether those detained are actually threats to society. One outside critic of preventive detention, who studied the cases of those detained in 1971, concluded "that virtually all of those detained had, in fact, been involved in terrorist activities; that the vast majority could not be tried under Israeli law; and that a considerable number would probably engage in future terrorism if released."[40] In any event, the number of those detained has never been great, and the overall trend within Israel was to reduce the number. From the figures announced sporadically, it appears that 315 detention orders were issued in 1956–1957, but that the number fell to twenty-three in 1970 and fifteen in 1971 (not including the West Bank and Gaza, where the number was much higher; see chapter 10). By 1978 the total, including the occupied territories, was thirty; in 1979 (when Regulation 111 was replaced by regular legislation) there were eighteen; and by 1981 the number had dropped to twelve in the occupied territories and none in Israel.[41] Since then the use of administrative detention has been limited almost entirely to the occupied territories.

In summary, the continuing existence of the 1945 British Defense (Emergency) Regulations raises serious problems from a civil liberties perspective, and hard questions can also be raised regarding some of the ways they have been applied. But at the same time, usage of the regulations has generally been selective and limited and has been softened in implementation by internal guidelines and court review that provide some protection against abuse. Critics ask why these guidelines, which actually define practice, could not be converted into laws that would remove the specter of colonial police powers from the books. This has been done with administrative detention, perhaps the most controversial of the "emergency" measures; it would not be so revolutionary to apply the same treatment to the remaining regulations.

There are two channels for replacing the British Defense Regulations with more regularized and more accountable provisions. The first is emergency regulations issued by government ministers under Section 9 of the

Law and Administration Ordinance of 1948; these are measures based on a grant of authority from the legislative branch and are not valid beyond three months unless extended by the Knesset. Finally, there is regular legislation whose period of validity is dependent on the existence of a state of emergency, or whose functioning is in some other way affected by the emergency. Such legislation may also give the government the right to carry out "emergency-type" measures, subject to review; this was the approach used in the Emergency Powers (Detention) Law, 1979, which replaced the detention provisions of the 1945 British regulations.

The Law and Administration Ordinance was the first law passed by the Provisional State Council of the new State of Israel, on May 19, 1948. It provides in Section 9 that, upon declaration of a state of emergency, the cabinet could authorize the prime minister or any other minister to issue emergency regulations "for the defense of the state, the public safety, and the maintenance of essential supplies and services." The major use of Section 9 emergency regulations since the mid-1970s has been in authorizing return-to-work orders to employees providing "vital public services." With the increase of such orders has also come a number of instances in which ministers have reissued emergency regulations, without Knesset action, in order to keep a particular group of employees working. In the 1977–1982 period, ten such renewed regulations were issued either before the end of the three-month period, or within three months after its expiration. In one of these cases, involving workers in the Ministry of Education, the reissue of the regulation without Knesset approval was successfully challenged in a district labor court.[42] On the whole, the use of emergency regulations under Section 9 was relatively noncontroversial, despite the broad wording of the statute, and declined over time (apart from their use in labor disputes). They were used primarily in wartime, reflecting the need, even under conditions of permanent crisis, to reserve some measures for the most threatening occasions only. It is interesting to note that during the 1982 Lebanese War, for example, the government made use of Section 9 to authorize the detention of non-Israeli citizens, but in doing so proclaimed a "special" state of emergency whose legal provenance was uncertain.[43]

The third channel for emergency measures, as noted, is directly through the Knesset. Since it is the act of a deliberative legislative body, Knesset "emergency" legislation represents the greatest degree of normalization in adjustment to permanent crisis. When a declared state of emergency is a permanent fixture, laws whose operation is dependent on its existence are difficult to distinguish from other laws. A number of Israeli laws fit this description, as do emergency regulations under Section 9 that were simply extended by the Knesset until the end of the state of emergency.[44] Many of these laws are "emergency" measures in name only, since in scope, procedure, reviewability in court, and other respects, they do not differ from ordinary legislation. An example of delegated powers that are genuinely emergency-related is the authority given the minister of defense, in the Law of Military Service, to order a mobilization and take other appropriate military measures in the face of an imminent threat. As befits genuine emergencies, these powers are limited to fourteen days without Knesset approval.[45]

All of the emergency regulations are subject to judicial review. Courts have generally applied two criteria: whether the procedural requirements of the law have been followed, and whether substantively the authority has acted in good faith and in accord with the stated purposes of the regulation. Regarding the merits of the case, however, the court has ordinarily declined to look at the content of orders under the Defense Regulations, beyond ascertaining that they were enacted in good faith and according to relevant considerations within the scope of the regulation (Alyubi v. Minister of Defense, H. C. 46/50, 4 P.D. 222).[46]

The realistic possibility of reversing an order has also been limited by the refusal of authorities to divulge evidence or the reasons behind their actions. This can make it almost impossible to show that an authority has acted in bad faith. This problem was alleviated to some degree by changes in the Law of Evidence, in 1968, which abolished absolute state privilege on disclosure of evidence and authorized courts to hear evidence *in camera* when state security was involved. Subsequently, judges on appeal have examined secret evidence to see if it really needed to be withheld from the defendant.[47]

Generally the judicial system has functioned as an independent guardian of civil liberties and the chief repository of the civic approach in Israeli life. Given the traditional strength of legal and judicial institutions in Jewish life, this is perhaps to be expected; the strongest resistance to the pressures of security come where Western liberal ideas and a deeply Jewish respect for the judiciary come together and reinforce each other. Other aspects of tradition that have worked to desanctify security fetishes are the habitual skepticism toward authority (the *lese majesté* of Jewish life), the tendency to practical bargaining rather than rigid hierarchies, the unstoppable flow of informal communication within the community, and the sheer lack of experience in carrying out the kind of controls associated with a garrison state. To this should be added the normal human tendency to normalize or routinize life during a protracted crisis, rather than to remain indefinitely fixated on the presumed threat.

On the other hand, where the dictates of security coincided with particular legacies of the Jewish experience, the challenge to democracy was greatest. The very ease with which the young and vulnerable state accepted the primacy of security concerns was testimony to the preoccupation—perhaps even the obsession—with security that is a part of the Jewish condition. And on issues like guarding secrets from the outside world, contracting civilly with an enemy minority, or dealing with acts of political violence, it was also too easy to slip into the particularist or communal frame of reference.

In summary, however, the overriding security constraints have not led to the sacrifices of civil liberties that has occurred in other democratic states during wartime or periods of protracted conflict:

1. Emergency powers have not challenged the normal functioning of government. The Knesset has operated undisturbed and has the formal power to change emergency measures as it sees fit (though the exercise of this right may depend on coalition politics); courts continue to function, and to review (within limits) the use of such powers. There is no general suspension of rights, even in wartime.
2. In practice, the use of emergency powers has fallen far short of what could be done, legally, under existing grants of authority. Many of the broad powers available have not been utilized, and others have been moderated in usage by self-imposed administrative guidelines. This reverses the common pattern among many nondemocratic governments, which stretch their emergency authority in various ways; while the law in such cases is better than the practice, in Israel the practice is better than the law.
3. Over time, there has been a trend to greater regularity in the use of emergency powers and greater reliance on legal and judicial procedures governing them. The role of judicial review, for example, has been expanded. In recent years there has been less automatic deference to security claims than in the early years of statehood.

In conclusion, the balance between the demands of security and the ideals of law and liberty is at least as problematic in Israel as in any other democratic state. Given the circumstances, Israel may even represent the extreme test case of such balancing. In the event, there are good arguments for criticizing the weight assigned to emergency powers and for wishing the balance moved somewhat in the opposite direction. But it is important to bear in mind that an act of balancing is taking place.

The picture up to the Six-Day War, therefore, was one of unusual continuity, despite (or because of) the extreme pressure under which the government operated. Israel had one of the few regimes—practically the only one in the region—that could claim such stability in leadership and policy over such a long period. But appearances were deceptive. Underneath the surface were forces for change that would eventually shatter the hold of the Labor Zionist establishment and call into question Israel's commitment to the civic, liberal, universalist conception of state-building.

SIX

The Erosion of Ideology

By the late 1960s Israeli politics was headed for fundamental change. But this is said with the advantage of hindsight; few if any observers foresaw the coming whirlwind at the time. As late as 1971, one of the more perceptive Israeli analysts could still claim that Israeli youth were more dovish than their elders and that "no liberal-centrist or right-wing opposition is likely to gain power within the foreseeable future."[1] Neither the stunning victory of the 1967 war nor the demoralizing impact of the 1973 war left a sense that basic transformations were underway.

Yet in retrospect the signs of erosion were evident. As time passed, the hold of ideology in daily life was being progressively loosened (in part because governmental services were replacing party functions). The gap between a secularized socialist elite, mainly of Eastern European origin, and a significantly more traditional public, much of it of Middle Eastern origin, was bound to assert itself. But the dominant elite did not bridge the generation gap within its own ranks, let alone reach out to alienated non-European and religious Jews.

Gradually a viable option to Mapai and its Labor Zionist allies emerged. The 1967 war, by reviving dormant territorial issues, contributed to the rise of the nationalist right's agenda, and the general malaise following the 1973 war cast a giant shadow over Labor's aura of invincibility. The culmination came in 1977, when the inconceivable occurred and a center-right government came to power after half a century of Labor Zionist hegemony.[2]

What was the significance of this "upheaval" in Israeli politics? Can it be seen as a reassertion of tradition, as the tide of universalizing ideology ebbed and those untouched by it reclaimed the center of national life? Certainly Middle Eastern and religious Jews became more active, more visible, and more influential in politics. The majoritarian features of the early

statehood period receded as political parties themselves became less coherent, as their role in the system declined, and as autonomous (and often
extraparliamentary) groups made their weight felt. More fundamentally,
there was increased challenge to Western liberal and rationalist values and
a resurgence of particularistic thinking. The post-1977 period was dominated, some believed, by a "New Zionism" rooted in primordial religious
and ethnic sentiments and focused on exclusivist territorial claims. There
was concern, as described in chapter 1, that this reassertion of tradition was
undermining the strength of democracy.

The overall picture, however, was not so simple. Other trends, connected directly neither to tradition nor to ideology, were also at work in Israel. Modernization brought new technologies, new social patterns, penetration of Westernization in many guises, and new styles of mass politics in
public life. Though these social forces contributed mightily to the undermining of classic Zionist ideologies, they also constituted a challenge to tradition no less potent than secular ideology at its peak. Thus, even while traditional forces were reemerging, the process of synthesis between Jewish
particularism and universalistic influences continued. But the universalizing
pressures came from "modernity" itself more than from spent or declining
ideological fervor.

DECLINE OF THE CLASSIC CONSENSUS

Protracted conflict imposes costs on any political system; emergency measures become routinized and security concerns become the defining issues
in politics. In Israel, the left-right spectrum is defined mostly by security
and foreign policy positions rather than by socioeconomic issues. In 1977
one survey found no difference between the self-identified left and the self-
identified right in Israel regarding socioeconomic gaps.[3] Economic issues
became blurred as security concerns dominated political debate. In such a
situation, the appeal of an ideology based on class interests is undercut by
the change in public priorities.

Paradoxically, the improvement in Israel's security brought about by the
1967 war also helped to undermine Labor by removing one of the stronger
motives to stand behind the existing government. As the risk of actual physical destruction receded, the need to maintain national unity at all costs also
lessened. Security remained a dominant fixation, but there was more willingness to bring differences out into the open and less deference to present
policies and leaders. Where choices in the past had been "strategic impera-
tives," dictated by circumstances over which Israel had no control, more policy options were now available. Sheer survival was no longer the yardstick of
all policy.

By the end of the 1970s, with a reduction of the Soviet role in the region and the signing of the Egyptian peace treaty, Israel's security position was better than it had ever been. The 1982 attack on the PLO in southern Lebanon and the decision to pursue the PLO forces to Beirut represented policy choices that, wise or unwise, would have been impossible in an earlier period. The Lebanon campaign was, as many Israelis saw it, the nation's first "optional" war—one that policymakers could have chosen to fight at a different time, or in a different way, or not at all.

With more leeway on security issues, the gap between a leftist elite and a more centrist electorate became more visible. In the 1960s the electorate was voting to the left of its opinions on the issues.[4] A large part of the public, despite support of Labor Zionist parties at the polls, had not been swept away by Western socialist or liberal visions. With regard to religious belief the public as a whole was much more traditional than the customary vote of about 15 percent for religious parties would indicate. Surveys done during the 1960s and 1970s showed that up to 30 percent observed most religious law, while an even larger percentage considered itself "traditional" if not wholly observant, and only a minority considered itself wholly secular.[5]

The gap was closing, however. From the 1950s there was a drift of religious Zionist voters to the nationalist right, as the precursor parties of the Likud (rather than Labor Zionist parties) became their preferred second choice.[6] Throughout the 1970s, opinions in the Knesset moved to the right.[7] This reflected both the increased number of Likud members (from twenty-six in 1969 to forty-three in 1977) and the increased hawkishness of the National Religious Party members of parliament.

Contributing to this was another demographic reality. From the 1950s, about half of the electorate consisted of refugees, or the descendants of refugees, from Arab countries. In a pattern common to refugees, these voters tended to be strongly anti-Arab and thus over time increasingly attracted to the more hawkish parties. Having endured as a minority in the Arab world, they saw no injustice in West Bank Arabs continuing to live under Israeli rule.[8] This tendency was reinforced by the identification of Labor Zionism with the privileged elite and the perception that socialism was an alien, Western doctrine not linked to the Jewish tradition. Jews from Arab lands were still basically tied to the Middle Eastern conception of politics, in which ethnic identity is everything and in which deprivation is seen in relation to established authority. As relative latecomers, the immigrants from Middle East countries had started at the bottom of the ladder and had often been exposed to an attitude of superiority on the part of the "Europeans." That the Establishment espoused an ideology of equality that favored the downtrodden did not seem to help; the fact was that, whatever its theories, the left was the Establishment. After a period of incubation, alienation from the Labor Establishment grew quickly among the younger Middle Eastern generation that had grown up in Israel.

The Likud was attractive to Middle Eastern Jews because it, too, was "outside" the system. They responded to Begin's warm appeal on traditional historic and religious grounds, as opposed to the cold rationalism of Western liberalism and socialism represented by the Labor Party. For a time Labor's superior mobilization of new immigrants, backed by its legitimacy as the ruling party and by Ben-Gurion's image as the founder of the state, succeeded in stemming the tide. But after Ben-Gurion, and with a second generation raised in Israel under Labor hegemony, the shift to the right become inexorable. While an estimated 35 percent of non-European Jews voted for the Likud in 1969, this rose to 45 percent in 1973, to 56 percent in 1977, and to 69 percent in 1981.[9]

What happened was the reassertion of human realities. But at the same time, Labor Zionism was losing its vitality. This may be the inevitable fate of all revolutions that have run their course; in any event, even its staunchest supporters admit that Labor Zionist institutions had become bureaucratized and ossified. As a generation of apparatchiks took over from the ideologues, ideas became less important than securing the benefits of power. There was less access to newcomers—the younger generation, Middle Eastern Jews—precisely at a time when expanded access was needed in order to keep Labor Zionism abreast of demographic changes. The dominant elite developed into what Amos Elon called a "Mandarin class," and when the concept of an "Establishment" was developed in other contexts, the term was translated into Hebrew and applied to the Israeli scene with no loss in translation.[10]

Symptoms of decay had appeared earlier, when Mapai tore itself apart over the Lavon affair in 1960 to 1961 and 1964 to 1965. This was the first major intraparty issue that did not cut primarily along ideological grounds but was basically a power struggle between party factions (though justified, of course, in ideological language). The unedifying spectacle of "The Affair" undermined Mapai's claims to moral preeminence and a monopoly on political legitimacy. It could be seen as a "tragedy of success"; Labor Zionism had accomplished its immediate aims and, left with little sense of purpose, sank into a state of organizational sclerosis, surviving in power until 1977 only because no viable alternative emerged before then.[11]

Like most ossified elites, Labor Zionists experienced a serious problem with succession. The transfer of top positions to the new native-born generation took place only in the 1970s, by which time it was overtaken by more profound changes. But in any event, the younger generation was not well-equipped to carry on. The founding generation had not inculcated its ideology deeply in its successors nor trained them adequately in leadership roles.[12] In fact this failure was not limited to the education of a new generation of party leaders; it reflected a broader failure in the socialization of youth to Labor Zionist thinking.

In pursuit of *mamlachtiut* (civic-mindedness), Labor Zionists undercut their own movement by putting national symbols and values ahead of socialist ideology and party institutions. Much of Labor's ability to recruit new immigrants had been tied to its ability to deliver benefits. Now this dependence—often the only bond to Labor Zionism—was broken by the growth of government services outside the party system. In particular, it is said, the integration of Labor Zionist schools into the state system robbed the movement of the principal means of passing on its distinctive values.[13] Not only did the new state educational system provide no socialist content, but it was even revised in 1957 to include a "Jewish Consciousness Program" that introduced more particularistic elements into the curriculum.

Secular ideology was under attack on a number of fronts. In 1953, it should be recalled, the integration of the socialist schools into the official network could still be delayed by controversy over the flying of the red flag and the singing of the workers' anthem on certain days, in schools where a majority of the parents so requested. But the ideologues lost that battle, and advocacy of socialist symbolism in an official setting became passé. Along with most modernizing societies, Israel was experiencing a general decline of ideology as new lifestyles challenged old doctrines. Urbanization and consumerism were replacing agrarian pioneering, and economic rewards were increasingly individual rather than collective.[14] Also, the fountainhead and reservoir that had continuously replenished the ideological vigor of Zionism no longer existed: Eastern European Jewry, as a meaningful source of inspiration and dedicated adherents, had been destroyed. Without roots in their new environment, and without reinforcement from the point of origin, the transplanted creeds of Eastern Europe withered in the alien and inhospitable soil.

External support and inspiration now came from Western Jews, particularly from the large Jewish community in the United States. There was little support for radical doctrines from these quarters. For that matter, by the time of Stalin and his successors, any refugees reaching Israel from Eastern Europe also tended to be congenitally hostile to anything bearing a socialist label.

The lines of social division that developed in Israel simply did not fit classic Labor Zionist thinking. Labor Zionists were the Establishment and paid the price of power by becoming the target of discontent from below. The discontented, many of them Middle Eastern Jews from traditional backgrounds, interpreted their grievances in communal terms or as resentment of established authority rather than in terms of class. In any event, most of the country's capital investment was in state or Histadrut hands, making organization of workers against private interests very secondary. The one respect in which Labor's worldview coincided with popular expectations was in the provision of a broad range of governmental services, but this welfare statism was accepted by most groups in Israeli politics.[15] All in all, socialist ideology appeared increasingly irrelevant to Israel's circumstances, and in time voting patterns became the reverse of what class analysis would predict: Labor veterans moved into the middle class and working-class voters turned to the right.

The erosion of ideology had many expressions. Among the youth, even on kibbutzim, the phrase "preaching Zionism" became a term of derision.[16] The influence of the kibbutz model receded, after its image of agrarian pioneering and collective endeavor had once enjoyed ideological supremacy. The prestige of middle-class occupations rose; by 1976 the highest-status professions in public opinion were biologists, dentists, lawyers, and judges, while kibbutz officials ranked far down in the list.[17] Inequality increased, moving Israel from one of the most egalitarian social structures in the world to a pattern more typical of developed countries, even as class consciousness actually decreased.[18]

Consequently, party- and movement-affiliated institutions declined or became less doctrinaire. The party press was supplanted by independent mass circulation newspapers. Affiliated youth movements, which had been a critical focus of political socialization, declined in importance. Parties themselves moved away from identification with a particular segment of society, becoming more heterogeneous in their composition and appeal. Mapai moved from a predominantly agricultural and pioneering orientation to a largely urban base, drawing in members of the growing middle class. The parties on the right (and especially Herut, with its populist streak) made inroads among the working-class population.[19]

The ideological loosening made it easier for parties to coalesce into larger blocs for electoral purposes, presenting a common list to the electorate. Mapai, Ahdut Ha'avoda, and Rafi (a splinter party established by Ben-Gurion toward the end of his career) merged to form the Israel Labor Party in 1968. From 1969 to 1984, the Labor Party and Mapam presented a single list (the Alignment) in all Israeli elections. The Liberals and Herut formed an electoral list (Gahal) in 1965, and in 1973 this was expanded, with the addition of some smaller parties, to establish the Likud (Unity). In all of this, cooperating parties overcame ideological differences that in an earlier period would have been considered insuperable.

By greatly enlarging the territory under Israeli control, the 1967 war also dealt a severe blow to the classic consensus (see Map 3). This consensus assumed that the 1948 war had settled not only the question of Israel's existence but also its borders and its character as a predominantly Jewish state. Of course some remained committed in theory to a claim to all of historic Eretz Yisrael, taken in practice to mean the British Mandate in Palestine. But this was not an active issue in political debate. If neighboring

Arab states had at the time offered to conclude a peace treaty based on the existing borders (the armistice lines of 1949), a majority in Israel would have readily agreed. The general expectation then was that peace would evolve along these lines, with Jordan assimilating the West Bank and becoming the de facto Palestinian state.

What the 1967 war did, in Avner Yaniv's words, was "to salvage from oblivion the twin ghosts of Jewish maximalism and Palestinian particularism."[20] Israel now occupied all of Mandatory Palestine, plus Egyptian Sinai in the south and the Syrian Golan Heights in the north. The war brought to life contentious questions that had been locked in cold storage for twenty years. These questions involved not just the future of territories occupied in war, but the very nature of Israel itself: a relatively compact and homogeneous state with a predominantly Jewish character, or a binational state of two peoples.[21]

Initially, Mapai/Labor policy continued the unofficial preference for a resolution based on de facto division of Palestine with Jordan. It was clearly contemplated that the West Bank (except for East Jerusalem and some minor claims) would be returned to Jordan in exchange for a peace treaty, and likewise the Sinai Peninsula would be restored to Egypt in exchange for a peace treaty, while the Golan Heights would be retained by Israel because of its strategic importance and because of Syrian intransigence. In line with these intentions, the Israeli government adopted a policy of minimal interference in the daily lives of the West Bank population, with one important exception: prohibition of local political organization, since development of a West Bank leadership would undercut the strategy of resolving the conflict by cutting a deal with Jordan.

Labor Zionists also found it hard to reverse past habits. The strength of "practical" Zionism, in the socialist version, had been its success in grassroots settlement, in creating facts on the ground. This had not ceased in 1948; efforts simply shifted to previously unsettled areas within the new armistice lines. Thus many Labor Zionists approached the results of the 1967 war in a similar frame of mind, falling back into a settlement mode. The government itself opened the door by establishing settlements in areas where border changes were anticipated, either for security reasons (the Golan Heights and the Jordan Valley) or because of Jewish settlement there before 1948 (East Jerusalem, the Etzion bloc of settlements near Bethlehem). Regarding the West Bank, this evolved into what became known as the Allon Plan, according to which Israel would establish a security frontier on the Jordan River, but most of the West Bank and nearly all of its Arab population would be demilitarized and returned to Jordan, to which it would be connected by a corridor through the Israeli security belt.[22]

Mapai/Labor also compromised its policy by hitching its wagon to Moshe

Dayan, an authentic national hero who had been made minister of defense at the peak of the 1967 crisis and emerged from the victory in a powerful position. Dayan had his own program, enunciated in various versions at various times, for maintaining a permanent Israeli presence in the West Bank. This involved using the West Bank as an opening to the Arab world by a policy of "open bridges" between the West Bank and Jordan, and integrating the West Bank economy and infrastructure with those of Israel.[23]

Thus the Labor Party itself laid the foundation for a program of permanent Israel control of the West Bank (or Judea and Samaria, as traditionally known). Backed by public opinion and legitimized by the actions of the Labor Party, the nationalist right was revitalized and provided with a galvanizing issue ideal to its purposes. It could even appropriate one of Labor's traditional methods—grassroots settlement activity—in pursuit of its own maximalist aims, over the opposition of Labor. At the same time, Labor faced the challenges of a new era in a state of unilateral intellectual and ideological disarmament.

As Labor's fortunes declined, the Yom Kippur War of 1973 dealt a punishing blow to public confidence in its ability to lead. As in all wars, there was at first a surge of unity behind the government, which enabled Labor to emerge relatively undamaged in the Knesset elections held a few weeks afterward. But the shock of the unanticipated Egyptian and Syrian attack and initial successes, together with the high casualty rate, undermined Labor's image as the party that had always successfully defended national security. A deep sense of malaise and demoralization pervaded the nation, and Labor's leadership came to represent complacency, deterioration, and lack of clear direction. On the eve of the 1973 war, around 60 percent of the Israeli public had perceived the general situation in Israel as positive; after the war, and throughout the 1974–1977 period, this dropped to 10 to 20 percent.[24]

The changing climate finally triggered the long-expected "changing of the guard" to a new generation of Labor leadership (Yitzhak Rabin, Shimon Peres, Yigal Allon). But the Rabin government, in the 1974–1977 period, was unable to reverse the trends already set in motion. Labor continued to suffer from the lack of a sense of direction, which was aggravated by bitter personal rivalries between Rabin and Peres. The general malaise was compounded by scandals in the ruling party, further strengthening the image of a leadership corrupted by its lengthy tenure in office. The evaluation of government performance, which had been 90 percent positive in 1967, had plummeted to 15 percent by mid-1977.[25]

Nevertheless, there was little expectation that the governing party would be cast into the wilderness. It might very well be weakened by the elections, as an angry electorate punished it for its sins, but it was still inconceivable that it would not continue as the core of the Israeli government.[26] However, the visible and not so visible developments that converged in May 1977 changed the face of Israeli politics irrevocably. After half a century on the outside, the Revisionist Zionists, under Menachem Begin, came to power.

The 1977 Likud victory marked in a dramatic way the broadening of the range of difference in relevant political debate, even as a general weakening of ideology was taking place on most fronts. A convergence of developments had undermined prevailing patterns of accommodation and sharpened the differences on standing policy issues. There were, to be sure, still many points of consensus: the primacy of security, dedication to nation-building, social and economic integration (at least within the Jewish community), and welfare statism. But there were also deepening divisions in the body politic, expressed in "a growing intolerance of opponents" and tendencies "to delegitimize them in terms of the seemingly common Zionist themes. . . ."[27] There was need of a new paradigm to describe Israeli society and politics, as the classic Zionist vision of the Jewish state—or at least its Labor Zionist version—became increasingly irrelevant. Such a new paradigm would need to encompass not only the emerging nationalist right but also the more assertive and visible religious communities, both Zionist and *haredi* (ultra-Orthodox) and—given the demographic realities since 1967— the growing Arab populations both in Israel and in the occupied territories.

There was a loss of consensus on the most basic issue: the very definition of the state that Zionism pursued. The nationalist right reopened the territorial issue and raised the prospect of a state without a Jewish majority. The gulf that opened between competing territorial and demographic conceptions was reinforced and sharpened by an overlapping communal (Ashkenazi-Sephardi) division that had not been politically significant before. The new combination of religion and nationalism, as expressed by the hawkishness of the National Religious Party and the activities of Gush Emunim and similar groups, made political compromise more difficult to achieve. The larger political role of the *haredi* community added to this difficulty by bringing to the political center groups that continued to challenge basic Zionist premises. Finally, at about the same time the Arab citizens of Israel, who had been politically quiescent for two decades, began to demonstrate increasing political consciousness and sophistication in pursuing their demands through the system (see chapter 9). All in all, the Israeli political system encompassed an extraordinarily broad spectrum of ideological differences, much broader than that of other democratic states.[28]

However, this increased pluralism did not lead to an increase of issue dimensions in Israeli politics. In fact, the dominance of the territorial issue actually led to a partial convergence of the three separate political axes of the past. With socialism on the decline, the socioeconomic dimension was subordinated to divisions on foreign policy. Ahdut Ha'avoda followed the lead of its Labor partners on both issues, while the Liberals and Herut overcame their differences on foreign policy. Choice between parties on economic issues became more and more difficult as party positions became incoherent or indistinguishable from each other. At the same time, as the National Religious Party and other religious groups became more hawkish, the religious dimension also came to parallel security issues to some extent. In the words of one analyst, there was a "gradual reduction of the multidimensional character of the political scene."[29] Theoretically this could make it easier to achieve coherent majoritarian government—but not when the divisions on the one overriding issue become insurmountable. In this case, the dominance of one political axis in the system produced polarization and deadlock.

REASSERTION OF TRADITION?

As classic Labor Zionist ideology declined and the somewhat atypical period of *mamlachtiut* became a memory, it appeared that traditional political habits—protest, civil religiosity, extraparliamentary politics—were reasserting themselves. Can post-1977 Israeli politics be interpreted as a resurgence of tradition? In some respects it can be, but with caution: other forces are also at work, and in any event the end result has not been a triumph of one worldview over another but polarization and stalemate. There has been no dominant consensus to shape the nation's response on the key issues of territory and security.

Politically, the deadlock was a result of the decline of Labor and the rise of the right. As Table 2 shows, there was a steady upward trend in Likud strength, from thirty-two seats in 1969 (counting the parties that later joined the Likud), to thirty-nine in 1973 and forty-three in 1977. The long-term steady slide of Labor, from fifty-six seats in 1969 to thirty-nine in 1988, is also apparent. But in 1977 this was magnified by the appearance of the Democratic Movement for Change, a reformist movement led by popular military commander and archeologist Yigael Yadin, whose fifteen seats came primarily at Labor's expense. This, more than its own electoral success, put Likud in a position to form a government in 1977—but given prevailing trends, this would have happened one or two elections later in any event. Once it had happened, however, the election served to legitimate the Likud in the public mind. There was a significant shift in polling data to support of Likud positions, bringing opinion polls and party support into closer correlation. On the eve of the 1977 elections 61 percent of one sample still claimed to be closest to the Labor position on foreign policy, against only 30 percent for Likud. But immediately after the election and before any other changes had taken place, the same question drew only a 38 percent support

TABLE 2   Knesset Seats by Party, 1969–1996

	Year of Election							
	1969	1973	1977	1981	1984	1988	1992	1996
Alignment/Labor[a]	56	51	32	47	44	39	44	34
Left[b]	—	3	1	1	3	8	12	9
Centrist[c] ·	10	4	17	4	7	2	—	11
Likud[d]	26	39	43	48	41	40	32	32
Far right	—	—	2	3	6	7	11	2
National Religious Party	12	10	12	6	4	5	6	9
Other religious-Zionist	—	—	—	3	3	—	—	—
Haredi	6	5	5	4	6	13	10	14
Radical left/Arab lists	10	8	8	4	6	6	5	9

SOURCE: Compiled by the author.

[a]Includes Labor and Mapam before 1988.

[b]Citizens' Rights Movement (1973–1988), Mapam (1988), Meretz (1992, 1996).

[c]Independent Liberals (1969–1977), State List (1969), Merkaz Hofshi (1969), Democratic Movement for Change (1977), Telem (1981), Shinui (1981–1988), Yahad (1984), Ometz (1984), Yisrael B'aliya (1996), The Third Way (1996).

[d]In 1969, electoral bloc of Herut and Liberals (Gahal). In 1973, Gahal joined with smaller parties to form the Likud (Unity) electoral bloc. In 1996, Likud formed an electoral alliance with the Tsomet, the major party of the far right, and with Gesher, a Likud splinter group.

for the Alignment's foreign policy, while identification with the Likud rose to 53 percent.[30] This was not just a change in parties but a watershed in Israeli politics. It brought a new orientation, with new values and political symbols, into equal political legitimacy and at least equal electoral potential with Labor Zionism. It marked the emergence of a truly competitive system, with clearly opposed options, as well as Israel's first successful transfer of power.

The thought that the 1977 elections might have been an aberration was put to rest by the 1981 elections. The Likud continued its slow but steady accretion of strength, gaining an additional five seats over 1977. Furthermore, although the Likud had only a one-vote edge, the remaining seats were held by parties that, by and large, preferred Likud to Labor (religious and nationalist parties accounting for sixteen of the twenty-five seats). Ironically, the election left the religious parties in a better bargaining position, despite a drop in seats, because of the close balance between the two major blocs.

Nevertheless, Likud Prime Minister Yitzhak Shamir (who had succeeded Menachem Begin in September 1983) appeared in a weak position when he was forced to call elections a year early, in July 1984. By this time the inflation rate was estimated at over 400 percent, and Israeli forces were still

bogged down in southern Lebanon following the controversial Israeli invasion of that country in 1982. Public opinion polls in the early phase of the
campaign predicted a decisive Labor victory—as they had in 1981. In any
event, it was widely expected that the election would provide a clear mandate to one or the other of the two major blocs and end the stalemate between the two opposed conceptions that they represented.

This was not to be, however. In defiance of expectations, the 1984 elections produced a balance even more delicate than 1981, forcing Labor and
Likud to embark on an era of power-sharing and mutual veto. While consensus on some pressing domestic issues—primarily the economy—proved
to be within reach of the two blocs, their shared control of foreign and defense policy was marked by mutual paralysis and rejection of any new departures. To the surprise of most observers and despite repeated threats of
collapse, this rickety structure actually lasted out its term of office. In part
this could be attributed to the inability of either bloc to form a government
on its own and the unwillingness of key parties, at crucial junctures, to face
new elections. But it also represented recognition of the need for unity in
addressing the country's economic crisis, a task that could not be accomplished unless both major blocs were willing to share the onus of institut-
ing the tough and unpopular measures required.

Paralysis in foreign policy seemed to be a price most Israelis were willing
to pay in return for unity on economic and other domestic matters. It was
also a luxury they could afford so long as no credible Palestinian negotiating partner, committed to coexistence with Israel, emerged. The government was thus under little domestic pressure, and only minimal international pressure, to offer any major concessions. In the mid-1980s, international conditions also favored inaction: the Iran-Iraq war preoccupied much
of the Arab world, and Egypt was reintegrating back into the Arab fold
without withdrawing from the Egypt-Israel peace treaty (though this remained a "cold" peace in most respects). These conditions changed, however, with the onset of sustained Arab unrest (the *intifada*) in the occupied
territories from the end of 1987.

The *intifada*, unlike the previous sporadic rioting against Israel's control of the territories, brought about a lasting change on this front. It threatened the country's international standing and its internal cohesion, posing a sharp challenge that the country's deadlocked political system was ill
equipped to handle. It did not become a blatantly partisan issue, since Labor shared responsibility with Likud, but the future of the territories could
no longer be shelved as a political issue. In this context, the scheduled elections of November 1, 1988, like those of 1984, were again a potential turning point that turned nowhere: the two blocs again emerged nearly equal in
the number of seats won. But the Likud had a slight edge in postelection
bargaining because the balance was held by a reinvigorated religious bloc

with eighteen of the 120 Knesset seats. Some of the religious parties were closer to the Likud position on foreign policy and defense, and none of them were likely to sit in the same government with Labor's secular leftist partners. As a result, Labor was forced to agree to a renewed National Unity Government on less-than-equal terms, with Shamir projected as prime minister for the full four-year term of office.

Basic disagreement over foreign policy still deadlocked the government, despite Shamir's stronger position. This became more critical after December 1988, when PLO leader Yasir Arafat made his highly publicized declaration renouncing terrorism and calling for a negotiated peace based on coexistence of Israel and a Palestinian state. This statement changed the rules of the diplomatic game, increasing pressure on Israel for something other than the standard negative response. Also, the *intifada* was having a mixed impact on Israeli opinion: while the public continued to favor severe measures against violence in the territories, there was also a slight but measurable shift in a dovish direction on key long-term questions in Arab-Israeli relations.

By early 1990, the popularity of the National Unity Government had plummeted to the point that three-quarters of the public were unhappy with it.[31] Finally, in March Labor Party leader (and Finance Minister) Peres succeeded in bringing down the government on a no-confidence vote. Bringing down the government did not mean, however, that Peres could offer a viable alternative. After long and intricate maneuvering, Shamir emerged as head of a "narrow" Likud-led government with a bare majority, marking the end of five and a half years of power-sharing by the two major blocs. But this government was also unable to pursue a coherent policy or serve out its full term of office. Shamir's agreement to participate in the U.S.-initiated peace talks that began in October 1991 led to the defection of the smaller rightwing parties and to the calling of early elections in June 1992.

The 1992 elections produced a narrow margin of sixty-one seats for Labor together with other parties on the left, a "blocking majority" that forestalled formation of another right-religious coalition. On the basis of this slim edge, the Labor-led government of Prime Minister Rabin and Foreign Minister Peres opened up direct negotiations with the Palestine Liberation Organization (PLO), initiating a process that led to the Israel-PLO Declaration of Principles in September 1993, agreement on Israeli withdrawal from Gaza and Jericho in May 1994, and an interim agreement on Palestinian autonomy in October 1995 (see chapter 10). But Israel remained deeply divided between a secular, modernizing, more dovish half and a traditional, conservative, more hawkish half. This was underlined by the 1996 elections where for the first time the electorate had to choose directly between two candidates for prime minister and in which Likud's Benjamin Netanyahu defeated Labor's Peres by less than 1 percent of the vote.

The delicacy of the political balance meant that while the public did overwhelmingly support the idea of a peace process, there was still no clear consensus on the nature of the peace. Labor and Likud offered clearly different visions of an overall settlement of the Arab-Israel conflict. The Likud consistently advocated the Israeli right to remain in Judea and Samaria and to expand Jewish settlement there; there would be no Arab sovereignty west of the Jordan River, and Arabs living there would be offered autonomy as individuals but not as a nationality or by territorial definition. Peace would be finalized by the simple signing of peace treaties with bordering Arab states on the basis of existing lines of demarcation. Labor leaders called for some amendment of the pre-1967 borders in Israel's favor, basically on strategic grounds, but favored withdrawing Israeli control over most of the West Bank in the framework of a permanent peace that would include demilitarization of the returned territory. Initially this meant the "Jordanian option," which would avoid a Palestinian state by inviting King Hussein back into the West Bank. But in July 1988, King Hussein relinquished all claim to the West Bank and to speaking for Arabs living there, and Labor was eventually forced to deal with the PLO as the only credible representative of the Palestinians.

On the surface, the Likud's conception was no less ideological than the Labor version: it proclaimed Revisionist tenets of the Jewish right to the entire Land of Israel and a veneration of ethnicity typical of modern nationalism (as described in chapter 3). In this sense, the post-1977 division simply marked the renewal of the intense ideological conflict of the pre-state period, which had been muffled in the first two decades of statehood. But the worldview represented by Menachem Begin also incorporated some new elements, leading some to describe it as a "New Zionism" or as "neo-Revisionism." In the aftermath of the Holocaust, the message became much more emotional, with an even stronger focus on assertive self-defense and a defiant rejection of the outside world.[32]

Revisionism in any variant was, of course, more receptive to claims of Jewish tradition than Labor Zionism had ever been. It embodied a militant and unapologetic affirmation of historical and ethnic roots and the rejection (in theory) of "non-Jewish" secular doctrines. Religious symbolism was assimilated and adapted to a nationalist ethos, creating a new "civil religion" synthesizing these two elements.[33] In its more extreme manifestations, it could even be seen as an atavistic response to modernity, similar to Islamic fundamentalism in rejecting the modern world and calling for a return to one's own roots.

Modernized secular Zionists saw this as a huge step backward. Uniqueness, rather than normalization, was becoming the watchword. Diaspora mentality "was forcefully returning, uninvited, to the house which Zionism built."[34] Instead of becoming a nation like other nations, Israelis were again seeing themselves, in the words of Balaam's blessing, as "a people who shall dwell alone" (Numbers 23:9). Israel was moving from a universalistic, secular, rational, civic orientation to one that was particularistic, religious, mystical, and primordial. It was reverting from an "Israeli" outlook, embodied in the concept of the State of Israel, back to a more "Jewish" self-identity, tied to the idea of Eretz Yisrael.[35] There was a reassertion of tradition after an interlude during which it had been temporarily submerged by a now-receding wave of secular ideology.

The reassertion of tradition could be seen on a number of fronts, from a strengthening of Jewish studies in secular schools to a revival of femininity in daily life. The impact on the role of women is especially instructive. Labor Zionism had taken pride in its progressive stance on women's issues, reflected in such images as women serving alongside men in the army and Golda Meir's election as one of the first women heads of government in the world. In truth these images were always overdrawn; Israel was in the forefront as far as legal equality was concerned but lagged behind many other states regarding de facto equality in public life, in the marketplace, and in society at large. Even some of the advances made were rolled back as progressive ideology yielded ground to more traditional attitudes associated with growing religiosity or imported non-Western folkways. For example, the representation of women in the Knesset fell from twelve seats in 1948 (and a high of thirteen in 1955) to a low of seven seats in 1988 and eight seats in 1996.

Religious revivalism and messianism were important dimensions of the new intellectual climate. The establishment of a separate state religious school system, as part of a network of institutions tied to the National Religious Party, had reinforced a distinct religious-Zionist subculture within Israeli society. The younger generation that passed through this network underwent intense socialization into the religious interpretation of Zionism. They served as the basis for Gush Emunim (Bloc of the Faithful), the group that spearheaded the establishment of Jewish settlements throughout the occupied territories.

Gush Emunim was not simply a religious faction but represented more broadly a "revitalization" movement of a type not unknown elsewhere.[36] In reaction to the threat of modern secular culture, such movements seek to revive traditional patterns (as they conceive those patterns). Gush Emunim adherents felt that the movement was acting to realize a divine purpose and that the return of Jews to Eretz Yisrael was the beginning of the final redemption for Jews and for mankind. In seeking to reclaim the entire Jewish homeland, therefore, they were performing a sacred mission. They did not seek the normalization of Jews among the family of nations but rather a return to the concept of chosenness that secular Zionists had tried to abandon. Jews, in this view, have a unique attachment to Eretz Yisrael that transcends the kinds of claims others may have there. The Western civic ideal is not applicable: equality among different peoples is not possible in these circumstances, and democracy is secondary to national rights. Arabs who live in Eretz Yisrael should have full civic rights only if they accept the essential Jewishness of the state; otherwise, they must choose between living there peacefully without full rights, or leaving.

Gush Emunim served as the ideological vanguard of the New Zionism, as the main force behind the settlement movement in the territories, and as a bridge between religious and secular nationalists. In some ways, it was co-opted and used by the leadership of Likud, which shared most of its immediate goals. In another sense, this connection with the ruling party gave Gush Emunim and the settlement movement an influence in public life well beyond what would be expected from the actual size of their membership. The influence of Gush Emunim-style nationalist ideology cannot account, however, for all of the overlap between religious self-identity and support of more hawkish parties. The core supporters of Gush Emunim, and the ideological expressions of nationalism generally, came disproportionately from Jews of European background. The religious orientation of Middle Eastern Jews is generally less doctrinaire and less messianic. In the style of the Middle East, religion is more a matter of traditions and customs tied to group identity than of inviolable sacred ideology. Religious Jews of Middle Eastern background were drawn to the Likud and other secular nationalist parties more by a general sense of ethnic particularism than by ideological fervor. But they were still predisposed more to support of Likud than of Labor, with its secular socialism and Western universalism.

This visceral attraction of Revisionism to many less Westernized Jews, religious and nonreligious, was apparent in some early successes. For example, the first place where the Revisionists gained a majority in a Zionist movement branch was in Tunis, in 1928.[37] This tendency was obscured in the early statehood period, for reasons already outlined (above and chapter 4). But it emerged more strongly as time passed, reinforced by the hostility of refugees toward their lands of origin. Many Middle Eastern Jews related easily to Menachem Begin's emotional appeal to ethnic sentiment and his unapologetic defense of Jewishness. Middle Eastern Jews also shared with the Likud (before 1977) common ground as outsiders facing a haughty and patronizing Labor Establishment.

The appeal of the right to Middle Eastern Jewish voters was not, therefore, ideological or intellectual primarily, but more attitudinal and emotional. Support of the Likud was a way of breaking the hegemony of a Western-oriented elite, of asserting full and equal membership in Israeli society, and even of turning the tables on those who had been disdainful of them (now it was Labor Zionists who were "less Zionist"). Belief in the historical or God-given right to the entire Land of Israel was less central to this than the social and demographic realities that had shaped the historical experience of Israelis from non-European lands.[38]

The loss of a dominant consensus meant, inevitably, the loss of coherence and strong direction in government. Though one bloc might control the government, it held no monopoly on legitimacy and its ability to make basic changes was limited. There were more autonomous forces to deal with, as new organizations and groups appeared to represent their own interests. The role of parties was weakened, and the cabinet was less able to act with unity and decisiveness. In some ways, these trends marked the reemergence of the pre-state coalition tradition, when power-sharing arrangements were broad and shallow with much less coalition discipline. There was also less coherence within the parties, however, as the hold of ideological camps and movements loosened. In a sense, what was happening was what Peter Medding has called "the breakthrough of society."[39] This moved Israeli politics closer to underlying human realities and fostered the reemergence of pre-civic patterns of behavior; in the words of one commentator, the loss of governmental coherence was "taking us back to the shtetl" (the Jewish village of Eastern Europe).[40]

The pattern of decentralized bargaining among semiautonomous agencies has emerged even more strongly. Kupat Holim Klalit (the Sick Fund of the Histadrut), which had been a direct participant in making health policy when the Labor Party was in power, became a "veto group" in the setting of that policy.[41] A proposal for a five-day work week was the subject of negotiations between the Histadrut and the Ministry of Finance. Reforms in energy policy were negotiated among the Ministry of Energy, the three major oil companies, and the corporation operating the refineries. The transfer of absorption services for new immigrants from the Jewish Agency to the government was the subject of difficult negotiations between the agency and the Ministry of Absorption, with the Ministry of Finance also involved. The examples could be multiplied extensively, involving a variety of public, semipublic, and private bodies according to the subject involved.

As a result of frustration over their inability to influence policy, Israelis turned—or, perhaps more accurately, returned—increasingly to unofficial and unstructured channels of political action. The level of protest and other forms of direct action had as noted been relatively low during the period of state-building on the civic model. But from the early 1970s there was a steep rise in direct public participation (or "hyper-participation") in politics, creating greater democracy (in a basic sense) at the cost of greater discord and disorder. As Itzhak Galnoor summarized the situation, "there has been . . . increased committed participation and more direct impact on steering, accompanied by less stability and greater difficulties in governing."[42] In short, by the 1980s the incidence of protest and demonstration in Israel surpassed that of almost any other democratic regime.

As measured by Sam Lehman-Wilzig, the frequency of "protest events" in Israel can be divided into four distinct periods. During the first six years of statehood, despite the enormous problems of state-building and mass immigration, there were on the average only fifty-four significant protests or demonstrations annually. With improvement in the economic situation and greater overall stability, this decreased to an average of thirty-nine protest events per year in the domestically quiescent period of 1955–1970. Beginning in 1971—a year marked by the end of an external threat (the war of attrition) and the breakup of the National Unity Government that had ruled since the eve of the 1967 war—the number of protests and demonstrations tripled to an average of 122 per year over the next eight years. At that point, corresponding with the Egyptian peace treaty and the onset of triple-digit inflation, this level of protest almost doubled again, to an average of 202 annually during the following eight years.[43] In 1986 Lehman-Wilzig concluded that Israel was "the most protest-oriented polity in the democratic world today," pointing out a 1981 survey which showed that 21.5 percent of Israelis had taken part in a protest event while the highest proportion anywhere else was 11 percent, in the United States.[44] Gadi Wolfsfeld, comparing Israel to eight other democratic states, found that only in Italy had a higher percentage of the public participated in a demonstration.[45] In this light, perhaps the most symptomatic political event of post-1977 Israel was the 1982 demonstration by an estimated 400,000 protesters—nearly 20 percent of the country's adult population—demanding an official inquiry into the Sabra and Shatila massacre in Lebanon (a demand that the government was forced to meet).

In these "old-new" patterns of direct action and confrontational politics, as with traditional Jewish politics, the prevalence of informal bargaining and unclear lines of authority led competing groups and interests to resort to tactics outside of normal procedure. Linking this contemporary surge of protest to classical Jewish "oppositionism," Lehman-Wilzig argues that "the modern *secular* State of Israel may be somewhat of a novum in Jewish political history, but the political culture animating it has roots deep in the past."[46]

The growing frustration with existing channels of political communication and influence, in the 1970s and 1989s, was reflected in the declining role of parties. From Zionism's earliest days parties had been the dominant channels in politics. But after 1948 the role of parties was undercut by the development of state institutions and bureaucracy, vast changes in demography, growing social and economic complexity, generational change, and the overall decline of ideology. One clear index of this development is the decline in party membership: in the mid-1950s over one-quarter of the Israeli population were members of a political party, but this figure declined to 18 percent in 1969, 13 percent in 1977, and only 8 percent in 1988.[47]

Together with this came a devastating increase in the percentage of those surveyed who said the government was performing "poorly" or "very poorly," from only 8 percent in 1967 to 81 percent in 1977 (and with similar high percentages for Likud governments in the 1980s).[48] Public frustration with existing channels led to more direct forms of communication, whether as protest or other forms of direct action. It was "the lack of formal opportunities for political communication" or the "blocked opportunities" that lay behind the resort to venerable patterns of confrontational politics. When asked to identify the reasons for Israel's high level of protest activity, the leading explanation chosen by Israeli respondents was that "the citizen does not have enough other ways to express himself to the authorities."[49]

There were of course other circumstances that pushed politics into irregular channels. The 1967 war had put on the table issues upon which there was deep division and toward which some groups put principle ahead of adherence to procedure. At the same time, the war also created greater room for such debate by reducing security fears that normally impelled Israelis to unite and submerge their differences. In addition, the second generation from the great influx of Middle Eastern Jews in the 1950s, born or raised in Israel, was less hesitant than its parents in challenging inequities, and this generation was coming to political maturity. Finally, modernization also reinforced the return of extraparliamentary politics; in particular, the introduction of television in the late 1960s greatly enlarged the potential of public drama as a means of getting the attention of nonresponsive leaders.

While there is something "democratic" about direct public involvement on the political stage, there are also drawbacks. As Wolfsfeld puts it, "Israel has developed a participatory democracy, but the modes of participation leave something to be desired."[50] Politics conducted in the street tends to be episodic, reactive, negative, and something of a blunt instrument. Rewards go to those groups that are best organized, most disruptive, and least ready to compromise, which hardly encourages a civil political discourse. Even in the best circumstances there is a potential threat of violence. Finally, increased recourse to such methods undercuts the ordinary processes of government and fosters disrespect for regular procedures and the rule of law.

All of this is part of a process in which the centralization of the system is challenged and a diffusion of power is taking place. Even in the area of local government, usually considered the most centralized feature of the Israeli system, there has been considerable diffusion of power. As local governments have almost no restriction on their borrowing, they often go deeply into debt and then bargain with the state for funds to repay the loans. So long as local expenditures do not violate state policy, the state usually ends up covering them (the Knesset passed a law to prohibit such practices, but it has not been effective). Even more importantly, there has been a trend in some of the larger municipalities toward increasing financial independence by increasing local taxes and forgoing the fiscal support of the national government upon which they had depended in the past.[51]

More is involved here than protest plain and simple; the diffusion of power and expansion of public involvement extend to other ways of bypassing formal channels of government. In this broader sense, it could be said that Israelis have a penchant for direct action as part of the informal bargaining that takes place. Perhaps this can best be seen by citing the direct actions reported in the Israeli press during one randomly chosen week:

> A right-wing group blocks the road between Gaza and Israel with burning tires in order to protest the entrance of Arab labor to Israel.
>
> Na'amat, the women's division of the Histadrut, conducts a national "referendum" on the issue of economic equality for women.
>
> Young Labor Party activists bring sacks of garbage to the twelfth-floor office of Tel Aviv's Likud mayor as a strike of municipal sanitation workers continues.
>
> Tel Aviv's striking garbage collectors try to physically block the work of private contractors hired to remove the accumulated refuse.
>
> Parents and children in a Jerusalem neighborhood stage an unlicensed demonstration to demand installation of traffic lights in a busy intersection (licenses to demonstrate are usually given for the asking).
>
> Also in Jerusalem, members of a right-wing group try to disrupt an open-air performance of a play they deem objectionable.
>
> A construction firm in Haifa occupies a building it has built for the municipality and refuses to transfer possession until its financial claims are settled.
>
> The municipal offices of Yokne'am, a development town, shut down for two hours to protest the loss of jobs at a local factory.
>
> Eighth-graders in Kiryat Shmonah barricade themselves on the upper floor of their school building following cancellation of a class trip.
>
> A national protest meeting is held in Jerusalem to press Bezek, the government communications company, to remedy defective telephone service.
>
> Right-wing demonstrators block a convoy of vehicles, organized by left-wing groups, that is carrying food supplies into the Gaza strip during a curfew there.[52]

Another dimension of the "old-new" pattern of direct action was the establishment of alternative social and economic networks. The Israeli public has often organized its own informal systems to address unmet needs. Under this rubric are phenomena as varied as the settlers' movement in the occupied territories, pirate cable television (operating, at one time, in a quarter of Israel's households), the black market, and private health insurance plans. In the 1970s and 1980s budgetary pressures forced serious cutbacks in government spending, leading to the emergence of "gray education" and "gray medicine" as families made their own arrangements for additional schooling or medical treatment. Likewise, dissatisfaction with police protection sparked an explosion of private security forces, which by the late 1980s outnumbered Israeli police three to one; even in the isolated *haredi* community, residents organized civil patrols to secure the safety of the streets.[53]

Another "old-new" pattern was the tendency to illegalism, or an attitude of expediency toward the law, a tendency which "is nourished by the venerable tradition of the shtetl."[54] During the Ben-Gurion period, this tendency remained largely under the surface as the government promoted its version of *mamlachtiut,* or civic-mindedness, as a cure for age-old habits of circumventing unwanted authority. After Ben-Gurion left the scene, familiar attitudes came back into the open as public scandals multiplied and corruption at higher levels became increasingly open. It appeared that the exploitation of a public position for private or party needs was "almost legitimate," or so widespread that no guilt was really involved. As extraparliamentary politics became more common, violations of the law by extreme movements were opposed only by political enemies; few figures in public life condemned the illegal acts of groups with which they sympathized.[55] The expansion of protest politics involved a paradox: greater acceptance of the democratic right of protest, but consequently a lessening of respect for orderly procedure and the general rule of law.[56]

To what extent can a decline in support for democratic values be documented? As summarized in chapter 1, the evidence is mixed:

1. Respect for political parties, the media, and some other institutions in democratic politics is remarkably low, though not substantially different from some other democratic nations.

2. A significant part of the public thinks that Israel is "too democratic," and such attitudes tend to increase with greater religiosity and decrease with greater education. Again, this is not radically different from other democracies, though Israel tends to the European approach permitting greater curbs on free speech, in the name of public order, than American thinking would customarily permit.[57]

3. Where Israeli belief in democracy seems relatively weak is in three particular areas: (a) deference to authority and support of strong leadership, especially when security issues are invoked; (b) sensitivity to the image being projected externally, and consequently demands for controls on the media; and (c) accommodation of non-Jewish minorities on a fair and equal basis. All three of these weaknesses reflect

in one way or another the impact or limitations of Jewish historical experience.

4. Israel is characterized by "focused intolerance" toward an Arab minority that is clearly identified and linked with a foreign threat, while democracies such as the United States, with a variety of target groups, demonstrate "pluralistic intolerance."

5. The *intifada* or Arab uprising in the occupied territories, from late 1987, led in the short term to demands for tougher policing, but in the long term to greater readiness for compromise (see chapter 10).

The New Zionism never became dominant in the way classical Labor Zionism had been at its peak. Vociferous debate over the future of the territories continued unabated, with the dominant tone in intellectual and academic circles still set by the doves. (The novelist Amos Oz taunted the hawks: "Why are most of the creative people in the country, heaven help us, 'leftists'? Is it a conspiracy? Has Damascus bought out Hebrew literature lock, stock, and barrel?")[58] The political success of the Likud from 1977 to 1992 served to legitimize it as a contender for power, but the effort to substitute Revisionist symbols and myths for established Zionist symbols and myths did not succeed: "The majority of the nation's educational and cultural elite and leading figures in the media are among the substantial number of Israelis who do not share the cultural definition of political reality staged by the Likud. . . ."[59]

The Likud's success in pulling even with Labor at the polls was not achieved on the basis of its ideological appeal alone; in fact, the ideology may on balance have been a handicap. There is substantial evidence that many of those voting for the Likud were actually closer to Labor on issues such as the territories.[60] In other words, by the 1980s the electorate was voting somewhat to the right of its beliefs, just as in the 1950s and 1960s it had voted to the left of its beliefs (see chapter 4). Menachem Begin's success in attracting votes did not come from his ideology, which he had learned to downplay, but from his appeal to the emotions and sentiments of traditional, religious, and above all Middle Eastern Jews who were alienated from the Labor Zionist Establishment. Begin's own party, Herut, had by this time completed the transition from ideological movement to modern, bureaucratized political party.[61]

What we have seen, in sum, is a reassertion of traditional Jewish occupational and social patterns, religious beliefs, and non-European influences that ended the dominance of Labor Zionism. Like other "new societies," Israel moved from ideology to patterns more reflective of its human and material realities.[62] There was a weakening of the "movement style of life" and an accentuation of occupational, economic, and ethnic differences.[63] While politics created society in the *yishuv*, the more common pattern is now emerging: social realities shape politics.

ECONOMIC TRANSITION

Israel's first twenty-five years also stand apart in economic terms. Before the 1970s, Israel was judged to be one of the world's true economic success stories. With the help of reparations payments from Germany and private aid from Jewish communities, economic growth averaged around 10 percent a year. This was achieved despite the pressures of massive immigration and a level of defense spending (8 to 10 percent of the gross domestic product, or GDP) heavier than that in any other democratic state. Israel did suffer from a chronic negative balance of trade, as well as an overall negative balance of payments, which helped to fuel a high rate of inflation. Nevertheless, until 1966 taxes were sufficient to cover domestic government spending, and taxes consistently took about a quarter of the GDP—not a particularly heavy burden by Western European standards.[64]

The wars of 1967 and 1973 ratcheted defense spending up to new levels where it remained stuck for the time being. After 1967 it rose to over 20 percent of GDP and to 28 percent or more after 1973, peaking somewhere above 30 percent (by most calculations) in 1975.[65] At the same time, with a sixfold increase in world oil prices during this period, the costs of imported energy skyrocketed. Yet there was no offsetting reduction in governmental social spending; in fact pubic services continued to expand, with real spending on health rising 60 percent per capita and on education 80 percent per capita during the 1968–1978 decade. By 1978 Israel ranked fifth in the world in public education expenditure as a proportion of GDP, at 8.5 percent.[66] Though growth had slowed down by this time, the standard of living continued to rise. The result was "the overburdened polity": a state with unrealistic goals on one side and limited resources, growing demands, loss of cohesion, and a protracted conflict on the other. Part of this problem was that the decline in the level of ideological commitment left the public less willing to delay personal gratification in order to achieve common goals (as earlier Zionists did).[67]

Though there were tax increases, they were insufficient to close the broadening gap between revenue and consumption. Many public services were being provided free of charge or well below cost, and reliance on external sources of funding inevitably grew. "A pattern of over-consumption was created"; in other words, the country was simply living beyond its means.[68] The government's response to this situation was described by one economist as "schizophrenia": pressing economic realities were being willfully ignored, and deficit financing was pursued as though large-scale foreign aid and massive borrowing could continue indefinitely into the future.[69]

The results were entirely predictable. As defense spending, public services, and private consumption all rose, gross investment fell from 33 percent of GDP in the 1973–1975 period to 24 percent in the 1980–1983 period.[70] The growth rate of the economy fell to an average of 3.2 percent in the 1976–1989 period, with a low point of 1 to 2 percent in the early 1980s.[71] Israel was not keeping pace with other developed countries; while per capita income stood at 83 percent of the average of the twenty-three most developed economies in 1960, this figure had dropped to 48 percent by 1978.[72] One index of the underlying problem was the level of governmental expenditure in relation to the size of the economy. The weight of public spending in Israel had always been impressive by world standards, running at around 50 percent of GDP, but by the early 1980s this had risen to 75 percent or more of GDP by most accounts, and for some years and by some measures even exceeded the official GDP.[73] The difference was made up by borrowing; net external debt increased from $500 million in 1964 to over $17.7 billion in 1983—a 35-fold expansion.

By the mid-1980s inflation was running at a 300–400 percent annual rate. Despite its supposed commitment to a market economy, the Likud after its 1977 victory found itself no more able politically than Labor to tame the runaway economy (indeed, the Likud's base of support was disproportionately, and paradoxically, among those most dependent on a continuing high level of government subsidies and services). Though taxes had risen from about 25 percent of GDP to around 50 percent and austerity measures were intermittently attempted (only to be abandoned before elections), the economy remained out of kilter. Inevitably, public services began to decline as the crunch grew more severe, contributing to the development of "gray education," "gray medicine," and the other alternative private social service networks described above.

The need for a massive restructuring of the economy was one of the major incentives for formation of the National Unity Government (NUG) after the elections of July 1984. This forced the two major blocs to share responsibility for the unpopular steps required, thus removing the issue from politics. After some false starts, the NUG used its emergency powers in July 1985, to impose a sweeping Economic Stabilization Plan (ESP) that was, like most larger economic policies, the result of hard bargaining among the government, labor, and industry. The ESP included dramatic cuts in government spending and subsidies, strict price controls, severe wage restraints, and devaluation, as well as measures to encourage private sector growth and the liberalization of trade restrictions in order to expose more of the economy to open competition. In part, cuts in government spending were made possible by the 1979 peace treaty with Egypt, Israel's most powerful enemy; defense spending had already fallen in the early 1980s to under 20 percent of GDP, and the downward trend continued as Israel disengaged from its heavy involvement in Lebanon in the middle of the decade.

The ESP set in motion a gradual turnaround in the Israeli economy. In the short term, of course, it accelerated the deterioration of public services, as well as threatening economic collapse in the agricultural sector (the kibbutz and moshav movements were overburdened with debt). But it was a textbook success in curtailing inflation to the low double-digits; the annual increase in the consumer price index averaged only 18.5 percent from July 1985 through 1991 and fell to 9.4 percent in 1992 (the first single-digit increase since 1970).[74]

In the short term, the ESP also cut the purchasing power of wages by about 30 percent. Wage increases that were intended to compensate for part of this loss were overly generous, however, because the likely rate of inflation was overestimated, and as a result private consumption rebounded and the previous imbalance reappeared in 1988–1989. Fortuitously this distortion was corrected by the wave of mass immigration that began in 1989, with 500,000 new Israelis, mostly from the former Soviet Union, arriving by mid-1994. This increase of roughly 10 percent in the population pushed wages downward again; together with lower interest rates and a more stable and predictable exchange rate for the Israeli shekel, this triggered a period of sustained and impressive growth.[75]

From 1990 to 1995 the Israeli economy grew by 42 percent, near the top among developed economies. The 1995 GDP was $86 billion or $15,500 per capita, putting Israel ahead of many European states. Government spending had returned to a more normal level of about 49 percent of GDP, with defense spending below 10 percent of GDP at that point and falling. Unemployment had fallen to 6 percent.[76]

Serious problems still remained in Israel's economy and in the scramble over scarce resources; Israel was still an "overburdened polity" by any standard. But after the dramatic economic turnaround it was clear that Israel of the mid-1990s was a modernizing state increasingly drawn into the converging social and economic currents that pull such states together. In some ways Israel, ranked very highly in the number of videocassette recorders and personal computers per capita, was even in the vanguard of the electronic age. More is at work here than economics alone; whether labeled as "modernization" or "Westernization," Israel, no less than other states and perhaps more than most, was becoming a part of the global village. Are cellular phones, Scandinavian vacations, and TV-age electoral campaigns replacing pioneering ideologies as the universalizing counteweight to reassertive Jewish particularism? Will hard disks rather than hard dogmas serve as the vehicle of civicness and secularization? The very success of Israel's economic transition calls attention to the changing nature of challenges to tradition in Israeli life and politics.

IMPACT OF MODERNIZATION

At its most fundamental level modernization is said to involve liberation from traditional authority, a new positive attitude toward change, and a turn from cultural orientations or values to social rationality. A civil society autonomous of the state emerges, as do new social strata (particularly professionals), more complex economic division of labor, and general bureaucratization. The weight of tradition, and its associated particularities, decline as objective forces mold all aspects of life. There is a convergence as societies respond to the same forces, a process which accelerates as these forces become internationalized. Of course, we are reminded, the dichotomy between tradition and modernity is not absolute; traditional societies also can undergo considerable change and modern societies retain considerable diversity, often incorporating traditional elements in a variety of ways. But modernization still involves a number of common universalizing tendencies.[77]

In terms of these basic definitions, Israel has long been a modernizing or modernized society. Zionism was itself part of a broad historical challenge to old identities and value orientations. Jews were to join other peoples in a process of nation-building, creating a new order consonant with the progressive currents of the time. Zionism, and Israeli society, were attuned to, and even fixated on, technological innovation and prevailing models of social and economic development. The *yishuv* and the state, like other modernizing societies, underwent increased social mobilization, organizational diversification and proliferation, rationalized regulation and allocation (market mechanisms, voting), greater division of labor and occupational specialization, enhanced social mobility, urbanization, secularization, expansion of media, and diffusion of political power.[78]

This process—long and slow but cumulative—was obscured by ideological habits of thought and revived resistance of traditionalists. But by the 1980s and 1990s, with the decline of ideology, the pressures of modernity were taking center stage. In the third great revolution of the modern era— that of information technology, following the earlier industrial and scientific revolutions—Israel was not only a full participant but was even at the forefront in certain respects. The electronic age was integrating Israel into the larger world in ways that the founders of Zionism could hardly have imagined, while at the same time rewriting the rules of Israeli politics.

The impact of modernization on politics, as generally understood, is to create a more diversified political structure, to extend the scope of law and administration into all spheres, to spread power more widely, to weaken traditional elites and traditional sources of legitimation, and to foster a new accountability in which the ruled participate more directly in selection of the rulers and in setting major policies.[79] In the Israeli case, this has been expressed by diffusion of power within and among parties, decline of party dominance, emergence of new kinds of political actors, a new "mass politics" based more on personalities and less on issues, greater electoral fluidity and volatility, and the strengthening of administrative and legislative regularity.

"Mass politics" meant appeals to a broad central spectrum of the electorate, to a large floating vote influenced more by the images of leading candidates and by general public mood than by ideological loyalties. This was closely linked to the changing role of the media. Since late 1968 television had come to play a large role in election campaigns and in shaping public images of candidates and issues, in place of the classic party-sponsored political rallies of the past. The party press, which had once dominated the newspaper scene, was pushed aside by the popular independent papers more closely tuned to the general public mood.

The correlation of voting to party platforms was strikingly weak; if voters had for certain historical reasons voted to the left of their beliefs during the glory days of Labor Zionism, they now deviated in the other direction because of a general weakening of ideology and the presence of personal and emotional factors that overshadowed the issues. About half of the voters remained loyal to their parties through several elections—a proportion higher than in other Western democracies—but this still left a considerable floating vote that could potentially cause a radical shift in power any time it flowed more in one direction than the other.[80] The shift from issue-centered politics to image-centered media campaigns sparked the emergence of populist appeals in election campaigns; in 1981, for example, the government in power made imported television sets and videocassette recorders much cheaper to buy—at the cost of great damage to the nation's balance of payments—in order to create a more favorable climate on election day. To some observers, there was even a risk that the system might become too responsive, moving from tight party control to unrestrained populism and demagoguery.[81]

Another aspect of the loosening party system, and one generally regarded positively, was the democratization that took place within the parties. In the past party leaderships had tightly controlled the selection and ranking of Knesset candidates, thus insuring fairly strong party discipline. By the early 1980s there was some loosening of this process as candidate selection, in at least its early stages, was passed on to broader and more representative party bodies. In 1988 the Labor Party chose most of its candidates through twenty-three councils of district branches with the final ranking done by the Central Committee (a body of 1,267 members), a procedure that led to the rejection of some prominent party figures (Abba Eban in particular).[82]

By 1992 Labor had moved all the way to a full-fledged primary system for both Knesset candidates and for selection of party leader, with all registered party members eligible to vote in the election that replaced Shimon Peres with Yitzhak Rabin. The ensuing general election was also unusually personalized, with Rabin's supporters and opponents both focusing on his personal strengths and weaknesses in the confrontation with the comparatively less popular Yitzhak Shamir. Other parties were undergoing similar transitions during this period; in March 1993, the Likud replaced Shamir as party leader with Benjamin Netanyahu in its first general party primaries.

The new open elections did change party slates to some degree, at least in bringing in younger candidates and increasing representation of Jews from Asia and Africa, though they were less successful in increasing the numbers of women and Arab candidates. More broadly, like modern parties elsewhere Israeli political institutions were becoming less ideological. In place of the old party ties centered around youth movements, newspapers, and other elements of the "movement" style of life, they now waged modern election campaigns aimed at the amorphous middle of the political spectrum with hired U.S. political consultants and public relations firms. Differences on issues were blurred, especially in the realm of economic policy where the gap between the two major blocs had long been narrowing. The Labor Party had long subsidized business interests, for example, and the Likud after 1977 continued to do so despite its supposed commitment to a free market. And while more voters identified with the right than had been the case before 1977, a majority (60 percent in one survey) continued to support socialism and to oppose reduction of the state's role in the economy.[83] Even differences on the occupied territories narrowed somewhat, as both Labor and Likud moved toward autonomy as at least an interim solution; debate now focused on the scope of autonomy and whether it would be the permanent solution. While "polarization" between hawks and doves was a major concern of the early 1980s, commentators a decade later were remarking over a lessening of distance between the two camps and the incorporation of more extreme groups back into the two major parties.[84]

Israelis were turning more to other bodies for services and channels of access previously provided by parties, as reflected in the expansion of governmental activities and the proliferation of other political, social, and economic groups. Parties, it seemed, were simply becoming less important. Or were they? It could be argued that it was primarily the parties' mode of operation and electoral behavior that changed, and that once an election was over they were no less important than before. Parties still held the key to forming governing coalitions and negotiating government policy.

In other respects, modernization or Westernization of Israeli public life also contributed to greater regularization and rationalization in areas where a predisposition in this direction existed. The best expression of this was in the legal and judicial sphere, though the picture regarding attitudes toward the law is somewhat contradictory; two opposed trends were operating at the same time. On one hand, "illegalism" accompanied the growth of extraparliamentary politics and the breakdown of the tight Ben-Gurion sys-

TABLE 3   Basic Laws of the State of Israel

	Year enacted
The Knesset	1958
Israel Lands	1960
President of the State	1964
The Government	1968
The State Economy	1971
Israel Defense Forces	1976
Jerusalem, Capital of Israel	1980
The Judicature	1984
The State Comptroller	1987
Freedom of Occupation	1992
Human Dignity and Freedom	1992

tem. Yet at the same time there was often more tolerance in practice, politics was more competitive, groups at the margin of the system were now drawn within it, and arbitrary procedures were reduced in a number of specific areas.[85]

To be sure, Israel remained one of only seven nations, and only three democratic nations (together with the United Kingdom and New Zealand), that have never had a formal, entrenched, written constitution.[86] But part of the progress toward a civic legal order was passage of nine of the eleven Basic Laws projected as building blocks for such a constitution, as well as two pieces of what was to have been the tenth Basic Law. Put together these Basic Laws are an impressive body of "constitutional" material (see Table 3).

The last two laws listed in Table 3 were to have been part of a Basic Law on Civil Rights, but they were passed separately when other parts of that proposed law bogged down in controversies over security concerns and religious opposition. The projected eleventh Basic Law, on Legislation, also raises religious objections since it affirms the legitimacy of nonreligious sources of law; thus, completing the process of writing Basic Laws is problematic. Only specified clauses in some of the Basic Laws are entrenched to any extent, requiring an absolute majority (or in one case a majority of 80 members) of the Knesset for any change; otherwise any of these provisions can, like an ordinary piece of legislation, be changed or invalidated by a simple majority of those voting (as they in fact have been). In essence, for the constitution as a whole to be entrenched the Knesset will have to vote away its own prerogatives, an act rare in the annals of legislative history.[87]

Nevertheless the net result of this process has been a steady growth of constitutionality over time. The basic contours of Israel's political and legal order has stabilized and are not going to be suddenly or arbitrarily changed. Apart from the Basic Laws, some other documents and Knesset laws also have an aura of basic definition of government about them: the Declaration of Independence, the Law of Return (1950) asserting the Jewish link to Israel, the 1952 law specifying the status of the World Zionist Organization and the Jewish Agency, the Equal Rights for Women Law (1951), and others.

The solidification of the court system also has advanced the rule of law. In this area tradition and modernity go hand in hand: courts and legal institutions have always played a central role in Jewish life, while in a contemporary context they are a prime vehicle for instilling the civic ethic.[88] Of course Israeli courts, like other features of public life, come in a variety of shapes and sizes. There is in fact a loosely coordinated set of court systems: civil courts, military courts, and religious courts (in fourteen different recognized religious communities). Of these the civil courts are the most instrumental in promoting democracy and the rule of law, while military and religious courts tend to draw on and strengthen group identity and solidarity.[89]

The judiciary remains one of the most important channels of Western influence. The Supreme Court is particularly important in promoting universalist values. Sitting as the High Court of Justice, it exercises an equity jurisdiction as a court of first instance as well as appeal, intervening to protect individuals from government arbitrariness. The court has increasingly applied principles of natural justice to legislation and administrative measures, adding safeguards to existing procedures and curtailing actions said to impinge on human rights. It has also expanded its jurisdiction to cover such areas as internal decisions of the Knesset and the substance of security claims made by the government.[90]

The Israeli system remains majoritarian in that a Knesset majority is still sovereign; ordinarily acts of the Knesset cannot be invalidated by the courts. But even in this regard the scope of judicial review has been expanded somewhat. In 1969 the Supreme Court, sitting as the High Court of Justice, invalidated an election financing law that conflicted with an entrenched provision of a Basic Law but had not been passed by the absolute majority needed to amend that Basic Law (Bergman v. Minister of Finance). The Knesset subsequently passed a new law consistent with the Basic Law, while at the same time mobilizing the necessary sixty-one votes. Similar court actions were taken in 1981 and 1982, again negating changes in entrenched provisions of Basic Laws passed without the absolute majority required by these provisions. In essence the High Court was simply forcing the Knesset to observe its own rules, while recognizing the right of the Knesset to change any legislation, including Basic Laws and the rules themselves, so long as proper procedure was followed. On the other hand the proposed Basic Law: Legislation would give all Basic Laws a superior status, requiring an absolute majority at all stages for changes and providing formally for judicial review; if passed this would again increase the constitutionality of the Israeli system.[91]

Finally, there was increasing resort to quasi-judicial official commissions of inquiry set up under the 1968 Commissions of Inquiry Law, empowered to require all officials—even the prime minister—to testify and supply evidence, and to issue specific recommendations that are generally implemented. Such commissions sorted out a number of front-page controversies, including lack of preparedness in the 1973 Yom Kippur War, failure to prevent the massacre of Palestinians in Lebanese refugee camps (Sabra and Shatila) in 1982, collapse of the bank shares market in 1983, controversy over the interrogation methods of the General Security Service in 1986, and the 1994 massacre of Moslem worshippers by a Jewish settler in Hebron's Tomb of the Patriarchs.

At the same time Knesset legislation accumulated over time, gradually replacing older Ottoman and British laws and creating the basis of a unified and rationalized code of law. The role of common law diminished as the gaps in existing laws were filled in. Executive discretion has been narrowed as laws become more detailed, and ministerial regulations are reviewed more consistently by Knesset committees. Knesset procedures have also been tightened, with committees meeting more often and maintaining a closer watch over government activities and finances.[92]

Among the areas in which governmental powers have been more carefully defined is wiretapping, where a 1979 act detailed procedures designed to prevent arbitrary or unjustified invasions of privacy. In addition, over time governmental secrecy loosened considerably: public debate over strategic issues (even nuclear weapons) became less restrained, the inner workings of government (never totally hidden) became more visible, and information on sensitive topics became more available.[93] For example, efforts to contain information about the 1986 arrest of former nuclear technician Mordechai Vanunu provide an interesting contrast to the Lavon affair some thirty years earlier. While details of the Lavon affair became public knowledge only years after the fact, the sensational story of Vanunu passing Israel's nuclear secrets to the *Sunday Times* (in London), and his subsequent abduction to Israel, swiftly became public knowledge (even though his trial was conducted in secret).

Progress was even made in regularizing some of the more controversial emergency regulations. Following the assumption of power by the right-wing Likud bloc in 1977, a law replacing Regulation 111 of the 1945 Defense Regulations (on administrative detention) with more circumscribed procedures and abolishing the deportation measures in Regulation 112 (within Israel itself), was enacted in 1979. In contrast to the British regulations, the new law required judicial approval of any detention within forty-eight hours (as with ordinary police arrests). Judicial review explicitly

includes examination of the "objective reasons of state security" that justify the detention. Amnon Rubinstein, who had been among the leading critics of previous arrangements, called the new law a "most liberal arrangement—almost without precedent in countries facing emergency situations
and war. . . ."[94] Judged by international human rights standards, the 1979
Emergency Detention Law meets the International Law Association standards on administrative detention: procedures set by law, the right to be in-
formed of grounds for detention, the right to consult a lawyer, judicial review, limited duration, and humane treatment. Only on publication of the
names of the detainees is Israeli practice remiss.[95]

According to the International Commission of Jurists, as of 1985 at
least eighty-five countries had laws permitting preventive detention.[96] Compared even to such nations as Great Britain (especially in Northern Ireland), Canada (where 450 French Canadians were detained in 1970), or the
United States in its treatment of the Japanese during World War II, the
1979 Israeli law, as applied, seems unexceptional. This, however, raises another question: if this most problematic part of the 1945 British Defense
Regulations can be successfully replaced by "ordinary" legislation, then why
are the rest of them still on the books?

The issuance of emergency regulations under Section 9 of the Law and
Administration Ordinance, on the other hand, seems at first glance to have
skyrocketed. The number of new regulations jumped to an annual average
of nearly twenty after the mid-1970s. But most of this quantitative leap is a
result of an explosion of regulations authorizing return-to-work orders to
striking public employees. Of the 144 new regulations in the 1975–1982 period, 124 were of this type, meaning that the underlying pattern had not significantly altered. At the rate of two to three a year, non-work-related emergency regulations were being enacted less frequently than during the first
fifteen years of the state's existence, and a large proportion of these came
during the 1982 Lebanese War.[97]

In 1985 Section 9 was used by the National Unity Government to enact
the broad-ranging and drastic Economic Stabilization Program. The emergency regulations, signed by both Shimon Peres of Labor as prime minister
and Yitzhak Modai of Likud as minister of finance, established strict controls
on wages, prices, conditions of employment, taxes, welfare, and number of
public employees, superseding all previous laws and agreements. Leaders
of both major parties defended the unusual use of emergency powers on
grounds that the economic crisis was threatening imminent disaster and that
getting such a program through the Knesset expeditiously was a practical impossibility given the range and importance of interests affected. Nevertheless, there were strong reactions from many sources, including condemnation by a former minister of justice and some calls for resignation of the
attorney general, who had approved the use of Section 9.[98]

Considering the amount of discretion available and the absence of firm institutional obstacles in a system without a written constitution or bill of rights, the use of emergency powers in Israel has been modest. The same might be said in comparison to other nations; for example, the British Emergency Powers (Defense) Acts of 1939 and 1940 (in Britain itself) went much further than Israeli laws or practice, and many of the provisions were continued after the war, until as late as 1959.[99] Nevertheless, an alert civil libertarian could easily identify several areas of weakness in the application of Israeli emergency powers. Among these would be the use of emergency regulations in nonemergency situations, the remaining limitations on judicial review, defective safeguards in the administrative process itself, the unequal application of emergency rules, and the use of measures questionable in themselves.

ISRAELIS VS. JEWS?

While policy differences between the two major blocs on certain issues may have narrowed, the pressures of modernity seem to have sharpened a more basic kind of polarization. As Myron Aronoff notes, the most serious division among Jews in Israel continues to be "the basic, conflicting, and even contradictory interpretations over what should be the exact Jewish character of Israel as a Jewish state. . . ."[100] Aronoff further defines this polarization in terms that echo the age-old struggle between particularity and universalism:

> The nation is polarized between those who emphasize the duty of the Jewish people to colonize and incorporate the ancient biblical heartland of the state of Israel (Judea and Samaria, or the West Bank) at any cost, and those who argue that to do so would threaten both the Jewish and the democratic character of the state and would make the perpetuation of war inevitable. There is an equally deep division between those who argue that the Jewish character of the state should be based on conformity with religious tradition and law, and those who strongly reject this position, arguing for a democratic, liberal, and humanistic adaptation of Jewish values to contemporary contexts.[101]

These two cleavages coincide to a great extent, though not completely. Those who celebrate particular Jewish values and traditions tend to be more hawkish on territorial issues, while those who feel comfortable as part of modern secular Western culture are more likely to apply a liberal critique to continued Israeli occupation of the West Bank and Gaza. There is also a rough correlation to the intensity of nationalism: the first approach, Nationalist or Ultranationalist Zionism, stresses "the singularity of the Jewish people and the isolation of Israel" because of irremediable hostility of non-Jews toward Jews, while the second orientation, Humanist Zionism, calls for the normalization and integration of the Jewish state into a world of states, with Israel as "a light unto the nations" in the achievement of universally recognized values.[102] This dichotomy also corresponds to Baruch

Kimmerling's two definitions of the collectivity: (1) Eretz Yisrael, based on primordial kinship ties among all Jews, historical borders, and traditional Jewish law; and (2) the State of Israel, stressing the Western civic model, negotiated borders, and Israeli secular law.[103] Or to put it on the simplest level, as some observers have suggested, the Israeli public may divide into "Jews," particularistic and tradition-oriented, and "Israelis," building a new national identity among the free nations of the West.[104]

The strength of the "Israeli" orientation is not entirely a product of modernization; it is also testimony to the continuing influence of secular Zionism, including the Labor Zionist variant. Labor Zionism has been undermined by the natural decline of ideology in a poststatehood society, a massive influx of immigrants indifferent or even hostile to socialism, the inevitable bureaucratic sclerosis of a long-dominant group and growth of resentment toward it, and a continuing preoccupation with military security and a hostile environment. Yet there is a tendency to exaggerate its decline, in part because the extent of its domination during its peak was also exaggerated. As we have seen, Labor Zionism never enjoyed real ideological hegemony, so its decline as ideology is hardly unexpected. At the same time, its institutions—the Histadrut, kibbutzim and moshavim, cooperative enterprises in the economy, the welfare state, much of the basic structure of government—survive as key elements in Israeli life. Though the agrarian ideal has to be seen in perspective in a country that is overwhelmingly urban, that part of European Zionism that represented a rebellion against traditional Jewish life in Eastern Europe still has an imprint on contemporary life. Old Jewish habits may be emerging as classic Labor Zionist ideology declines, but it can be argued that without this ideology, there would have been no state.

Will polarization between "Jews" and "Israelis" continue and deepen? Or will the pressures of modernity bring about renewed synthesis, parallel to the earlier de facto synthesis between tradition and change? There are signs that many Israelis are in fact beginning to reconcile the conflicting forces in ways that make sense to them. A religious peace movement defines itself as a choice between secular liberal humanism and religiously based nationalism. Similarly, a Sephardi group advocates both Jewish values and peaceful integration into the region.[105] The growth of "civil religion" (see chapter 8) is testimony to dissatisfaction with both total secularism and unchanging orthodoxy. Religious schools teach computing skills—and revolutionize talmudic scholarship by computerizing it—while free-thinking kibbutzim build their first synagogues.

Both universalism and particularism are basic to Jewish history; the tension between them may be the key dynamic in the unfolding of this history. In the end, Israel will, no doubt, develop into a society and a polity that is both modern *and* Jewish. Jews are a people who live by their traditions, even when rebelling against them.

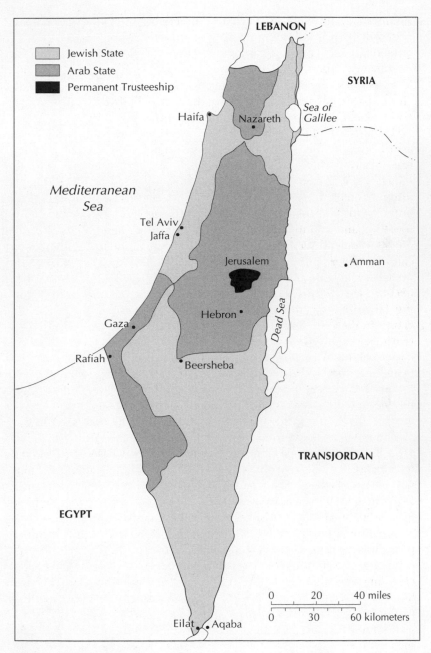

Map 1. UN Partition Plan, 1947

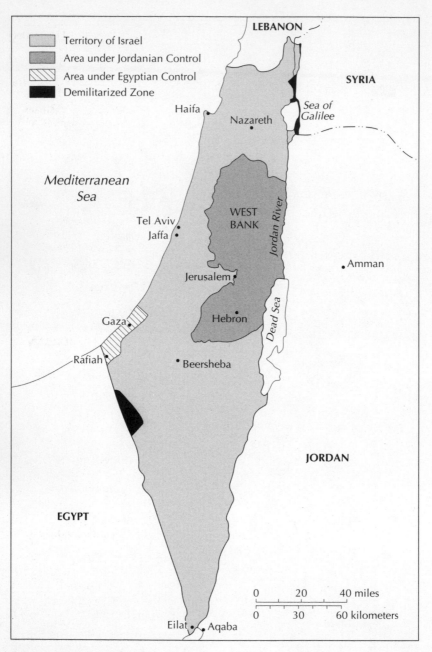

Map 2. Armistice Agreements, 1949

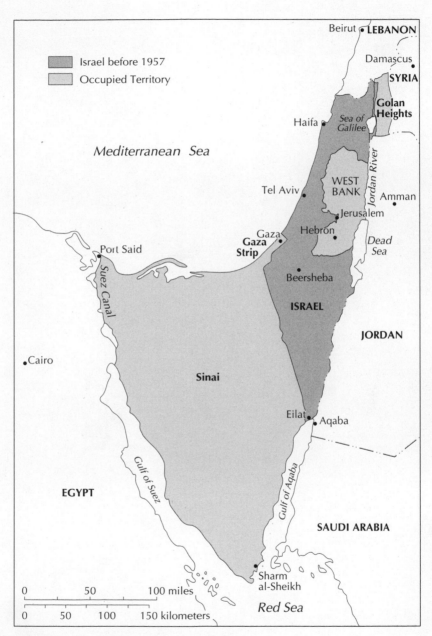

Map 3. Israeli-controlled Territories, 1967

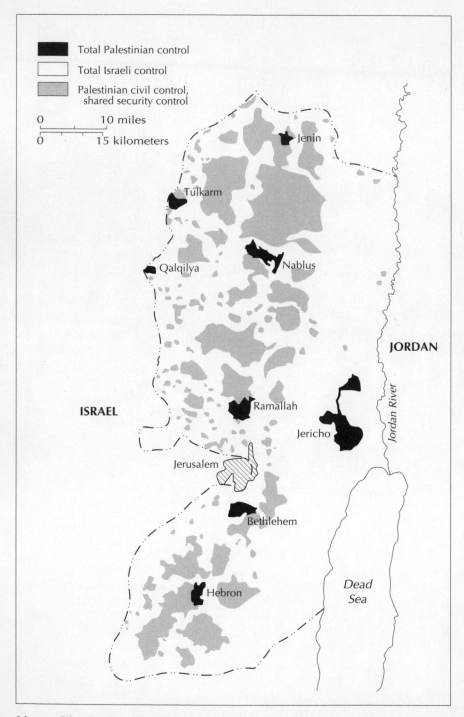

Map 4. West Bank under the Interim Agreement, 1995

PART TWO

Challenges to
Israeli Democracy

SEVEN

The Communal Split

The major cleavages in Israel illustrate the interplay of tradition, ideology, and modernization. They also illustrate the successes and failures of power-sharing based on consensus rather than undiluted majority rule, which is in theory more suitable to deeply divided societies like Israel. Israel is marked by a communal division between Jews of European background and those from the Middle East, Africa, or Asia, by a religious division between Orthodox and non-Orthodox Jews, and by an ethnic division between Jews and Arabs. The "Jewish" patterns of politics play out differently in these three different contexts, covered in the following three chapters: the comparison helps show where such patterns are relevant and where they are not.

Division among Jews from different communities is an inescapable result of Jewish history. Since the inception of Zionism, Jews have immigrated to Palestine or Israel from over a hundred countries of origin, bringing with them vast cultural, social, linguistic, and—by some definitions—ethnic differences. The most obvious distinction is between "Western" Jews from Europe, the Americas, or British Commonwealth nations, and "Eastern" Jews from Asia or Africa. This corresponds roughly to the traditional division between "German" (Ashkenazi) and "Spanish" (Sephardi) Jews. Ashkenazi Jews trace their origins and language (Yiddish) to medieval Germany and were concentrated historically in Eastern Europe, especially Poland and Russia, where by the late nineteenth century they constituted about 90 percent of world Jewry. Sephardi Jews are by strict definition the descendants of Jews forced out of Spain in the fourteenth and fifteenth centuries (most notably in the 1492 expulsion), who were dispersed around the Mediterranean world and often spoke a Spanish dialect (Ladino).

These traditional terms have been applied in Israel to the division between West and East: Jews of European cultural background are labeled

"Ashkenazim," while those of non-European background are referred to as "Sephardim" or as "Easterners." The terms do not really fit; some European or American Jews are actually Sephardim, while many Jews in the Middle East, Asia, and North Africa were not linked historically with either Ashkenazi or Sephardi dispersions. But whatever terms are used, there is a very real division between Jews whose background was European—including the Eastern European and American variants—and those, largely from the Middle East, who came from a non-European (usually Islamic) environment. It is a bit superficial to divide Jewish Israelis simply into Western Jews and Eastern Jews, but the division is a reality in the life of the country and in struggles over secular ideas and particularistic tendencies.

The potential for conflict among Israeli Jews from different backgrounds should not be underestimated. European Jews founded the Zionist movement, dominated it, and overwhelmed the long-existing Sephardi community in Palestine. They imposed their institutions and values on the politics, society, and culture of the *yishuv* (the Jewish community in pre-1948 Palestine) and the State of Israel, assuming that Jews from "backward" non-European areas would simply have to adjust to the established order. The bulk of Asian and African Jews, on the other hand, arrived on the scene only after the state was established, often as uprooted refugees who had been stripped of their property and other resources. Initially the gap—economically, socially, politically, or on any other dimension—was enormous, and resentment was further fueled by attitudes of paternalism and contempt for non-European culture on the part of the Ashkenazi elite.

THE REALITY OF THE GAP

Jewish-Arab differences are usually characterized as an "ethnic" division. That being the case, then for the sake of clarity differences among Jews should perhaps be termed "communal" or "subcultural" rather than ethnic. The difference may only be one of degree, but the interactions between Western and Eastern Jews are marked by less rigid boundaries, more common bonds, and less fundamental conflict than is usually associated with "interethnic" relations.[1] In any event, in this study Arab-Jewish differences are termed an "ethnic" split, while divisions between Western and Eastern Jews are characterized as "communal" (which is also the term used in Hebrew).

This is not to minimize the differences between the two communities. Jews of European ancestry had both different cultural baggage and a different ideological point of departure from their Middle Eastern counterparts. This starting point was their "pioneering, revolutionary orientation largely couched in Western secular terms" and aimed at creating a new kind of Jewishness, in contrast to the continuing adherence of non-European Jews to the Jewishness they had always known.[2] Not having been shaped by the currents of Western modernism, Jews from Asia and Africa were still attached to custom and ritual and viewed Zionism as, if anything, a reinforcement of traditional Jewishness rather than a revolution against it.

There was also an important difference in the time and character of the Western and Eastern immigrations. The European Jews in the early *aliyot* (waves of immigration) did not arrive as communities including all elements from the most traditional to the most radicalized. They were in large part an intellectual vanguard, highly Westernized and fairly unrepresentative of the Jewish world. Their Zionism was expressed in the secular language of European liberalism, nationalism, and socialism. As Conor Cruise O'Brien remarks, "it was not in practice possible for Zionists of European origin to teach Zionism to Orientals [Eastern Jews] without also trying to Europeanize them."[3]

As the dominant element among early Zionists, European Jews established their own style as the accepted model for becoming a Zionist or, eventually, an Israeli. Apart from the universalistic elements of this style, many features of it were actually quite specifically Eastern European, though its practitioners often did not realize the extent to which this was true. Consequently a process of "Ashkenazation" became a norm to which Jews of other backgrounds were expected to adjust, abandoning their "primitive" folkways for the more progressive patterns to which they were now exposed. The cultural linkage of most Eastern Jews to Middle East societies was also a factor, since the Arab-Jewish conflict also increased hostility toward Arab culture. The attitude of veteran settlers was expressed in a Western-oriented educational system that ignored the heritage of Middle Eastern Jews and dismissed non-Western cultures.[4]

The starting point for Middle East Jews was quite different. Most came in mass migrations of entire communities in which the more traditional segments were not only fully represented but in some cases overrepresented. In North Africa, much of the educated elite moved to France while the bulk of the community immigrated to Israel. And of course these communities were far more traditional anyway, not having been deeply touched by Westernization or modernization.

The Zionist movement began in Europe and was dominated by Eastern European Jews. But that does not mean that Zionism, in the sense of a love of Zion and the idea of a return to Zion, was less intense among non-European Jews. Sammy Smooha points out that on a per capita basis, Iraqi Jews contributed to Zionism two to three times as much as Polish Jews in money and in immigrants during the Mandatory period.[5] European Jews dominated Zionism because they constituted 90 percent of world Jewry, not because they gave the movement greater proportional support. But while European Zionists formulated their program in the language of liberal democracy and national self-determination, Middle Eastern Jews had a more messianic vision expressed in traditional historical and religious terms. In Daniel Elazar's words, "the former was a Zionism that demanded internal revolution as much as a transformation of the Jewish condition, while the latter was a Zionism of redemption, which sought continuity with a tradition that was not perceived as requiring revolution."[6] There was never any doubt about the strong Jewish identity of Eastern Jews who arrived in Israel, whether as voluntary immigrants or as refugees, and the centrality of Jewishness on both sides made a "Jewish" approach to their differences inevitable.

In some ways Middle Eastern Jews were closer to the host cultures from which they came, and unlike many European Zionists they felt no ideological compunction to repudiate or reject patterns identified with *galut* (Diaspora) life or goyish (Gentile) influences. Their traditional lifestyles were not regarded as a threat to the realization of Jewishness; many of these customs and folkways were long identified with the Middle East, of which Eretz-Yisrael was an integral part, and seemed as authentically Jewish as they were authentically Arabic or Islamic. From this perspective Eastern Jews could not really comprehend the upheaval, and wholesale rejection of *galut* patterns, through which Eastern European Jewry had passed in the late nineteenth century.[7] In the Middle East setting religiosity was simply assumed and woven into the fabric of daily life, while rabbinical leaders retained their customary role as respected elders and leaders of the community. Since religion was not under attack, it remained relaxed and nondefensive, never developing the suspicion of innovation and the fortress mentality that marked the emergence of reactive ultra-Orthodox (*haredi*) Judaism in Europe.[8]

The result was a dichotomization along Western/Eastern lines; differences among various groups on both sides were subordinated to the central feature of European or non-European cultural background. European Jews stereotypically lumped all others together as "Sephardim," whether accurate or not, obscuring specific community differences and legacies. Similarly all Western Jews became "Ashkenazim." The great divide also corresponded to those whose specific cultural traditions were associated with "Israeliness" and those who were expected to adjust to this model. As noted in a number of studies, this was to some extent even internalized by Eastern Jews, leading to self-rejection and denigration of their own traditions.[9]

A number of objective realities reinforced this dichotomization and the inferior status assigned to Eastern Jews. Most Middle Eastern immigrants came into an already existing system, and as newcomers were forced to start at the bottom of the ladder. Most lacked the educational background or skills that would have enabled them to compete successfully in the new setting, even against European immigrants, and certainly not against veteran settlers with their mastery of the language and the system, their established networks, and their accumulated resources. The dispersion of many Middle Eastern Jews to development towns on the periphery deepened their isolation and limited their mobility. At the same time the large influx of Eastern Jews in the 1950s, as Israel tripled its population within a decade, helped bring about mass upward mobility among Western Jews who moved up on the social ladder in a process of "deproletarization." As Smooha notes, "the substantial mobility of *Ashkenazim* was predicated on the channeling of Oriental newcomers to the lower rungs of society."[10]

This link between the Western/Eastern split and socioeconomic status has proved to be persistent over time, in contradiction to the long-dominant "nation-building" paradigm that postulated the "absorption" of all immigrants into a modernizing society. In retrospect this model appears Eurocentric and overly rational, ignoring the forces that work to perpetuate a gap between the two communities.[11] Despite signs of greater cultural similarity, evidence indicates that socioeconomic differences have been passed on from generation to generation. The lower levels of society remain overwhelmingly Eastern, despite the influx of immigrants from the former Soviet Union, while European Jews are overrepresented in the middle and predominate among the elite. While Eastern Jews have advanced in absolute terms, European Jews have in some ways advanced more. There has been a certain homogenization within each major community, with differences between subgroups (Moroccan and Iraqi Jews, or Polish and Romanian Jews) becoming less distinct. Most but not all of this seems explainable by the usual mechanisms that tend to reproduce class differences: disparities in family size, social environment, and access to opportunities, together with lack of effective intervention to overcome these structural impediments.[12]

This persistent gulf is less apparent in income than in other measures. By 1994 the average income of Jews born in Asia and Africa was actually higher, at 112.5 percent, than that of Jews born in Europe or the Americas, against only 65 percent in the 1956–1958 period and 80 percent in the 1978–1980 period.[13] (The 1994 income of European Jews was, of course, somewhat deflated by recent immigrants from post-Soviet states.) But differences in housing density, for example, were still substantial despite the influx of Russian Jews at the bottom; the average density for Israeli Jews born in Asia or Africa was 1.04 persons per room, while the density for those from Europe or the Americas was .88 persons per room.[14] In education, Western Jews on the average had about three more years of schooling than Eastern Jews in the late 1970s and still 2.4 more years in 1988, and this figure was back up to 2.8 years in 1993 after the immigrant influx. In the late 1970s Western Jews were five times as likely as Eastern Jews to have studied at a university, and this figure remained almost as high in 1994.[15]

The continuing disparities between the two communities, correlated with socioeconomic class, became a greater cause of resentment as expectations changed. As living standards improved generally and Eastern Jews themselves became "old-timers," remaining inequalities were more visible and less easily tolerated. This was particularly true of the second generation of Eastern Jews, born in Israel, who were much less patient with handicaps that could no longer be dismissed as the fated destiny of newcomers. Those raised in Israel were more sensitive to the structural disadvantages they faced, in comparison with Jews of European background, especially given the official egalitarian ethos and their potential numerical strength (constituting, by most definitions, over half of the population by the 1980s). This created a level of intercommunal tension, usually submerged but occasionally erupting, that was a serious source of social conflict.[16]

THE IDEOLOGY OF INTEGRATION

Despite the persistence of the communal split, a strong sense of common Jewishness on both sides of the divide outweighed subgroup identities in most contexts. The importance of this shared Jewishness was greatly reinforced by the existence and intensity of the conflict between Israel and the Arab world and the fact that many Eastern Jews were refugees from Arab lands.

Jews of all backgrounds share a common religion (with minor differences between Ashkenazi and Sephardi practices), some common traditions, and by and large the sense of a common history. They also had in common strikingly similar experiences as a minority in a non-Jewish context, whether Christian or Islamic, and most of those who reached Israel, from West or East, shared the refugee experience. Jewishness had been central to their identity in nearly all countries of origin, and certainly no less so in the Middle East, where group identity was central, than elsewhere. All new Jewish Israelis could immediately relate to national symbols and myths, in everything from language to the holiday calendar, as well as a sense of shared fate in a critical struggle with a common enemy.

Contrary to some impressions, Jews outside the European orbit were not less receptive toward Zionism. They understood it, however, in terms of a traditional return to Zion rather than as a reaction to Diaspora existence or as a rejection of the Jewish past. Unlike the pious Ashkenazi Jews in the old *yishuv,* they had no ideological problems with Zionism as such or with participation in Zionist undertakings. As noted, in some cases they contributed more to Zionism on a per capita basis than did their Western counterparts. The role of non-European Jews in early Zionism was to some extent obscured by their smaller numbers in absolute terms, by the nature of their immigration (a slow, steady flow rather than waves of communities), by their joining urban communities rather than the agricultural settlements at the heart of the new *yishuv,* and by their lack of connection to "official" Zionist ideology and leadership.

Despite European attitudes of superiority and contempt toward non-European cultures and immigrants,[17] the universal goal of integration, accepted by all parties, limited the scope of conflict and helped define methods for dealing with it. The ideal of *mizug hagaluyot* (integration of exiles) was universally accepted as a point of reference. Thus Western Jews were ready in principle to co-opt Eastern leaders into the system, and both sides tended to avoid group bargaining that might have suggested the permanence and sanctification of communal divisions. This may be the most decisive factor in the way the system has handled communal divisions: such divisions were regarded as transitional. It was easier to deal with a division that is seen as an artifact of history, and not as a legitimate and substantive split to be perpetuated in the institutions of the nation. Whatever the relative impact that European and Middle East inputs come to have on the final product of integration, striving to realize a common Jewishness is not challenged. Given the centrality of immigration to the raision d'etre of Zionism itself, the failure to achieve social equality in the course of time between Jews from East and West would be perceived by those on both sides as a failure of the entire enterprise.[18]

Consequently, demands of Eastern Jews do not focus on the perpetuation of differences. As Smooha has noted, "My survey of pronouncements by Oriental spokesmen, ethnic publications and programmes of ethnic election lists shows a broad consensus with the established ideologies. The stated target is definitely ethnic integration, and separatism is out of the question. The emphasis is on uniculturalism with minor subcultural pluralism."[19]

This acceptance of integration as the desired goal has been matched by an expectation, perhaps unrealistic, that a fusion of the communities would indeed take place fairly quickly. In a 1967–1968 survey, 86 percent of Eastern Jews and 81 percent of Western Jews felt that significant differences between the two groups would disappear within twenty years.[20]

The "subcultural pluralism" to which Smooha refers has become more of an issue as Easterners strive for better recognition of their particular Jewish cultures, within the framework of a shared "Israeliness." Even in this regard there is no strong ideology behind the preservation of particular cultural legacies from countries of origin (except, perhaps, in the religious sphere). If earlier European settlers brought such legacies with them, it was not done as a matter of belief or even done consciously, but was more a matter of habit and inertia. But growing awareness of such differences has led to de facto acceptance, and even encouragement, of particular traditions in folklore, music, and other areas of popular culture, as part of a broader shift in recognizing the legitimacy of the non-Western Jewish experience.[21] This remains, however, a consensus for pluralism on a relatively superficial level; on a more basic level both sides share a developing core culture that is basically Western in political and legal norms, consumerism, patterns of leisure activity, the role of mass media, and other important features.

Also, while communal differences do often correspond to class differences, there are cross-cutting affiliations that undermine the East/West division. Middle Eastern Jews may be disproportionately religious, but the Israeli-born generation is markedly less so and European Jews run the spectrum on religiosity. Given the greater prominence of religious issues (see chapter 8), such divisions often supersede communal distinctions. Both communities also represent a variety of political views, even if not in the same proportions; few political parties have focused exclusively on one community, and European Jews are again disproportionately represented on the two ends of the spectrum, accounting for most of both the extreme doves and the extreme hawks. On economic and social issues, as well, both Eastern and Western Jews are likely to find themselves divided from many in their own community and allied with some in the other. In the inclusive picture, other cleavages help to break down the boundaries between Jews from differing backgrounds or at least reduce them to secondary importance (the contrast with the Jewish-Arab division is striking).[22]

The centrality of the security threat is perhaps the most important mitigating factor. The Arab-Israeli conflict is a "cross-cutting affiliation" that put all Jewish Israelis, whatever their background, on the same side of a deep chasm. The perception of a threat to existence makes other issues appear inconsequential, if not trivial, in comparison. Not surprisingly, surveys taken during wartime or crisis periods have shown surges in feelings of communal solidarity.[23] Furthermore, the existence of the conflict and of an Arab minority within Israel enabled Middle Eastern Jews to be part of the majority on the really critical issues, and impelled them to demonstrate distance from an enemy with whom they had cultural similarities. In addition, their experience as refugees created by the Arab-Israeli conflict embittered many Middle Eastern Jews and further reinforced their hawkishness on issues related to the conflict. In Smooha's survey, for example, 72 percent of Eastern Jews, but only 48.6 percent of European Jews, fell on the hawkish side of the spectrum as "hard-liners" or "exclusionists," while in a study by the Israel Democracy Institute the mean score on a scale of hostility toward Arabs was 69 percent among Eastern Jews and 46 percent among Western Jews.[24]

The experience of facing a common threat, together with other reassuring developments over the course of time, eroded the fears some European Jews had expressed about the "Levantinization" of Israel. Consequently, overt prejudice and discrimination also diminished over time. Middle Eastern customs that had at first appeared threatening became less so with familiarity, and many accepted the notion that integration might entail synthesis as well as assimilation (for example, festivals associated with particular communities, such as the Moroccan *mimouna,* became a legitimate part of public life). But the bottom line was that such differences were tolerable because, in contrast to similar situations elsewhere and to the Arab-Jewish division, no strong forces in Israel were working to perpetuate the basic distinctions with which they were associated.

Most recent studies, in the words of one review, present "an array of evidence for homogenization and social fusion of European and Afro-Asian Jews."[25] Middle Eastern Jews, by integrating into Israeli life, have acculturated to Western society. Families have become smaller and less patriarchal; fertility rates have decreased; women have entered the job market; "Western" consumer patterns and leisure activities have been adopted; religious observance and traditional customs have declined.[26] Differences remain, of course: residential patterns are still segregated to some degree, religious observance and traditional gender roles are still stronger among Eastern Jews, and families are still somewhat larger.[27] But the "social distance" between the two communities has diminished dramatically. For example, the percentage of high school students with reservations to "intermarriage" between the two communities dropped from 60 percent in 1965 to 21 percent only ten years later; in 1991 only 6 percent of an adult sample opposed marriage of their son or daughter to someone from a different community.[28] Other measures of intercommunal contacts and friendship show similar change. Strikingly, in a 1981 survey 69 percent of Eastern Jews said they were *not* being discriminated against, even though only 50 percent of Western Jews shared this belief.[29] Thus it is not surprising that communal identity is not considered very important to most Israelis; when asked recently to rank nine different components of collective identity, only 2.7 percent ranked their communal identity first, while 75.3 percent said it was not important at all.[30]

Some analysts have even concluded that the category of Eastern Jews is a "phantom," since it is not based on significant observable cultural differences.[31] Not only do the general categories of Western and Eastern Jews lump together different groups, but the rapid assimilation to prevailing Israeli values and lifestyle has, in this view, removed all meaningful differences on the general level. The younger generation of Eastern Jews, in particular, appears to an anthropologist or ethnographer to be indistinguishable from its counterparts of European origin in any respect that would be considered culturally significant.[32] In some ways this is not reassuring, as it may be taken to imply that gaps remaining between the two communities cannot be explained as a product of objective cultural differences but only as the result of discrimination that persists despite the disappearance of any basis for discrimination. It may even be, as the "theory of perceived inequality" would have it, that the decline of real cultural differences sharpens the perception of inequality and the sense of outrage at such discrimination, intensifying frictions rather than relieving them.[33]

What seems most likely, however, is that the linkage between communal identity and class will continue to blur, with socioeconomic status gradually becoming independent of origin or background as these factors become less visible. Already much behavior associated with the Eastern working class seems more working class than Eastern, and there may be an emerging working-class culture cutting across communal lines; increasingly, "Israelis in the same socioeconomic level think and behave in the same way."[34]

The ultimate outcome may be foreshadowed in the increasing rate of intermarriage between Jews of Western and Eastern background. Marriages between persons born in Europe or North America, or whose fathers were born in Europe or North America, and persons born in Asia or Africa, or whose fathers were born in Asia or Africa, have increased steadily over the years and in the 1975–1979 period stood at 20.0 percent of all marriages (a purely random distribution of marriage partners, it should be recalled, would raise this only to about the 50 percent level). By 1986, this percentage had increased to 24.3 percent.[35] Intermarriage in itself does not guarantee the disappearance of distinct communities; Calvin Goldscheider points out that it can even reinforce these identities when out-marriage involves mainly the more loosely affiliated and leaves a core of the more strongly identified.[36] By 1994 fully 61 percent of Israel Jews were actually born in Israel, and even if "origin" is defined as the father's place of birth, fully 24 percent were Israeli by origin, 36 percent were from Asia or Africa, and 40 percent from Europe or the Americas.[37] Given these trends, statistics over communal differences become less reliable and less meaningful as an index of what is happening.

THE POLITICAL RESPONSE

Given the potentially disruptive impact of the communal division, the Israeli political system has avoided the worst. With some delay, Eastern Jews have gradually been integrated into Israeli politics and are no longer grossly underrepresented in the corridors of power. Despite their arrival in an already established system, their lack of prior experience in democratic politics, and weaknesses in organization and leadership, Sephardim have become an integral part of the system and key players within it.

In contrast to the situation on the religious-secular front, this integration was not achieved by classic consociational methods of power-sharing; that is, by social bargaining and diffusion of power among contending elites (the rise of Shas, as a party representing Sephardi interests, is an exception to this statement). Before the rise of Shas there was little bargaining with and accommodation of Middle Eastern Jews as a group. Nevertheless the process of integration did reflect Jewish habits of communal solidarity, inclusion, informality, and compromise. Entrance into politics has usually proceeded on an individual rather than a collective basis, often by a process of co-optation, which was a hallmark of traditional Jewish politics.

Power-sharing between Western and Eastern Jews was institutionalized in only one limited sphere, in election of both Ashkenazi and Sephardi chief rabbis and a Chief Rabbinical Council explicitly composed of equal numbers from each community. Even this dualism is limited, extending to the election of two chief rabbis in the larger towns but not to most other religious offices and bodies. The official recognition of communal division in the religious hierarchy has a certain legitimacy because of long-standing historical differences between the two traditions in some matters of religious practice and because of the prior existence of a Sephardi rabbinate, recognized by the Ottoman government, before Ashkenazim arrived on the scene in large numbers.

Group bargaining might have suggested the permanence and legitimization of communal divisions generally, outside the religious orbit, and both sides hesitated on this score (apart from the fact that Eastern Jews were initially not organized for such bargaining). Instead, when discontent erupted (as with a "Black Panther" movement in the 1970s), the tendency was to look for ways to bring the outsiders into the system. One observer, discussing the response to those group protests that were made, identifies a number of typical measures: the protest is allowed, symbolic reassurances are given, benefits are dispensed, and some of the demands are actually fulfilled. At the same time, group protests were undercut by the upward social mobility and co-optation of their leaders.[38]

These responses are, however, reactive and piecemeal. Political representation lagged far behind reality both demographically and in comparison to progress in reducing the gap in other areas. Even reduction of economic differences proceeded more quickly; in the late 1970s Smooha could still note a "striking imbalance" between the achievement of material progress by Eastern Jews and their lack of success in gaining political power.[39] Their earliest success began in the development towns, where they constituted an overwhelming majority; from the 1960s Middle Eastern Jews began to dominate local council and mayoral elections in these areas, but they remained vastly underrepresented on the national level.

To use Knesset membership as an index, only 6 percent (seven seats out of 120) in the First Knesset (1949) were of non-European origin, and in the Eighth Knesset (1973) this had risen to only 10 percent (twelve seats)—at a time when Eastern Jews outnumbered Western Jews. This number rose to twenty-three with the electoral "upheaval" of 1977, and thereafter increased steadily: thirty in 1981, thirty-two in 1984, thirty-eight in 1988, forty in 1992, and forty-one in 1996.[40] By the late 1980s Eastern representation on the ministerial level had also improved considerably. In the government established after the 1988 elections, nine of the twenty-six cabinet posts were held by Eastern Jews, after the 1992 elections the figure was five of seventeen, and in 1996 it was seven of eighteen. Israel has had a Sephardi president, chief of staff, deputy prime minister, Speaker of the Knesset, and chairman of Histadrut. In the economic sphere, Sephardim have served as minister and director-general in the Ministry of Finance, and as managers of Bank Leumi and Bank Discount. Representation in the top echelons of the civil service, Histadrut, party central committees, and other centers of power, while not yet proportionate to numbers in the population at large, also increased substantially.[41]

In some respects the electoral system made it more difficult to increase representation of Eastern Jews on a national level. The single national list puts the focus on national issues rather than communal concerns, and tight control of party lists (at least in the past) made it difficult for Easterners to make good use of their advantage in numbers. Nor did the Eastern community constitute a well-defined voting bloc that could force the parties into intense competition for their favors. The logical response to this situation might be separate Eastern or Sephardi party lists, a strategy for which the system seems designed and the favored approach of other (especially religious) groups. Yet the efforts to establish such lists enjoyed little success in the past; Sephardi lists gained five seats in 1949 and three in 1951, but thereafter failed to win a single seat in elections over the next three decades. Only in 1981 did Tami, a Sephardi religious party, finally win three seats, and in 1984 Shas—also Sephardi and religious—appeared on the scene, supplanting Tami and winning four seats (and subsequently six seats in 1988 and 1992, and ten seats in 1996). Middle Eastern Jews have generally preferred to vote for mainstream parties, which moved to attract their votes by putting Middle Eastern candidates on their own lists, first in a kind of tokenism but increasingly as serious representation. Cross-cutting affiliations also undercut the separate lists, as Eastern Jews were pulled in different directions on religious, ideological, and socioeconomic issues that outweighed the communal considerations.[42]

Eastern Jews did, however, use the electoral system by another route as a vehicle of protest. The alienation of Middle Eastern Jews from the Labor Party, described in chapter 6, led them not to a separate, Sephardi party but to support of the major alternative—Likud—in disproportionate numbers.[43] This was especially true of the Israeli-born generation in development towns, who in the 1970s and 1980s turned in record numbers to the Likud and helped bring it to power.[44] This voting pattern, though sometimes overstated, remained consistent and cannot be explained on the basis of class, age, education, and other variables alone; clearly there was a communal component to it, based on a common belief that the Likud better represented the interests of Middle Eastern Jews.[45] This could, however, be a result of preference for Likud policies as much as a protest vote. Which factor is more important?

Eastern Jews were more hawkish on Israeli-Arab issues. However, they had no particular affinity for the Revisionist ideology of Likud true believers (at least those of the older generation), nor to other aspects of official Likud doctrine. The most penetrating study of the hawkishness of Middle Eastern Jews concludes that socioeconomic facts alone cannot account for it, nor is it a matter of intellectual predilection, but that it must be seen as an expression of discontent: a response to alienation, a path to integration, a bar against further deprivation, and an escape from ethnic identity. The case of Eastern Jews in Israel indicates, in short, "that sentiments, expectations, and frustrations emanating from ethnic affiliations may serve as important factors in determining foreign policy (in this case, hawkish) attitudes." This is reinforced by the fact that "the object of the hard-line policies is the same people with whom the ethnic groups associated" before acquiring their current status.[46] The predominance of evidence indicates, in short, that communal voting among Middle Eastern Jews in Israel is more a function of domestic issues than foreign policy and that "hawkish" tendencies among this group are not ideologically determined.[47]

Observers tend to describe the political culture of Eastern Jews as non-ideological and practical, rather than doctrinaire or dogmatic. Eastern Jews, it is argued, have not opposed peace with the Arab world as a matter of principle, but have focused on security issues to which they are particularly sensitive because of their background as refugees or children of refugees, usually from Arab lands. If they have tended to favor the Likud, it is "because they see in it, rightly or wrongly, a means for social mobility and status attainment."[48] If they are less willing to contemplate withdrawal from territories occupied in the 1967 war, it is in part because incorporation of the large Arab population there into the Israeli system had the same impact that their own immigration had on European Jews: it gave them massive upward mobility by creating a new underclass of unskilled workers.[49]

The important motivations in Eastern Jewish voting can also be read in the nature of the one party that has established itself successfully on a communal basis. As a religious party Shas appeals to traditional Sephardi religiosity while at the same time avoiding the stigma of separatism that would apply to any nonreligious appeal. By focusing on domestic issues of direct concern to Eastern Jews and taking a pragmatic, centrist, and somewhat vague position on security issues, the party also reflects the agenda of its constituents. The formula has worked very well, enabling a rabbinical leadership of *haredi* leanings to build a faithful constituency among traditional religious Eastern Jews. Thus, while party leaders do not teach Zionist history or observe Zionist holidays, Shas has never labeled itself as a "non-Zionist" party, and most of its voters are enthusiastic supporters of Israel, who serve in the army (unlike many *haredim*) and fulfill all other civil obligations. The party platform rejects the secularism of Israel, but not the state itself. Most critically, it treats foreign and security issues as secondary to its main concerns as an ethnoreligious party.[50]

Shas has not taken a firm position, for example, on the central issue of the future of the occupied territories. Party leaders, reflecting their *haredi* leanings, take the position that withdrawal is permissible if it saves Jewish lives, while party voters tend to be more hawkish, though on anti-Arab rather than ideological grounds. It would therefore be prudent for party leaders to downplay such issues, even if their own priorities did not already dictate this. But they are already focused on other issues, such as funding for their own institutions (including their own school system), that are connected to the renewal and revitalization of the Eastern Jewish community.

The appeal of the Likud to Eastern Jews was noticeably weaker in the 1992 and 1996 elections, with large numbers defecting to parties of both the left and the right. The remaining Likud voters were still predominantly Easterners, but in 1992 the defection of some to Labor helped tilt the overall balance of power.[51] The correlation of voting to communal lines was blurred yet a little more, and the vote for Labor (35 percent from Eastern Jews, 50 percent from Western Jews, 15 percent from those whose fathers were born in Israel) was only a few percentage points from the actual population distribution.[52] In 1996, the separate vote for prime minister and for Knesset led many in the Sephardi community to split their vote, supporting Netanyahu for prime minister but turning to religious parties (especially Shas) in the party vote.

PROSPECTS FOR SYNTHESIS

The communal split in Israel parallels, to a great extent, the clash between the hold of tradition, on one side, and the challenges of both secular ideology and modernization on the other, in Israel's development. It may even represent the kind of synthesis taking place more broadly: while the impact of ideology on the traditionally inclined was limited and is now receding, more general forces of modernity have replaced it as the main vehicle of civicness and secularization. The pioneer generation of Eastern European true believers may have had limited success in inculcating Labor Zionism among non-European Jews, but in the end television, computers, and Western-style consumerism may do much more to weaken customary patterns and lifestyles.

In other words, Western (or "Ashkenazi") culture will continue to dominate in Israel, even after the reassertion of tradition and of pluralism in which Eastern Jews have played a key role. Though its grip may be loosening, the Western, secular model of Zionism is still the officially sanctioned version taught widely and systematically. The impact of modernization is almost synonymous with the penetration of values and models associated with the West. Furthermore, Western Jews established the overall framework that remains the basic point of reference, and they continue to dominate it in all important respects even as the division between the communities begins to blur. Almost all future influence, support, and immigration from the Diaspora will reinforce this Western orientation, since most Eastern Jews are already in Israel and the Jewish world outside Israel is today concentrated almost entirely in Europe, the Americas, and Commonwealth nations. Even within Israel itself the majority status of Eastern Jews has been reversed by the massive immigration of Russian Jews, and this influx has also undercut the upward mobility of Eastern Jews by sharpening competition for mid-level and professional positions.

The question is whether the underlying trends toward accommodation and assimilation will proceed quickly enough to prevent a buildup, and possible eruption, of discontent based on perceived communal differences. As the categories of "Western" and "Eastern" (or Ashkenazi and Sephardi) themselves become increasingly irrelevant with more Israelis possessing a mixed heritage, discontent will be defined differently. Inequalities and disparities will be expressed more in class or socioeconomic, rather than communal, terms. Or communal differences may meld into the distinction between modernizing "Israelis," likely to be disproportionately of European background, and more traditional "Jews," who would include most Middle Easterners (see chapter 6).

This distinction would, however, have to be seen in the context of the strong sense of commonness among Jews in Israel that is apparent in any examination of communal relations. An important index of this has been the use of power-sharing methods common to Jewish experience—inclusion, co-optation, informal bargaining and compromise, toleration of diversity, and appeal to common ties—without needing to resort to more formal consociational procedures (formal group bargaining, guaranteed representation, mutual veto) often used in more serious societal splits. It is also likely that moderation of the Arab-Israel conflict will serve to reduce communal tensions yet further, as Israel reorients itself to an Arab world and culture no longer seen as innately hostile and threatening, improving the status of Eastern Jews and giving them a key role as bridge between the two cultures.

At bottom, the communal split is not a major threat to Israel because both communities regard it as an artificial division that is transitory or at least ought to be transitory. There is no loud call for the preservation of basic cultural differences and no significant opposition in principle to integration of the various dispersions into a common society and culture. The importance of this can be seen by comparison to a sphere in which different world-views are perpetuated from generation to generation as a matter of deeply held conviction. In dealing with religious divisions, in particular, the power-sharing capacity of the system has been stretched to the limit despite the same reality of common Jewishness that tempers communal grievances.

EIGHT

Religion and Politics

It is rare to find a hopeful view of relations between the religious and secular communities in Israel. Both academic and nonacademic analyses paint a dismal portrait of sharpened conflict, unyielding dogmatism, and impending catastrophe. One observer notes that "far more than the Sephardi/Ashkenazi split, the conflict between the varying demands of religious observance is the most potentially disruptive threat to the unity of Jewish Israel."[1] An academic analyst concludes that the demands of religious parties may be as serious as the Arab threat: "Indeed, the latter groups may be more willing to compromise their demands than the religious parties have ever shown a willingness to do."[2] An Israeli long active in opposing religious demands states that "we are now witnessing the Judgment Day of the State's domestic affairs."[3]

Opinion surveys seem to indicate that most Israelis may feel the same way. In March 1988—soon after the onset of the Palestinian *intifada* against Israeli occupation—58 percent of a sample of Jews in Jerusalem considered religious-secular relations to be the most critical problem in the city, while only 23 percent identified Jewish-Arab relations as the most critical.[4] In 1991 a national sample showed that 71 percent of the Jewish population thought that religious-secular relations were "not so good" or "not good at all."[5]

In some ways religious differences do seem less amenable to resolution than other cleavages in Israeli society. The split between Jews of European and those of African and Asian background, though serious and persistent, is regarded by both sides as a temporary phenomenon, the result of historic accident, that will eventually be erased or at least blurred in the forging of a common Israeli identity. The sharp differences between Israelis and Arabs can at least in theory be settled through compromise on the basis of mutual recognition. But religious differences seem less susceptible to such compromise; they are deeply rooted in opposed ways of life that often deny the legitimacy of coexistence and seek to undermine the enemy. Nor are these divisions a transitional phase; different degrees and definitions of religious observance and competing religious authorities have characterized Jewish life over the centuries.

The social distance between the religious (meaning Orthodox in the Israeli context) and nonreligious publics, reinforced by residential concentration and educational segregation, has been amply documented. One study of eleventh-graders in 1973 found, for example, that 65 percent of nonreligious respondents were unwilling to have a religious friend, and 81 percent did not want a religious neighbor; among religious respondents 68 percent rejected a nonreligious friend and 65 percent a nonreligious neighbor.[6] Such attitudes reflect not only the inconvenience of conflicting lifestyles in situations of close social proximity but also the fear that one's own lifestyle might be threatened by changes in the neighborhood (a problem raised, for example, by the expansion of religious neighborhoods in Jerusalem). From the religious side, it seems normal to maintain sharp boundaries protecting the integrity of religious life, since "separation and distinction are characteristic of the halakhic legal system that lies at the heart of the Jewish world view."[7]

Religious-secular relations are of special significance for the political system because of the historic blurring of civil and religious matters in Jewish life and the lack even today of strong support for the principle of separation of religion and state. In Jewish tradition, "religious" and "secular" matters overlapped; in fact, the very distinction would have made little sense to premodern generations. The weight of tradition was reinforced, in the Zionist and Israeli experiences, by the practical necessity of compromise on religious demands in order to preserve unity. Ultimately, this developed into ingrained habits of coexistence according to formulas that fit neither side's worldview squarely but also impinged on neither's basic way of life unduly.[8]

Of course this invites constant struggle and uneasy compromise over the role of religion in politics. But that is hardly novel in Jewish history; in fact, the traditional patterns of accommodation help to explain how the Israeli system has coped with religious cleavages and why these cleavages have not torn the system asunder. Religious politics in Israel, as much as any part of the system, reflect the bargaining pattern in Jewish political tradition. This tradition has enabled Israel to deal with religious division more successfully than most observers would credit, and certainly more successfully than those actively engaged in the conflict would concede.

The resemblance of religious-secular politics in Israel to the consociational pattern has been noted by several observers. Sammy Smooha points to the maintenance of separate institutions, the organization of religious Jews to procure a share of the resources and benefits of government, the ability of religious parties to cast a veto on religious issues, and the general pattern of accommodation and negotiation rather than confrontation and decisive outcomes.[9] Eliezer Don-Yehiya concludes that the consociational democracy model helps to explain, to a large extent, how "the Israeli political system has managed to resolve religious conflicts by peaceful means, while preserving its stability and democratic character."[10]

In order to appreciate these arrangements, we should first look at the relationship of religion to politics in Israel and compare it to other states. Clearly Israel is not among the states committed to the maximum separation between religion and state (recognizing that even these states—for example, the United States—have never achieved total governmental neutrality toward religion). But neither is the modern Jewish state a theocracy, governed by religious clerics or religious laws. Rather, Israel ranks somewhere in the middle of the spectrum, together with European states that have "established," state-supported religions but strong respect, at the same time, for religious freedom. Actually Israel does not even have a single state religion, as legally Judaism is but one of fourteen established and state-supported religions (together with Islam, Baha'i, the Druze faith, and ten Christian denominations).[11]

Thus, despite the absence of formal constitutional guarantees, the protection of minority religions is not the major issue; Israeli practice in this regard may even be superior to that of the United States, despite the latter's written constitution.[12] The main controversy involves the application of Jewish religious law to the Jewish public. Secular Israelis characterize existing arrangements (such as the rabbinical monopoly over Jewish marriage and divorce) as a form of religious coercion. Non-Orthodox Jewish movements complain that only in Israel, among all democratic states, are they subject to legal discrimination. On the other hand, Orthodox advocates argue that without protection by the state (for example, guarantee of the right not to work on Sabbath), those faithful to religious precepts are effectively denied equal rights and full integration into the nation's social and cultural life.[13]

This debate is complicated by the lack of clarity in Jewish law on its relationship to the state and by preexisting patterns of religious governance in the Middle East that carried over into Zionism and the State of Israel. Furthermore, both major groups within the religious population refused in principle to recognize the supremacy of state law over religious commandments: religious Zionists did so because their Zionism was linked to the state's religious mission, while non-Zionist Orthodoxy disputed the state's legitimacy from the outset.[14]

TENSION BETWEEN ZIONISM AND RELIGION

Observers unfamiliar with Zionism's inner history are sometimes astonished to learn that the movement was not an expression of religious impulses and that it actually developed in an atmosphere of mutual hostility between Zionists and religious authorities.

This antagonism was part of the larger struggle between those seeking to make Jewish communities part of modern secular European society and those clinging tenaciously to Jewish separatism and particularity. As noted in chapters 2 and 3, the Enlightenment and its Jewish echo (the Haskala) had seriously undermined the autonomy of the traditional Jewish community and the role of religious law in Jewish life. In reaction, much of the rabbinical establishment in Eastern Europe turned inward, rejecting the lures of the outside world and focusing religious law (halacha) increasingly and inflexibly on matters of ritual observance.[15]

In this context, Zionism was simply another threat to Jewish integrity from an alien and menacing universe. Religious leaders regarded it, with considerable justice, as a continuation of the secularizing Haskala movement; it was no accident that most early Zionist leaders were *maskilim* by background. Zionism was part and parcel of the Western secular nationalist tradition. It was a movement for Jewish national self-determination in the same mode as other nationalist movements of the nineteenth century. Furthermore, like other nationalist movements of the period, Zionism was anticlerical, opposed to basing public life on religious principle. Just as the nationalists of Europe sought to liberate themselves from all traditionalism, including clerical control of politics, Zionism sought new political paths free of religious restraints.

Consequently, the established religious leadership opposed Zionism with near unanimity, in defense of both their prerogatives and their principles. Naturally they saw it as a threat to their own position within the Jewish community, where their authority had long been accepted on matters both sacred and mundane. They also opposed it on theological grounds because Zionism aspired to create a Jewish state outside the religious framework, as a result of the endeavors of humankind rather than the intervention of God. They opposed such undertakings as the rebirth of Hebrew as a spoken language, preferring that it remain a sacred liturgical tongue. Traditional religious authorities were the most vocal opponents of Zionism within the Jewish community. While a religious version of Zionism did develop in the early twentieth century, it remained a minority both among Zionists and—until much later in the century—among Orthodox Jews as well.

Secularization of public life, it should be recalled, is a Western invention that does not appear even in Western history before the last few centuries, and it has probably been totally achieved only in a handful of avowedly "materialist" regimes (most of which no longer exist). Historically Judaism viewed itself as a way of life and not simply as a religion (originally there was no word for "religion" in Hebrew). Like Islam, it centered on a code of law that encompassed what we would now consider civil or political matters (consider the Ten Commandments). The traditions of Judaism provide little basis for the modern idea of separating religion and politics.

The same can be said about Middle East custom and practice, embodied particularly in Islam. Islam affirms religion (or what the West calls "religion") as the organizing principle of state and society. In the Ottoman Empire this link between religion and politics was expressed in the *millet* system, under which each religious community governed itself in certain respects. Even before the British Mandate in Palestine, the rabbinical establishment in the area exercised certain governing powers within the Jewish community (the so-called "old *yishuv*"), particularly in matters of personal status such as marriage and divorce.

The old *yishuv* was divided between a Sephardi community, led by a chief rabbi, and an Ashkenazi community, with its own rabbinical courts, that was supported by outside contributions (*haluka*) and led a largely isolated existence centered around acts of piety. Though both groups opposed Zionism, the Ashkenazim in the old *yishuv* were particularly antagonistic to this latest and most insidious challenge to their besieged way of life. It was this group that set the basic patterns for the non-Zionist and anti-Zionist *haredi* communities in Palestine and Israel.[16]

In some respects, the division between non- or anti-Zionist *haredim* and Zionist Jews, religious or nonreligious, was more fundamental than the more common distinction between religious Jews (whether *haredi* or Zionist) and nonreligious Jews. Apart from a much smaller number on the far left, the *haredim* were the only Jewish group in Israel outside the "Zionist consensus"; religious Zionists often had more in common with nonreligious Zionists than they did with religious Jews outside the Zionist fold. Despite their shared religiosity, the worldview of those who work fervently for the Jewish state—even one with secular leaders—differs in essence from the worldview of those who view that same state as an alien and illegitimate entity. In contrast to the *haredim,* religious Zionists stress the national as well as the religious aspect of Judaism, reject separatism as a way of life, and seek in many ways to become part of modern society.

Had members of the old *yishuv* been the leading element in the expansion of the Jewish settlement in late nineteenth-century Palestine, the governing principles of the new settlement would have been quite different. In fact, the settlers of Petah Tikva, the first settlement outside the old *yishuv* (1880), drew up regulations making their rabbi sole judicial authority within the settlement, with powers to enforce all religious laws (many of the settlers were from the old *yishuv*).[17] But the Zionist settlers of the "new *yishuv*" did not adopt this model (nor, eventually, did Petah Tikva itself); they made use of experience with self-government in Eastern Europe and elsewhere to create autonomous, but basically secularized, villages and communes. When the new settlers finally convened a body to represent Palestinian Jewry—the Knesiya of 1903—they excluded from the electorate all those who subsisted on *haluka,* meaning most of those in the old *yishuv*, though they still constituted the bulk of the Jewish population.[18] Jews in the homeland were now sharply divided into two communities, neither of which respected the values or way of life of the other.

The division between old *yishuv* and new *yishuv* corresponds roughly to the division between *haredi* and Zionist, which has reemerged in recent years as a source of increasing trouble for Israeli politics. It is important to understand the depth of this divide. The leading analyst of *haredi* society, Menachem Friedman, describes its worldview as "a comprehensive historiographic conception which perceived of the central historical processes of the modern era—from the inception of modernization and secularization (i.e., the Haskala or Enlightenment), through the development of the Zionist Movement up to the establishment of the State of Israel—as a totality of a cause and effect expressing the great 'rebellion' against the unique essence of religious Judaism. . . ."[19]

Haredim are "fundamentalist" according to the definition developed by Martin E. Marty and R. Scott Appleby: "a tendency . . . which manifests itself as a strategy, or set of strategies, by which beleaguered believers attempt to preserve their distinctive identity as a people or group." This involves the selective retrieval of "fundamentals" from a sacred past and their use as a bulwark against the dislocations of modernization. It is not a simple return to the past, but an innovative recreation of a political and social order characterized by authoritarian leadership, strong discipline, a rigorous moral code, clear boundaries, and an identified enemy.[20] All of these elements appear in *haredi* society, whose roots go back over two centuries to Jewish resistance to the Enlightenment and the prospect of integration into European culture.

As noted, most Jewish religious authorities initially saw Zionism as part and parcel of this threat. While religious Zionists came to terms with a largely secular process by ascribing messianic significance to the Jewish state as "the Beginning of Redemption," anti-Zionists turned this on its head by labeling Zionism a "false Redemption" and promoting a messianism based on its rejection. The return of Jews to the Land of Israel may be a part of the process, but genuine redemption cannot take place in a secular framework. Some even believed that "the great sin which has prevented the coming of the Messiah is none other than Zionism!"[21] Cooperation and accommodation with the Zionist state was regarded by many anti-Zionists as a practical or tactical necessity but did not necessarily indicate recognition of its legitimacy.

ROOTS OF RELIGIOUS-SECULAR ACCOMMODATION

Despite the obvious problems, the Zionist movement from its earliest days made efforts to reach religious Jews, either by enlisting them as Zionists or (in the case of anti-Zionists) by drawing them into practical cooperation in the rebuilding of the homeland. Though religious delegates to the First Zionist Congress, in 1897, were a small minority, Theodor Herzl made an important gesture in their direction by attending services (for the first time in years) at a Basel synagogue on the Sabbath before the Congress opened.[22] The Zionist movement, which lacked even the slight aura of governmental authority enjoyed by Jewish community leaders, could attract religious Jews only by offering them a sense of participation and a proportional share of influence and benefits. By the early years of the century religious Zionists, or "national-religious" Jews, had organized as the Mizrahi movement and were participating in power-sharing arrangements within the World Zionist Organization. During this period there were acrimonious battles over efforts to establish a secular program of cultural education not controlled, as Jewish education had been historically, by religious authorities. The compromise eventually reached was to establish a dual set of cultural institutions, one Orthodox and one nonreligious. The same patterns carried over into the Mandatory period as Zionist institutions came to dominate there in the post-World War I period. Beginning in the 1930s, the secular leadership of the new *yishuv* made explicit arrangements with religious Zionist parties on the proportionate division of jobs and other benefits, beginning a forty-year period of partnership between Labor Zionists and religious Zionists.

Following World War I efforts were also made to bring Agudat Yisrael, the party representing what had been the old *yishuv*, within the purview of the new communal institutions. Zionist officials extended some funding to traditional religious schools (yeshivot) and offered additional assistance if the yeshivot would teach Hebrew as a language (the offer was refused). By late 1918 it became necessary to convene representatives of the entire *yishuv*, old and new, in order to select Palestinian Jewish delegates to the Paris peace talks and to prepare for the election of a constituent assembly. The gathering convened in Jaffa in December of that year with the participation of the non-Zionist old *yishuv*, who by that time constituted a minority within the Jewish population. Participation of the old *yishuv* in election of the assembly remained problematic, however, because of their objection to giving women the rights to vote and to be elected.

When elections for the Assembly of Delegates were finally held in April 1920, non-Zionists in Jerusalem held their own polls from which women were excluded. Nevertheless, the elected non-Zionist delegates were admitted to the Assembly, where they constituted 16 percent of the membership (religious Zionists, still a tiny part of the movement, received only 4 percent of the seats in a strictly proportional system, with the remaining 80 percent divided among non-religious Zionist parties). However, Agudat Yisrael and other groups in the non-Zionist religious community boycotted subsequent elections, and many in that community withdrew their names entirely from the registered Jewish electorate.

The continuation of the Turkish *millet* system, under which religious communities operated their own court systems, made the continuing separatism of non-Zionist religious Jews easier. The terms of the Mandate actually enjoined Great Britain to retain this arrangement, in order to avoid controversy. In the Jewish case, the office of Sephardi chief rabbi had been established in pre-Zionist days and continued to serve all Sephardi Jews, whatever their position on Zionism. The office of Ashkenazi chief rabbi was only created, however, in the early days of the Mandate, and fell at once under the control of religious Zionists. Consequently the non-Zionist Ashkenazi ultra-Orthodox, having previously rejected the authority of the Sephardi chief rabbi, also refused to recognize the new Ashkenazi chief rabbi and continued to maintain their own independent court systems as established under the Ottomans. This basic structure of religious life—unitary among Sephardim, divided along Zionist/*haredi* lines on the Ashkenazi side—persisted until the rise of Shas(see below).

Throughout the 1920s Chaim Weizmann, as head of the World Zionist Organization, sought to bring Agudat Yisrael into the Assembly of Delegates and the National Council that it elected, exploiting the fact that these bodies controlled the allocation of official funds within the Jewish community. In the first stage this led to a compromise providing for funding of institutions of the old *yishuv* but no active cooperation; finally, in 1934, an agreement of formal cooperation between Agudat Yisrael and the World Zionist Organization was reached.

The pressures of the Nazi era brought Zionists and non-Zionists into closer cooperation. All factions recognized the importance of Mandatory Palestine as one of the few havens to which European Jews might flee. After the Holocaust, most non-Zionists also came to accept the practical necessity of an independent Jewish state, even if that state (initially) was not religiously correct. Before supporting Zionist goals even on this conditional basis, however, Agudat Yisrael and other *haredi* groups sought assurance that this "Jewish" state would not publicly desecrate religious law.

David Ben-Gurion provided such assurance in a June 19, 1947, letter to the leadership of Agudat Yisrael; this letter became the basis of complex bargaining in which a status quo acceptable to both sides was defined.[23] This status quo, serving as a point of reference for future bargaining, included recognizing the Jewish Sabbath as a day of rest, maintaining *kashrut* (Jewish dietary laws) in governmental institutions, state funding of religious public schools, and leaving jurisdiction over marriage and divorce in the hands of religious authorities. On other matters the status quo meant recognition of anomalous situations that had developed; for example, banning public transportation on the Sabbath in the country as a whole but allowing it to continue in localities where it already existed.

On the basis of this understanding, Agudat Yisrael joined the provisional government of Israel in 1948, even receiving one of thirteen cabinet seats (the Ministry of Welfare). Mizrahi, representing religious Zionists, was allotted two ministries; by this time the relative strength of Zionist and non-Zionist Orthodoxy had been reversed. Furthermore, the two factions of the religious camp managed to form a joint list for elections to the first Israeli Knesset in 1949, and Agudat Yisrael continued to serve in the Israeli government until 1952.

For all this, however, Agudat Yisrael still recognized Israel only on a de facto basis, and other elements in the *haredi* community did not even go this far. None of them accepted Israel as a legitimate state and government according to Jewish law; the difference lay in the willingness to make practical, temporary accommodations—and thereby receive state funding—while working to transform the secular order into a truly Jewish state based solely on the laws of the Torah as authoritatively interpreted by their own rabbinical establishment. While accepting the validity of Knesset legislation as "temporary" laws, therefore, Agudat Yisrael opposed the drafting of a man-made constitution for Israel (as did, for that matter, the religious Zionists). Unlike the religious Zionists, however, *haredi* authorities also opposed the celebration of Israeli Independence Day (including the recitation of Psalms—*Hallel*—on that occasion), use of the Israeli flag or other national symbols, or service (at least by their own youth) in the Israeli army.[24] By the time of the 1951 elections to the Second Knesset, the fault line between Zionist and non-Zionist religious camps had reasserted itself; the joint list fell apart and has never been restored. A year later Agudat Yisrael left the government over the issue of military conscription of women (even though the religious population was to be exempted), and since then has never again accepted a ministerial post, even when supporting a government in the Knesset. The difference between religious Zionists and *haredim* is thus basic to Israeli politics, though both are a part—in differing degrees—of the broader religious-secular accommodation on religious issues.

ELEMENTS OF THE ACCOMMODATION

There are three major elements in the accommodation that have characterized Israeli secular-religious relations, as identified by Eliezer Don-Yehiya. The principle of proportionality, as implemented through "party key" arrangements, is of primary importance. The party key extends the idea of proportional representation beyond the electoral system and applies it to the division of offices, patronage, public financial support, access to state lands, and so on—in fact to all the "goods" that the political system has at its disposal. In this regard both Zionist and non-Zionist religious parties, as well-organized groups representing distinct subcultures with their own networks of institutions, have been very successful in getting benefits from the political system.[25]

The religious minority in Israel, more than the Sephardi community or even the Arab minority, has chosen the path of separate party lists to secure its interests. Occasionally there has been debate on this score, within religious circles, from those who argue that making the secular parties compete for an uncommitted religious vote would be more effective in gaining concessions.[26] It is argued that a comparison of the army to the educational system demonstrates the advantages of integration over separatism: in the integrated army kosher food is served to everyone, while in the divided educational system, the secular schools typically take no account at all of religious sensitivities (for instance, scheduling social events on the Sabbath). But the political system seems designed to reward the separatist strategy, and most religious political activists feel (with some justice) that the strategy of forming religious blocs able to play off the major parties against each other has proven itself over the years.

The second major element of accommodation is the autonomy of religious institutions and culture, which protects the religious subculture from the threat of assimilation by secular society.[27] This is especially marked in education but extends through a network of institutions designed to preserve the integrity and vitality of religious life within the national-religious community. There is even greater separation of the *haredi* community, which has its own courts, welfare institutions, religious authorities, and independent schools. This autonomy is not only an expression of Jewish traditions and customs, of course, but is also in some ways a continuation of the *millet* system of the Ottoman Empire. The existence of these networks gives most parties an additional stake in the status quo, since most of these institutions are state-supported despite their autonomy (even the "independent" schools in the *haredi* community receive government funding).

From the secular side, autonomy means that religious authorities make little effort in practice to impose their rulings on the secular majority, even when they are committed in principle to doing so. Despite considerable grumbling about secular patterns of entertainment on the Sabbath, for example, there is a de facto tolerance of secular diversions so long as they do not intrude directly on religious neighborhoods (and sometimes even when they do). To some extent, this element of accommodation is achieved by the unwritten practice of not enforcing statutes and regulations on the books. If the government were to enforce to the letter all legal provisions that have been enacted at one time or another as part of bargains with religious parties, the secular public would react strongly. Instead, those laws most likely to cause a backlash are simply ignored: a supposed ban on pork is not enforced, restaurants and places of entertainment defy local bylaws, and work permits for "essential public services" on the Sabbath are issued with a free hand (making possible radio and television broadcasts, for example). This arrangement may damage public respect for the rule of law, but it is also part of the modus vivendi by which secular and religious publics coexist.[28]

The third element in the basic secular-religious compromise is mutual veto: the recognition by each side that it cannot push the other past a certain point without threatening Jewish unity—which all regard as a supreme value—as well as endangering its own interests. Religious spokesman deny any intention of trying to use state power to regulate citizens' private lives, while even ardent secularists agree that Israeli state and society should in some way reflect its Jewish roots. In this acceptance of informal limits, the status quo serves an almost sacred role as a "constitution" or "social contract" that forbids basic challenges to the existing order.[29] It serves as a basic point of reference that both sides respect in its essential features, though this does not rule out efforts to nudge current arrangements slightly in one direction or the other (particularly with new issues not covered clearly in the original understanding).

The veto power of the religious minority does not, contrary to conventional wisdom, rest primarily on its ability to deny a majority to government coalitions. Religious parties (and especially the National Religious Party, the successor to Mizrahi) participated in nearly every government since 1948, but in most cases their participation was not actually necessary for a majority. It is rather the fear of a broad-ranging *Kulturkampf* that has reinforced the respect for boundaries: "The religious minority's veto powers in religious matters are not due to coalition politics but rather to their institutional capability to resort to mass dissent and disruption if necessary."[30]

Fear of a strong backlash likewise deters religious leaders from pushing measures that would impinge significantly on the secular public. Being in a minority, religious parties have limited prospects of forcing their will on a recalcitrant majority. In addition they must consider that aggressive demands will undermine efforts to attract votes from the marginally religious or traditional, forfeit concrete gains they could make by cooperating, and create internal conflict when national unity is essential. Therefore religious parties, even the *haredim*, typically make modest demands and tend to focus on narrow interests (funds and patronage) rather than broader issues of principle.[31]

The limits to what religious parties can reasonably expect was clearly indicated in the aftermath of the 1988 elections, when *haredi* parties more than doubled their representation in the Knesset. Trying to make use of their increased leverage, these parties put on the table a new set of demands on Sabbath observance and other religious issues as a condition for helping to form a government. When these demands brought about a backlash in public opinion, Prime-Minister-designate Yitzhak Shamir backed away from a coalition based on their support and returned to a National Unity Government in which religious bargaining power was considerably reduced. And when the National Unity Government finally collapsed in early 1990 and Shamir turned once more to the formation of a narrow, right-religious, government, the *haredi* and religious parties did not renew their more far-reaching demands.

The reality of these arrangements, then, is that implied or open threats to disrupt the tenor of public life and charges that the other side is encroaching upon or endangering the status quo are built into the bargaining process on secular-religious issues. The constant jockeying for position over the status quo generates heated and noisy debate, and even violence, all of which creates the impression that the existing order may be torn apart at any moment. Both sides express dissatisfaction with the status quo, though neither is in a position to challenge it seriously, and the expressed fear of both is that the other side will challenge it. Nor within the status quo is there expressed any coherent and logical position on the issues in contention, since it simply registers the point beyond which neither side can push the other, given their relative strength (why, for example, should there be public transportation on the Sabbath in Haifa but not in Tel Aviv?) In such a situation, it may be that the mutual and roughly comparable dissatisfaction on both sides is in fact an index of the success of existing arrangements in balancing opposed worldviews.

Other moderating influences also operate on secular-religious relations. For national-religious Jews, at least, there are cross-cutting affiliations, as they are integrated fairly well into the economy, governmental service, the army, and the media (this is, of course, offset by separatism in education, culture, political parties, and to some extent residential patterns). The politicization of religious issues is itself a moderating factor since it means that these issues are threshed out in bargaining between party leaders rather than being worked out directly on the popular level. Also, the very existence of a vociferous debate on religious issues indicates an underlying sense of commonness and shared destiny: neither side is prepared to write off the other.

THE QUESTION OF RELATIVE POWER

The success of religious parties in the consociational politics of Israel has, however, given rise to a widespread perception among secular Israelis that these groups enjoy more-than-proportional power over Israel politics and society and that the role of religion in public life is expanding. Although religious parties have never won more than 19 percent of the Knesset seats, they have won concessions in nearly every coalition agreement since the state was established. The power of the rabbinate in matters of personal status, marriage, and divorce impinges on every Israeli, no matter how secular. In everyday life, the expansion of religious neighborhoods and greater assertiveness in religious demands both reinforce the perception of a rising tide of religiosity. One 1986 poll found that 66 percent of Israelis felt that *haredi*-religious influence was increasing, and 67 percent characterized the *haredim* as "unacceptable," against only 48 percent who put Israeli Arabs in that category.[32] The visible expansion of *haredi* presence and influence fed fears among the secular population, since the *haredim* represent a much

more basic challenge to prevailing lifestyles than do modern religious Zionists. Thus the "haredization" of religious life in Israel, as seen in the victory
of *haredi*-favored candidates for both chief rabbi posts in 1993, appears omi-
nous both to the defeated religious Zionists and to the nonreligious public.

In a 1987 poll, 83 percent of those polled said they had little or no confidence in religious parties and the rabbinate—a level of respect below that
toward nearly any other public institution.[33] Clearly the low respect for religious figures is partly a function of their involvement in politics. The aura of
spiritual leadership is quickly dissipated by the posturing, electioneering,
and bargaining inherent to the political process. Even the elections of the
chief rabbis themselves have been politicized, presenting an unedifying spectacle of manipulation and protection of special interests.[34] This led some
members of the religious community—Yeshayahu Leibowitz being the most
prominent—to attack organized religion as "a kept woman of the secular
power" and to call for a separation of religion and politics that would remove the former from the corrupting influence of the pursuit of power.[35]

The discontent about the role of religion in Israeli life is real, but it
needs to be seen in perspective. The status quo represents no one's preferred solution but is simply a compromise that most Israelis accept for
want of a better option. Clearly the long-term goals of secularists and Orthodox are incompatible, but in the meantime the level of mutual dissatisfaction is in reasonable balance. Despite dissatisfaction, there is little actual
challenge to the basic elements of the status quo or to the general division
of territory between the secular and religious spheres of life. The only religious arrangement that impinges in a major way on the "freedom of conscience" of a secular Israeli is the monopoly of marriage and divorce matters
in the hands of an Orthodox rabbinate; most other pieces of "religious legislation" are either matters of minor inconvenience, or are unenforced, or
in practice affect only religious Jews. Furthermore, there is widespread support, or at least tolerance, among secular Israelis for many of the symbolic
expressions of religion in public life (as will be seen below).

A close look at the specific issues on the religious-secular front shows that
few, if any, of them involved real challenges to the status quo. They are either
minor issues where the existing guidelines are murky or efforts to move the
line very slightly to one side or the other; they represent border skirmishes
rather than full-scale warfare. Typical examples include controversy over
bathing suit ads in bus shelters, questions about organ transplants in Jewish
law, proposals to include women on local religious councils, decisions on
whether newly built facilities should be open on the Sabbath, charges of ar-
cheological digs desecrating ancient Jewish cemeteries, and controversy over
the right of physicians to conduct autopsies without consent of the family.
None of these questions are earthshaking; the only issue with broad significance for religious-secular relations is the "Who is a Jew?" issue: this is the

question of recognizing non-Orthodox converts as Jews in immigration policy and legal status. This issue is critical to non-Orthodox religious groups in Israel and elsewhere and acquired wide practical significance with the high number of mixed marriages among immigrants from the former Soviet Union.

On these "border skirmishes" the religious camp was, contrary to secular Israeli belief, seldom victorious. Battles against radio and TV broadcasting on Sabbath and against public swimming pools with mixed bathing were lost long ago. In the area of Sabbath closings, the overwhelming trend has been toward the opening of more restaurants, theaters, and other places of entertainment; even in Jerusalem, dozens of establishments opened on Friday night and Saturday. The *haredi* community in Jerusalem lost battles to close a road and a swimming pool in Ramot on the Sabbath and to prevent the building of a new soccer stadium in Manahat.[36] From the religious side, in fact, there have been numerous complaints of "regressions from the status quo" over the years, on matters ranging from the increased number of Sabbath work permits issued by the minister of labor, to the inclusion of women on religious councils, to the continuing failure to resolve the "Who is a Jew?" issue according to Orthodox criteria.[37] Those few victories that religious forces could claim, in such matters as separate education and exemption from conscription for yeshiva students, came for the most part from Israel's first few years.

Even the violence of extremists is usually seen by them as defense of the status quo. Only a small fraction of *haredim* engage in violence, and most of this is in-group, aimed at enforcing community norms on the occasional dissident or deviant. When violence is directed externally, it is also usually at targets seen as threats to the *haredi* lifestyle: Christian missions, intrusions of what the *haredi* categorize as pornography, and the like. In this case the militancy may even be a function of the "siege mentality and sense of fighting a perennial uphill battle"; the *haredim* are surrounded by what they regard as a hostile and secular culture that is stronger politically, economically, and in many other respects.[38]

Rather strikingly, therefore, there is not even agreement on which side is gaining. Both secular and religious Israelis tend to perceive themselves as losing ground to the other side. Both sides claim defeat. This mutual dread of impending loss undoubtedly helps to account for some of the bitterness and desperation in public rhetoric. For example, in the 1986 poll cited, those opposed to an expansion of *haredi*-religious influence (59 percent of the total) thought by a 6 to 1 margin that such expansion was nevertheless taking place, while those who welcomed such expanded influence (25 percent) believed by a 3 to 2 margin that it was not taking place.[39] It is difficult to understand such a gap in basic perceptions, except on the basis of deeply rooted habits of pessimism on all sides. But whose pessimism is more factually correct?

THE REALITY OF SECULARIZATION

Modernization has in most societies been associated with secularization and decline of traditional religious practices. If Israel were indeed undergoing a growth of religiosity, it would be exceptional among modernizing states. But there is considerable evidence that Israel is not exceptional. Changes in leisure and recreation patterns have clearly undercut traditional religious practices, and the growth of Sabbath entertainment reflects this.[40] Challenges to strict observance abound in every sphere of modern life: in the sexuality and escapism of mass culture, in cosmopolitan cuisines that challenge dietary laws, in social and recreational activities that involve travel on the Sabbath, and in the penetration of Western cultural models and values.

There is a basic difference between this kind of secularization and the classical secularism of Labor Zionism. The classical secularism (characterized by Charles Liebman as "nationalist-secularism") was an ideology: "a program of living and not simply an absence of religious observance." Religious forms and authority were rejected as a matter of principle, but a strong Jewish consciousness and sense of identity remained.[41] Though secularism as ideology still exists, particularly in kibbutzim and other socialist strongholds, it has clearly declined along with Labor Zionist ideology generally. The more recent wave of secularism is "universalist-secularism," which is more of a lifestyle than an ideology and which involves the dilution of Judaism in everyday life as Israel integrates more fully into modern Western society. This secularism as lifestyle, or secularism of "convenience," is prominent among intellectuals and civic groups such as the Citizens' Rights Movement; it is also clearly gaining ground as modernization proceeds.[42]

A closer look at demographic data indicates that religious observance, by Orthodox definition, is at best holding the line. For this purpose the simple division into religious and nonreligious, while having a certain reality in popular perceptions and in political divisions, does not adequately capture the range of practices. Most surveys of Israeli religious observance use a threefold self-categorization of "religious" (*dati*), "traditional" (*masorti*), or "secular" (*hiloni* or *lo dati*) to describe the population. The label of "traditional" describes a group in the middle, predominantly Sephardi Jews, who follow many time-honored Jewish practices as a matter of custom but are not devout or strict in a religious sense. Some of the data using these definitions are summarized in Table 4.

These figures show remarkable stability in the percentage of Israelis who describe themselves as religious.[43] Apparently a higher birthrate among

TABLE 4   Religious Self-Identification among Israeli Jews
(in percentage)

	1979	1986	1989*	1992
Religious	17	15	17	20
Traditional	41	38	33	29
Secular, nonreligious	42	47	51	51

SOURCES: 1979 data from Yehuda Ben-Meir and Peri Kedem, "Index of Religiosity of the Jewish Population of Israel" (in Hebrew), *Megamot* 24 (February 1979): 353–62; 1986 data from a poll by the Smith Research Center, *Jerusalem Post,* 15 May 1986, and personal interview with Hanoch Smith, 11 June 1988; 1989 data also from a Smith poll, reported in Hanoch Smith and Rafi Smith, *Judaism in the Jewish State: A 1989 Survey of Attitudes of Israeli Jews* (New York: American Jewish Committee, Institute of Human Relations, 1989); 1992 data from Yochanan Peres, "Religiosity and Political Positions" (in Hebrew), *Democracy* (Winter 1992): 26–31.

*Column totals more than 100 because of rounding.

religious families and a higher percentage of observance among immigrants have been offset by attrition due to secularization. In addition, there is movement from the "traditional" category to a secular lifestyle, which reflects increased secularization among the Israel-born Sephardi population. In addition, the influx of largely secularized Jewish immigrants from the former Soviet Union adds large numbers to this category.

Further evidence for a decline in self-identification as religious can be found in surveys carried out among youth. In one poll reported in 1985, only 12.3 percent of fifteen- to eighteen-year-olds described themselves as religious, 27.3 percent as traditional, and fully 59.5 percent as secular.[44] In 1991, 37 percent of the youths surveyed reported that they were less religious than their parents, 46 percent that they were just as religious, and only 17 percent that they were more religious than their parents.[45] By 1996 roughly 20 percent of all marriages took place outside the official Orthodox framework, either as unrecognized marriages or as marriages abroad.[46] Polls among youth cannot be regarded as conclusive, since religiosity may increase with age, but clearly these surveys support the thesis of secularization more than the image of growing religiosity.

Study of voting patterns tells a more complicated story. The total vote for all religious parties together, Zionist and *haredi,* has never exceeded 19 percent (twenty-three seats of 120) in Knesset elections, and this was only after the changed electoral system in 1996 gave a boost to smaller parties (the previous high was eighteen seats). The real story has been a shift of power within the religious camp, with *haredim* gaining ground at the expense of religious Zionists. The *haredi* success has been due, in particular, to unusual success in attracting large numbers of Sephardi voters. At first glance this development seems highly unlikely, given the heavily Eastern European flavor of *haredi* culture (the use of Yiddish as a spoken language, for example). But in some ways Sephardi religiosity—conservative, traditional, nonideological—was more compatible with this lifestyle than with that of religious Zionists, who were seen as part of the modern Western world. Though Sephardi religious voters had initially supported the National Religious Party in great numbers, over the years a Sephardi-*haredi* subculture materialized, especially in largely Sephardi development towns and suburbs. In reaction to the dominant Ashkenazi character of Agudat Yisrael, leaders of this constituency established a separate party in the 1984 elections, Sephardi Torah Guardians or Shas, and captured a surprising four seats, the best showing for any explicitly Sephardi party since 1948. Building on this success by developing their own institutional network, Shas made an even stronger showing in 1988 and 1992, winning six seats, and, with the help of the new electoral system, ten seats in 1996.[47]

Other developments also challenge the notion that the power of the religious establishment is on the rise. One threat perceived by Orthodox circles in Israel is a "softening" toward non-Orthodox (Reform, Reconstructionist, and Conservative) forms of Judaism. In the past the general public attitude toward these movements, even among secular Israelis, was fairly negative, and only a tiny percentage of the public joined non-Orthodox congregations. This has been changing; a representative survey conducted for the Ministry of Religious Affairs in 1988 (and later leaked to that Ministry's critics) reportedly showed that 12 percent of the respondents identified themselves as Orthodox, 3 percent as Conservative, and a surprising 9 percent (far beyond the movement's actual members) as Reform. The self-described Reform even included 19 percent of those who said they observed most of the religious commandments.[48] In 1991, 79 percent of a national sample favored giving equal status to non-Orthodox movements.[49]

Furthermore, beginning in 1989 Reform and Conservative Jewish movements won a series of court cases regarding government funding, membership in religious councils, recognition of non-Orthodox conversions, and provision for non-Orthodox burial. Following the success of the religious parties in the 1996 elections, the new coalition government, in which they controlled five ministries, was committed to rolling back some, but not all, of these "changes in the status quo."

Overall, therefore, the (Orthodox) religious establishment in Israel is justified in feeling threatened from several quarters. But why have these developments not been perceived more clearly by the nonreligious public? The forces of secularization or liberalization have been disguised by a number of factors. First, with the much closer balance between the two major blocs since 1977, the bargaining leverage of the religious parties has actually

increased even when (in 1981 and 1984) the number of seats they controlled declined. This has been reinforced by the greater visibility of religious figures, including some from the *haredi* camp, in positions of responsibility as ministers, deputy ministers, chairmen of key committees in the
Knesset, heads of government corporations, and other positions where the
religious community was underrepresented (in part by its own choice) in
the past.

A second factor is the increased vitality and assertiveness of the religious
subculture, as expressed in the scope of its activities, the proliferation of
new institutions and publications, and its higher visibility in public life.
The new prominence of the *haredi* community is important in this regard,
since the *haredim* appear to the secular public as more visible and more vocal champions of religious causes viewed as a threat to secular patterns of
life.[50]

A third development that contributes to an appearance of greater religiosity is the growth of what has been labeled a new "civil religion" in Israel,
in which traditional religious symbols assume an increasing importance in
public life.[51] This does not indicate a higher level of religious observance as
such but, to the contrary, the appropriation and secularization of religious
elements as part of national identity. As Liebman and Don-Yehiya put it,
"whereas religious symbols play an increasingly important role in Israeli public or collective life, Judaism has no great significance to the individual in
terms of spiritual and personal self-definition or his behavior."[52] Holidays
once observed mainly in prayer have become national commemorations
marked by public ceremonies and events, while holidays that were once only
secular (such as Independence Day) have begun to acquire some religious
connotations and symbols.[53] The greater mixture of secular and religious
does indeed make religion more visible in public life but at the cost of di-
luting its religious content—and it is therefore of small comfort to many
religious leaders. Israelis are not becoming more religious but simply more
traditional in some collective rituals.

The rise of the new civil religion is also made more significant and more
visible by the general decline of ideology in Israeli society. The decline of
Labor Zionist and "statist" ideologies, which served as competing civil religions, left a vacuum for the reassertion of symbols rooted more deeply in
Jewish history and ritual.[54] Tied to this, and accounting for much of it, has
been the growing Sephardi contribution to Israeli culture and politics. Israelis of African and Asian background never engaged in the same revolt
against tradition that marked much of European Zionism (especially for
Labor Zionists) and thus have clung to traditional Jewish symbols and customs even while undergoing a process of secularization.

This reality is reflected in continuing support for Jewish religious expressions in Israeli public life, going well beyond the community that de-

TABLE 5   Degrees of Religiosity of Israeli Jews (in percentage)

	1962	1989*	1993	Range
Observe strictly	15	12	14	8–17
Observe to great extent	15	17	24	11–24
Observe somewhat	46	40	41	37–48
Don't observe at all	24	30	21	21–38

SOURCE: All data originates from the Guttman Institute; the 1962 figures were reprinted in Aaron Antonovsky and Alan Arian, *Hopes and Fears of Israelis: Consensus in a New Society* (Jerusalem: Jerusalem Academic Press, 1972); the 1993 data is taken from Yosef Goell, "Religious Differences: A Chasm or a Crack?" *Jerusalem Post International Edition*, 22 January 1994; the remainder of the data was supplied directly by the institute.
   *Column totals less than 100 because of rounding.

fines itself as religious. In the 1991 Guttman Institute survey, respondents split almost evenly, 54 percent in favor and 46 percent opposed, on the question of separation of religion and state.[55] The widespread support for religious symbolism on the national level was also expressed in a 1987 survey that found that only 47.5 percent of the nonobservant supported the idea of making civil marriage available and only 41.1 percent of the same group wanted to end the ban on public transportation on the Sabbath.[56]

Again, this does not demonstrate the rise of Orthodoxy but rather the broad acceptance of religious symbolism in a civil religion mode. It also shows that customary frameworks for measuring religiosity in Israel do not capture all the dimensions of the subject. The dichotomous division of Israelis into "religious" and "nonreligious" has been superseded by the common, threefold self-classification as "religious," "traditional," and "secular" (or "nonreligious"). Even greater definition of actual observance is available in data from the Guttman Institute, which has been tracking religious observance for over two decades; respondents are asked to describe their observance of Jewish religious law on a scale of four categories. Some of the results are summarized in Table 5.

Clearly there are many degrees of religious observance, and important differences in what such observance signifies. Many who observe "to a great extent" think of themselves as "traditional" rather than "religious," and some who observe religious practices "somewhat" tend to identify themselves as "secular." In both cases it seems likely that much of this observance would fit the model of civil religion (that is, the appropriation and secularization of religious symbols as part of national identity). As this demonstrates, the threefold division into religious, traditional, and secular does not capture the real complexity of Israeli reality; apart from the division of the religious into national-religious Jews and *haredi*, the secular category

TABLE 6   Religious Identity of Israeli Jews
(in percentage)

Religious-*haredi*	3.9
Religious	11.0
Traditional	26.7
Secular, observe traditions	23.3
Secular	30.2
Antireligious	4.6

SOURCE: Baruch Kimmerling, "Yes, Returning to the Family," *Politika* (in Hebrew), no. 48 (1993): 43.
NOTE: Total is less than 100 because of rounding.

includes different degrees of nonobservance. Kimmerling carried out a survey that identified six different patterns of religious observance (summarized in Table 6).

There is in fact a broad range of religious practice. In an important study published in 1979, Yehuda Ben-Meir and Peri Kedem checked the observance of specific religious practices and found a broad range of responses: only 6 percent went to synagogue every day, but 14 percent put on tefillin every morning, 22 percent refrained from travel on the Sabbath, 44 percent separated milk and meat utensils in their homes, 53 percent lit candles on Sabbath, 79 percent did not eat bread during Passover, and fully 99 percent participated in a Passover Seder. In conclusion: "The results of this study demonstrate that there is no clear-cut dichotomy in Israeli society between religious and non-religious Jews, but that there exists a continuum of religiosity, ranging from the extremely religious through various degrees of religious and traditional behavior, to the completely nonreligious."[57]

It is doubtful that the development of civil religion in itself poses a serious threat to democracy; a recent poll of the Israel Democracy Institute (which surveys public opinion on matters relating to democratic values) found that only 12.6 percent of the respondents would "generally" or "always" give priority to rulings of the rabbinate over acts of the Knesset.[58] If this is the case, and if the general picture painted here is accurate, what if anything is the threat to the status quo?

THE TWO THREATS

The major threats to the stability of secular-religious relations in Israel at the present time are (1) the rise of *haredi* influence within the religious camp, and (2) the strong link that has been forged between religious Zionism and uncompromising territorial nationalism.

The significance of the *haredi* resurgence was apparent in the May 1993 ceremony to install a new Sephardi chief rabbi elected with strong Shas support. Since this was a state occasion, marking the filling of a state office by official electors, the president of Israel was present and the national anthem (*Hatikva*) was to be sung. A number of those present, however, tried to prevent the singing of the anthem. As a television camera recorded the turbulent scene, Rabbi Ovadiah Yosef—spiritual and political leader of Shas and a former Sephardi chief rabbi himself—ostentatiously hid his face behind a pamphlet.

This refusal to acknowledge the State of Israel, even when one of their number was being inducted into a state office, fed the apprehensions many had about the increasing political leverage of *haredi* leaders. In the words of one editorial, Shas "treats the state as if it were a foreign entity, and it participates in its government for strictly materialist reasons." A Labor member of the Knesset put it less elegantly: "The more tightly they are connected to the teat the more they kick the milk bucket."[59]

When the State of Israel was founded, most secular Israelis assumed that the *haredi* way of life was disappearing and looked on the *haredi* neighborhoods of Jerusalem and B'nei Brak as living museums to be visited before they vanished entirely. To be sure the birthrate in these communities was very impressive (six to eight children per family on the average), but the experience in Eastern Europe and Palestine before the Holocaust had been one of rampant assimilation. Few of these children, it was felt, would resist the pull of the modern world. In this spirit, it was easy to be tolerant and even generous in granting *haredi* demands: military exemptions for yeshiva students, funding for their separate educational networks.

It was precisely under these conditions, however, that the *haredim* managed to halt the demographic erosion and to build the kind of closed community that could shut out unwanted influences. Though appearing to be a continuation of tradition, this "society of scholars" was in some respects a new phenomenon. For the first time, young men were kept in school not only through their childhood and adolescence but long past their marriage, and in an environment from which all secular education and influences were carefully excluded and a fairly complete social and cultural segregation was enforced. For example, *ba'alei tshuva*—"born-again" Jews—are not accepted into *haredi* schools because of apprehension that their previous exposure to secular life would be a source of contamination.[60] What made this isolation possible, paradoxically, was a greater flow of funds from the outside. In the Israeli case, most of these funds came from the state, either through direct subsidy of "independent" *haredi* schools or through the employment of *haredi* women as teachers in state religious schools.[61]

Observers speak of "the apparent retreat of modern Orthodoxy" before the *haredi* resurgence, noting that "the distinction between an ultra-Orthodox and a modern religious person is as basic today as it once was in Eastern Europe."[62] The particularism of the *haredi* lifestyle, with its hermetic closure to the outside world, has enabled it to withstand assimilative pressures better, while the ranks of the modern Orthodox, being exposed more fully to the inroads of modern secular culture, have been progressively thinned. Some religious Zionists have moved to a more nationalist stance, leading them to desert the National Religious Party (NRP) for Likud and the smaller nationalist parties of the right. As indicated, many Sephardi voters also deserted the NRP for Shas, as well as for secular parties; consequently, the NRP fell from twelve Knesset seats in 1977 to only four in 1984.[63] Religious Zionists were also being directly challenged by the *haredim* on a number of fronts, from the employment of *haredi* teachers in state religious schools to control of rabbinical institutions and the sale of newspapers in religious neighborhoods.

The gap in worldview between the *haredi* community and the rest of Israel—secular and "modern Orthodox" alike—constitutes a challenge to the nation's integrative capacities. The *haredim* do not intend to be integrated. They reject modern Western society (apart from its technology) and proselytize for their own lifestyle as an alternative to secular Israeli culture. From the *haredi* perspective, there is no validity to a secular Jewish identity; as one of their leading intellects put it, "if they are Jews—they are not free, and if they are free—they are not Jews."[64] Sometimes *haredim* reserve the label of "Jews" for themselves, as opposed to the "Israelis" who live in the surrounding society; secular Israelis, in other words, are equivalent to the goyim among whom Jews lived in the past.[65] Nor are *haredi* political parties committed in principle to democracy, even when playing Israeli politics according to the rules of the game. Agudat Yisrael had initially opposed establishment of a Jewish state based on majority rule, since this would deny the sovereignty of the Torah (in its authoritative rabbinical interpretation) as the only legitimate source of Jewish laws. The *haredi* parties (Agudat Yisrael, Shas, and Degel Hatorah during its brief existence) have never been operated by democratic procedures but rather have been governed by rabbinical councils whose decisions are final—a rare if not unprecedented situation for a democracy. This in return reflects the reality of *haredi* society, which makes no pretense of being democratic nor of recognizing a realm of personal freedom: "Though people join the *haredi* society voluntarily, it is a totalitarian system which does not recognize privacy."[66]

The *haredi* position on security issues has often been characterized as relatively dovish. Those who rejected the idea of a secular Israeli state were not likely to seek its expansion or promote its aggressive defense; many did not even serve in the army. And indeed, many *haredi* leaders (Rabbis Schach and Yosef in particular) have decreed that peace and saving lives come before the acquisition or retention of territory. But the complete picture of *haredi* views on these controversial issues is actually more complex.

Haredim may avoid the use of state symbols, but most of them do relate to Israel as a Jewish society and to the Land of Israel as the sacred and inalienable legacy of the Jewish people. Arab hostility and attacks can also be seen as a continuation of classic patterns of antisemitic persecution, calling for Jewish resistance and defense. In this context *haredim* can identify with the Jewish struggle against an external enemy, support Jewish control of ancestral lands, and even oppose the withdrawal of Israeli forces from occupied territories while continuing to challenge the legitimacy of Israel itself.[67] The late Rabbi Menachem Mendel Schneerson (the Lubavitcher Rebbe, leader of Habad Hasidism) refused even to visit Israel during his lifetime, but his followers mobilized in vehement opposition to the Israeli-Palestinian agreement of September 1993. Furthermore, rank and file *haredim* are notably less dovish than leaders like Rabbis Schach and Yosef. In particular, Shas voters (many of them non-*haredim*) are more hawkish than the party's leadership.[68] But even among the *haredim* alone, a survey in 1992 demonstrated that they were in fact more hawkish than religious Zionists on the issue of exclusive Jewish rights to the Land of Israel.[69]

Furthermore, while the *haredi* community is not committed in principle to the political system, it has nevertheless learned how to use it effectively and with increasing skill. In fact this community scores very highly on scales of access to and participation in the political system (even before the 1988 election).[70] They use the rules of the game to maximize their own benefits and to influence the entire system more in their direction, if only slightly. In playing this game, however, they also become a part of the system, however conditionally, and run the risk of a two-way flow of influences.

There remains the central contradiction in the *haredi* relationship to Israel: their isolation from secular Israeli society is made possible by the resources they receive from it. The more they impinge on this society, the greater the danger of a backlash that will force them to choose between their principles and their economic viability. Already they have been drawn into more active participation in the public life of Israel; while Agudat Yisrael has refused (since 1952) to become full partners in any Israeli government, ministers from Shas served in all the governments from 1984 to 1993 and again from 1996. Increasingly, pragmatism in pursuing political goals seems to characterize the leadership of all the *haredi* parties.[71] On a broader scale, observers also note the subtle ways in which the imprint of modern Israel penetrates into *haredi* society despite its attempted isolation.[72]

Other problems also face the *haredim:* there is no guarantee that the success of the last four decades will continue indefinitely. Particularism and rivalry among different *haredi* groups, intensified by involvement in politics, is on the rise and threatens the capacity for common action. For example, when Shas established its own Council of Torah Sages, the position of the Sephardi chief rabbi as the recognized rabbinical authority in that community was undercut—as that of the Ashkenazi chief rabbi had been from its inception. Also, despite the infusion of outside funds, economic pressures increase as the *haredi* community grows. Teaching jobs for *haredi* women, a major economic prop, have become increasingly hard to find, in part because of growing resistance among religious Zionists to *haredi* teachers in state religious schools. Women are therefore being prepared for jobs that involve greater contact with the outside world, creating the possibility of a culture gap between working wives and their still-cloistered husbands. Poverty is a serious problem and is getting worse; the chronic housing shortage forces some families to beg in order to provide for their married children. In Jerusalem, particularly, *haredi* separatism collides head on with the need for territorial expansion into areas where prevailing patterns of land use undermine such separation.[73]

Finally, success in sealing off the exits from the community also involves certain costs. Previously those who did not fit in could simply pass over to religious or secular Israeli society, but the chasm between the two sides now makes this difficult. For one thing, the lack of general education leaves young *haredim* with no marketable skills in the secular workplace. Those who are unsuited by temperament or by intellect for a life of Torah study find themselves with no viable options, and they constitute a growing group that strains the harmony of the *haredi* world.[74]

In light of these problems, the leading authority on *haredi* society asks: "Is the existence of a society of scholars that requires all its male members to study in *yeshivot* . . . for many years, to the exclusion of general or vocational education, viable in the long term?"[75] Its very dependence on outside support makes this society vulnerable to the influences it seeks to keep out, and every success that it achieves raises the level of resentment and opposition among the secular majority. Whether *haredim* can avoid becoming part of the modern world remains to be seen; as fundamentalists elsewhere over the last two centuries, they may win some battles but ultimately lose the war.

The second major problematic aspect of religion and politics in Israel is tied to broader political issues. Many Israelis have felt threatened by Orthodoxy not because of religious issues per se, but because of the linkage between religious fervor and exclusivist nationalism. The highly charged issues connected with Israeli-Arab relations, including such questions as Jewish settlement in the territories held by Israel after 1967, are widely seen as religious issues since many of the more fervent nationalists come from religious Zionist circles. With the decline in secular ideologies, the crusading commitment of such groups as Gush Emunim filled a spiritual vacuum.

Of course not all religious leaders espouse the sacralizing of territory in

the name of religion. As noted many *haredi* leaders explicitly reject interpretations of tradition that forbid Israel withdrawal from the occupied territories, and some religious Zionists agree with them.[76] But the dominance
of the religious-national view among religious Zionists (in the NRP) contributed to a fundamental shift in the Israeli political system. This development will be studied more closely in chapter 10.

Finally, there are some indications that the two threats to Israeli democracy may be merging. Despite past differences between non-Zionist *haredim*
and religious ultranationalists, a growing number of people describe themselves as "nationalist-*haredi*." Contributing to this are twin processes of na-
tionalization among *haredim*, as they come to identify with territorial claims,
and the haredization of religious Zionists as they turn to stricter standards
of religious observance. In the latter case religious Zionists, who in the past
showed "an accommodationist rather than a rejectionist orientation toward
modernity and secular culture," have in Charles Liebman's view come increasingly to show "signs of rejecting modernity and adopting a rather reactionary interpretation of the religious tradition."[77]

What is emerging from this is a new Jewish fundamentalism that transcends old divisions between Zionists and anti-Zionists and which on
religious-national grounds preaches a "higher law" that sanctions civil disobedience and threatens the principles of democracy. The two strands together promote an ethnic particularism "which includes suspicion of and
hostility toward non-Jews, cultural isolationism including a suspicion of universalist moralist values, and . . . territorial irredentism."[78] Can the Israeli
political system continue to accommodate elements that make use of the
existing framework while denying the universalistic premises upon which it
is grounded?

The convergence of fundamentalism with nationalism is not surprising
since both are "essentially modern constructs" that use similar language to
engage in a process of self-definition and self-assertion against a hostile
Other.[79] Like nationalism, fundamentalism is theoretically capable of universal extension as others also establish their sacred communities, but in
practice it is "irredeemably particular" as each fundamentalism insists on its
own exceptionalism. Thus, in the eyes of *haredim* and religious nationalists,
their claims take precedence over those of others—secular Jews, Palestinian
Arabs—because only theirs are authentic. Such a view is in its essence inimical to pluralist democracy, but in the case of Israel this is countered by
the finding, among students of comparative fundamentalisms, that fundamentalists operating in democracies typically find it necessary to compromise and to confine their aspirations to the private sphere of life.[80] Whether
this holds true for Israel will depend on its success in contending with the
cleavage that traditional power-sharing has not bridged: that between Jew
and Arab.

NINE

Arabs in Israel

One of the central puzzles of Israeli politics is the general strength of democratic institutions, given the fact that relatively few of the immigrants to Palestine or to Israel over the last century came from countries with a viable democratic tradition. A second puzzle is that one of the weaker aspects of these democratic institutions is respect for minority rights, though it is precisely as a minority group that Jewish historical experience is most extensive.

A number of influences have contributed to this outcome. The general currents of Western liberalism, the role of the British model, and populist aspects of East European socialist ideologies all pushed the Zionist movement and Israeli governance in a democratic direction. On the other hand, Zionism, like contemporary nationalisms to which it was both an imitation and a reaction, focused on the rights of those who shared a Jewish identity rather than their relations with those who did not. As Jews knew all too well from their own experience with modern nationalism, the place of minorities in a state based on the principle of nationality was highly problematic. Furthermore, Zionism functioned in a Middle Eastern context where ethnoreligious particularism—the delineation of rights and privileges according to group identity—was the rule even before the advent of modern nationalism. And finally, Zionism and Israel both have contended with an ethnic group viewed as a basic threat to the security or survival of the Jewish community.

The British Mandate experience did nothing to develop common frameworks or shared institutions transcending ethnic identities. The idea of a "civic realm" indifferent to ethnicity, in which all are equal as individuals, did not take root among Jews or Arabs. During the 1930s various schemes for developing "neutral" state machinery above both communities were floated, but none could resolve the clash between two nationalisms that were each bent on full self-determination. The idea of "binationalism" attracted few on the Jewish side and even fewer Arab Palestinians, while Jewish suggestions of "parity" between the two communities, with neither dominating the other, held little appeal to an Arab population that still constituted a clear majority. Ideas for power-sharing between Arabs and Jews withered before the fierce determination of each community to develop its own political identity, its own communal institutions, and ultimately its own unfettered sovereign state.

All of the institutions inherited by the new State of Israel were, therefore, ethnically defined. The political bodies—the Knesset, the National Council—were elected by Jewish voters only, and the Jewish Agency, the Histadrut, political parties, and other enterprises of the *yishuv* did not include Arabs (nor did Arabs seek to join them). The establishment of Israel theoretically created a civic space where none had existed: Arabs within the state became "Israelis" by citizenship without becoming Jews by nationality. But the name "Israel" had meaning only in a Jewish context; previous to this, the idea of "Israeli Arabs" was as self-contradictory as "Hindu Arabs" or "Persian Arabs." Efforts were made to stretch the idea of "Israeliness" to encompass non-Jews, or to invent a new all-encompassing identity. Among Arabs, Rustum Bastuni led an early movement for a common Israeli identity, while on the Jewish side the advocates of a "Canaanite" or "Semitic" nation sought the same basic goal. Neither movement made any headway.[1]

Given this lack of a common identity, the Jewish-Arab split represents a bigger challenge to Israel than either the communal or religious cleavages. This is also clearly the public perception: in 1990, 85 percent of the Jewish public rated Ashkenazi-Sephardi relations as either "very good" or "good," while 38 percent gave the same ratings to relations between religious and secular Jews—and only 10 percent thought that relations between Jews and Arabs in Israel were this good.[2] In Sammy Smooha's words, "the Orientals are not-separate-but-unequal, the religious Jews are separate-but-equal, and the Israeli Arabs are separate-but-unequal."[3] The accommodative and power-sharing features of Israeli politics in other contexts do not apply to relations between Jews and Arabs. Why should this be the case?

MINORITY RIGHTS AFTER STATEHOOD

Despite all that had transpired before, only in 1948 did the problem of Arabs in a Jewish community become an operational issue. At this point both the confusion of the historical legacy and the lack of consensus on the issue became all too apparent. But another result of the new situation was, paradoxically, that the Arab minority within Israel became a secondary concern.

The 1948–1949 Arab-Israeli war shifted the focus of the Arab-Israeli conflict from interethnic strife within Palestine to a state-to-state confrontation between Israel and its Arab neighbors, who had previously played a marginal role in the conflict. Most of the Arab population in areas under Israeli control had fled or been expelled; the roughly 150,000 who remained were demoralized, largely leaderless, and cut off from contact with other Arabs. Their situation was now but a minor aspect of a much larger picture, and the new government of Israel instinctively tried to keep the internal Arab problem separate from the larger issues of Arab-Israeli diplomacy and war.

At the same time, these new circumstances did seem to offer a propitious opportunity to try integrative approaches to Arab-Israeli relations. Leaders of the new state were aware that, as Histadrut General Secretary Pinhas Lavon said in early 1948, "this state will in some ways be a glass house, and every time we yawn, and anything that we do, big or small, will be photographed by the entire world."[4] The smaller size of the remaining Arab population would make integration easier. Finally, one of the strengths of Jewish and Israeli politics was precisely its capacity to deal with deep cleavages through techniques of inclusion and power-sharing, which performed remarkably well in keeping potentially explosive social and religious divisions from tearing the country apart.

But the place of the Arab minority in Israel—19 percent of the population in May 1948, and still 19 percent in 1996—is quite different from that of any part of the Jewish population. While Israeli Arabs enjoy the formal rights of citizenship, including voting and access to the political system, they stand outside the sphere of traditional Jewish politics. There has been no meaningful power-sharing with the Arab community, and, despite the great absolute progress made by Israeli Arabs since 1948, there is still significant material inequality. For the first four decades there was no independent nationwide Arab political party or organization, dedicated to the vigorous pursuit of Arab rights within the Israeli political system and speaking credibly for the Arab community or a large part of it. Nor were there truly independent Arab newspapers of significance or Arab leaders of national stature. In the bargaining process that characterizes Israel politics, there was, in short, no Arab negotiating partner: "There simply does not exist an elite cartel within which leaders of the Jewish and Arab communal groups engage in quiet ethnic bargaining and careful apportionment of social, political, and economic resources."[5]

Perhaps Israeli leaders truly believed that achieving a Jewish majority would easily resolve minority issues in democratic style. Before statehood, the question of a non-Jewish minority had seemed very remote and had received scant attention, and when it was discussed the tendency was to invoke the principle of "equality" as a self-evident solution. In 1943, for example, David Ben-Gurion called for a policy of "complete equality of all inhabitants," together with independent Arab municipalities and a gradual equalization of living standards.[6] Jewish leaders repeatedly referred to "absolute"

equality as a standard, sometimes qualified as civic or legal equality in recognition of the fact that equality in objective conditions might take time,
and Israel's Declaration of Independence promised "complete equality of
social and political rights to all inhabitants irrespective of religion, race, or
sex." There seemed to be little recognition at the time, despite long Jewish
experience as a minority, of possible tension between this promise and the
declared mission of Israel as the state of the Jewish people.[7]

The definition of Israel as a Jewish state is expressed in a number of
ways. The national flag is inspired by the Jewish prayer shawl and features
the Shield of David, and the national emblem is the seven-branched cande-
labra associated with the First and Second Temples. The national anthem
(*Hatikva*) actually has no legal status, but is sung on most official occasions
and is decidedly Jewish in content ("As long as a Jewish soul beats . . ."). The
1950 Law of Return, which grants all Jews the right to Israeli citizenship, is
the very embodiment of Israel as a Jewish state and will be discussed below;
however, it is not the only legal reflection of Israel's Jewishness. A 1952
statute gives the World Zionist Organization and the Jewish Agency special
status, while the State Education Law (1953) invokes "the values of Jewish
culture." The Foundations of Law Act (1980) calls for reference to "Israel's
heritage" when courts face a gap in existing statutes. Though all religious
communities in Israel have their own courts in matters of marriage and divorce, the Jewish Chief Rabbinate has unique statutory status and powers.
The Jewish Sabbath and holidays are official days of rest (though non-
Jews observe their own days of rest), and laws dealing with cultural, educational, and memorial institutions (for example, the Holocaust Memorial,
Yad Vashem) relate to Jewish culture and history.[8] As a second official language, Arabic may be used in courts, Knesset, and governmental transac-
tions, but naturalized citizens are required to know Hebrew; furthermore,
outside of Arab localities few government documents, official announce-
ments, or street signs actually appear in both languages.

This Jewishness of the state has clear implications for the proposition of
civic equality for all Israelis, Jewish or non-Jewish. Before the event, however,
little thought appears to have been devoted to fitting these two elements together. When equality was discussed, it was usually in terms of individual
rights that would be guaranteed equally to Jews and Arabs: the right of voting and political participation, due process of law, freedom of speech and assembly, the right to practice one's religion, the right to education in one's
own language. The fact of a collective national identity, and demands stemming from it, raised issues for which this approach had few answers and
for which Jewish tradition and experience, prior to 1948, offered no precedents or guidelines. It is hardly surprising, therefore, that when the problem of dealing with a large non-Jewish minority within a Jewish setting first
arose, there was tremendous intellectual confusion and incoherence over

how to go about creating a previously nonexistent category of "Israelis" who would be equal while remaining non-Jewish.

Those who appreciated the strength of Arab national identity sometimes pursued far-reaching schemes of integration as a means of weakening it. Lavon proposed integrating Arabs into all spheres of life including the army, stressing the army's "political function in national and social education."[9] Yitzhak Ben-Zvi, later the second president of Israel, called in 1950 for the integration of Arabs into Hebrew culture and language so that "Hebrew will become the state language also for them."[10] As late as 1951 Prime Minister David Ben-Gurion himself convened a group of experts to discuss the possibility that Israeli Arabs might be "Judaized."[11]

Policy proposals ran the gamut from such fantasies of total assimilation to arguments for total separation between the two communities. But no Israeli government followed a clear, consistent policy of either integration or separation, or a clear, consistent policy of any kind, toward the Arab minority. The main feature of government policy in this area, in the eyes of most observers, has been its lack of coherence. Suddenly faced with a large non-Jewish minority and without clear guidelines based either on traditions or experience, the government's policies reflected this confusion. The formative stage in particular was a period of contradictions, with differing tendencies—separatist and assimilationist, Revisionist and socialist, conciliatory and hard-line—all competing for influence. The lack of coherence was magnified by the lack of clear lines of authority, with responsibility for issues involving Arab citizens diffused among a number of ministries and other governmental actors. This brought into play not only differing bureaucratic perspectives but also the differing worldviews of the competing parties controlling the various ministries.

The result was that no one overriding conception or approach was adopted and that nearly all of the competing perspectives were, at some time and to some degree, reflected in actual policies. In fact, says one historian, "it is impossible to talk about 'the Israeli Arab policy' as a clear-cut notion in the early 1950s."[12] A former advisor on Arab affairs has confirmed that "no government in Israel has ever formed any plan or any comprehensive policy towards [Israeli Arabs]. No government in Israel thought the Israeli Arabs' position abnormal enough to merit even one session of the cabinet."[13] In the absence of an agreed-upon overall strategy, it is also difficult to characterize the intent of Israeli policy as *primarily* "modernization," "internal colonialism," "exclusionary domination," or "control," to mention some of the paradigms that have been suggested.[14]

The policies (in the plural) actually followed have vacillated and often contradicted each other. Benziman and Mansour argue that four different tendencies have at various times and to varying degrees been observable: expulsion ("transfer"), arbitrary imposition of inferior status, Arab-Jewish coexistence based on recognition of differences, and full integration of Arabs into public life.[15] Policies have swung from the pole of integration to the pole of isolation, defying any single logic and operating at cross-purposes to defeat the achievement of either set of goals.

In part, this confusion prevailed because of an astonishing lack of attention on the policymaking level. Consistent with their failure to recognize the dilemma of Arab citizens in a Jewish state, and also with a natural desire to keep the issue quiet, top policymakers devoted little time and energy to internal Arab issues. Like some early Zionists, they adopted a posture of avoidance. Reportedly the Israeli cabinet has never held a comprehensive discussion or review of policy toward the Arab sector; specific Israeli Arab issues have been discussed in regular cabinet sessions on perhaps a dozen occasions, but no overall decisions or guidelines have ever been adopted by the government as a whole.[16] The tendency to avoidance can be further documented with any number of quaint illustrations; for example, in the 1952 Israel Government Yearbook Prime Minister Ben-Gurion wrote that the new state of Israel "was virtually emptied of its former owners."[17] Ben-Gurion's failure to notice the state's remaining Arab citizens was perhaps understandable in light of the fact that he did not visit any Israeli Arab community until eleven years after the establishment of the state.[18]

In the light of such indifference and in the absence of clear and agreed-upon guidelines, short-term security interests became the touchstone of government policy. Security became, in a sense, the "default setting" on minority policy: when there was no consensus on a coherent alternative policy—and in most cases there was not—the security interest became the basis of decision, even when it was relatively trivial. Sometimes very marginal security considerations outweighed all political, diplomatic, and human factors, as in the case of Biram and Ikrit, two small Arab villages on the Lebanese border whose inhabitants were evacuated after the fighting in 1948 and were not allowed to return.

Security was in any event the dominant concern in Israeli thinking, especially in the early years. In the context of the recent Holocaust and a war for survival, Israeli Arabs were seen first as part of a Palestinian Arab community with which the *yishuv* had been in violent conflict for decades, and second as part of a vast Arab world that was threatening a "second round" to destroy Israel. Israeli Arabs were also bound by both ethnic and family links to a hostile refugee population increasingly involved in infiltration and violence against Israeli targets, and they were concentrated in border areas where control was most difficult.

These circumstances, added to underlying assumptions of a hostile external world, produced an attitude of deep suspicion toward Arabs who remained in Israel. Fears regarding Israel's survival, given Arab superiority in numbers, were easily transferred from the external realm to the population at hand. To some extent, Israeli leaders may also have been extrapolating from their own politicized and ideologized worldview, expecting Arabs to behave "as Arabs" in the same way that Zionists were expected to adhere to a fervent and self-sacrificing nationalism. Phrases such as "fifth column," "Trojan horse," and "completing Hitler's work" characterized official discourse regarding Israeli Arabs.[19] A favored historical analogy was the German minority in Czechoslovakia's Sudetenland, which had presumably paved the way for Hitler's conquest of that land. Little account was taken of the actual weakness of Israeli Arabs in the aftermath of the 1948 war, of their continuing fear of being expelled as others already had been, or of their experience in dealing pragmatically with alien governments. The prevailing attitude was deep suspicion; in David Grossman's words, "sometimes it seems as if Israeli-Jewish DNA, after being modified by long generations of oppression and pogroms and blood libels and mass extermination, contains no gene for any other attitude toward people who might also be dangerous, even if their deeds, for almost half a century, prove the exact opposite."[20]

Consequently, military authorities and military considerations prevailed in almost every decision affecting the Arab population. Initially a Ministry of Minority Affairs—the only entirely new government ministry not based on *yishuv* institutions—was set up to handle Jewish-Arab relations within Israel. The new ministry was headed by Behor Shalom Shitrit, born in Ottoman Palestine and speaking native Palestinian Arabic, who was the only Sephardi Jew in the first government. Shitrit was a career police officer who served simultaneously as minister of police; he was therefore very sensitive to security concerns and in fact shared prevailing doubts about the likely loyalty of Israeli Arabs.[21] Nevertheless, as Minorities minister he tried to promote the integration and civil equality of the Arab community, and during its brief period of existence his ministry found itself in a constant, and usually losing, struggle with the Military Government, established in October 1948, which held actual military control of most Arab areas after the war.

The military establishment, including the Military Government, was answerable to Prime Minister and Defense Minister Ben-Gurion, as was the General Security Service (*Shin Beit* or *Shabak*, the Israeli equivalent of the American FBI), which was also very active in the Arab sector. Thus the institutional arrangements gave Ben-Gurion, backed by a military and security apparatus in actual control of Arab areas, the decisive voice in determining what transpired there. The Prime Minister's concerns were exemplified by his long list of occupations which, for security reasons, were to be closed to Arabs; he also vetoed Shitrit's proposal for an Arab advisory council in the Ministry of Minority Affairs, and within a few months (in July 1949) Ben-Gurion eliminated the nettlesome ministry itself. From this point on coordination of Israeli Arab matters was handled by an advisor on Arab affairs working directly out of the office of the prime minister.[22]

The appointees who filled this position through the years often derived their credentials as Arabists from a security or intelligence background. Despite this predisposition, by virtue of their role as liaison with the Arab community many advisors made serious efforts to arouse governmental interest in Israeli Arab issues and to reduce some of the obvious inequalities. These efforts were generally ineffective, however, because of the weak bureaucratic position of the advisors and the lack of continuity from one advisor to the next. The dominance of security concerns was also expressed in the structure of the Central Committee, which set and implemented specific policies; on this committee the advisor was outnumbered by representatives of the army, police, and General Security Service.[23] Only under the National Unity Government (1984–1990) did these issues again get ministerial-level attention, as three consecutive ministers without portfolio (Ezer Weizman, Moshe Arens, and Ehud Olmert) were assigned responsibility for Israeli Arab affairs, working with the advisor on Arab affairs.

With security as the touchstone, the army continued to expel Arab residents from sensitive areas up to two years after the war, as in the Biram and Ikrit cases already cited or in the general eviction of Arabs from Majdal (Ashkelon) in 1950. The spirit of the times was conveyed by Foreign Minister Moshe Sharett—generally one of the more conciliatory members of the government—in his reminder to his fellow ministers that all dealings with Arab citizens should be channeled through local military government officers and should be "in full cooperation" with them.[24] Such policies, as a practical consequence, distanced Arabs from the regular government machinery, localized the focus of Arab-related issues, and helped to block the emergence of a unified Arab leadership. These results fit the deliberate goal of those key policymakers who explicitly promoted separation as the answer; Yehoshua Palmon, the first advisor on Arab affairs, later stated that "I opposed the integration of Arabs into Israeli society. I preferred separate development."[25]

Those pushing integration in theory were slow to act in practice. The Histadrut, which as a labor federation might have been expected to embrace "the principle of binational class solidarity," was more concerned at first with the protection of Jewish jobs and did not accept Arabs as full members until 1959.[26]

The government thus found itself working at cross-purposes, having never made a clear choice between integrative and isolating strategies. Had it been decided, for example, to counter discontent by a concerted policy of assimilation and material well-being, then the unequal distribution of benefits would have been addressed. Had it been decided, on the other hand, to maintain the peace by working with, and even reinforcing, the traditional social structure of Arab village life (with which it was always easier to bargain), then modernization and other outside forces would have been kept out as much as possible. As it happened, the mixed and inconsistent policy that was followed—combining some modernization with continuing systematic discrimination—created a desire to achieve real equality without providing the means to do so.

Because of this inconsistency, criticism of Israeli policy may also overstate that policy's coherence and purposefulness. The Israeli government can be charged justifiably with both neglect and overly tight control, with policies of both isolation and co-optation, with creating dependence on one side and refusing assistance on the other—but identifying these often opposed tendencies as part of a coordinated design is as illogical as the policy itself. Ian Lustick, in his 1980 study, described "a sophisticated system of control" in which apparently conflicting elements of governmental actions are seen as mutually reinforcing elements of a conscious policy.[27] The components of this system were defined as segmentation (isolating and fragmenting the Arab population by various means), dependence (blocking Arab development and independence), and co-optation (using favors and benefits to encourage cooperation and neutralize opposition). Certainly specific government actions can be identified with each of these themes, but this does not mean that these actions were carefully coordinated with each other according to a coherent master plan. Though his framework tends to suggest a purposeful and consistent policy, Lustick added that it was not "a massive and brilliant conspiracy on the part of Jewish officials responsible for Arab affairs."[28]

Many of the obstacles to Arab integration did not result from government policy but stemmed from such structural factors as the nature of Arab society, the vastly different starting points of the two communities, and prevailing attitudes among the Arab public (see the following section). Israeli policy exploited some of these obstacles, but a more telling criticism would be that it made almost no effort to accommodate or overcome them. There is little evidence of a sustained, coherent strategy to prevent Arab social and economic development, but there is likewise little indication that Israeli policymakers felt that it was urgent, or even worthwhile, to address the structural impediments that perpetuated the gap between Jews and Arabs. For example, not only did the Arab population receive a disproportionately low share of governmental benefits but in addition support from world Jewry continued to flow exclusively to the Jewish community, thus helping to maintain or enlarge, rather than close, the gap. Related to this is the fact that much of the actual governance in the Israeli political system is carried out by quasi-governmental or nongovernmental bodies, such as the Histadrut, the Jewish Agency, the Jewish National Fund, the kibbutz movement, religious bodies, and major banks and economic organizations, most of which predate the state and are conceived as strictly Jewish institutions, in which Arab participation is not seriously proposed. In this situation economic development of the Arab sector, however impressive on an absolute scale, did little to relieve the sense of relative deprivation.

OBSTACLES TO POWER-SHARING

The objective difficulties in achieving equality were tremendous by any account. Palestinian Muslims lacked any experience or precedent for living as a minority under the rule of Jews, who had always been a subject minority (*dhimmi*) in Muslim lands. In fact the legitimacy of non-Muslim rule over Muslim populations is problematic in the Islamic tradition and relatively infrequent in the historical record.[29] This matched the lack of precedent on the Jewish side, which had no historical experience and few useful guidelines on how as a majority to rule over a well-defined minority from which it differed in ethnicity, language, religion, culture, and economic development.

The two communities lived in near-total separation before 1948 and began from vastly different starting points. The Arab population, under the Ottoman *millet* system and the British Mandate, was not included in any of the institutions established by the Zionist movement. As a result, no groundwork had been laid for Arab participation in frameworks organized and dominated by Jews. Israeli Arabs lacked an understanding of how Jewish politics worked and of how organized groups within the system could fight to protect their interests. They began with an almost total ignorance of Jewish society and politics; in the words of one prominent Arab writer and activist, "in general, few of us knew what was happening in the Jewish community. People mostly ignored what was happening there."[30] Even more important perhaps, they lacked an inclination to pursue the possibilities that were at least partly open, not being a part of the Zionist consensus upon which Israeli politics was premised. As another Israeli Arab literary figure has put it, "Our failure to struggle against discrimination and humiliation . . . [derives mostly] from the feeling that this is not our country. We are strangers to it. So what should we protest about? Who has any expectations of this country?"[31]

Related to this is the tendency, in traditional Arab political culture, to accommodate rather than rebel when subjected to alien rule; though hardly accustomed to Jewish rule, Palestinians had for centuries contended with non-Arab governments. There was also a continuing fear of expulsion if they openly challenged the Israeli government, as well as the belief or hope (at least in the early years) that the existing situation was not permanent and might be reversed in the near future.[32] And even after Israeli Arabs became more familiar with Israeli politics and began to seek access to it, the sense of alienation remained: "It became apparent to me that not only newspaper advertisements but also most other things in this country, apart from laws and taxes, were not for Arabs. . . . It was as though we did not exist."[33] Subordinated suddenly to an alien order that they neither understood nor accepted (and until 1965 subjected to direct military control of most areas in which they lived), their reticence to play the game by the rules was understandable. But it was equally inevitable that, as a result, they would lose out in the shuffle, even if no special obstacles had been placed in their way. In the Israeli system, resources tend to be distributed to groups according to their success in playing the game.

Other circumstances reinforced this "quietism." While the Jewish community had developed and operated a nearly full set of governmental institutions, the Arab community had relied on the Mandatory government to provide most local services. Unaccustomed to organizing on their own behalf beyond the limited and largely confessional institutions of the *millet* system, Israeli Arabs were prone to take a passive posture toward the government, expecting continued delivery of services provided in the past (a highly unrealistic expectation, in view of how the Israeli system operates). In addition, the Arab community had been decimated and demoralized by the departure of most of its members, including nearly all of its natural leadership. The community remaining was fragmented and dispersed, mostly in small villages. Only one city of significance, Nazareth, remained; otherwise villages were cut off from their natural centers in the West Bank and isolated from the Arab world generally, while a large part of their economic infrastructure was either destroyed by the war or (in the case of land) confiscated afterward.[34]

Beyond this, Arab political culture was even less prepared than Jewish political culture to move beyond particularism toward the Western idea of a civic state that transcends ethnic and other differences (the idea that Ben-Gurion tried to promote as *mamlachtiut*). As in traditional Jewish thought, basic differentiation by religious or communal identity was a given, and Arabs were themselves slow to push for equality as citizens in a state that, committed to democratic ideals, was in theory committed to equal civil rights. Nor did they organize to bargain with the Israeli government as a community. The tendency, instead, was to pursue particular or local interests in the form of favors from the government, a strategy that made it relatively easy for government officials to play off Arab groups against each other and to buy peace with minimal concessions.

Government policy alone does not explain such things as the underrepresentation of Arabs in the Knesset. Even though there are informal obstacles and national political organization is weak, there is no formal obstacle to Arabs voting for Arab party lists and achieving a level of representation proportionate to their share of the population. Only one suggested Arab party list—the El Ard movement in the 1960s—has been disqualified from participation in the elections (on grounds that the movement rejected the legitimacy of the State of Israel as a Jewish state). Yet in the 1996 elections only eleven Arabs were elected to the Knesset, as opposed to the fifteen to sixteen that could have been elected if Arab voters all mobilized behind Arab lists. Furthermore this represented a high point in Arab representation, which had never risen above six seats until 1992, when eight Arabs were elected. Many Arab votes have gone to Jewish parties that "bought" Arab support in various ways, or to joint Arab-Jewish parties (principally the Communist Party) whose Knesset candidates were disproportionately Jewish (compared to their voters). The Arab public is politically fragmented and has consistently failed to unite behind a single list. Some remain opposed in principle to participating in Israeli politics, at least on the national level; the turnout among Arab voters has averaged around 70 percent in recent elections, as opposed to roughly 80 percent in the Jewish sector, though in 1996 it rose to 76 percent. Those who do vote remain divided not only ideologically but also tactically, with many voting for Jewish parties because the Arab lists are not likely government coalition partners and are therefore not considered an effective route to influence. Consequently the Arab public has not exploited the possibilities of a proportional representation system almost perfectly designed for the interests of minorities, and only slowly has a new leadership attuned to this possible strategy emerged and made its mark.

Arab unpreparedness or unwillingness to join in the scramble helps to explain why their share of the spoils has been so meager. But another major obstacle is Jewish opposition to the idea of sharing power with the Arabs. Surveys of Israeli public opinion consistently show that strong support for democratic values in principle is often dramatically contradicted on specific policy questions involving the Arab minority. In a 1980 survey, for example, 90 percent of Jewish Israelis supported minority rights generally but only 40 percent were willing to extend full civil equality to Israeli Arabs.[35] In another poll 36 percent of the Jewish public would deny the right of Israeli Arab citizens to hold demonstrations, and 37 percent had reservations on the subject. In 1988, fully 43 percent of a sample favored denying the right to vote to Israeli Arabs, and 68 percent would deny the vote to "non-Zionists who support the formation of a Palestinian state in the West Bank and Gaza alongside Israel."[36] These patterns have been confirmed in numerous studies and have remained fairly consistent since the first serious survey research was carried out.[37]

This attitude is not simply a product of security concerns but is reinforced by strong ethnocentric sentiments. Surveys have repeatedly shown that a majority of the Israeli Jewish public have not had Arab visitors in their homes and do not want Arab families living in their building or neighborhood (though most are ready to have friendly personal relations).[38] There is widespread sentiment that the government does "too much" for Arabs, and a vast majority (74 percent in a 1988 poll) believe that Israel should, in fact, prefer Jews to Arabs in the allocation of resources.[39]

The legal limit, foreshadowed by the El Ard case, was formalized in a 1985 law that was initially aimed at Kach, the racist party of Rabbi Meir Kahane. In addition to barring any party with a racist or antidemocratic program from Knesset elections, this law also ruled out any list that denied the existence of Israel "as the state of the Jewish people." This represents a dilemma for Arab groups that accept the State of Israel as a point of departure but challenge its "Jewish" character; they must either frame their aims in sufficiently ambiguous language or else forego the use of the parliamentary channel (as the Islamic Movement party did before 1996). In the 1992 elections the Progressive List for Peace (PLP), a joint Arab-Jewish party on the dovish end of the spectrum, was challenged on these grounds and was allowed to run only on the basis of the factual determination that there was insufficient evidence that it denied the legitimacy of Israel as a Jewish state; had such evidence existed, it would presumably have been disqualified. In deciding this case, a majority of the judges on the Israeli Supreme Court held that a minimal definition of Israel as the state of the Jewish people included maintenance of a Jewish majority, preference for Jews in immigration (the Law of Return), and recognition of ties with Jews outside of Israel. By this standard a list that advocated the repeal of the Law of Return by regular parliamentary procedures would be disqualified, which narrows the permissible range of debate more than in other democratic states, where only violent challenges to the existing order are ruled out.[40]

Furthermore, this weakness on minority rights, like Zionist attitudes toward Arab nationalism in the past, shows a particular sensitivity toward recognition of Arab rights and activities as a group. There is less reluctance to accord rights on the individual level, particularly in matters of personal advancement, fair treatment by institutions and courts, and material well-being. Even on a group basis, questions related to cultural differences, such as religion and language, are less contentious. The problem arises in moving from these "ethnic" aspects of minority status to collective political and civil rights of Arabs as a national minority. The image of Palestinians as a competing national movement within the same territorial domain arouses some of the deepest insecurities within the Jewish public; dealing with Arabs on a humane basis as individuals is much less problematic. There is strong instinctive resistance to the emergence of autonomous or independent Arab entities in any form, which conflicts with the opposite impulse—to keep the two communities separate. Majorities of 75 percent or more consistently oppose the formation of independent Arab media, universities, unions, or parties and oppose the idea that "Arabs in Israel should organize independently, like Orthodox Jews, in order to advance their vital interests."[41]

Even though access to organized political activity is formally open, therefore, the government has acted in a variety of ways to discourage truly independent national organization. El-Asmar states that "any independent
initiative was met with resistance. Everything was done to ensure its failure
and to present it in a bad light."[42] Political activity was directed to approved
channels, rivalries within the Arab community were exploited, some groups
and leaders were "bought off" by minor concessions, and any effort at organization above the local level was likely to encounter obstruction (the universities, for example, generally refused to recognize separate Arab student
unions). Even after the National Committee of Heads of Local Arab Councils began operating as a de facto representative of Arab interests, government spokesmen refused to meet with it except on municipal issues. Given
this resistance to recognition of, and power-sharing with, the Arab minority
as a group, neither full integration nor separate development proved to be
a workable path to meaningful Arab participation in public life.

INEQUALITY IN LAW AND PRACTICE

The separateness of Arabs as a linguistic and cultural minority is accepted as
a fact of life, and group rights that follow from this—in language, education,
religion—are not challenged. But in the political arena Arabs remain, in
Menachem Hofnung's apt phrase, in the "outer circle" of the system, excluded in ways that go beyond the formal provisions of law.[43] There are no
laws that discriminate explicitly against non-Jewish citizens, but the statutes
that uphold Israel's Jewishness promote inequality by legitimizing preference for Jews. In addition, other laws and arrangements that are formally indifferent to ethnicity nevertheless operate de facto to differentiate between
Jews and Arabs. For example, Israeli citizenship law was formulated to make
the principle of citizenship by descent (*jus sanguinis*) applicable to Jews everywhere, while to Arabs was applied a carefully limited version of citizenship by physical presence (*jus solis*) designed to prevent a massive influx
of Arab refugees (in 1980 a new naturalization law adopted more equal
terms).[44] As noted (chapter 5), emergency regulations have been implemented disproportionately against the Arab minority.

The importance of quasi-governmental institutions in Israeli life also contributes to de facto preferential treatment for Jews. The World Zionist Organization, the Jewish Agency, the Jewish National Fund, the United Jewish
Appeal, and other organizations that grew out of the Zionist movement are
all explicitly Jewish organizations, funded by world Jewry (not the Israeli tax-
payer) and serving Jewish goals. Yet given their role in the development of
Israel, they have a legal status defined by special statutes, and they continue
to provide services that are a government responsibility in most modern
states. The Jewish Agency, for example, is central in support of immigration

and rural settlement, coordinates a massive urban renewal program, and provides numerous other cultural, social, and educational services to the Jewish population. The Jewish National Fund (JNF) acquires and leases land in the name of the Jewish people; even though these lands are administered by the Israel Lands Authority (a government body), under established JNF policy they cannot be "alienated" to non-Jews. This precludes Arab purchase or long-term lease of most land in Israel, and with the remaining non-JNF lands there is still considerable de facto discrimination in favor of Jewish agricultural movements.[45]

Army service is another basis for de facto discrimination, since nearly all Jews but very few Arabs (apart from the Druze community) do the obligatory tour of duty. The military interlude is not only a defining rite of passage for both men and women in Israeli society but is also the source of important benefits in employment, housing, and education during the critical years of young adulthood. Though few in either community suggest compelling Arabs to serve in the army, many Jewish Israelis justify the lack of equal rights on grounds of lack of equal duties. And there is a general tendency to regard the structural impediments, such as JNF land policy or soldiers' benefits, not as discrimination against Arabs but as legitimate preferences accorded Jews in a Jewish state. Preference for one group logically means relative disadvantage for others, but public attitudes often do not admit this logic.

The most significant use of "neutral" state machinery in de facto discrimination was the widespread appropriation of Arab land for public use, which almost always meant Jewish settlement or cultivation. During the first three decades of statehood a substantial portion of land owned by Arab citizens was expropriated under these procedures.[46] Other lands of Arab residents were put under the control of the custodian for Absentees' Property, who in theory dealt only with the abandoned property of Arab refugees; these lands were made available (like refugee land generally) for Jewish settlement. The legal basis in this case involved creating the oxymoronic category of "present absentees" for Arabs still living under Israeli jurisdiction who had not been in their regular place of residence when official registration took place. The Military Government generally prevented such people from returning to their homes and reclaiming their property, based in part on the assumption that their absence was proof of hostility to Israel.[47]

The end result was that major disparities in political power, economic well-being, and most other measures remained substantially unchanged over time. Though in 1992 Arabs constituted 19 percent of Israel's population, they held only seventeen of 1,300 senior government positions, and only ten of 5,000 university posts. In total government employment in eight governmental departments, according to a cabinet subcommittee report of 1987, they held only 5 percent of the positions. There has never been an Arab cabinet minister or Supreme Court justice, nor has any large economic institution in Israel ever been headed by an Arab; the highest positions achieved have been as district judges, deputy ministers, and (once) as Deputy Speaker of the Knesset. Even more striking was the lack of Arab appointees as head of the Arab Department in the Ministry of Education, as head of the Department of Muslim Affairs in the Ministry of Religious Affairs, or as director of Arabic-language broadcasts on radio.[48]

The economic gap also remains substantial; for example, in 1994, the average density in Jewish homes was .99 persons per room, compared to 1.70 persons per room in non-Jewish homes. Among Jews, 32.9 percent held scientific, professional, or managerial positions, while among non-Jews the figure was 14.4 percent. The median years of education for persons fifteen years and over was 12.1 for Jews and 10.0 for non-Jews.[49] In 1991 a report to a Knesset committee concluded that Arabs constituted 55 percent of those below the poverty line in Israel.[50]

Measured against the situation in 1948, on the other hand, there was dramatic progress in absolute terms and significant progress in reducing the gap between the two communities. In 1961, for example, the median years of schooling had been 8.4 for Jews and only 1.2 for non-Jews.[51] The economic gap, though substantial for a developed economy, was considerably reduced over time, and Israeli Arabs were higher on most measures than the West Bank Arab population with whom it shared a common point of departure (though not in all regards; West Bank Arabs had a far higher rate of participation in higher education, for example).[52] Of course comparison to the West Bank and Arab countries does not relieve the sense of relative deprivation that Israeli Arabs feel toward the Jewish society with which they are in closest contact. In addition, integration into the Israeli economy has high costs: as a recent survey demonstrated, the shift from agriculture to a service-based economy has meant less self-employment, greater dependence on jobs in the Jewish sector (involving large-scale commuting), and a growing problem of lack of opportunities for better educated and better skilled young Arabs.[53]

Since the Jewish and Arab school systems are inevitably separate, if only because of language, they provide a clear index of de facto discrimination despite formal equality and impressive advances in the Arab sector. As Kretzmer notes, by almost any measure—expenditure per pupil, teacher training, facilities, dropout rate—"the system still has a long way to go" before Arab schools are "separate but equal."[54] Government policy toward Arab schools has been more concerned with control of content than with the overall quality of education, while the inequality in budgetary allocations is part of the general inequity in public services.

The inferiority of Arab schools puts graduates at a double disadvantage on the university level; as there is no Arab university, they must continue their studies in Hebrew and at a level geared to Jewish secondary schools. This factor together with the lack of jobs for college graduates as well as psychological and practical obstacles (such as the difficulty of finding housing near Israeli universities) help account for the low rate of university attendance compared both to Israeli Jews and to Arab populations elsewhere.[55]

The shift from self-employment to jobs in the Jewish sector has also exposed more of the Arab work force to job discrimination. Though Israeli law explicitly forbids discrimination in employment on religious, ethnic, or national grounds, there is no enforcement mechanism outside normal criminal procedures. Consequently such discrimination is basically unchecked and prevails widely; in practice it is sanctioned by the norms of Jewish economic and social life.[56] Of course Jewish workers begin with enormous educational and social advantages, to which are added "security considerations" and "local preferences" that exclude Arabs. While the occupational structure has changed radically, therefore, this in itself has done little to improve Arabs' relative economic standing. As they enter the general Israeli labor market, Arabs are segregated into low-status jobs. While the percentage of employed Arabs engaged in agriculture dropped from 46.8 percent in 1960 to 7 percent in 1990, the percentage of skilled and unskilled workers grew from 31.7 percent to 52 percent (among Jews, agriculture fell from 14.4 percent to 3.4 percent and manual labor from 32.6 percent to 23.3 percent). While Arabs in the professions grew from 4.2 percent to 12.2 percent of all working Arabs, the proportion in the Jewish labor force went from 12.3 percent to 26.9 percent.[57]

In short, despite considerable improvement in absolute terms, Arabs within Israel remain on the periphery of the system. While inequality between the two communities has been reduced, it remains substantial. Israeli Arabs occupy a position similar to that of Diaspora Jewry seen through Zionist lens: not actors in history but the objects of actions by others. Would the response to this perceived weakness be assimilation to prevailing patterns or assertion of particularity and independence? The Zionist response had been a complex synthesis of both responses; trends among Israeli Arabs are no less complex.

ISRAELIZATION OR PALESTINIZATION?

One clear trend among Arabs in Israel has been variously labeled as "Palestinization," "radicalization," or "politicization." It includes the growth of solidarity with Arab Palestinians outside Israel, the rise of radical movements, and a generally greater level of political activism and self-assertion, with the choice of label reflecting the relative emphasis among these elements. The trend results from both external and internal forces: the growth of Palestinian nationalism as represented by the Palestine Liberation Organization (PLO), and important transformations within the Arab community in Israel.

The resurgence of "Palestinianism" among Arabs outside Israel, following the 1967 war, was bound to touch Israeli Arabs also. The war brought the two populations back into direct contact after two decades of artificial separation. Arabs in the West Bank and Gaza, and Arabs in Israel, were now part of a single "control system."[58] Inevitably the line that had been drawn became increasingly blurred over time as contact was renewed and deepened, not just in politics but also in social, cultural, and economic spheres. Furthermore, contact with Israeli Arabs did not greatly moderate the attitudes of other Palestinians to Israel, as some Israeli Jews hoped. Instead, what developed was largely a "one-way channel," with the West Bank and Gaza influencing the attitudes of Israeli Arabs.[59]

Changes within the Arab community include a higher level of education, rapid growth of professional and middle classes, emergence of new leadership to fill the initial vacuum, accumulation of grievances and frustrations over time, and development of political skills and tactics geared to Israeli reality. Increased resort to radical tactics, including extraparliamentary methods, was a predictable response not unlike that of Jewish groups seeking to secure their interests. Those who see the process more as "politicization," such as Sammy Smooha, emphasize these internal developments and the efforts to achieve concrete results.[60] In any event the trend in Arab voting, at least since 1959, was abandonment of establishment-oriented "moderate" Arab parties (which eventually disappeared) and growing support of "radical" parties, first the Communists and after 1984 the Progressive List for Peace. Both of these parties, while formally offering joint Jewish-Arab lists, appealed primarily to Arab voters, spoke the language of Arab nationalism, and sought the unofficial favor of the PLO.[61]

Even more radical movements had appeared by the 1970s, among them the Sons of the Village and the National Progressive Movement. These groups not only supported the undiluted original PLO program, which called for armed struggle and refused any Jewish claims in Palestine, but also denied any distinction between Palestinian Arabs on both sides of the border. During the 1980s resurgent Islam, nourished by contact with Islamic life in the territories and the general advance of Islamism in the Arab world, became the rallying point for rejectionists among Israeli Arabs. Paradoxically given an operational freedom in Israel not enjoyed by its counterparts in most Arab states, the Islamic Movement established a firm foothold in Arab towns and villages by the end of the decade, winning control of several municipalities. Though stating its goals in terms that did not directly challenge Israel's right to exist as a Jewish state, the Islamic Movement did not enter Knesset elections until 1996. According to some estimates, the Islamic

Movement had the allegiance of one-quarter to one-third of Israeli Muslims and was "poised to become the leading force" among Israeli Arabs generally.[62] But later in 1995 an Israeli Arab researcher reported that Islamism had peaked and was now waning; in 1988, 28 percent of Israeli Muslims had declared themselves as "very religious," 43 percent as "traditional," and 24 percent as "not religious," while in 1995 the respective figures were 22 percent, 27 percent, and 52 percent—not that different from the figures among Israeli Jews.[63] Furthermore, when the Islamic Movement finally did compete in the 1996 Knesset elections in coalition with the Arab Democratic Party (ADP), it won only four seats (the ADP alone had won two in 1992).

Whatever the extent of Palestinization or radicalization, it is only one dimension of the total picture. Arabs in the Jewish state were also subject to a process of "Israelization" that over time differentiated them from their fellow Palestinians in the West Bank and Gaza. However imperfectly integrated into Israeli economy and society, Arab citizens were exposed to Israeli life and to the cultural patterns of a modernizing state. They could not totally identify with Israel, but its impact on their thinking and behavior was undeniable, and over time they came to recognize that their future was tied to Israel.

Despite the lack of a consistent policy promoting integration, assimilative influences made their mark over the decades. Participation in what had been exclusively Jewish frameworks gradually increased; by the end of the 1980s, Arabs accounted for almost 15 percent of Histadrut membership, close to their proportionate numbers in the work force.[64] Almost three-quarters of Israeli Arabs could speak Hebrew (among men eighteen to twenty-five years old the figure was 92 percent), and nearly as many (72 percent) could also read and write Hebrew. Over 53 percent claimed to read Hebrew newspapers regularly.[65] The number of Israeli Arabs who are literate in the Jewish national tongue is clearly greater than the number of non-Israeli Jews who can speak, read, and write modern Hebrew. In addition, despite the recent visibility of the Islamic Movement, Israeli Arabs (like Israeli Jews) have as noted become more secular over time.

Smooha's surveys of Israeli Arabs in 1976, 1980, 1985, and 1988 represent the most extensive study of attitudes within that community. While opinion surveys do not tell the entire story, they are clearly one important measure and certainly provide a sense of trends over time when the same questions and methods are repeated. Smooha's results provide massive evidence of Israelization, as well as Palestinization.[66] By 1988, for example, 55.5 percent of Israeli Arabs surveyed felt that their style of life and daily behavior was more similar to that of Jews in Israel than to that of Arabs in the West Bank and Gaza.[67] Fully 64.3 percent said that they felt more at home in Israel than in an Arab country, and only 13.5 percent rejected Israel's right to exist (down from 20.5 percent in 1976). This did not mean that fundamental disagreements disappeared; a consistent majority in all surveys continue to regard Zionism as racism and to oppose Israel as a Jewish-Zionist state.[68] In other words, while they accept Israel as a state and their own citizenship within it, they object to aspects of Israeli ideology that they see as exclusivist principles barring Arabs from true civic equality. In the words of an Israeli Arab researcher, they generally accept "the legitimacy granted by the international community . . . to Israeli sovereignty over the part of Palestine that became Israel. This is the distinction between Israel's *a priori* right to exist and its right to exist *ex post facto*."[69]

Consequently there is also general consensus that the fight to achieve equality should be conducted within the limits of Israeli law. Other surveys have confirmed that nearly all Israeli Arabs consider themselves strongly loyal to the state, and a majority even favor the conscription of Arabs to some form of national service as a parallel to military service among Jewish Israelis.[70] The number of Israeli Arabs convicted of security offenses has been very small; even during the peak periods of unrest and violence in the West Bank and Gaza, comparatively few Arabs within Israel chose to challenge Israeli rule outside normal channels.[71]

Israeli Arabs certainly identify with West Bank and Gaza Arabs and favor the establishment of a Palestinian state in those territories, but they also distinguish between this issue and their own interests within Israel. Only a small minority (14.4 percent in 1976 and 7.5 percent in 1988) stated a definite willingness to move to a Palestinian state alongside Israel.[72] As observers of Israeli Arab politics repeatedly note, priority is given to local issues such as unequal budget allocations rather than to broader nationalist issues, and speakers who dwell on the latter are often interrupted by demands for attention to "peace at home." In certain respects the aspirations of Arabs within Israel have diverged significantly from those of Arabs living under occupation, reflecting the substantial difference in their status, experience, and prospects.[73]

Arab residents on both sides of the border separating Israel from the West Bank and Gaza testify to its continuing importance despite decades of Israeli presence in the territories and the assertion of Palestinian identity among Israeli Arabs. In spite of increased contact, there has been little social and cultural integration and very little intermarriage between the two communities. As a leading Israeli Arab intellectual remarks, "the gap between us and them has never closed. They are, for most of us, foreigners."[74] While supporting the drive of Palestinians outside Israel to independence and statehood, most of those within Israel distinguish this sharply from their own fight for recognition and equality as a national minority. There is a sense of different situations with different goals and different strategies. Since accepting the framework of a two-state solution to the Israeli-Palestinian conflict (instead of single Palestinian state in all of Palestine), the PLO has also dealt with Israeli Arab issues as an internal Israeli matter and not as part of the international negotiating agenda.[75]

Palestinization and Israelization appear at first to be contradictory processes, and indeed they often do pull in different directions. Yet both trends are clearly taking place at the same time, and in some senses they may even reinforce each other. Growing skill in Israeli politics, for example, makes possible more effective assertion of Arab or Palestinian identity; "nationalistic awakening shows an integrative as well as a divisive pattern of behavior."[76] Many are in any event influenced simultaneously by both developments, while others are pushed more in one direction than the other. This helps account for the spectrum of attitudes that exists within the Israeli Arab community.

Based on his surveys, Smooha divides Israeli Arabs into four major groups politically: roughly 11 percent are "accommodationists," who are ready to work through the system as it is; about 39 percent are "reservationists," who seek to change some aspects of the system but are reconciled to doing so within the existing framework; 40 percent are "oppositionists," who accept Israel as a state but not its Jewish-Zionist character; and 10 percent are "rejectionists," who oppose Israel's existence and advocate replacing it with an Arab Palestinian state, if necessary by extralegal or even violent means. This division has been fairly stable over the period of the surveys, with some drop on both ends of the spectrum—accommodationists and rejectionists—and some increase in the oppositionists in the middle, reflecting the growth of militancy without radicalization of goals.[77] The typology also corresponds roughly to Arab voting patterns since 1977, with about half (accommodationists and reservationists) supporting Jewish parties and the other half backing "outside" parties (in the case of oppositionists) or not participating (the rejectionists).

Before the 1970s, fewer than a quarter of Arab voters voted for oppositionist parties (the various Communist lists), while around half had supported minority lists affiliated with Jewish parties and the rest had voted directly for Jewish parties. The major shift took place in the 1970s when, as the minority lists disappeared, the remaining accommodationists and reservationists voted for Jewish parties, the ranks of the oppositionists grew, and the rate of participation dropped. This pattern remained fairly consistent thereafter, though new groups appeared within the various camps.[78] The results of the 1967 war had helped to stir the Arab population out of its previous passivity and fragmentation. The renewed contact with other Arabs, and especially the spillover from unrest in the West Bank and Gaza, served as stimulus and inspiration. The growth of a deep split among Israelis over the future of the territories also created a greater opportunity for Arabs, voting as a bloc, to gain political power. Arabs could, in theory, act as holder of the balance (the historic role of religious parties) or at least form part of a "blocking majority" keeping narrow right-wing governments out of power.[79]

The rise of Arab protest followed patterns of Jewish protest: both had a practical focus, a low level of violence, and an emphasis on "self-help," and both took forms indicating "that sector's acceptance of the country's democratic norms."[80] Much Arab political activity focused on the local level where it could be more effective, given the concentration of Arab population geographically and the fact that, unlike elsewhere, Arabs remained in villages after they left agriculture. The localization of politics is also tied to the strength of kinship structure (*hamula* or clan) in towns and villages, which was initially revived by Israeli authorities as a tool of control but survived the end of military rule.[81]

From its local base Arab politics inevitably moved to develop independent organizations and voices on a national level. The Committee for the Defense of Arab Lands, established before Land Day, became prominent as a result of it. Land Day—March 30, 1976—was a day of protests against land expropriations and marked the emergence of Israeli Arab protest. By 1980 leading figures in Arab public life across the political spectrum planned a "Congress of Arab Masses" to organize politically; as minister of defense, Menachem Begin banned the congress under the 1945 emergency regulations, but the momentum continued to build.[82] The most important body, the National Committee of Heads of Local Arab Councils, emerged directly from the local Arab governments. The National Committee evolved into a national body bargaining with the government over budgetary allotments and other practical issues, using such accepted techniques as work sanctions, strikes, and demonstrations. As the most representative and truly national Arab body, it became the de facto spokesman for the community and its most influential voice, even though the Israeli government formally refused to deal with it on anything but local issues. During the 1980s a "Higher Surveillance Committee of the Arab Population," based on the National Committee together with Arab Knesset members and representatives of other Arab bodies, was formed to coordinate demands and strategies in the Arab sector.[83]

The outbreak of the uprising or *intifada* against Israeli rule in the territories, in December 1987, immediately raised the prospect that the spirit of rebellion would spread into Israel itself. Would Israeli Arabs follow the lead of Arabs in the West Bank and Gaza, blurring the line that had divided the two communities? There was little doubt of a strong sense of identification with fellow Palestinians: the Israeli Arab press and leaders praised the *intifada* and condemned Israeli occupation in language hardly different from that used in the territories. A one-day general strike, called as a demonstration of solidarity, was almost universally observed in the Arab sector; some thirty-five strikes and demonstrations linked to the uprising took place in its first eighteen months. The number of politically related acts of violence attributed to Israeli Arabs rose from sixty-nine in 1987 to 208 in 1988.[84]

At the same time, this sense of solidarity did not translate into a significant shift in basic political aims and attitudes. Most of the protests were organized locally and followed the legal requirements for demonstrations. The level of violence, though increased, was still very low—a tiny fraction of that in the West Bank and Gaza. Israeli Arab leaders perceived themselves not as having joined the *intifada* but as extending moral support to it within the limits of Israeli law. Events in the territories strengthened their belief in independent organization to secure their own interests by democratic means, but this was already the direction of their thinking. Some Arab observers asserted that the *intifada* actually brought differences between the two communities into sharper focus and pushed Israeli Arabs to the periphery in the Palestinian arena.[85]

By the early 1980s, the decline of affiliated lists led Jewish parties to put Arab candidates on their regular party slates instead. But Arab Knesset members elected by this route, though relatively moderate in their aims, tended to be more assertive in their style.[86] The question was a practical one: would it be more effective to work through Jewish parties or to establish totally independent frameworks? In either case, Arab leaders were becoming more proficient in playing the political game according to the rules. In June 1989, Arabs used their numbers in the Union of Local Authorities (representing 48 of 173 localities) as a bargaining lever in elections, demanding proportional representation in all the union bodies. In March 1990, a strike of local Arab councils led to the rescheduling of municipal debt payments, and in July and August of 1994, Arab mayors held an extended protest opposite the Knesset, in classic Israeli style, to secure implementation of promised parity in Arab municipal budget allocations.

The question was whether to make Jewish parties compete for Arab votes or to organize Arab lists that were truly independent but still moderate enough to work within the system, unlike the oppositionist Communist lists or Progressive List for Peace. The second strategy was natural and logical under the conditions of Israeli politics, but would be effective only if such lists could win enough seats to bargain as potential members of a governing coalition and if Jewish parties would in fact bargain with them. The *intifada* sparked a move in the second direction when Labor Knesset Member Abd el-Wahhab Darawshe resigned from his party in protest over the army's handling of the uprising and formed the Arab Democratic Party to contest the 1988 elections. If such a party were to gain half a dozen seats—less than half of the potential Arab vote—it could conceivably put Israeli Arabs in an unprecedented position to bargain in consociational style. The ADP platform stressed this strategy, presenting itself as a potential coalition partner within the broad Israeli consensus while at the same time supporting Palestinian statehood in the territories and trying to gain favor with the PLO.[87]

The ADP won one seat in 1988, two seats in 1992, and (in coalition with the Islamic Movement) four in 1996. During the extended governmental crisis of 1990 Shimon Peres had invited Darawshe, as the sole ADP Knesset member, to join a projected (but stillborn) Labor-led government, lending encouragement to proponents of this approach. But in 1992 Yitzhak Rabin, new leader of the Labor Party, was able to form a center-left government without the ADP, knowing that in any event he could count on their two votes and the three votes of the Democratic Front for Peace and Equality (DFPE, the Communist list) as part of a "blocking majority" that would prevent Likud from forming a narrow government with right-wing and religious parties. Rabin could also count on ADP and DFPE support on critical votes involving the peace process, such as the narrow 61 to 59 approval of the Interim Peace Agreement on October 6, 1995, without including them in the government. Arab political forces were not yet real players in the system, despite greater recognition of their presence.

THE TEST OF ISRAELI DEMOCRACY

Israeli Arabs are not yet partners in the political system, but if present trends continue the power-sharing patterns of Jewish politics could come to encompass the non-Jewish population. From an initial situation of overwhelming suspicion and de facto domination on one side, against overwhelming alienation and demoralization on the other, the overall trend was toward gradual, if halting and incomplete, liberalization. The passage of discriminatory laws (though not their application) ended in the early 1950s. The Military Government in Arab areas, and most related "security zones," were phased out by the early 1970s (one particularly controversial zone, Military Area 9 in the Galilee, was finally opened in 1986). The expropriation of land, beyond legitimate public need, came virtually to a halt. Laws and procedures were regularized over time; by the 1980s little use was made of emergency regulations in the Arab sector.[88]

By the early 1990s there was visible representation of Arabs in some fields of public life, especially health, education, police, media, arts, and the Histadrut. The first Arab ambassador representing Israel (to Finland) was appointed in 1995. Though the Rabin government did not take Arab parties into the coalition, it was more active in the Arab sector than its predecessors. It established a Committee of Directors-General of Ministries, under the director-general of the prime minister's office, to oversee implementation of its commitments toward Arab citizens. The post of advisor on Arab affairs was abolished; instead, a new head of minority affairs was given the more modest role of coordinating the Committee of Directors-General. The idea was to put Arab citizens on the same footing as Jewish citizens, dealing directly with governmental ministries rather than being relegated to a special supervised channel.[89]

Civic organizations became more active in pressing the government on these issues. Sikkuy (the Association for the Advancement of Equal Opportunity), a joint Jewish-Arab body promoting equality and integration, began to monitor government performance systematically on the model of human rights groups elsewhere. By 1996 it could report considerable progress: committed to closing the disparity in allocations to local governments, the government had in fact increased the budgets in the Arab and Druze sectors almost threefold in 1996 as against 1992. The process of equalizing education budgets and child allowances had nearly been completed. The number of Arabs in the civil service, though still low, increased as specific slots were created for qualified Arab applicants.[90]

Jewish-Arab relations within Israel are the acid test of Israeli democracy. Critics on both ends of the spectrum argue that Israel cannot be both Jewish and democratic if it has a large Arab minority; either it must shed its Jewishness in order to remain democratic (the position of Arab oppositionists), or it must exclude or expel Arabs in order to remain Jewish (as Israeli ultranationalists urge). Posing this as a stark "either-or" choice, however, ignores the reality that all nation-states must in some fashion balance the demands of cultural, ethnic, and historical particularity against universalistic principles. Israel faces the difficulty, in Kretzmer's words, of managing the tension between two conceptions of nationhood: "As a democratic state Israel must serve the needs of all its citizens; as the state of the Jewish people its function is to pursue particularistic goals."[91] This tension helps explain the contradiction between formal equality, where laws reflect universal standards, and informal discrimination where Jewishness serves as the de facto point of reference. But Israel is hardly the only state facing this dilemma.

Sammy Smooha has suggested that Israel belongs to a category of "ethnic democracies" that combine a dominant ethnic character with democratic rights for all. He posits this category as a third democratic alternative for deeply divided societies, in addition to majoritarianism and consociationalism, and defines it as "the extension of political and civil rights to individuals and certain collective rights to minorities with institutionalized dominance over the state by one of the ethnic groups," or as "a system that combines a genuine democracy for all with institutionalized dominance for one of its constituent groups."[92] Yoav Peled has developed the idea of ethnic democracy, in the Israeli case, as a confluence of two types of citizenship: "republican" citizenship with communal dimensions for Jews, and "liberal" citizenship with civil and political rights, but no share of communality, for Arabs.[93]

But does "ethnic democracy" represent a third type on the majoritarian-consociational axis? The distinction between majoritarian and consociational (or consensus) democracies is in the broadest sense a question of undiluted majority rule against a broader diffusion of power, and operationally it is defined by such measures as the size of governing coalitions, the presence of checks and balances, unicameralism or bicameralism, two-party or multiparty systems, the number of important political dimensions, proportional vs. nonproportional electoral systems, federalism or centralization, and entrenchment of basic laws. These are features in terms of which any democratic government, including those "with institutionalized dominance of one ethnic group," could be measured. Ethnic democracies do not, in other words, constitute a third type opposed to majoritarian or consociational democracies but may like other democracies be measured in terms of their majoritarian or consociational elements. We expect successful ethnic democracies to tend to consociationalism, but in fact some have majoritarian features (such as parliamentary dominance, district elections, or weak federalism).

Ethnic democracy as defined does not measure the mechanics of majority rule but addresses the relationship of nations to states. In this role it is an extremely useful concept in discussion of minority rights. The basic idea—dominance by one ethnic group in a democratic framework—comes suggestively close to the classic definition of a nation-state. A "nation" has been defined as "a people connected by supposed ties of blood generally manifested by community of language, religion, and customs, and by a sense of common interest and interrelation."[94] As the idea became prevalent that every such nation had a democratic right of self-determination, the dominant model became the nation-state: "A state organized for the government of a 'nation' (or perhaps two or more closely related nations), whose territory is determined by national boundaries, and whose law is determined, at least in part, by national customs and expectations."[95] Since ethnic borders seldom correspond perfectly to political borders, the "national" majority in any given state constitutes a dominant ethnic group with respect to minorities not identified with that nationhood, no matter how democratic the procedures. All nationalisms have a potential problem with minority rights, as Jewish history demonstrates very well; a hostile majority can suppress a minority by democratic as well as nondemocratic means. The critical question is how far ethnonational identity is intertwined with the very definition of the state, and this is a matter of degree.

In theory liberal democracy is indifferent to distinctions among citizens. But no political system exists in a social, cultural, linguistic, and historical vacuum; even the most liberal regime is shaped by its particular context. A nation-state, formed around a central "nation" however defined, bears some particularistic features. This imprint will be lighter where the prevailing model of nationality is assimilative and where it corresponds to the concept of citizenship. In this "New World" model, state forms nations: there is a territorial focus, citizenship is extended to those born within its borders (*jus solis*), and naturalization is not tied to ethnicity, culture, or descent. Such a pattern predominates not only in New World nations formed by immigration but also in some states with natural borders (for example, islands), in some older states where borders shaped identity (France, Britain), and in newly emerging states where "artificial" borders are beginning to shape identity. Even here, however, a sense of particularity—Americanness, Australianness, Frenchness—remains and may be a strong political factor.

Clearly this sense is stronger in the "Old World" model, where nation forms state: there is an ethnic focus with citizenship distinguished from nationality and often extended on grounds of descent (*jus sanguinis*), while naturalization is more difficult since it is tied to ethnicity, culture, or language. This pattern predominates in some areas with well-defined historical nations (Central and Eastern Europe, Asia), in newer states formed when the concept of nation-state was at its peak (post- World War I), and in some situations where the mismatch between ethnic and political borders is especially dramatic (Vietnam, Korea, Bangladesh, Yugoslavia).

As a product of the nation-state idea at its most intense, Israel ranks toward the more ethnic end of this continuum. It is not, however, in a category by itself; there are other states in which ethnicity is likewise closely intertwined with the definition of the state. Many states, for example, confer citizenship by descent or ethnicity (or both) to those who can establish an ancestral link.[96] The Israeli Law of Return is an unusual case of *jus sanguinis* in that it recognizes an ancestral link over two millennia, but other states have similar policies. Germany, which generally follows the concept of a community of descent, has as part of its 1949 Basic Law a provision granting the right of return to refugees of German ethnic stock, which led to a massive influx of "Germans" from Eastern Europe whose ancestral link was measured in centuries.[97] The Soviet Union, following World War II, adopted similar laws of return for persons of Armenian, Russian, Ukrainian, or Byelorussian national origin who wished to enter the Soviet Union and receive Soviet citizenship. During the decolonization process the imperial powers (Britain, France, Netherlands, Italy, Belgium) readmitted "nationals" who were generations removed from the home country.[98]

Israel's link to ethnicity is not unique. But the Law of Return and other explicitly Jewish features do place it among the more ethnic nation-states, and thus among the more problematic in terms of ethnic minorities. How does it compare in this regard to other ethnic democracies? In 1995 there were approximately seventy-one states in the world with a dominant ethnic group, defined by language, of over 50 percent but less than 95 percent (less than 50 percent would indicate a multiethnic society, while states with less than 5 percent linguistic minorities can be considered homogeneous).[99] Of these seventy-one states with a dominant ethnic group but a significant minority or minorities, twenty-six were ranked as "free" on political rights and civil liberties in the annual Freedom House survey of 1994–1995.[100] This could serve as an operationalized, if somewhat relaxed, definition of "ethnic democracies," but by any label it is a relevant comparison group.[101]

From Israel's perspective an important question is how many of these twenty-six states (which include Israel) practice some form of ethnic power-sharing and how many do not, and whether this is related to the size of minorities. Arend Lijphart's four basic characteristics of power-sharing are (1) participation in the governing coalition or executive, (2) a high degree of group autonomy, (3) proportionality in representation and allocation, and (4) a formal or informal minority veto on matters of fundamental importance.[102] Addressing only ethnic divisions, eleven of the twenty-six states meet at least three of these four conditions (see Table 7: the numbers following each state indicate the size of the dominant ethnic group, or linguistic majority, as a percentage of the total population; for each state, linguistic minorities larger than 5 percent of the total population are listed in descending order of size).

In the fifteen ethnic democracies without ethnic power-sharing, the average size of the dominant group was 79 percent, while in the eleven power-sharing states the dominant group averaged only 67 percent (64 percent without the exceptional case of Finland). Put differently, only one (Finland) of the twelve democratic states with linguistic minorities smaller than 20 percent of the total population used power-sharing techniques in its ethnic relations, while ten (all but Belize, Cape Verde, Estonia, and Latvia) of the fourteen democratic states with minorities larger than 20 percent did so.[103] Clearly accommodation of ethnic groups above this threshold, in an ethnic democracy, ordinarily involves the use of explicit power-sharing techniques that by their nature dilute the prevailing ethnicity of the state. With an Arab minority of about 19 percent, Israel stands near this threshold, or fulcrum: close to the upper limit on the size of minorities that states have generally been able to incorporate successfully into functioning majoritarian democracies, and already in the range where most states have found consociationalism more applicable.[104] To judge by experience elsewhere, it would appear that Israel could conceivably integrate this minority without wide use of power-sharing techniques, but that such techniques may be advisable and would have been absolutely essential if Israel had tried to incorporate the occupied territories democratically.

Does the existence of a broader Arab-Israeli conflict make Israel's minority issue unique? One of the more curious defenses of de facto discrimination is the argument that Israeli Arabs, as an ethnic minority linked to an external threat, represent a unique security problem. This is not a unique case: there are Greeks in Turkey and in Turkish Cyprus as well as Turks in Greek Cyprus; Hindus in Pakistan and Moslems in India; Tamils in Sri

TABLE 7   Ethnic Democracies with Linguistic Minorities Larger than
5 Percent (in percentage)

No Ethnic Power-Sharing			Ethnic Power-Sharing		
	Size of Dominant Ethnonational Group	Sizes of Linguistic Minorities		Size of Dominant Ethnonational Group	Sizes of Linguistic Minorities
Bahamas	85	15	Belgium	58	39
Belize	60	25, 8, 7	Benin	66	14, 13, 5
Bulgaria	85	8	Botswana	75	12, 6
Cape Verde	70	30	Canada	62	25
Ecuador	93	7	Finland	94	6
Estonia	65	32	Guyana	78	21
France	87	7	Malawi	59	15, 14
Israel	81	19	Mauritius	54	39
Latvia	54	33	South Africa	55	20, 16, 9
Lithuania	80	11, 6	Spain	70	21, 7
Mongolia	90	7	Switzerland	65	19, 12
New Zealand	81	9			
Panama	81	14			
Slovakia	87	11			
U.S.	89	6			

SOURCES: *Maps 'N' Facts* (Broderbund Software, 1994); *Freedom in the World: The Annual Survey of Political Rights and Civil Liberties 1994–1995* (Freedom House, 1995), 683–84.

Lanka; Arabs in Iran; Albanians in Macedonia; Chinese in Vietnam and elsewhere in Southeast Asia; Somalis in Ethiopia; and many potentially hostile tribes with cross-border links in Africa. In the past, the presence of ethnic Japanese in the United States and Canada, Armenians in Turkey, of Germans throughout Eastern Europe, and of various "suspect" ethnic groups in the Soviet Union has been a source of concern to these governments.

The treatment of these "enemy minorities" has usually been dismal. The fate of Armenians during World War I, of Japanese in the United States during World War II, and of German minorities during and after World War II all testify to the corrosiveness of wartime suspicions. In recent decades the expulsion of suspect minorities has been commonplace, long before civil strife in the former Yugoslavia gave "ethnic cleansing" a bad name. It is noteworthy that among the twenty-six ethnic states rated as democratic, only the Baltic states parallel Israel in having sizable minorities linked to a potentially hostile neighbor. Clearly such links do put minority groups in a more complicated and vulnerable position.

One useful index related to this pattern is the exclusion of ethnic minorities from military service; again, Israel is not unique in selective conscription. Among democratic nations, Britain did not apply the draft to Ireland in World War I or to Northern Ireland in World War II, while in Canada the conscription of French Canadians was a contentious issue in both world wars. Elsewhere minorities have been excluded from the armed forces, in whole or in part, in Burma, Fiji, Guyana, Iraq, Malaysia, Pakistan, Sri Lanka, and a number of African states.[105] Military service often serves minorities as a path to gaining legitimacy and acceptance, as it has with the Druze community in Israel.

Given the depth of the ethnic division, lessons from experience elsewhere, and the particular strengths of Israeli politics, the growth of consociationalism in Arab-Jewish relations seems inevitable. Israeli Jews wish to remain Jewish: that, after all, was the basic idea of Zionism. By the same token, Israeli Arabs are a nonassimilating minority with their own culture, language, and identity. Democratic governments—and even many nondemocratic regimes—usually achieve long-term stability in such cases by power-sharing based on the explicit recognition of two or more ethnic communities.[106]

This may require development of an overarching identity, a common framework that transcends the division into Jew and Arab, to counter the feeling of Israeli Arabs that they do not belong. Though the name *Israel* is decidedly Jewish in origin, Arab citizens have often expressed interest in expanding the concept, as a territorial label, to encompass non-Jews as well. This would in essence create the common civic space that has existed only in theory. Israeli Arab novelist Anton Shammas has asked for "a new definition of the word 'Israeli,' so that it will include me as well. . . . " Responding from a Jewish perspective, A. B. Yehoshua—a leading Israeli literary figure—noted that during the First Temple period "Jewish religious identity was not at all a necessary element of Israeli identity" and projects a gradual cultural symbiosis leading to a common Israeli identity.[107]

Introduction of power-sharing would be eased by the fact that it already works on the Jewish side. Power-sharing among Jewish groups, messy and contentious yet effective, already serves as a model of independent organization, collective bargaining, and direct action within the framework of law. On the municipal level, a "system of elite consultations" kept Arab-Jewish peace in Jerusalem for many decades, providing another model.[108] Survey data show that support for consociationalism has risen over the years both among Jews and Arabs.[109]

Whether conceived as consociationalism or as reform of ethnic democracy, specific proposals for Jewish-Arab accommodation tend to be similar. Most involve explicit recognition of Israeli Arabs as a national minority with rights as a group, such as an act of the Knesset affirming that "the Arab minority in the State of Israel is an integral part of the Jewish State and is entitled to full recognition of its specificity within the framework of law."[110] Recognition of Arabs as a minority could involve making state symbols and practices more inclusive; for example, by having "Israeli" holidays that draw in both communities.

Second, following from such recognition would be group autonomy in cultural and educational affairs, with election of a representative body for the purpose and possibly including establishment of an Arab-language university. Functional autonomy in these areas may be necessary to counter the growth of support for territorial autonomy or total separation.

Finally, interethnic consociationalism will get a tremendous boost when Arab parties that accept the framework of a Jewish state are brought into government coalitions. Nothing else would provide as clear an index of the extension of Israeli power-sharing to the Arab community.

This is in addition, of course, to a fair allocation of resources and equality before the law. Nothing in the "Jewish" nature of the state inherently compels discrimination in local government budgets, health and welfare services, education, economic opportunities, or treatment in the courts. In fact all of the above measures could be implemented without renouncing the essential Jewishness of Israel as a nation-state or ethnic democracy. What they involve is some dilution of the relationship between ethnicity and statehood, moving Israel more toward the center of the spectrum on this dimension. There always remains some sense in which an ethnic minority "does not fully belong" in a nation-state with a dominant ethnic group, but Israel would become more of a "normal" nation-state with "normal" minority problems.

A majority in both communities—roughly two-thirds, in fact—believe that a solution based on Israeli statehood and recognition of Arab rights as a national minority is both preferable and workable.[111] This assumes, of course, that the process of delinking the Israeli Arab situation from developments in the West Bank and Gaza continues. The 1988 acceptance by the PLO of a two-state solution to the Israeli-Palestinian conflict, based on mutual recognition between Israel and a Palestinian state in the West Bank and Gaza, accelerated this process—even at the peak of the *intifada*—by setting clearly different courses for Arabs in the occupied territories and Arabs in Israel. Subsequent progress toward Palestinian self-rule in the territories (the 1993 Declaration of Principles, the 1994 Gaza-Jericho agreement, and the 1995 Interim Agreement) separated the two situations further. The idea of Palestinian statehood or self-governance also helps to legitimize

Israel as a Jewish state; a Palestinian state as a homeland for Palestinian Arabs (perhaps with its own "Law of Return") would mirror Israel as a nation-state with a dominant ethnic character. It would lend a sense of symmetry to the situation, helping Israeli Arabs achieve a sense of equality (and providing them with an option if they wanted to live in an Arab state). Palestinian spokesmen on the West Bank have declared that they would recognize Israel's right to exist as a Jewish state if a Palestinian state is established.[112] In this framework, PLO leaders prefer to keep issues of the Israeli Arabs off their agenda—which is complicated enough—and to have Israeli Arabs work on their behalf as a pressure group within Israel.

For Arabs within Israel, the sense that the basic conflict is being resolved also frees them to focus further on their own problems and demands. Resolution of broader Arab-Israel issues could conceivably intensify their struggle, in the sense that they could no longer be put off by security arguments. But on the whole, peace and stability on the international level should reduce tensions within Israel, remove legitimate security issues, help expand civil rights, and make Israelis more willing to accept independent Arab organizations and Arabs' control of their own education and internal affairs. In such a setting Arabs could also perform military service, or another form of national service, as a path to integration and equality.[113]

Reading in the other direction, this implies that there is no real solution to ethnic relations within Israel as long as the larger problem impinges. The future of Israeli democracy is inextricably linked to continued moderation of the Arab-Israeli conflict and in particular to the fate of the larger Arab population in the territories that Israel has occupied since 1967.

TEN

The Impact of the West Bank and Gaza

From 1948 to 1967 the issue of integration with or separation from Palestinian Arabs was dormant in Israeli politics. The Arab minority in Israel had not become part of the power-sharing arrangements in the country, and beyond Israel's borders the reality was one of stark separation. Partition was reinforced by the 1949 armistice lines, which acquired legitimacy and permanence as lines dividing Israel from the Arab world. On the Arab side of those lines, what was to have been the core of Arab Palestine was under Jordanian or Egyptian rule.

The 1967 war, however, revived the pre-1948 debate; old divisions and dormant claims were reopened. Once again those who favored a largely homogeneous Jewish state in part of Palestine contended with those who promoted a Jewish presence and claim in an undivided Palestine with a large Arab population. Even the terminology was disputed; proponents of partition tended to use the political term "West Bank" as defined by the Jordanian presence before 1967, while the opponents of division preferred "Judea" and "Samaria," the historic Jewish geographic designations for roughly the same area.

Lack of clear consensus on an underlying conception was bridged by unspoken agreement to live indefinitely with a "temporary" military occupation that presumably did not prejudice the final resolution of the political issue. Occupation could end either with a negotiated withdrawal (in return for a credible peace treaty) or with a more permanent Israeli status in the territories. Where there was consensus on remaining, as in East Jerusalem and the Golan Heights, the government did extend Israeli jurisdiction in 1967 and 1981 respectively. Where there was no consensus, the matter could wait; in any event, there was no bargaining partner at the time.

But as occupation stretched into decades, did options really remain open?

As time passed and patterns hardened, wasn't de facto fusion of Israel and the territories taking place? Increasingly, it made more sense to describe this total area as a political unit, as a single "system of control" in which the land of the occupied territories was being integrated while its population served as a source of labor and as a market.[1] This posed a dilemma: if this population was not to be integrated politically into Israel with full civil rights—a solution favored by very few on either side—how could such a control system remain stable over time? Those who favored permanent Israeli control offered two categories of answers: some form of functional Jordanian link for Arab residents of the territories, or some form of autonomy. Both answers sought to address West Bank and Gaza populations on an individual basis rather than as a community with collective rights, thus avoiding the need to redraw boundaries. But neither proved to be a workable basis for a mutually acceptable solution, and eventually a majority in Israel came to favor renewed separation as the basis for stability. Consequently Israel began to disentangle its system of control, attempting to remove itself from the role of occupier of a hostile population without sacrificing its essential security.

LEGAL ISSUES

Legally the status of the West Bank and Gaza fell under the international law of belligerent occupation, as distinguished from nonbelligerent occupation that follows an armistice (as with Germany or Japan after 1945) or a peace treaty (as with foreign troops in the Rhineland after 1919). In the absence of anything more than a cease-fire, belligerent occupation assumes the possibility of renewed fighting and accords the occupier broad leeway; there are few precedents for such situations enduring for more than a brief period, with the German occupation of Belgium from 1914 to 1918 being the most prominent case.[2] A second singular feature of the occupation was that neither the West Bank nor the Gaza Strip were generally recognized as part of the territory of any sovereign state: Jordan's annexation of the West Bank had been recognized only by Britain and Pakistan, and Egypt had made no claim to the Gaza Strip. There being, in legal parlance, no "reversioner" for these two areas, sovereignty was generally held to be in suspension, and Israel (as the only successor state to the Palestine Mandate) was held by some to have a status there beyond that of military occupier alone.[3]

The Israeli government recognized the applicability of customary international law, including the Hague Conventions, to its occupation, but not that of the Fourth Geneva Convention of 1949, on grounds that acceptance of this convention would imply recognition that the West Bank is the sovereign territory of another state (Jordan). This reading of the Geneva Convention is disputed by many legal experts,[4] but in any event Israel announced that it would abide by the "humanitarian" provisions of the convention; the document is routinely cited in Israeli court cases dealing with occupation powers and is incorporated into many military orders and other occupation directives.

Another legal issue concerned the applicability of the Defense (Emergency) Regulations issued by Great Britain, as the Mandatory authority in Palestine, in 1945. These regulations, most of which are still in effect in Israel itself, gave the government wide and controversial powers in such areas as deportations, detentions, and censorship. Israel claimed they were also in effect in the West Bank and Gaza, since these areas had been part of Mandatory Palestine. The Jordanian government and West Bank residents argued that they were implicitly annulled on the West Bank, first by a 1948 proclamation of the Jordanian military commander that canceled any laws in conflict with the Jordanian Defense Law of 1935, and second by two Jordanian acts that also invalidated any conflicting provisions.[5]

Israeli jurists replied that the conflict with these laws was nonexistent, that the 1948 and other Jordanian proclamations all provided that existing regulations would remain in force, and that in the absence of explicit repeal they were therefore part of Jordanian law when Israel assumed control in 1967. In 1979 the Israeli High Court of Justice reviewed the arguments and concluded that the Defense Regulations were indeed still in force. Among other things, the court cited two Jordanian court decisions that had upheld the validity both of the regulations and of detention orders issued under them.[6]

But even if the Defense Regulations were set aside, the latitude of Israeli authorities would hardly be reduced. First of all, Jordanian laws provide draconian measures against political unrest or opposition, including trials in military courts not bound by ordinary procedures and use of the death penalty. But even more important, the customary international law of belligerent occupation allows a wide range of measures without legislative or judicial review. An occupier, in the words of one authority, "may take such measures of control and security in regard to protected persons as may be necessary as a result of the war."[7] This may include freezing political activities, curtailing freedom of speech and assembly, limiting free movement, limiting the right to return, requisitioning material and services from the population, increasing taxes to cover occupation expenses, using state property, or issuing currency. An occupier may control the content of educational curricula, change local laws, establish military courts in place of the local courts, and control the media and the mails. Those who resist this authority as members of "resistance movements" are not granted the status of prisoners-of-war unless they are members of "a Party to the conflict" and meet four conditions: (1) command of a person responsible for his subordinates, (2) distinctive insignia recognizable at a distance, (3) open carrying of arms, and (4) conduct of operations in accordance with the law and customs of war.[8] In sum, as the leading authority puts it, "it is unfortunate but true that severity will and must appear a dominant characteristic of the military government of any occupied enemy area."[9]

Given such wide latitude in the customary powers of an occupier, the question of the validity of the British Defense Regulations assumes a secondary importance. The occupying power can simply restate the content of such regulations in the form of military orders. In fact, Israel did this soon after the 1967 war; Military Order 224 (1968) explicitly reaffirms the Defense Regulations, and Military Order 378 (1970) repeats the provisions on administrative detention.[10]

The wide powers of military commanders under the law of belligerent occupation constitute an open invitation to excess and abuse, whatever the political system of the occupier. Furthermore, this law was designed for a short-term situation rather than a protracted occupation extending over decades, and for the relationship between an army and an occupied civilian population rather than frontal contact between two societies. Inevitably, serious legal and political issues regarding the rights of occupier and occupied grew sharper over time.

MILITARY OCCUPATION AND HUMAN RIGHTS

Since the international law of belligerent occupation is designed for temporary situations, the implications of prolonged occupation for the population involved are very problematic. Israeli military and civil administrations in the territories responded by proclaiming an enlightened and "benign" occupation that operated with a light hand, interfering minimally with the daily life of inhabitants, and that was symbolized by the "open bridges" that enabled the West Bank to maintain contact with Jordan and the broader Arab world. They pointed out that Israelis at the top of the Civil Administration comprised less than 5 percent of the staff, that they essentially exercised the powers that Jordanian ministers had exercised, and that at lower levels (especially municipalities) Arab administrators actually had more power than in the past.[11] The idea of devolving authority to local Arab bodies actually meshed well with the idea of fostering integration between the territories and Israel, which was especially prominent under Likud governments. While at one level Likud occupation policy tried to make renewed separation difficult or impossible, at another level it sought to make a permanent Israeli role in the territories acceptable by developing as much de facto autonomy or self-rule on the local level as possible.

The integrative processes were documented in painstaking detail by the West Bank Data Project, which between 1982 and 1989 published about three dozen studies of the West Bank and Gaza under occupation. These studies focused attention on the scope of Israeli government activity and spending in the territories, on the extent of land appropriation (about one-third of the total area), and on the growing degree of interdependence due to interlocking infrastructure, Jewish settlement, economic integration, and other aspects of occupation over time. In the view of Meron Benve-nisti, director of the project, these trends pointed to the increasing irreversibility of Israeli control and incorporation of the territories, a conclusion welcomed by the advocates of integration and resisted by its dovish opponents.[12]

Official occupation policy, particularly in its earlier years, stressed the benefits imparted by Israeli values and expertise. Municipal elections held in 1976 were said to be the most democratic ever, with the entire adult population including women enfranchised for the first time (after a pro-PLO sweep, however, no further elections were held). Freedom of religion and worship was not contested; for the sake of peace, Jewish claims in contested holy sites were not pushed strongly. The only interference in the education curriculum was the removal of anti-Israel content, while in the first twenty years of occupation schools expanded to cover 87 percent of school-age children, against 56 percent in 1967. By this time there were also eight academic universities and colleges, where none had existed before. Health care was also better by most (if not quite all) measures; infant mortality was roughly half the previous level.[13]

In terms of economic development, occupation authorities proclaimed (on the eve of the *intifada,* as it happened) that there had been "unprecedented" economic growth in the two decades of occupation: an increase of 400 percent in the Gross Domestic Product (GDP) of Judea and Samaria and of 430 percent in the Gaza Strip. Agricultural production had increased by an average of 10 percent annually. The percentage of households with electricity had climbed from 23 to 91 in Judea and Samaria and from 18 to 88 in Gaza; of households with a refrigerator from 5 to 74 in Judea and Samaria and 3 to 77 in Gaza; of households with television from 2 to 72 in Judea and Samaria and 3 to 78 in Gaza; and private car ownership from 2 to 10 in Judea and Samaria and 3 to 14 in Gaza.[14]

Growth in private consumption is not, however, the only measure of economic progress. Improvement in living standards was due more to income from work in Israel than from economic development in the territories themselves, while the growth of a large unskilled or semiskilled commuter labor force brought its own political and economic problems. The Israeli government had little incentive to invest in West Bank or Gaza industries that would compete with Israeli producers in the new captive market they had acquired. The industrial work force in the territories increased from 16,500 to 25,000 in the first twenty years, but this was actually a decrease as part of the total work force; industry as a share of GDP fell from 9 percent to 8 percent during this period.[15]

The onset of the *intifada*, shortly after completion of the self-congratulatory twenty-year report, revealed the hollowness of the occupation's social and economic benefits in two respects. In the first place, more refrigerators and more schools would not buy Arab acquiescence to continued Israeli control of their lives. Second, the economic relationship that had been nurtured was itself ruptured by the *intifada*. Arab workers were cut off from their jobs, Israeli goods were boycotted in the territories, and Israeli employers found new sources of cheap labor. Surprisingly, some indices of consumption continued to rise in the West Bank and Gaza even during the *intifada*,[16] but the paternalistic optimism of earlier years was dead. Military occupation was still military occupation, even if carried out by a democratic state and even if it included material benefits.

There were safeguards against abuse in the Israeli system. First was the open nature of Israeli society itself: open access to the press and human rights groups, vigorous domestic criticism, and questioning and publicizing of occupation policies and practices by critical Knesset members. Second were internal regulations of the army and police, which are often quite explicit and quite restrictive (in the first six years of the *intifada*, the army indicted 260 soldiers for intifada-related criminal offenses, of whom 225 were convicted and 25 acquitted as of October 10, 1993).[17] Finally, there were quasi-judicial appeal boards, and eventually an actual Court of Military Appeals, to contest military orders in the occupied territories, and these decisions could be appealed to the Israeli High Court of Justice. At the peak of the *intifada* about 40 percent of the petitions to the High Court came from the occupied territories.[18]

But some practices violate international standards even when they are strictly governed by well-established and consistent internal directives. A major criticism of Israeli occupation involves methods of interrogation used to extract information. As William V. O'Brien notes, there is a "notorious gap" between law and practice in this area: "Torture, while clearly illegal, has occurred in most contemporary revolutionary/counterinsurgency wars. . . . the issue is the control and minimization of physical and mental 'pressure' on prisoners of war and detainees."[19]

Following two public scandals involving the General Security Service (*Shin Beit*) in the mid-1980s, a governmental inquiry (the Landau Commission) in 1987 set guidelines for interrogation of security suspects that allowed "moderate physical pressure" but not "torture" by standard international definition. Israel maintains officially that the Landau Commission guidelines do not contradict the 1984 International Convention against Torture, to which it is a party, or other prohibitions in international law, and the High Court of Justice upheld the guidelines in a 1993 decision on grounds that they were subject to legislative oversight.[20] However, the precise definition of methods of "pressure" that are allowed remains classified, reflecting the inherent tension between an obsession with legal precision and the use of interrogation techniques that cannot withstand public scrutiny. Furthermore, the adoption of such guidelines on the eve of the *intifada* served to legitimize and regularize practices that soon became more widespread and routinized than ever. While according to Amnesty International about half the governments of the world sanction systematic torture in some form,[21] few if any have perfected its rationalization and bureaucratization as Israel has.

Reports of various monitoring bodies make it clear that standard procedures include sleep and food deprivation, verbal abuse and threats, intense noise, hooding, forced standing, binding in painful positions, solitary confinement, enclosure in tight spaces, exposure to extreme temperatures, denial of access to toilets, genital abuse, "shakings," and beatings.[22] Revealingly, a leaked form for examining physicians asks whether there are any medical limitations to the prisoner's stay in an isolated cell, to chaining, to wearing head or eye cover, or to prolonged standing.[23] The conclusion of the U.S. Department of State annual report is that "Israeli security forces are responsible for widespread abuse, and in some case torture, of Palestinian detainees," while Amnesty International reports that "Palestinian detainees continued to be systematically tortured or ill-treated during interrogation."[24]

Another frequently questioned practice is the use of undercover units, disguised as Palestinians, to seize suspects. Though the government claims that such units observe the standard rules of engagement, they are often accused of "extrajudicial executions" in the killing of targeted individuals who could have been apprehended alive. According to the U.S. Department of State, these units killed ten Palestinians in 1995, a decrease from thirteen in 1994 and twenty-seven in 1993.[25]

Many Israeli policies are not invalid on their face but have to be measured against the security concerns of the occupier. This is especially true of restrictions on speech, assembly, and movement, of the various economic measures, and of the changes in existing laws. In addition, some of the restrictions are more apparent on paper than in reality. For example, in theory any printed matter requires a permit, and the occupation regime maintains a list of publications that are explicitly prohibited. But while most expressions of Palestinian nationalism are censored, considerable material finds its way into circulation anyway. In fact, given the movement across the Jordan River as well as constant penetration of radio and television from neighboring countries and the relatively freer press of East Jerusalem, censorship efforts on the West Bank are often an exercise in futility.[26]

Some of the more controversial measures merit a closer look. The practice of demolishing or sealing off the homes of presumed security offenders has been one of the most heavily criticized methods both inside Israel and abroad, as the Geneva Convention allows for destruction of property only when "rendered absolutely necessary by military operations." It is also a collective punishment, which is just as clearly forbidden by the Geneva Convention and other international law. An Israeli court case in 1979 upheld the legality of demolitions and sealings under the British Defense Regulations, but legally the measure seems indefensible. Only in 1990 did the High Court of Justice seriously limit it by requiring a judicial hearing before any house demolition, because of the irreversible nature of the punishment.[27]

Another controversial Defense Regulation used in the occupied territories was deportation. The close ties between the West and East Banks of the Jordan made expulsion across the river a convenient way of dealing with problematic individuals. During the 1967–1978 period, according to one compilation, 1,151 individuals were deported from the West Bank and the Gaza Strip (an official Israeli source actually gave a slightly higher figure: 1,180).[28] Most of these deportations came in the first four years, with 406 in the peak year, 1970. By the end of the decade the figure had fallen to fewer than ten each year. Israeli authorities claim that the majority—whether originally from the area or not—had infiltrated back into Israeli-held territory after the 1967 war, and that some of the others chose deportation as an alternative to serving prison sentences.

Deportation is difficult to reconcile with Article 49 of the Geneva Convention, which forbids "individual or mass forcible transfers, as well as deportations of protected persons from occupied territory to the territory of the Occupying Power or to that of any other country." Israeli authorities responded that, as Jordanian citizens, the deportees were not being transferred to the occupier's territory or to "another country," but merely to a different part of their own country. It was also argued that Article 49 had been aimed at the kinds of mass deportations, for purposes of forced labor or physical annihilation, that had taken place during World War II, and not at the expulsion of individuals, acting as enemy agents, to the territory of that enemy.[29] But the wording of Article 49 would seem to forbid even a forcible transfer to one's own country. It is also a well-established principle that no country can be forced to accept deportees from another state, so that deportation to Lebanon or elsewhere (as became the practice after Jordan began turning back deportees at its border) clearly has no legal basis. Moreover, with Jordan's relinquishment of claims to the West Bank in July 1988, even the thin claim of returning "Jordanian citizens" to "their" country was undercut.[30]

The Israeli Supreme Court upheld deportations from the occupied territories, arguing that the prohibition was aimed at mass deportations rather than individual deportations for cause.[31] But this was seriously challenged in December 1992, when the Israeli government expelled 415 leaders of

Hamas and the Islamic Jihad from the territories to Lebanon. In this case the Supreme Court again upheld the expulsions as a series of individual orders rather than a mass deportation but required that a right to be heard be granted on an individual basis.[32] Because of the intense international reaction to this deportation, however, the Israeli government permitted the piecemeal return of the deportees over the course of the following year, and no further deportations were ordered in the ensuing period.

The use of administrative detention is a more complicated issue. Detention as a legal measure is regarded as preventive rather than punitive; it exists in a number of democratic countries, where it is used to restrict individuals who, according to good evidence, plan to commit a crime or otherwise threaten public order. It ordinarily involves a judicial proceeding involving an independent review of evidence and some avenue of appeal, even if it does not have all the safeguards of a criminal trial. In Israel itself, the administrative detention provisions of the British Defense Regulations were replaced in 1979 by a regular legislative act.

Prior to the period of the *intifada,* the use of administrative detention on the West Bank was most extensive in the period immediately after the 1967 war. In 1970 Defense Minister Moshe Dayan put the total number of administrative detainees at 1,131, all but thirty-four of them from the occupied territories. In later years this dropped to fewer than a hundred, and eventually the use of detention was temporarily phased out both in Israel and the territories, with the last detainee released in March 1982.[33]

Following the enactment of the 1979 Israeli law that replaced the British regulation, changes were also made in the West Bank and Gaza. A new military order brought practice there into line with the reforms of the 1979 law: more limited authority for issuing orders, the requirement of approval by a qualified judge at the time of detention, and expanded judicial review of detention orders.[34] As noted, these changes occurred simultaneously with an overall phasing out of administrative detention in Israel and the territories. However, a series of violent incidents in late 1985 led to its reintroduction, after a lull of over three years.

The legal criticisms of administrative detentions involve loose rules of evidence, withholding of evidence from the accused, and the unwillingness of courts to substitute their own judgment for that of the military officer on the merits of the case.[35] Perhaps a more serious problem, however, is that the entire administrative detention system breaks down when it is flooded with large numbers of detainees; rather than the individual consideration that each case receives in theory, the process becomes a parody of proper legal procedure.

The legality of Jewish settlement in the occupied territories is also challenged on the basis of the Fourth Geneva Convention, which forbids an occupying power from transferring its own population into occupied territories.

Some observers make the argument that, since Israel is the only successor state to the Palestine Mandate, Israeli citizens may move anywhere within the former Mandate lines, and that in any event the prohibition in the Geneva Convention was aimed at the kind of massive population displacements carried out by Nazi Germany in World War II.[36] But Esther Cohen makes a more convincing argument that such movements are legal only if they are (1) voluntary, (2) individual, (3) based on military necessity, (4) temporary in duration, and (5) not a prelude to annexation or displacement of the existing population.[37] Few of the existing settlements, if any, would meet these criteria. Furthermore, the presence of Jewish settlers beyond Israel proper raises the issue of two systems of law, since Israeli law has been extended to the settlers on a personal basis while the Arab population remains under the occupation regime.[38]

Israeli courts have been asked to rule on the requisitioning of land "for military purposes" as a step in making it available for Jewish civilian settlement. One such expropriation, at Beth-El (near Ramallah) was upheld by the Israeli High Court of Justice, which accepted the claims of military necessity. But in a subsequent case, involving land at Elon Moreh, near Nablus, the court ruled otherwise. Reviewing the security claims made by the chief of staff, the judges concluded that the motives were primarily ideological rather than military and ruled the requisition illegal. Of some importance was the fact that the minister of defense did not back the chief of staff and that prominent former military commanders disputed the claims of military necessity before the court.[39]

Finally, there is the question of whether school or business closures, curfews, restrictions on movement, and similar measures constitute "collective" punishment, which is expressly forbidden in international instruments. There can be no definitive answer; if used legitimately to ensure the security of the occupier's forces and general public order, such measures are defensible, but if the primary intent is punitive, they are not. By this standard some of the measures used would seem legitimate and others would not.[40]

The onset of the *intifada* in December 1987, did not change this general picture. Measures used against the *intifada* did not differ in kind from those used before 1987; what changed was the ability of the Israeli army to maintain, within its stated guidelines, order within the territories and discipline among its own troops. Guidelines on the use of live ammunition and other forms of force broke down in the face of massive demonstrations. Administrative detention was used as a broad weapon rather than as an individual measure; in the first six years of the *intifada,* over 105,000 Palestinians passed through the detention or prison system, and in mid-November 1995, some 4,000 remained (2,751 sentenced, 1,059 awaiting trial or detention proceedings, and 203 in administrative detention).[41]

Also in the first six years of the *intifada,* 434 houses were demolished and 314 were sealed. However, the 1990 court decision requiring a prior hearing caused a shift from demolition to sealing of houses—a reversible procedure—and the new Rabin government reduced demolitions to isolated cases (three in 1994, six in 1995). Also some sixty-six Palestinians were deported from the territories during the *intifada* prior to the mass deportation of December 1992, which as noted marked an end to that measure.[42]

The *intifada* underlined, however, that legal issues were not the core of the conflict. Even if deportation, demolition, Jewish settlement, and other questionable measures were halted, while such methods as administrative detention were to be employed strictly within acceptable legal standards and all Israeli soldiers were to adhere strictly to the "rules of engagement" and other accepted norms of law enforcement, basic demands on both sides would remain unmet. Palestinians would continue to oppose the very fact of Israeli occupation, however civilized and refined it might become. But for Israelis also the basic issue was not legal; while there was vigorous debate within the country over the legality of particular measures, the legality of the occupation itself was not an issue on the public agenda. The issue was the political question of what was to come after the occupation, and this debate was in essence a replay of the historic debate between the partisans of partition and the advocates of a unitary solution in various forms. This became the defining issue of Israeli politics and for over two decades deadlocked the Israeli political system.

THE OCCUPIED TERRITORIES: POLITICAL ISSUES

Israel's Labor Party leadership emerged from the 1967 war still committed to the principle of partition. They envisioned limited changes in the 1949 armistice lines: Jerusalem would be reunited under Israeli sovereignty, and there would be minor rectifications in Israel's favor on the West Bank. The Straits of Tiran, for which Israel had fought twice, and the Golan Heights, from which the Syrians had bombarded Israeli settlements, would also remain under Israeli control. Jordan was seen as the key to future negotiations, based on the return of the bulk of the West Bank (particularly the Arab population centers) to King Hussein. But there would be no withdrawal except as part of a final peace treaty. With the West Bank and Sinai as leverage, Israel could afford to wait for the Arab states to come to the negotiating table.

As a consequence, the Israeli government adopted an open-bridges policy on the Jordan River and discouraged the emergence of independent Arab leadership on the West Bank. Both of these measures served to protect the Jordanian presence in the territory, in anticipation of a peace treaty with

Hussein. The government established settlements in those areas where border changes were anticipated. Policy in this area was guided by what was called the "oral law," since Israel's claims could not be presented formally at this stage. In accordance with the oral law (a concept borrowed from Jewish tradition), settlements were concentrated in the Jordan Valley, on the Golan Heights, and on the border between Egypt and the Gaza Strip. The settlements in the Jordan Valley were also connected to what became known as the Allon Plan. In this conception, Israel would establish a security frontier, distinct from a political boundary, on the Jordan River. Most of the West Bank and nearly all its Arab population would be demilitarized and returned to Jordan, to which it would be connected by a corridor through the Israeli security belt on the Jordan.

But the Labor approach was challenged from the outset by Herut and others who opposed any return of the West Bank to Arab rule. Herut, which came to dominate the Likud bloc after its formation in 1973, represented the historic position of the Revisionist movement. In this view, Israel had a claim to Judea and Samaria on both historic and security grounds, and should act toward realizing this claim. Palestine west of the Jordan River should not be redivided, no "foreign sovereignty" should be reintroduced in this area, and there should be no restriction on Jewish settlement anywhere in the historic homeland. Arabs in the occupied territories would be offered autonomy as individuals but should express their national identity in the framework of one of the existing Arab states (especially Jordan, seen as basically a "Palestinian" state). The peace process was thus basically conceived as a negotiation between Israel and these Arab states, on the basis of existing lines of demarcation; the Palestinians did not appear as an independent body.

Behind these opposed conceptions, there was a fair degree of consensus on certain basic issues: both major parties (and most of the Israeli public) opposed the creation of an independent Palestinian state between Israel and Jordan, and both opposed recognition of and negotiation with the Palestine Liberation Organization as then constituted and represented. Also, Likud, like Labor, favored the continuation for the foreseeable future of the "temporary" military occupation in the West Bank and Gaza, given the fact that immediate annexation (a course favored only by small groups on the right) would at once pose the question of the civil rights of Arab inhabitants, who still comprised 95 percent of the population there after two decades of Jewish settlement. Nevertheless, the basically opposed conceptions of Labor and Likud prevented development of a coherent foreign policy during periods when the two parties shared power, and the Likud's opposition in principle to Israeli withdrawal from the occupied territories stymied diplomacy based on this quid pro quo—the only one in which Arab interlocutors were interested—during periods of Likud dominance.

Interwoven with the opposition to withdrawal was the rise of religious nationalism, representing "the first attempt by a religious community to determine political-religious objectives for the entire Jewish People since the beginning of the *Haskala* [the Jewish Enlightenment, at the end of the eighteenth century]."[43] The main expression of this perspective came from Gush Emunim, an extraparliamentary movement founded in 1974 to secure Israeli sovereignty over the West Bank (Judea and Samaria) through massive Jewish settlement there. Religious nationalism in the Zionist context shares the characteristics of other fundamentalist movements, drawing selectively from tradition to formulate an activist ideology that challenges modern secular culture.[44] It differs, however, from the fundamentalism of the ultra-Orthodox (*haredim*) in Israel, which draws strictly from religious sources; Gush Emunim advocated a "political theology" that drew from both religion and from modern nationalist thinking, and its success was in large part due to a simultaneous rise of secular nationalism.[45]

Consequently religious Zionists, who had been marginal players in classical Zionism, emerged as the most fervent practitioners of the pioneering Zionist settlement ethic. This gave them an ideological importance far beyond their actual numbers, as Israelis in general respected an ideological commitment and intensity that were increasingly hard to find in secular Israeli society. The ability of Gush Emunim to incorporate values and methods of secular Zionism, together with the rise of "civil religion" that increased receptiveness to traditional Jewish symbols, created a favorable atmosphere for religious nationalism and a "permissive" attitude toward settlement in the territories. Though activists numbered only in the thousands, a large part of the public supported their endeavors in spirit.[46]

The key figure in the development of religious nationalist ideology was Rabbi Zvi Yehuda Kook, whose father—Rabbi Avraham Yitzhak Hacohen Kook—was the first Ashkenazi chief rabbi in Palestine. The elder Rabbi Kook had provided important intellectual underpinnings to religious Zionism by defining secular Zionists as unwitting agents of a divine plan for Jewish restoration and redemption. Rabbi Zvi Yehuda Kook took this traditional messianism further, declaring that redemption was to be achieved in the present age by restoring Jewish rule to the remaining areas of the Land of Israel that had been by divine providence captured in the 1967 war. A religious vision thus became a radical political program to carry out the sacred task of reclaiming Judea and Samaria by intensive Jewish settlement in all areas of the historic homeland. Land itself became a supreme moral and religious value; Israeli authorities were forbidden by religious decree from relinquishing control over any part of the ancestral domain.

As with other fundamentalisms, this worldview posed issues for democratic governance. In the first place, the idea of a "higher law" legitimizes or even requires resistance to a government that derives its authority from society; in this context, the commandment to settle the land takes precedence over the democratic procedures of Israeli government. In the eyes of Gush Emunim settlers, it is the government that acts illegitimately when it abandons any part of the homeland.[47] Second, there is no sense of Arab rights to be measured against Jewish claims, since the latter are absolute. Given the focus on Jewish rights, religious nationalists do not have an agreed-upon position on the future of the Arab population in Judea and Samaria. Some would grant citizenship to those who accepted the Zionist framework, leaving others in a second-class status. Others argue that even granting autonomy or limited self-rule to Palestinians in a Jewish state is not permitted, and some openly urge voluntary or compulsory "transfer" (that is, expulsion). The most extreme position, expressed by Rabbi Yisrael Hess in a student publication of Bar-Ilan University in 1980, is that Arabs are descended from Amalek and that the Bible therefore commands their destruction.[48]

THE STRUCTURE OF ISRAELI OPINION

Given the influence of both secular and religious nationalism, there was a substantial gap between support of the "land-for-peace" formula, as espoused by the Labor Party, and a more hawkish public opinion. Already in the period immediately after the 1967 war, most of the public (up to 95 percent in some polls) were unwilling to return most of the West Bank to Arab rule. This stood in stark contrast to a government policy based precisely on leaving such a possibility open. Yet, rather paradoxically, 80 percent of the public (on the average) also said they were satisfied with the government's general performance.[49]

Some of the seeming contradiction is explained by general disbelief in the possibility of a peace treaty, which was regarded as a necessary condition for return of the West Bank. The persistence of a basic pessimism in Israeli opinion is striking. The Continuing Survey of the Israel Institute of Applied Social Research (IIASR) has tracked Israeli opinion on the territories since 1967, asking what territorial concessions respondents would be willing to make "in order to arrive at a peace agreement with Arab countries." A closer look at this data contradicts much conventional wisdom.[50] In the first place, opposition to Israeli withdrawal did not grow slowly over time but appeared in full force almost at once; overwhelming majorities opposed territorial concessions in the West Bank, Gaza, or the Golan Heights (though not, it should be noted, in the Sinai Peninsula). The general long-term trend has actually been toward greater willingness to make territorial concessions.

Second, opposition to withdrawal differed greatly according to the area in question. The greatest opposition, initially, was to giving up the Golan Heights or the Gaza Strip, confirming the dominance of security considerations over ideology in public attitudes. Though the West Bank was the focus of ideological aspirations and also had strategic significance, there was greater reticence to leaving the Golan Heights or Gaza, where the perceived strategic risk was greater because the states involved, Syria and Egypt, were Israel's most dangerous military foes.

Third, there was great sensitivity to dramatic events such as the Yom Kippur War in 1973 or the Sadat initiative in 1977. Apparently sudden jolts, whether positive or negative from Israel's perspective, tended to increase willingness to withdraw, while periods of relative quiet increased opposition to such withdrawal by making the status quo appear both more livable and more inevitable. Short-term shifts in opinion also show considerable fluidity, if not volatility, in Israeli opinion and voting patterns. Much of this fluidity has been masked by the fact that shifts take place in both directions, leaving the appearance of stability in the overall pattern. But much of this stability is illusory; for example, Katz and Levinsohn found on the very eve of the 1988 election that 40 percent of those polled claimed to be undecided not just between parties within the same bloc, but between the blocs themselves.[51]

A fourth point is that poll results in Israel, as elsewhere, show great sensitivity to the wording of the question. This is nowhere more apparent than in questions on the occupied territories, where the choices as seen by Israelis ranged, in Avner Yaniv's words, "from the unfeasible to the unthinkable."[52] The wording in the earlier IIASR surveys pushed somewhat in a hawkish direction by leaving open the possibility that the suggested withdrawal would not necessarily lead to a satisfactory peace agreement. Polls that made the return of territory explicitly conditional on conclusion of a satisfactory peace had different results; for example, in a 1975 poll commissioned by *Ha'aretz* almost 50 percent of the respondents said they would be willing to return to the pre-1967 lines, with only minor adjustments, in the context of a peace treaty.[53] This contrasts with the fewer than 20 percent willing to concede "all" of the territories, in IIASR data during the same period.

On the eve of the *intifada,* close to half of the Israeli public continued to oppose any territorial withdrawal in the West Bank and Gaza. A poll in April 1987, recorded 46.4 percent opposed to withdrawal, and other polls were similar. At the same time, a large part of the Israeli public, clinging to visions of a Jewish presence in all of Palestine, took a permissive approach to Jewish settlement in the occupied territories: 37.9 percent opposed the idea of a freeze on new Jewish settlements, and only 35.2 percent were willing to evacuate existing settlements.[54] A clear majority of the public favored leaving the rights of West Bank inhabitants as they were, in the absence of an overall solution; in a 1984 survey, only 23.2 percent favored increasing their civil rights under prevailing conditions, while 59.7 percent wanted to leave the situation as it was, and 17.1 percent wanted to decrease existing rights.[55]

There was no clear consensus on what kind of an "overall solution" the Israeli government should pursue, and in the absence of such a consensus a majority preferred the status quo. Israeli Jewish public opinion toward the territories divided into four ideal types, each of which corresponded to key defining positions.

On one end of the spectrum were the *ideological doves,* who took a principled position against permanent occupation, called for withdrawal from all or most of territories, and tended to favor a Palestinian state alongside Israel. These positions, represented by parties of the left and the dovish wing of the Labor Party, drew the support of 20 to 30 percent of the electorate.

The *ideological hawks,* on the other end of the spectrum, argued in principle for permanent control of the territories, opposing withdrawal and favoring annexation or integration in one form or another. These positions, also supported by 20 to 30 percent of the public, were identified with parties of the far right and with the hawkish wing of Likud, including most of the traditional leaders from Revisionist backgrounds.

Those in the middle, amounting roughly to half the electorate, took positions on the territories according to practical security considerations more than issues of principle. Consequently their opinions were less rigid and more reactive to events, changing over time as realities and threat perceptions changed. They were themselves divided, roughly equally, into *pragmatic doves* and *pragmatic hawks.* The former, corresponding to much of the Labor Party including traditional leaders such as Rabin and Peres, historically favored a Jordan-based solution that would involve withdrawal from most or at least some of the territories and eventually came to support such an arrangement with the PLO. The pragmatic hawks, on the other hand, argued that security needs required permanent Israeli control of most or all of the West Bank, combined perhaps with autonomy for its Arab population; much of the Likud electorate, and some of its leadership, supported these positions.

The lack of consensus was reflected in the evenness of the balance between the two major blocs. By the time of the 1984 elections, most observers expected that the pendulum would swing back to Labor's direction: the unpopularity of the Lebanese war and continuing Israeli occupation there, economic crisis with inflation well into three-digit figures, and the resignation of the colorful Menachem Begin as standard-bearer, all seemed to indicate a break in the deadlock in Labor's favor. This was not to be, however. In defiance of expectations, the 1984 elections produced a balance so delicate that Labor and Likud were forced to embark on an era of power-sharing and mutual veto, rotating the prime ministership within the framework of a National Unity Government. On foreign policy issues the National Unity Government was stalemated by the opposed approaches of its components. No major diplomatic initiative could gain the support of both Labor and Likud; in early 1987 Shamir (recently "rotated" to the prime ministership) blocked the effort of (newly rotated) Foreign Minister Peres to convene an international conference that would sponsor talks between Israel and a joint Jordanian-Palestinian delegation.

THE INEVITABILITY OF SEPARATION

Throughout this period, it seemed, time was working in favor of integration of the territories with Israel. Despite the political deadlock, developments on the ground were erasing the "Green Line," which separated pre-1967 Israel from the West Bank and Gaza. The main wedge of this integration was Jewish settlement beyond the Green Line, and in this case the nature of Jewish politics favored the settlers. Apart from the sympathy they gained by laying claim to Zionist pioneering values, the settlers benefited from the inability of the government to take a clear negative position on settlement, from the ability of independent groups to force the issue, from the tendency to view the issue simply in Jewish terms and ignore the Arab presence, and from compromises that inevitably gave expansionists at least some of what they demanded. Furthermore, settlement was a cumulative process; so long as it inched forward even in the absence of consensus, the end result would be a new reality.

In light of this ongoing "organic" process, arguments against settlement sounded like a loss of faith in the Zionist enterprise. If the original settlers had been so easily discouraged, would Israel ever have come into existence? Furthermore, the territorial minimalists were making the case for a narrowly Jewish state, presenting Zionism as exclusivism at its worst, while the settlers were keeping alive the old assimilationist ideal of a state in which Jews and Arabs could leave together peacefully.

The Labor Party itself favored Jewish settlement in areas that were considered strategically important and had few Arab inhabitants, and therefore set the process in motion during the first decade after 1967. These efforts focused on border areas: the Golan Heights opposite Syria, the Jordan Valley opposite Jordan, and the Rafiah salient (Gush Katif) between Gaza and Egypt (plus the Etzion bloc south of Jerusalem, where Jewish settlements had existed before 1948). When the Likud came to power in 1977, there were already seventy-six Jewish settlements in the territories, with a total of about 8,500 settlers.[56] Though most of these were "security" settlements in the above areas that fit within the context of the Allon Plan, there were also a few established in the heart of the West Bank, over initial government opposition, that challenged these limits; Kiryat Arba, on the outskirts of Hebron, was established in 1971, and Gush Emunim began its efforts in 1974.

Likud governments favored Jewish settlement throughout the territories in order to integrate them demographically and make the reestablishment of Arab rule impossible. By 1992, there were 175 settlements: 128 in the West Bank, 32 on the Golan, and 15 in Gaza, with a total population of 115,000–120,000.[57] However, the focus of settlement efforts shifted in the early 1980s as it became clear that the potential number of ideologically committed settlers willing to live in isolated outposts amidst a hostile population was limited. Instead, the government subsidized "bedroom communities" just across the Green Line, within commuting distance of greater Tel Aviv and greater Jerusalem, making new homes available on financial terms far more favorable than comparable housing within Israel. These new suburban settlements, based more on economics than ideology, actually contained a majority of the total number of settlers.

This strategy did not, however, produce a new demographic reality. Though Jewish settlers constituted almost 10 percent of the West Bank population, they were concentrated in areas bordering Israel, and in Gaza they were about 0.5 percent of the population. The entire settler population was offset within two years by the natural increase of the West Bank and Gaza Arab population.[58] Even with financial inducements it was difficult to attract settlers to scattered and often besieged sites with an uncertain future, with hostile neighbors, with no economic viability on their own, and with no real roots in their immediate environment; Prime Minister Rabin said of one such settlement, "if Netzarim is a settlement, I'm a kugalager [ball bearing]."[59] Jewish settlements in the heart of the West Bank were blocked from contiguity with each other and "contained" by existing Arab towns, villages, and cultivated fields; furthermore, having learned from past experience, the Arab population in these areas was now fully mobilized to block Jewish expansion by their own building, cultivation, and resistance to land sales or transfers. By the end of the 1980s it was clear that the hope of transforming the demography of Judea and Samaria was hollow.[60]

Moreover, the effort to integrate the territories threatened to dilute the Jewishness of Israel itself. In the total area of Israel plus the West Bank and Gaza, Arabs constituted about 39 percent of the population by 1995, and various projections (including those of the government itself) predicted an Arab majority within twenty to thirty years, due to the higher Arab birthrate.[61] The influx of Jews from the former Soviet Union, by these calculations, only delayed the inevitable; each 100,000 new immigrants pushed back the date of parity by one year. Consequently, if Israel chose to integrate the territories politically, it could not remain both Jewish and democratic: it would either become a binational (Arab-Jewish) state, or it would have to deny full civil rights to non-Jewish residents. In order to drive home this dilemma, West Bank leaders proposed, in mock seriousness, that Israel annex the territories and extend citizenship to all inhabitants—following which a democratic majority would eventually vote to change the name, symbols, and very character of the state, creating "Palestine" in place of Israel.[62]

How could Israel remain both Jewish and democratic while absorbing the occupied territories with their hostile populations? Opponents of withdrawal responded to this question in various ways, many of them reminiscent of initial Zionist reactions to the Arab issue. Avoidance was a common feature; many arguments for integration simply focused on the positive security, historical, religious, and other grounds for continued Israeli control, skirting the issue of the Arab population or addressing it in very general terms. Often, in the eyes of critics, proponents of Greater Israel seemed to be relying on a miracle to resolve the dilemma, based on their perception that all of the historical successes of Zionism had been miraculous achievements against great odds.

Denial of the reality of the threat was a second line of argument. In 1988 Benjamin Netanyahu, on the rise to leadership of the Likud, pointed out that according to official government numbers, Arabs comprised 37 percent of the total population of the Land of Israel (including Judea, Samaria, and Gaza) in 1967 and only 38 percent in 1987; with an increase of only one percent in twenty years, where was the demographic threat? Clearly the higher Arab birthrate had been offset by Jewish immigration and an outflow of Arabs from the territories. Demographers were quick to point out, however, that there had been an unusually large net Jewish influx, and an unusually large Arab exodus (largely a rush to jobs in the oil-producing states), during the first decade after 1967, and that during the 1980s these trends were reversed as Jewish emigration increased (sometimes offsetting immigration) and the collapse of the oil boom brought Arab workers back from the Gulf. If 1977 were used as the base, then the increase in the Arab population was three percent within a decade, a rate that would indeed create an Arab majority within about three decades. The aftermath of the 1991 Persian Gulf War brought a further influx of returning Palestinians to the territories; this was offset by the renewal of mass Jewish immigration from Soviet successor states, but as noted this influx at most postpones the day of parity by another decade.[63]

Denial was sometimes succeeded by wishful thinking: perhaps the Arab birthrate would fall as their standard of living rises and "drowns them in luxury," as one West Bank settler leader predicted.[64] (Given the age structure of the two populations, this would not prevent an Arab majority.) Perhaps low Jewish fertility could be raised by campaigns and policies to raise the birthrate—though such programs have never succeeded in other developed urbanized societies and have failed in the past in Israel. Strongest hopes were pinned on immigration: perhaps new waves of Jewish refugees would preserve a Jewish majority. This was, after all, how a Jewish majority was achieved in the first place, despite faster Arab population growth.

Comparison to past patterns leads, however, to pessimism rather than optimism on future immigration. Past immigration came largely from Jewish communities under pressure, from "push" rather than "pull" factors. With the exhaustion of the last major reservoir in the former Soviet Union, there remain only a few relatively small Jewish populations that are "in distress" or likely to become so. Over 80 percent of Jews outside Israel are in the advanced industrialized states of the West, and these communities have never contributed significantly to immigration to Israel. Furthermore, given current assimilative trends, they are not likely to: "Any effort to increase the Jewish population [of Israel], or at least to preserve the current demographic balances, will have to turn to other sources of growth."[65]

Even when pools of potential immigrants existed, moreover, Jewish settlement historically was successful only in areas with sparse Arab populations. Efforts to penetrate Arab population centers and alter their basic demography generally failed. If this was the case in earlier years, there is even less reason to expect success when the Palestinian population has been thoroughly aroused and mobilized and when international attention is fixed on every major or minor development in the Arab-Israel conflict.

Integrationists who moved beyond avoidance, denial, and wishful thinking and who recognized the need to choose tended to prefer Jewishness over democracy. If the numbers couldn't be changed, then Arabs in Judea, Samaria, and Gaza would have to be given something less than equal status with Jews in the integral Land of Israel. Usually such proposals involved autonomy or local self-rule for Arabs, or a two-tiered system of citizenship in which only those accepting Zionism would have full citizenship; in either case, there was no recognition of Palestinian national rights on a par with the rights of Jews as a people. A more sophisticated variant would begin with Jordan as the Palestinian state, leaving the West Bank to be divided between this new Palestine and Israel along pragmatic lines, and with Arabs remaining on the Israeli side given the two-tiered choice of Zionism or limited rights.[66] There is no evidence, however, that any significant number of Palestinians ever have been, or ever will be, willing to accept a solution that does not include total equality on a national level between Israelis and Palestinians.

This left the advocates of a negotiated withdrawal—the Labor Party and other groups on the left—and the advocates of expulsion—the late Meir Kahane's Kach and other groups on the far right—as proponents of a state with a clearly Jewish population.

No one has skewered right-wing solutions to the demographic problem better than Kahane:

> In this the "hawks" are as hapless as the "doves"; they have no answer for what
> to do with either the Arabs of Israel or the liberated lands. . . . Those who
> demand annexation of the liberated lands, no less than the "doves," blithely
> ignore the question of Arab population or fall back on evasive answers. . . .
> [W]e hear evasions such as: No clear demographic projections are really pos-
> sible (why it is not made clear); the past is no guide to the future (why not is
> again not spelled out); Jewish immigration to Israel will make up for the
> higher Arab birthrate (a delusion of major dimensions). The truth is that,
> having no answer to problems, the "hawks," no less than the "doves," ignore
> them.[67]

In Kahane's view, to the contrary, *any* significant number of Arabs in a
Jewish state—even if not a majority—constituted a serious threat. In this
he shared the basic assumption of the radical anti-Zionist left: any Jewish-
Zionist state must inherently be exclusivist and undemocratic. He drew,
however, the opposite conclusion: to achieve its Jewish calling, Israel must
abandon democratic pretenses and get rid of non-Jews. The idea of expulsion, or "transfer" in sanitized language, came to be legitimized in political
discourse and varying percentages of the public (in the 15 to 40 percent
range) expressed some degree of sympathy for the idea, depending on the
wording of the survey.[68] Much of this support can be taken, however, as expression of the wish that the Arabs would simply go away (a wish no doubt
reciprocated in Arab feelings toward Israelis) and did not necessarily reflect
active support for such a program; no party explicitly advocating "transfer"
has ever won more than three seats in the Knesset.

If expulsion is unthinkable and integration is impossible, logic leads back
to partition: to separate, independent (though intertwined) political desti-
nies for Jews and Arabs in the Land of Israel/Palestine. There was also growing awareness of the costs of occupation, which, like some of the integrative
processes, were cumulative over time. Was Israel, perhaps, worse off with the
occupied territories than without them? In the words of Jonathan Frankel,
occupation had recreated the troubled "Pale of Settlement" that had existed
a century earlier in tsarist Russia; Jews lived insecurely among a hostile
population, and a cycle of violence (this time in both directions) was turning the Zionist dream into the Zionist nightmare.[69]

Efforts to expand the area of control ran the risk of weakening Israel
within the pre-1967 lines. The diversion of human and material resources to
the territories meant less for development and basic needs at home, such as
absorbing the new wave of immigrants from the former Soviet Union. It also
had an adverse impact on the demographic balance within Israel itself, as
"reverse penetration" brought more Israeli Arabs into Jewish areas; better to
put the Jewish settlers, demographers argued, into the western Galilee and
other areas of Israel that were becoming more Arab.[70]

There was also a more general, "spillover" impact on the position of the

Arab minority within Israel. In a reasonably stable environment, a permanent minority of 20 percent could be accommodated peacefully within an ethnic (Jewish) democracy, judging from experience in Israel and elsewhere (see chapter 9). But as part of a much larger minority poised to become a majority, Arabs within Israel present an altogether different kind of challenge. Jewish Israelis would no longer enjoy the luxury of numbers and would be less willing to share power. Continued confrontation between Jews and Arabs in the territories also clearly intensified hostility to Arabs as such, increased readiness to curtail minority rights within Israel, and made Israeli Arabs themselves less inclined to reach accommodative solutions.

Another cost was the spillover into Israeli democracy generally. Can democracy coexist indefinitely with domination of a neighboring people, especially when strong efforts are being made to erase the border between the two sides? If democratic principles are not applicable in the "administered" territories, then why in the long run should they be so valued within Israel? Some Gush Emunim activists indeed drew the logical conclusion: "If democracy becomes inimical to the fundamental interests of the State of Israel, then it has to be reconsidered and analyzed and maybe eliminated."[71] Prolonged occupation erodes the rule of law in subtle ways: external threats are increasingly viewed as internal threats that justify internal restrictions; use of emergency powers becomes more deeply routinized both without and within; continued violent confrontation fortifies the tendency to give primacy to security considerations in political and judicial decisions; a legal double standard between Jews and Arabs becomes rooted in practice and thought; the political system realigns along this single burning question, with cross-cutting cleavages reduced and particular issues becoming "too sensitive" to be settled by mere majority rule. In short, the legitimacy of democracy as the authoritative arbiter in society is undermined.[72]

Observers also identified spillover from the occupation into Israeli society, in popular attitudes toward democracy and toward Arabs. There was particular concern about the impact on youth, who because of their army service were most exposed to the raw edge of the conflict. The steady drumbeat of conflict and hostility was likely to coarsen attitudes and create a more permissive climate toward the use of violence generally. Society became more polarized and confrontational, with a weakening center and increasingly rabid fringe groups.[73] The growth of intolerance, and delegitimization of political opponents, climaxed in the minds of most Israelis in November 1995, when Prime Minister Yitzhak Rabin was assassinated by an opponent of Israeli withdrawal from the territories.

Critics of occupation argued that over the course of time the domination of others inevitably corrupts the dominator. Those with the upper hand come to see their advantaged position, and the subordination of the unfavored, as the normal state of affairs. Standards of conduct decline over time;

the "benign" occupation of the West Bank and Gaza evolved by the time of the *intifada* into a brutalizing experience in which torture was routinized and hundreds of Palestinians were killed. Other symptoms of growing dehumanization included explosions of violence and vigilantism among West Bank settlers and the appearance, in the early 1980s, of a Jewish terrorist "underground" targeting Arab civilians and Muslim holy sites.[74]

By the standards of Western liberal democracy, denial of individual and national rights of others undermines one's own claim to self-determination. If the legitimacy of Zionism and of Israel as a nation-state is grounded in a universal right of all peoples to freedom and self-expression, then how can others, including the Palestinians, be excluded? Those who relied on Jewish law to make such distinctions also met strong objections: though Judaism does distinguish between Jews and non-Jews, mainstream rabbinical opinion from Maimonides through Rabbi Avraham Yitzhak Hacohen Kook regards an Arab in the Land of Israel as a *ger toshav,* with the right to remain and the right to equality under the law. Furthermore, leading rabbinical authorities (particular Rabbi Ovadiah Yosef, former Sephardi chief rabbi) have ruled that an Israeli government may relinquish control over parts of the Land of Israel in order to save human life, the highest value in Jewish law.[75]

Continuing rule over another people also runs counter to the traditional Jewish suspicion of power and resistance to strong authority, from within or without. Though the experience of being powerless and persecuted does not necessarily produce tolerance and virtue once one has acquired power, the weight of Jewish history could not be entirely ignored. It is no surprise that the most telling critiques of Israeli occupation came from within Israel itself. In a debate that could hardly have taken place anywhere else, Yehoshafat Harkabi, former chief of military intelligence, attacked the "mystical orientation of unrealism" in post-1967 Israel by drawing a historic parallel to the disastrous Bar-Kochba rebellion against Rome in 132–135 C.E.[76] Harkabi and others, in "speaking truth to power" and in reaffirming the priority of prudence and morality toward others over hubris and temporal power, harkened back to the classic prophetic tradition in Jewish history.

Even in the realm of security, the case for separation rather than integration looked stronger with the passage of time. While an independent Palestinian state in the West Bank and Gaza would pose serious strategic issues, so did continued occupation of that area. Jewish settlements did not contribute to strategic depth but stretched the resources of the Israeli army in providing protection to scattered and isolated outposts. The army itself was diverted from its basic missions by the tasks of occupation and the increasing need to focus on control of civilians rather than training and readiness for military combat. The lack of internal cohesion within Israel was reflected in growing confusion over a security policy torn by conflicting demands and pressures. Strategists pointed out that a settlement with the

Palestinians, by furthering the trend among Arab states to drop out of the conflict, would lessen the greater dangers that Israel faced. It would also strengthen Israel's international position immeasurably, leading to final universal acceptance and legitimacy. At some point, security arguments alone became a strong incentive for "territorial compromise" (under the right conditions) in the territories.[77]

By the mid-1990s it was clear that, in the words of one study, "the overall tendency among the Israeli political elites is to support greater separation between Israelis and Palestinians."[78] Even the Likud was not totally assimilationist, in that its proposed program of autonomy aimed for maximum separation consistent with continued Israeli sovereignty over the West Bank and Gaza. The strategy of separation was also a strategy for reducing the Arab-Israeli conflict to its pre-1948 intra-Palestinian core: by allowing Palestinian Arab self-determination to be realized within Palestine, alongside Israel, the major cause and incentive for external Arab involvement would be neutralized. Israel would remain in a very strong position in dealing with a separate Palestinian entity that in itself posed no military threat (apart from the problem of terrorism, to which continued occupation was also not a solution). Within such a state it was reasonable to expect that native West Bank and Gaza residents, rather than the refugee community, would dominate and would choose to coexist with Israel.

The missing ingredient was a negotiating partner willing to deal with Israel on this basis. The preferred partner for Israeli doves was Jordan, but King Hussein was never in a strong enough position to play the role, and finally in July 1988, he renounced any Jordanian claim to the West Bank. This left the Labor Party and others favoring separation in an awkward position, since the only body that could credibly represent West Bank and Gaza Palestinians—the PLO—remained committed to a unitary Palestine achieved by armed struggle. The PLO had adopted a program of "phases" in 1974, under which a state in part of Palestine might be established as an interim step toward total liberation of Palestine, and through the years its public declarations focused increasingly on Israeli withdrawal from the occupied territories. But it still rejected the Camp David agreement of 1978, which called for Israeli withdrawal in the framework of an autonomous elected Palestinian authority and a five-year period of transition—essentially the terms finally accepted by the PLO in the 1993 Declaration of Principles and the 1995 Interim Agreement. In theory, the five-year transition could have ended as early as 1983.

During the 1980s the PLO continued to move toward the option of a political and diplomatic, rather than military, solution. Its fighting forces were expelled from Lebanon, which meant the loss of the last actual fighting front against Israel. The *intifada* after 1987 instilled confidence needed to face negotiations, while it also shifted power among the Palestinians from the 1948–1949 refugees to West Bank and Gaza residents, who were generally readier to consider a two-state solution. But while the *intifada* could put the Palestinian issue back on the agenda and impose higher costs on Israel, it could not force unilateral Israeli withdrawal. The *intifada* might make Israelis more willing to leave the territories, but in order to reap this benefit the Palestinians would have to negotiate.

In December 1988, PLO leader Yasir Arafat renounced terrorism and called for a negotiated peace based on coexistence of Israel and a Palestinian state. This statement clearly changed the rules of the diplomatic game, leading to the opening of direct contact between the United States and the PLO, but it did not go far enough to qualify the PLO as a bargaining partner in the eyes of most Israelis. The Persian Gulf War in 1991 put further pressure on the PLO, as Palestinian support for Saddam Hussein led to loss of support from the oil-producing states and a severe financial crisis for the organization. The end of the Cold War and the collapse of the Soviet Union also changed the rules, as the PLO and other former clients could no longer count on Soviet diplomatic, political, and military backing. Instead, they would have to deal directly with the West, and with the United States in particular. Finally, the rise of Islamic fundamentalism (Hamas and other groups) in the occupied territories gave both the PLO and Israel reason to move while the window of opportunity was open and before religious extremism could slam it shut. The stage was set for a new chapter in the Arab-Israel conflict.

The onset of the *intifada* in December 1987, also had a major impact on Israeli opinion. With striking consistency about half of the respondents in different polls claimed that the *intifada* had made them either more hawkish or more dovish—but the proportion pushed in each direction was roughly similar, resulting in a very small net change for the sample as a whole. This pattern is illustrated with remarkable consistency in the three polls reported in Table 8.

The perception of a slight net shift in a hawkish direction, in response to the *intifada,* was true only in certain respects. It was most apparent on "short-term" issues in which emotions aroused by the *intifada* were most likely to be evident. The reaction of most Israelis to the *intifada* was colored by a tendency to see Palestinian violence and hostility in nonpolitical terms: not as opposition to occupation but as simple anti-Jewish hostility. The first response, therefore, was a demand for order. There was a clear hardening of public responses; throughout the *intifada* about half of Israeli Jews thought that the army was "too soft" in dealing with the uprising, while only about 10 percent thought it was "too hard."[79]

But at the same time, and despite the seeming contradiction, there was a discernible trend in a dovish direction on "long-term" questions such as preferred solutions to the conflict. As Asher Arian summarized these trends:

TABLE 8   Impact of the *Intifada* on Israeli Opinion (in percentage)

	Arian et al. October 1988*	Peres January 1990	Goldberg et al. May 1990
Intifada did not change opinion	49.9	51	50.2
Became more dovish	20.8	21	17.6
Became more hawkish	29.4	28	32.2

SOURCES: Asher Arian, Michal Shamir, and Raphael Ventura, "Public Opinion and Political Change: Israel and the Intifada," *Comparative Politics* 24 (April 1992): 323 (survey conducted by Dahaf Research Institute); Yochanan Peres, "Tolerance—Two Years Later," *Israeli Democracy* (Winter 1990): 17 (survey conducted by Dahaf Research Institute); Giora Goldberg, Gad Barzilai, and Efraim Inbar, *The Impact of Intercommunal Conflict: The Intifada and Israeli Public Opinion,* Policy Studies No. 43 (The Leonard Davis Institute for International Relations, 1991), 9 (survey conducted by Modi'in Ezrachi).

*Column totals more than 100 because of rounding.

"The reaction for most of the public seemed to be twofold: to tighten the grip and to be harsh in the short term, but to find a long-term solution which would extricate Israel from the dilemmas of the territories."[80] For most Israelis the *intifada* showed that maintenance of the status quo was not tenable over the long run; support for the status quo as a permanent solution, which had previously ranged from 11 to 47 percent in various polls, dropped to around 2 percent in one survey.[81] Even if the occupation brought material benefits to West Bank and Gaza residents, and even if the denial of civil and political rights were no worse than in most Arab states, continued Israeli occupation was unacceptable to Arabs in a way that suppression by their own regimes was not. It was the underlying ethnic conflict, not the flaws of the occupation regime, that fueled violent resistance to the continuing Israeli presence. And often it was military commanders, responsible for dealing with the *intifada,* who were first to point out that there was no military solution to this conflict and that a political solution must be found (Yitzhak Rabin, minister of defense during this period, personified this shift of views). In a 1992 survey of retired military and intelligence officers, 75 percent felt that Israel's security could be adequately maintained in a withdrawal from the West Bank and Gaza.[82]

Within a year or so after the onset of the *intifada,* surveys recorded a dovish shift of about 10 percent on the basic question of territorial compromise. Some of these results are shown in Table 9. In response to a slightly different question asked by Asher Arian, the percentage of those willing to return territories increased from 43 percent in 1986 to 60 percent in 1993.[83]

The dovish trend on basic issues can also been seen in regard to the controversial question of Israeli negotiations with the PLO. Support for negotiation with the PLO, provided it recognized Israel and renounced terrorism, grew from 43 percent in September 1986, to 58 percent by March

TABLE 9   Impact of *Intifada:* Territorial Concessions
(in percentage)

"What concessions would you make on the West Bank (Judea and Samaria) in order
to reach a peace settlement with the Arab states?"

	March 1987*	January 1989	May 1991
Some, most, or all of the territories	54	65	69
None of the territories	45	35	31

SOURCE: Continuing Survey of the Israel Institute of Applied Social Research, reported by
Elihu Katz, *Jerusalem Post International Edition*, 27 August 1988; Katz, "Majority Hawkish, But
Dovish Trend Seen," *Jerusalem Post International Edition*, 18 February 1989; Katz and Hannah
Levinsohn, "Poll: 75% Support the Return of Territories for a Peace Agreement" (in He-
brew), *Yediot Ahronot*, 21 June 1991.
    *Column totals less than 100 because of rounding.

1989, in figures from the Smith Research Center.[84] Conditional support for
talking with the PLO thus moved from a minority to a majority opinion after
the *intifada.*

Support for an independent Palestinian state in the West Bank and Gaza,
as a solution to the Israeli-Palestinian conflict, also grew from roughly 10
percent at the end of the 1970s to 25 to 30 percent a decade later. The
IIASR survey of April 1990, for example, showed 25 percent support for
a Palestinian state, while Asher Arian's survey of March–October 1990 recorded 28 percent in agreement with this solution—and 61 percent who
thought that a Palestinian state would come whether they supported it or
not (against 51 percent with this view before the *intifada*).[85]

Both Labor and Likud moved very gradually in a dovish direction in apparent response to shifting public opinion and, on a deeper level, to changes
in the Arab world.[86] In Labor, the Allon Plan (for the return of most of the
West Bank to Jordan), once championed by those on the left in the party, became the position of those on the right. The focus for resolving the conflict
shifted from Jordan to the Palestinians. The Likud dropped its earlier call
for eventual annexation (present in its 1969 and 1973 platforms), moving
to advocacy of various autonomy schemes, and also accepted UN Resolu-
tions 242 and 338, which it had originally rejected. During its long tenure
in power, it also accepted the previous international border with Egypt and
legitimized the role of Arab states as parties to negotiation over the future of
the West Bank (in the Camp David accords). Even where the substance of its
positions remained hawkish, Likud arguments over the years became notably less ideological and more oriented to security issues.

The electorate was still divided between those who favored partition solutions in their various versions (a Palestinian entity of some kind, redivi-

sion with Jordan, or a Palestinian-Jordanian confederation) and those who favored unitary solutions (autonomy or other forms of functional compromise based on continuing Israeli control of the territories), but the tide was running in favor of the former. Even 27 percent of those who voted for Likud and other right-wing parties in 1988 favored a compromise based on territory withdrawal in return for peace, indicating the potential for a mobilizable majority in Israel for territorial compromise.[87]

THE PROCESS OF DISENGAGEMENT

Pragmatic security concerns are the dominant variable in Israeli opinion. This opinion is remarkably sensitive to Arab words and actions; events and changes in the Arab world seem to provide the best explanation for the long-term moderation of Israeli thinking since 1967. Positions supposedly based on deeply held beliefs and convictions have shifted with startling rapidity in response to dramatic developments. Furthermore, the experience of the *intifada* demonstrates that changes can take place in contradictory directions simultaneously and that the impact of violent or negative events in the short term does not necessarily undercut or reverse positive trends in basic attitudes.

By the early 1990s there was a mobilizable majority of the Jewish Israeli public behind practical measures to moderate the conflict by disengaging from the occupied territories. The status quo enjoyed next to no support in principle from any segment of Israeli opinion; ideological doves and pragmatic doves, working together, could potentially dominate. The decisive consideration was security, not ideology. What once sounded radical had become less so; negotiation with the PLO and the idea of a Palestinian state, once outside the mainstream of political debate, became part of it.

How did the political system process the anomaly of increased dovishness on territorial issues—the dominant issues of Israeli politics—with little or no change in party loyalties? Clearly the electorate was voting somewhat to the right of its opinions on security issues.[88] A number of reasons for this anomaly can be suggested: the influence of other issues that favored Likud, continuing Sephardi alienation from the Labor Establishment, and—not least— the appeal of Likud as tougher bargainers who would better defend Israeli interests in any negotiations that took place (Likud electoral slogans and other moves to establish its credentials as a serious peace negotiator lent additional credence to this interpretation). Whatever the causes of this inconsistency, the phenomenon of an electorate voting to the right of its opinions on substantive issues provided an ironic contrast to the earlier pattern, in the 1960s and 1970s, of an electorate that voted to the left of its fundamental beliefs in a number of respects (see chapter 6).[89]

Elections in 1992 and 1996 confirmed a continuing split right down the middle of Israeli politics. In 1992 Labor and other parties of the left secured a bare majority of sixty-one in the Knesset, and in the first direct vote for prime minister (in 1996), Benjamin Netanyahu defeated Shimon Peres by less than 1 percent of votes cast. Netanyahu's victory also illustrated the continuing success of the right in attracting pragmatic hawks from the middle of the spectrum; his platform called for "making secure peace" and promised a continuation of the peace process.

In 1992 Yitzhak Rabin, returning to the prime ministership after a hiatus of fifteen years, had a narrow but workable advantage in the Knesset. Even without including the two far-left parties (Democratic Front for Peace and Equality and the Arab Democratic Party) in the governing coalition, he could count on their five Knesset votes as part of a "blocking majority" of sixty-one to bar any alternative government of right-wing and religious parties, who together could muster only fifty-nine votes. In addition, an even balance does not necessarily prevent decisive government action in Israel, given the amorphous state of opinion and the tendency to defer to strong leadership. Israel leaders have considerable latitude as long as party discipline holds; public opinion is responsive to strong direction on security issues, and especially to peaceful initiatives (such as the 1977 Sadat visit and the 1993 breakthrough with the PLO).[90]

In negotiating withdrawal from the territories, however, Israel faced two structural problems. The first was that, even in the framework of separation, there was initially no agreed-upon endpoint acceptable to a majority of both Israelis and Palestinians. Israelis who were ready to part with the territories tended to prefer a Jordan-based solution or some form of self-rule short of a Palestinian state; Palestinians who now accepted a state alongside (rather than in place of) Israel would not accept anything less than total sovereignty and independence from all Israeli control. Thus the interim solutions had to be open ended, leaving a number of possible outcomes on the table; it was indeed a peace *process,* as it was labeled, since it was only with the completion of each phase that sufficient agreement was built for the next.

The second problem is that, from Israel's perspective, the "Land-for-Peace" formula involves the surrender of tangible assets (territory, strategic advantages) for intangible commitments that can be quickly and easily renounced. For this reason, Israeli negotiators try to structure any agreement so that territorial withdrawal will be balanced by compensating security arrangements making renewed belligerency unappealing to the other side. It might be more accurate to term this approach "land for security" rather than "land for peace." In the peace treaty with Egypt, the return of the Sinai was combined with its demilitarization under international verification; in essence, given the superior mobility of Israeli forces, the Sinai serves as hostage for Egyptian adherence to its commitment of nonbelligerence.

Following the 1991 Persian Gulf War the United States had brokered a diplomatic effort that produced a formal framework for negotiations. At the Madrid Conference in October 1991—the first direct Arab-Israeli peace talks with representation of all major parties—separate but parallel multilateral and bilateral tracks were set in motion. The multilateral forums, which included the nations of the Middle East and some outside powers, met periodically in the following years to discuss the issues of water, environment, arms control, refugees, and economic development. The real action, however, was focused in four sets of bilateral talks between Israel and Jordan, Israel and Palestinians, Israel and Syria, and Israel and Lebanon. (Initially the Palestinians appeared as part of a joint Jordanian-Palestinian delegation, but this quickly became a polite fiction.)

With the Likud government unwilling to move beyond autonomy for West Bank and Gazan Arabs, early negotiations between Israel and the Palestinians made little progress. But continuing pressures on the PLO, together with the change of government in Israel, led to a breakthrough following months of secret contacts between the two parties. In September 1993, Israel and the PLO extended mutual recognition to each other and, in a dramatic ceremony on the White House lawn, signed a Declaration of Principles on Interim Self-Government Arrangements (DOP) to serve as an open-ended framework for a settlement.

The DOP was strikingly similar to the Camp David "Framework for Peace in the Middle East" negotiated between Israel and Egypt fifteen years earlier and rejected by the PLO at the time. Both agreements called for a five-year transition period in the West Bank and Gaza, during which Arabs in these areas would enjoy full autonomy under an elected Self-Governing Authority (which emerged as the "Palestinian Authority"), Israeli military and civil government would be ended, and Israeli troops would be redeployed out of Arab population centers and into specified security locations. Both agreements called for final status talks, covering borders, security measures, refugees, and other unsettled issues, to begin no later than the third year of the transition. The major difference was that Camp David had reserved a major role for Jordan and a lesser role for Egypt, while the DOP treated the West Bank and Gaza as a bilateral Israeli-Palestinian concern. The DOP also specified an early Israeli withdrawal from Gaza and from the Jericho area as a first step.

In a sense the DOP marked the "re-Palestinization" of the conflict, as Israel reestablished the border that had been blurred since 1967, recognized the Arabs within historic Palestine as its major negotiating partner, and reduced the role of external Arab states in the conflict.[91] This strategy gained strong public support, even though the Likud—sponsors of the Camp David accords—found grounds as an opposition party to reject the DOP and the subsequent agreements negotiated within its framework.

The timetable for implementation of various stages of the agreement was very ambitious, due to Palestinian pressure for quick Israeli withdrawal. Agreement on the details for the first-stage withdrawal, from Gaza and Jericho, was reached only in May 1994, rather than as scheduled in December 1993. Agreement on "Early Empowerment" of the Palestinian Authority throughout the territories was reached in August 1994, and finally in October 1995, the full Interim Agreement of some 400 pages, known as Oslo II, was finalized. Under this intricate arrangement, Israeli forces redeployed out of Arab cities and towns, the Palestinian Authority assumed control of the Arab population (total control in the cities, civil control in rural areas), and elections were held for a Palestinian council with legislative and executive powers, headed by an elected president (Yasir Arafat). Israeli forces still controlled 70 percent of the West Bank, however, including for the time being all of the Jewish settlements, a fact that gave the Palestine leadership a strong interest in not allowing the process to stall at this stage (see Map 4).

Support for the peace process within Israel fluctuated significantly in response to events, including the ups and downs of the process itself but, even more, a wave of suicide bombings perpetrated by Islamic extremists, who sought to derail the process. Nevertheless a strong, and even growing, majority of 60 to 65 percent continued in principle to support talks with the PLO, the return of territories, and the peace process in general. Support for the DOP in particular was eroded by the perception that the PLO was not acting in good faith to prevent terrorism, and support fluctuated in early 1995 between 30 and 35 percent (with a similar proportion opposed explicitly and up to a quarter of the respondents on the fence).[92] This support rose when Oslo II was signed, and the assassination of Prime Minister Yitzhak Rabin, on November 4, 1995, caused a strong backlash of support both for the peace process (to over 73 percent) and for the Oslo agreement in particular (to 58 percent).[93]

By this time the Israeli government could also enumerate concrete benefits of the peace process. Normalization of Arab relations was progressing: the Arab boycott was withering, and Israel was developing economic ties with a number of Arab states. The "cold" peace with Egypt seemed to be warming, and the 1994 treaty with Jordan promised full normalization, the repeal of anti-Israel laws, and a number of joint development projects along the Israel-Jordan border. The "Eastern front" threat diminished considerably with Jordanian guarantees against the stationing of hostile forces on its territory, while the detachment of Jordan from West Bank issues also lessened the risk of eventual Palestinian dominance on the East Bank. Lower-level relations were established with Morocco, Tunisia, Mauritania, and Oman; by late 1995 Israel had diplomatic relations with nearly all non-Arab Muslim states, and with 155 nations altogether (against only 68 a decade earlier). The changed political climate also helped the economy, with big jumps in tourism and foreign investment (following upgraded credit ratings in international markets).

Rather strikingly, the vast majority of Israelis—74 percent by 1994—had come to believe that a Palestinian state would in fact be established, whether it was their preference or not.[94] As the Israeli army moved out of Arab population centers, it seemed very unlikely that it would move back in, barring a total breakdown of law and order that spilled across Israel's frontiers. Public figures spoke with increasing candor about the likelihood that self-rule for the West Bank and Gaza was, as the opponents of the peace process charged, leading to eventual Palestinian statehood. It might appear under a different label and be constrained by demilitarization and other security arrangements, as Sinai had been and the Golan Heights would be in any settlement with Syria, but a Palestinian state in one form or another appeared as the logical outcome of the process that had been set in motion.

As for borders, the intentions of the Rabin and Peres governments could best be gauged by policies toward Jewish settlements across the Green Line: where was continued building encouraged, where was it frozen, and in what other ways was the government redrawing the boundaries? Initially the Rabin government had differentiated "security settlements" from "political settlements" and had retained generous government benefits only for the former while freezing public expenditure and new housing starts elsewhere in the territories. Consequently it seemed likely the government would try to include the bedroom communities of western Samaria and greater Jerusalem, the Etzion bloc south of Jerusalem, and the Jordan Valley settlements on the Israeli side of the final border. According to a study by the Jaffee Center for Strategic Studies, a redrawing of the Green Line to incorporate 11 percent of the West Bank in Israel could bring in 60 to 70 percent of the Jewish settlers (and very few Arabs), thus making this thorny issue less contentious.[95]

Netanyahu's razor-thin victory in 1996 put the process back on the slow track, however. The new government's opposition in principle to further Israeli withdrawal from the occupied territories, to Palestinian statehood in any form, or to any compromise on Jerusalem, made further agreements with the PLO, or any agreement with Syria, much more difficult. But while the process could be stalled, or even disrupted, it did not seem to be reversible. Despite detours and heartaches, it would inch forward.

It is possible that we are in the last phase of the Arab-Israel conflict. Its re-Palestinization encourages the gradual, grudging acceptance of Israel as a fact by Arab states, based on their recognition that it cannot be defeated militarily and by their own shift of focus to domestic problems and priorities. This acceptance is not based on conviction but on necessity; it will not be a "warm" peace in the near future (with the possible exception of Jordan), but it can be a workable and stable long-term settlement.

The detachment of external enemies requires settlement of Israeli-Palestinian differences in a way acceptable to most Palestinians; this in turn requires, realistically, a disentanglement of the two peoples. After flirting with other conceptions, the Israeli public has returned to the conventional wisdom that good fences make good neighbors; roughly 75 percent agreed in 1995 with the statement that "from Israel's point of view, also in a state of peace, it is preferable to have a clear and closed border between it and the Palestinian entity, in order to create maximum separation between Israelis and Palestinians."[96] Even more striking, perhaps, is the public response to the closures between the territories and Israel periodically implemented since March 1993, in response to terrorist incidents. Despite the fact that these closures contributed substantially to the process of disengagement, they were supported wholeheartedly by all segments of the population except the ideological hawks.

Separation is seen by some as the defeat of Jewish values, as failure to fulfill a historic mission. But disengagement may be the key to the preservation of a newly created Israeli culture within a re-created Jewish state. There is, as most observers on both sides note, a struggle between the universalistic values of the peace process and particularistic claims of those aspiring to an undivided Land of Israel, paralleling a presumed choice between democracy with limited Jewish character or an ethnic state with limited democracy. History rarely proceeds by such clear choices, however; Jewish history in particular is a continuing synthesis of the universal and the particular. Disengagement clearly preserves democracy, but it may also be the strongest bulwark of Jewishness.[97]

Epilogue

The May 1996 Israeli elections underlined, in a way previous elections had not, the continuing struggle between two different Israels. Since 1977 the body politic has been roughly divided into two halves, between left and radical/Arab blocs on one hand and right and religious blocs on the other (see chapter 6). This bifurcation had been obscured somewhat by the usual kaleidoscopic shifts among parties and by conflicting preferences for prime minister and for party. But in 1996 voters could for the first time vote separately for prime minister, and the two-way race between Labor's Shimon Peres and Likud's Benjamin Netanyahu forced voters to identify with one or the other of the two Israels (though a surprising 5 percent cast blank ballots). Netanyahu's narrow victory, by 50.5 percent to 49.5 percent, provided a clear if momentary measure of the continuing close division between "traditional" Israel, looking distrustfully on the prospects of Israel becoming "a nation like other nations," and "civic" Israel, fervently pushing the normalization of Israel's domestic life and external relations.

Clearly the precise outcome of the prime ministerial vote also reflected the personal appeal of the two candidates, the skill of their campaigns, and recent dramatic events such as Rabin's assassination seven months before the election (which created a wave of support for Peres) and the "Nine Days of Terror" in February–March (which created a backlash against Peres). But what was evident throughout the campaign was the polarization of the political scene down the middle as traditional Israel mobilized behind Netanyahu and civic Israel rallied to Peres. Religious and *haredi* leaders and parties came together behind Netanyahu despite his personal nonobservance and fervent appeals from the other side; leftists and Arab voters gave Peres overwhelming support despite their dislike of his "Grapes of Wrath" campaign in Lebanon just before the election. The flavor of the campaign reflected not just opposed views of the Oslo peace accords but opposed life-styles: on the one hand, appeals to tradition, attacks on pop culture and "yuppies," the blessing of amulets and of Netanyahu himself by an aged kab-balistic scholar, and the slogan that "Netanyahu is good for the Jews"; on the other hand, the argument of economic prosperity, the vision of Israel's integration into the Middle East, popular comedians and a pop "Song of Peace," and the call for an Israel that would be "the state of all its citizens."

Israel still struggles between its calling as "a nation that dwells alone," in the words of Balaam's blessing, and the natural attraction of normality. Tra-ditional Israel is more particularist, primordial, communitarian, religious, conservative, and hawkish where civic Israel—the "New Israel" created in the century since Herzl—is more universalist, modernist, cosmopolitan, secular, liberal, and dovish. Traditional Israel values affective thinking ("from the heart") as embodied in traditional cultures; civic Israel subscribes whole-heartedly to rationalist models ("from the head") associated with Western civilization. Traditional Israel conceives of collective identity in terms of eth-nicity ("Jewishness"); civic Israel tends to define identity in terms of territo-riality ("Israeliness").[1] In traditional Israel one is usually a Jew first and an Is-raeli second, while in civic Israel the order is reversed.

Of course these correlations are not perfect; real life is multidimensional. Israel has religious doves and secular hawks, antimodernists of European origin and "Westernizers" from non-Western backgrounds. But it is still pos-sible, given a very few variables, to predict with reasonable accuracy which Is-rael a particular voter will choose, especially when these variables all point in the same direction. A lower-income Sephardi religious voter did not tend to back Peres in 1996, just as Netanyahu did not get the support of the av-erage college-educated, native-born, higher-income secularist Ashkenazi (a category that he fit himself).

The basic division was most evident in the almost-even polarization of the 1996 prime ministerial vote, but the party vote in the Knesset also reflected it. While parties of the left and far left together lost their blocking majority of sixty-one, dropping to fifty-two, the parties of the right also lost nine seats (from forty-three to thirty-four). The new electoral system drained votes from the larger parties by enabling voters to cast a ballot for *both* their prime minister of choice *and* for the party closest to their heart. Smaller parties accordingly urged voters "not to put bread into pita" (that is, "don't vote twice for the same party"). The religious parties benefited greatly, moving from sixteen to twenty-three seats, but the real news was the appearance of a previously nonexisting centrist bloc, with eleven seats, consisting of the Third Way, a splinter group from Labor, and Yisrael B'aliya (Israel in As-cent), led by former Soviet dissident Natan Sharansky, which made history as the first immigrant-based party to gain representation in the Knesset and even seats in the cabinet.

The impact of the electoral reform, therefore, was to put more coalition bargaining power into the hands of smaller centrist and religious parties; Netanyahu's coalition was built of eight parties (including three in the Likud electoral alliance), and only twenty-three of his majority of sixty-six were members of the Likud itself. This was balanced by the increased powers given the prime minister in the reform, and in particular the fact that only the elected prime minister could form a government. The potential coalition partners thus had either to deal with Netanyahu or force new elections— never a popular option among newly elected legislators. The overall impact of the reform was thus limited; Netanyahu formed a government committed in principle to the peace process, though a majority of its members had opposed the Oslo accords in practice.

The balance of power between the prime minister and the Knesset was not changed profoundly, nor did the system as a whole shift more perceptibly to majoritarianism because of the reform. In fact, it seemed increasingly unlikely that any electoral reform would or should dilute the basic consociationalism of the system, as one *sine qua non* of any proposed reform, in practice, has been that it would maintain the representation of key groups (religious, minorities).[2] Following an election in which the power of smaller parties was further enhanced, it was unlikely that they would willingly yield the additional ground gained, let alone retreat beyond the original line.

Does this mean that Israel is doomed to paralysis by indecision between its two halves? Can it not overcome what has been termed by various observers "a *Kulturkampf,*" "a deadlock [between] opposing camps of nearly equal strength," or "two contradictory unbridgeable conceptions"?[3] Are these conceptions indeed unbridgeable—or will there be "a creative synthesis of both primordial loyalties and universalistic values inherent in traditional Jewish culture that have been vital aspects of Zionism in the past"?[4]

Haven't Jewish history and the Zionist enterprise both been characterized by an ongoing synthesis of the tribal and the universal? Increasingly in Israel one sees signs of a blurring in the middle, of a less sharp dichotomy between "Jewish" and "Israeli." The outcome of the two-person prime minister's contest was decided by appeals to the large group of voters in the middle of the spectrum; Netanyahu was forced to emphasize his commitment to the peace process while Peres stressed his toughness on security. With the general decline in ideological commitment there is added fluidity in politics, and the emerging center is where the game is won or lost. In the center particularism and universalism meet, and Israel finds it can neither live in isolation nor cut itself off from its Jewish roots.

No nation these days can totally ignore the civic principle that all citizens ought to be equal before the law despite racial, ethnic, religious, social, or political differences. This idea is now near-universal as a standard (if not as a practice), and Jews have always been among those foremost in promoting it. Indeed no people has gained as much from application of the civic ideal, or have as much continuing interest in furthering it, as the Jewish people; it would be inconsistent with Jewish history and with Jewish interests to suggest that a Jewish state is somehow exempt from this standard.

Nor can Israel escape being part of an increasingly interdependent and technologically oriented world. In Israel no less than elsewhere, modernization involves challenges to tradition, the decline of ideology, and convergence with other societies. Some describe contemporary Israel as "post-Zionist," though the term has been used in so many contexts—as loss of ideology, as critique of Zionist historiography, as attack on pop culture, as argument for a nonethnic state—that it has no commonly agreed-upon meaning.

But conversely Israel cannot cut its ties to Jewish tradition. As one secular critic concludes, "a Hebrew national consciousness will always have affinities to Judaism."[5] Without Jewish tradition, what would Israel have of its own? "A few Jewish Agency songs, a bit of Palmach style, some pioneering memories, and the idea of the *kibbutz* . . . ," in the words of Amos Oz?[6] Zionism drew heavily, if selectively, on Jewish tradition, and the human reality of a population *not* in rebellion against this tradition guaranteed the reemergence of much more of it.

The result is not so far from that envisioned by Ahad Ha'am, who saw Zionism as a higher stage in the development of Jewish civilization rather than as a break with the past. Ahad Ha'am personified the synthesis that has emerged and is yet emerging: "secular, liberal, but nonetheless embedded . . . in the fundamental teachings of Judaism. . . . because anything else would be humanly inauthentic, intellectually deadening, itself a curious and perverse exercise in parochialism."[7]

Speaking of the two opposed conceptions now at war in Israel, *The Economist* declares: "Which is the true Zionism? Both."[8] By extension: Which is the authentic Judaism? Both. Judaism, like other traditions, includes both particularist and universalist elements. Some on the nationalist fringes have selectively ignored the humanistic dimension, interpreting Judaism in wholly parochial terms. But if selectivity is inevitable with such a complex legacy, why not choose to stress the universalist ethics as Israel integrates into the family of nations? When tradition offers contradictory messages, why choose limited visions of the past rather than the timeless truths of the Hebrew prophets?

Perhaps the most valuable legacy of Jewish history is the principle of pluralism itself. Diversity was not only a central reality of Jewish life but was also a principle in Jewish law. As the Talmud says regarding differing schools of thought, "these *and* these are the words of the living God." But Judaism in Israel has resisted pluralism in its broader aspects. Clinging to a narrow view of tradition, "it is much the poorer for failing to develop non-Orthodox models of authenticity, for failing to extend adequately the meaning of Judaism to the personal domain, and for failing to engage and adapt for Jewish purposes non-Jewish cultural elements."[9] The growth of non-Orthodox religious movements—Reform, Reconstructionist, Conservative—seems inevitable in light of the fact that patterns of observance among large segments of the Israeli public already fit into these molds, being neither totally secular nor totally Orthodox.[10] Even staunch secularists have proposed enriching the religious studies in state secular schools by, among other things, including all the streams of modern Judaism in the curriculum and stressing Jewish heritage and history broadly.

Of what, minimally, does the "Jewishness" of the Jewish state consist? Interestingly the Israeli Supreme Court, in dealing with the eligibility of parties to participate in elections, has tried to answer that question. Acceptance of "Israel as a Jewish state," the court ruled, means at the least: (1) maintenance of a Jewish majority, (2) the right of Jews to immigrate (the Law of Return), and (3) ties with Jewish communities outside Israel.[11] None of these features are inherently inconsistent with liberal democracy, and none of them are in fact unique to Israel. As detailed in chapter 9, there are at least two dozen ethnic democracies in the world (among several dozen ethnic states), and a large number of states grant citizenship on the basis of ethnic identity or descent. Nor is the existence of a dispersion peculiar to the Jewish people, save perhaps in duration and extent, and the growth of sentiment for "normalizing" Israel-Diaspora relations would lessen any remaining differences (by limiting the Law of Return, reducing the role of world Jewry in Israel, or even reversing the flow of influence as Israel becomes the dominant force in the Jewish world).

As for non-Jews in Israel, pluralism may actually mean creating a new distinction between "Israeli" and "Jewish." Is it possible to develop an Israeliness that includes, but is not limited to, Jewishness? Can Palestinian citizens be made a part of "us" on at least one level? No nation-state, indeed, is entirely neutral in matters of particular ethnicity or culture, but this does not mean that a Jewish state by definition must be inhospitable to other ethnic groups. The acid test of Israeli democracy will be whether it can take Arab citizens into full partnership.

This should not be impossible. The genius of Jewish politics has always been its power-sharing, or consociationalism in political science terms. Consociationalism is a concept that itself synthesizes the civic and communitarian dimensions of politics; its point of departure is a clear recognition of the permanence and legitimacy of diversity within society. In the Jewish context it has functioned reasonably well even where the lifestyles of groups were so diametrically opposed as to defy comparison. It has enabled the *haredi* (ultra-Orthodox) community in Israel, for example, to become increasingly involved in the system even while questioning some of its basic premises. A balance of mutual dissatisfaction preserves stability, though it is sometimes hard to perceive this through the clamor of complaint.

Can Israel be both Jewish and democratic? The answer is yes, though there will be continuing tension between the two ideals. Furthermore, there is no precedent for a stable ethnic democracy with a minority of 40 percent or more, as would be the case in an Israel extended over the whole of Mandatory Palestine. Successful accommodation of Arab citizens within a Jewish Israel clearly assumes a divorce from broader Israel-Palestinian and Israel-Arab issues, if not an overall resolution of the broader conflict. Separation of Israel from the West Bank and Gaza is a process begun but not concluded, and even when concluded a high degree of mutual dependence will remain. But good Zionist principles would indicate that only independent nation-states, interacting as equals, can hope to achieve relative stability. The dilemma of post-Rabin politics in Israel is that the current situation cannot be reversed and can hardly be advanced, but also cannot be left as it is. In the end it will have to advance.

Another basic element of continuity in Jewish history is that insecurity still permeates Jewish politics. The establishment of a Jewish state displaced this fear and mistrust onto a new and unaccustomed plane, but the sense of being "a people that dwells alone" still pervades the nation. Israelis are reluctant to recognize success even when it is apparent; the historic achievement of at least de facto acceptance by most of the Arab world and contractual peace on the country's two longest borders are hardly felt. Despite tremendous change for the better in Israel's security position, and enviable success economically and otherwise, the *gevalt* syndrome still prevails. The capacity to extract gloomy premonitions from even the most promising turn of events remains undiminished.

In his inaugural address to the Knesset on July 13, 1992, Prime Minister Yitzhak Rabin addressed this sense of insecurity:

> It is our duty, to ourselves and our children, to see the new world as it is now—to discern its dangers, explore its prospects, and to do everything possible so the State of Israel will fit into this world whose face is changing. No longer are we necessarily "a people that dwells alone," and no longer is it true that "the whole world is against us." We must overcome the sense of isolation that has held us in thrall for almost half a century.

The stunning irony is that while "dwelling alone" Jews have had perhaps the most interactive experience of any nation in human history. Jews have been a part of most major world civilizations while still maintaining their own identity and essential unity. The maintenance of separation amidst dispersion has been the central dynamic of Jewish life and has produced a wide variety of responses. In this context Zionism was simply another attempt to resolve the dilemma, this time by reinventing Jews as a normal nation in order to make possible a positive assimilation into human history. It was an attempt at assimilation through insistence on identity; in Hannah Arendt's words, "it represents the only logically consistent effort at assimilation."[12]

In this sense, also, it is of a piece with Jewish history. As Leonard Fein has characterized this history:

> We are the tribe that proclaimed the universality of God, but insisted on remaining a tribe. Others, not understanding why we have felt such urgency about remaining apart, have asked—and sometimes demanded—that we follow our universal insight to its logical conclusion and ourselves become universal. We have steadfastly refused.[13]

NOTES

1. DEMOCRACY IN ISRAEL

1. Noam Chomsky, "Foreword," in Sabri Jiryis, *The Arabs in Israel* (Monthly Review Press, 1976), xi.

2. Ibid., viii.

3. The tension between universalism and particularism in the four major ideological sources of Zionism is discussed by Baruch Kimmerling, "Between the Primordial and Civil Definitions of the Collective Identity: *Eretz Yisrael* or the State of Israel?" in *Comparative Social Dynamics: Essays in Honor of Shmuel Eisenstadt*, ed. M. Lissak, E. Cohen, and U. Almagor (Westview Press, 1984), 262–83; see also Zeev Ben-Sira, *Zionism at the Close of the Twentieth Century* (Edwin Mellen Press, 1993).

4. This is not to imply that Herzl's political instincts were entirely democratic; see chapter 3.

5. Avineri, *The Making of Modern Zionism: The Intellectual Origins of the Jewish State* (Basic Books, 1981), 12.

6. Ibid., 13, 226.

7. Avishai, *The Tragedy of Zionism* (Farrar, Straus & Giroux, 1985), 10.

8. Ibid., 325; see also 11.

9. Ibid., 305.

10. Ibid., 304, 305. *Democracy* (and its cognates) is of course a borrowed word in every language but Greek and sounds no more alien to the native Hebrew speaker than to an English speaker.

11. Another instance of ethnic defense, in the most "open" of modern societies, has been the rash of laws in U.S. state legislatures affirming English as the "official language" of the state.

12. Benyamin Neuberger, "Does Israel Have a Liberal-Democratic Tradition?" *Jewish Political Studies Review*, nos. 3 and 4 (Fall 1990): 96.

13. Israel, Central Bureau of Statistics, *Statistical Abstract of Israel 1987*, 8–11; according to these figures, in the 1919–1948 period 45,010 of 482,857 immigrants, or 9.3 percent, came from countries generally recognized as democratic, while in the

1949–1987 period, 206,209 of 1,791,423, or 11.5 percent, came from democratic states. The study by B. Gil, *Chronicles of Aliya: Thirty Years of Aliya to the Land of Israel, 1919–1949* (in Hebrew) (Jewish Agency for the Land of Israel, 1949–1950), 28, gives a comparable figure of 89,552 of 805,216 (11.1 percent) for the 1919–1949 period.

14. A quick perusal of the figures of the Central Bureau of Statistics indicates that some 76.6 percent of the 1919–1948 immigrants and about 75.7 percent of the 1948–1967 entrants, would meet this definition. The figures in Gil for the 1919–1949 period lead to an estimate of about 82.2 percent refugees.

15. Daniel Shimshoni, *Israeli Democracy: The Middle of the Journey* (The Free Press, 1982), 452.

16. Yoram Ben-Porath, "Introduction," in *The Israeli Economy: Maturing through Crises*, ed. Yoram Ben-Porath (Harvard University Press, 1986), 5; see also Eitan Berglas, "Defense and the Economy," 173–91 in the same volume.

17. Eisenstadt, *The Transformation of Israeli Society* (Westview Press, 1985), 152; see also 344–45, 403, 557–58.

18. This is one of the theses in Yonathan Shapiro's important book, *Democracy in Israel* (in Hebrew) (Masada, 1977), 36; see also Asher Arian, *Politics in Israel: The Second Generation*, rev. ed. (Chatham House Publishers, 1989), 260.

19. Yochanan Peres, "Most Israelis Are Committed to Democracy," *Israeli Democracy* 1 (February 1987): 16–19; Yochanan Peres and Mira Freund, "Tolerance Israeli Style," *Israeli Democracy* 1, no. 3 (Fall 1987): 35–39; Ephraim Yuchtman-Ya'ar, "The Test of Israel's Arab Minority," *Israeli Democracy* 2, no. 1 (Spring 1988): 42–46; Ephraim Ya'ar and Yochanan Peres, "Democracy Index," *Israeli Democracy* 2, no. 4 (Winter 1988): 15–19; Yochanan Peres, "Tolerance—Two Years Later," *Israeli Democracy* (Winter 1990): 16–18; Ephraim Yuchtman-Ya'ar and Yochanan Peres, "Public Opinion and Democracy after Three Years of Intifada," *Israeli Democracy* (Spring 1991): 21–25; Yochanan Peres and Ephraim Ya'ar, "Postscript: Democracy under Fire," *Israeli Democracy* (Spring 1991): 26–29. See confirming data in Asher Arian, *Security Threatened: Surveying Israeli Opinion on Peace and War* (Cambridge University Press, 1995), 233; Arian points out that the Israeli public has consistently ranked "democracy" below "maintaining a Jewish majority" and "peace" as a value priority (211–16).

20. Peres, "Most Israelis Are Committed to Democracy," 16.

21. Peres and Freund, "Tolerance Israeli Style," 39. In research comparing U.S. and Israeli attitudes, Michal Shamir and John Sullivan note that "the percentages supporting the general norms of democracy were high in both the United States and Israel, with one exception: 89 percent of the Americans supported minority rights, but only 63 percent of the Israelis did so." The authors also note that "in Israel, 'minorities' means Arabs . . ."; Shamir and Sullivan, "The Political Context of Tolerance: The United States and Israel," *American Political Science Review* 77 (December 1983): 914.

22. Peres, "Tolerance—Two Years Later," 17.

23. S. Ezra Austern, Letter to the Editor, *Jerusalem Post*, 22 September 1985.

24. A sampling of such articles along these lines, in Hebrew, would include: Yisrael Eldad, "Zionism against Democracy," *Nativ* 2, no. 1 (January 1989): 54–60; Mor-

dechai Nisan, "The Zionist Sacrifice to the Moloch of Democracy," *Nativ* 3, no. 4 (July 1990): 16–21; Paul Eidelberg, "Demophrenia: Democracy in a Madman's Straightjacket," *Nativ* 4, no. 3 (May 1991): 46–51. These arguments are summarized and critiqued by Susan Hattis Rolef, "A Threat to Democracy Is a Threat to Zionism," *Jerusalem Post*, 20 May 1991, with responses from Eidelberg ("Democracy Doesn't Have All the Answers") and Nisan ("No Need to Apologize") in the *Jerusalem Post*, 10 June 1991.

25. The case for a comparative perspective is made convincingly by Benyamin Neuberger, "Israel's Democracy and Comparative Politics," *Jewish Political Studies Review* 1 (Fall 1989): 67–75, and by various authors in Michael N. Barnett, ed., *Israel in Comparative Perspective: Challenging the Conventional Wisdom* (State University of New York Press, 1996).

26. Arend Lijphart, *Democracies: Patterns of Majoritarian and Consensus Government in Twenty-One Countries* (Yale University Press, 1984), 37–45; Lijphart, "Democracies: Forms, Performance, and Constitutional Engineering," *European Journal of Political Research* 25 (January 1994): 1–17.

27. Shamir and Sullivan, "Political Context of Tolerance," esp. 917. This was confirmed in a study by Rita J. Simon, using surveys carried out by the Israel Institute for Applied Social Research, which found regard for civil liberties in Israel comparable to that of Western countries; see Simon, "Assessing Israel's Record on Human Rights," *The Annals of the American Academy of Political and Social Science*, no. 506 (November 1989): 115–28. Also see Rita J. Simon, Jean M. Landis, and Menachem Amir, "Public Support for Civil Liberties in Israel," *Middle East Review* 21 (Summer 1989): 2–8.

28. Shamir and Sullivan, "Political Context of Tolerance"; John L. Sullivan, Michal Shamir, Nigel S. Roberts, and Patrick Walsh, "Political Intolerance and the Structure of Mass Attitudes," *Comparative Political Studies* 17 (October 1984): 319–44; Michal Shamir and John L. Sullivan, "Jews and Arabs in Israel: Everybody Hates Somebody, Sometime," *Journal of Conflict Resolution* 29 (June 1985): 283–305; John L. Sullivan, Michal Shamir, Patrick Walsh, and Nigel S. Roberts, *Political Tolerance in Context: Support for Unpopular Minorities in Israel, New Zealand, and the United States* (Westview Press, 1985). The two studies by Rita Simon, cited above, also show that support of civil liberties in the abstract does not carry over to specific situations of threat and that tolerance declined over the period from 1975 to 1987 precisely on security-related issues.

29. Freedom House Survey Team, *Freedom in the World: The Annual Survey of Political Rights and Civil Liberties 1994–1995* (Freedom House, 1995).

30. Rustow, *A World of Nations: Problems of Political Modernization* (Brookings Institution, 1967); Dahl, *Polyarchy, Participation, and Observation* (Yale University Press, 1971), 246–47; Powell, *Contemporary Democracies: Participation, Stability, and Violence* (Harvard University Press, 1982), 5; Lijphart, *Democracies*, 37–45. See the similar listings in Alex Inkeles, ed., *On Measuring Democracy* (Transaction Books, 1991).

31. Dahl, *Polyarchy*, 106–21. See also the study by Pierre Van den Berghe, "Pluralism and the Polity: A Theoretical Exploration," in *Pluralism in Africa*, ed. Leo Kuper and M. G. Smith (University of California Press, 1969), 67–81.

32. Lijphart, *Democracies*, 1–9. Peter Medding has also made extensive use of the

Lijphart categories in his study of the early Israel statehood period: Peter Y. Medding, *The Founding of Israeli Democracy, 1948–1967* (Oxford University Press, 1990), esp. 4–7, 204–10.

33. Lijphart, *Democracies,* 21–30; Lijphart, "Democratic Political Systems: Types, Cases, Causes, and Consequences," *Journal of Theoretical Politics* 1, no. 1 (1989): 33–48.

34. Lijphart, *Democracy in Plural Societies: A Comparative Exploration* (Yale University Press, 1977), 25–44; Lijphart, "Democratic Political Systems," 39–41.

35. Lijphart, "Israeli Democracy and Democratic Reform in Comparative Perspective," in *Israeli Democracy under Stress,* ed. Ehud Sprinzak and Larry Diamond (Lynne Rienner, 1993), 110.

36. Speaking basically of the same phenomenon, Daniel Elazar has characterized consensus democracy as a form of federalism. Since the term "federalism" has strong specific connotations in the minds of most readers, I have retained Lijphart's terminology. Elazar, *Israel: Building a New Society* (Indiana University Press, 1986), 36–37, 261.

2. JEWISH POLITICS

1. Mark Zborowski and Elizabeth Herzog, *Life Is with People: The Culture of the Shtetl* (Schocken Books, 1952), 216–17. Though Zborowski and Herzog draw heavily on fictionalized accounts by such authors as Sholem Aleichem, Mendele Mocher Sforim, and I. L. Peretz, this picture of shtetl politics is confirmed by other sources.

2. David Biale, *Power and Powerlessness in Jewish History* (Schocken Books, 1986), 6; Biale cites Baron's views (from "Ghetto and Emancipation," *Menorah Journal* 14 [June 1928]: 515–26), 211, fn. 4.

3. In the words of the Mishnah (Talmud), "Do not become intimate with the ruling power" (*Pirkei Avot* 1:10).

4. Biale, *Power and Powerlessness,* 6.

5. M. Silberfarb, *The Kehillah Work, Its Potentialities and Prospects* (in Yiddish) (1911), quoted in A. L. Patkin, *The Origins of the Russian-Jewish Labour Movement* (F. W. Cheshire, 1947), 246; see also Dan V. Segre, *A Crisis of Identity: Israel and Zionism* (Oxford University Press, 1980), 58–59; and Mitchell Cohen, *Zion and State: Nation, Class and the Shaping of Modern Israel* (Basil Blackwell, 1987), 47–48.

6. A 1939 report of the Royal Institute of International Affairs noted that "special historical circumstances caused the Jewish people to assume, at an exceptionally early date, some of the characteristics which have since been associated most closely with the modern concept of a 'nation' "; quoted by Baruch Kimmerling, "Between the Primordial and Civil Definitions of the Collective Identity: Eretz Yisrael or the State of Israel?" in *Comparative Social Dynamics: Essays in Honor of Shmuel Eisenstadt,* ed. M. Lissak, E. Cohen, and U. Almagor (Westview Press, 1984), 263. Boas Evron, in *Jewish State or Israeli Nation?* (Indiana University Press, 1995), argues that a true Jewish "nation" developed only in late nineteenth-century Eastern Europe, which is in any event the focus of the analysis here.

7. Daniel J. Elazar and Stuart Cohen, *The Jewish Polity: Jewish Political Organization from Biblical Times to the Present* (Indiana University Press, 1985), 7–8; see also Daniel J. Elazar, ed., *Kinship and Consent: The Jewish Political Tradition and Its Contemporary*

Uses (University Press of America, 1983) and Daniel Elazar, *Israel: Building a New Society* (Indiana University Press, 1986). For development of a normative Jewish political theory from classical sources, see Martin Sicker, *The Judaic State: A Study in Rabbinic Political Thought* (Praeger, 1988), and Sicker, *What Judaism Says about Politics: The Political Theology of the Torah* (Jason Aronson, 1994).

8. Daniel Elazar has developed this theme most extensively; see, for example, Elazar, *Kinship and Consent*, 10–11; the importance of the covenantal relationship is also stressed by Shmuel N. Eisenstadt, *Jewish Civilization: The Jewish Historical Experience in a Comparative Perspective* (State University of New York Press, 1992).

9. Salo W. Baron, *The Jewish Community*, vol. 1 (Jewish Publication Society of America, 1942), 73; see also M. Cohen, *Zion and State*, 46–47; Elazar, *Kinship and Consent*, 31.

10. Elazar, *Kinship and Consent*, 23–27, 36–37.

11. The general picture of Jewish governance in the Middle Ages is based on Louis Finkelstein, *Jewish Self-Government in the Middle Ages* (Greenwood Press, 1972); Jacob Katz, *Exclusiveness and Tolerance: Studies in Jewish-Gentile Relations in Medieval and Modern Times* (Oxford University Press, 1961); and Katz, *Tradition and Crisis: Jewish Society at the End of the Middle Ages* (Schocken Books, 1971).

12. Finkelstein, *Jewish Self-Government*, esp. 33–34, 49.

13. Katz, *Tradition and Crisis*, 81–82; Eli Lederhendler, *The Road to Modern Jewish Politics* (Oxford University Press, 1989), 26. Lederhendler notes that "in the Polish Commonwealth Jewish communities struggled, survived, and flourished under those conditions for the greater part of five hundred years . . ."(154).

14. Katz, *Tradition and Crisis*, 122–27.

15. Katz, *Emancipation and Assimilation: Studies in Modern Jewish History* (Gregg International Publishers, 1972); Katz, *Out of the Ghetto: The Social Background of Jewish Emancipation, 1770–1870* (Harvard University Press, 1973).

16. While this analysis focuses on Eastern European political traditions, Jewish experiences everywhere had in common certain patterns derived from the fact of minority status. This included, in most cases, a remarkable degree of communal autonomy within the existing political framework, whatever it might be. In the Ottoman Empire, for example, each ethnoreligious group had considerable self-government in religious, legal, social, and economic affairs, and as elsewhere Jews did not have to deal with the collective rights of other groups within the Jewish context. Otherwise there were significant differences between the European and non-European traditions, of course; non-European immigrants to Palestine and Israel were likely to be more fully identified with their traditions than their European counterparts, who were in some senses engaged in a "revolt" against age-old patterns of Jewish life.

17. Mead, "Foreword," in Zborowski and Herzog, *Life Is with People*, 16.

18. Baron, *The Russian Jew under Tsars and Soviets* (Macmillan, 1976), 99–100.

19. Katz, *Tradition and Crisis*, 227, 248–49.

20. Isaac Levitats, *The Jewish Community in Russia, 1844–1917* (Posner and Sons, 1981), 10; Baron, *Russian Jew*, 101–2.

21. Patkin, *Origins*, 246; see also Levitats, *Jewish Community in Russia*, 56–57, 61; and Zborowski and Herzog, *Life Is with People*, 214–15.

22. Vladimir Medem, *Otliki Bunda*, no. 1, quoted in Patkin, *Origins*, 245.

23. Lederhendler, *Road to Modern Jewish Politics*, 14, 36–37, 46–47, 82–83, 154–57; Yosef Salmon, "The Emergence of a Jewish Nationalist Consciousness in Europe during the 1860s and 1870s," *Association for Jewish Studies Review* 16 (Spring/Fall 1991): 107–32; Evron, *Jewish State or Israeli Nation?* 56–57.

24. Avineri, "The Historical Roots of Israeli Democracy," Second Annual Guest Lecture, Kaplan Center for Jewish Studies and Research, University of Cape Town, March 31, 1985; see also Avineri, "Israel as a Democratic State" (in Hebrew), *Skira Hodshit* (May 1973): 25–37.

25. Jay Y. Gonen, *A Psychohistory of Zionism* (Mason/Charter, 1975), 32.

26. Katz, *Tradition and Crisis*, 27.

27. Oz, "The Discreet Charm of Zionism," in Oz, *Under This Blazing Light* (Cambridge University Press, 1995), 107–8; Evron, *Jewish State or Israeli Nation?* 36; Charles S. Liebman and Steven M. Cohen, *Two Worlds of Judaism: The Israeli and American Experiences* (Yale University Press, 1990), 13, refer to this sense of solidarity as "quasi-familial sentiment."

28. Kimmerling, "Between the Primordial and Civil Definitions"; Liebman, "Conceptions of 'State of Israel' in Israeli Society" (in Hebrew), *Medina, Mimshal, V'yahasim Benle'umiim* [State, Government, and International Relations], no. 30 (Winter 1989): 51–60.

29. Lederhendler, *Road to Modern Jewish Politics*, 66; see also Katz, *Exclusiveness and Tolerance*, 52; and Baron, *Russian Jew*, 103–4.

30. Katz, *Tradition and Crisis*, 98.

31. Lederhendler, *Road to Modern Jewish Politics*, 12–13. In Lederhendler's analysis, the collapse of this monopoly (and the increased resort to outside authorities by those other than the "official" leaders) was one of the hallmarks in the breakdown of the classic *kahal*.

32. Eisenstadt, *The Transformation of Israeli Society* (Westview Press, 1985), 46. See also Segre, *Crisis of Identity*, 77–78; Elazar, *Kinship and Consent*, esp. 6; and Rabbi Natan Zvi Friedman, "Guidelines of Democracy and Jewish Law" (in Hebrew), *Tehumin*, 4 (1982–1983): 255–58.

33. Benyamin Neuberger, "Does Israel Have a Liberal-Democratic Tradition?" *Jewish Political Studies Review* 2, nos. 3 and 4 (Fall 1990): 90; the case for a specifically Jewish theory of the state, particularistic and essentially theocratic, is made by Sol Roth, *Halakha and Politics: The Jewish Idea of a State* (Ktav and Yeshiva University Press, 1988).

34. Bernard Susser, "Jewish Political Theory," in *Public Life in Israel and the Diaspora*, ed. Sam N. Lehman-Wilzig and Bernard Susser, vol. 1 of *Comparative Jewish Politics* (Bar-Ilan University Press, 1981), 19.

35. Eisenstadt, *Transformation of Israeli Society*, 45–46.

36. Baron, *Russian Jew*, 105; see also Katz, *Tradition and Crisis*, 98–101.

37. Katz, *Exclusiveness and Tolerance*, 161.

38. Katz, *Tradition and Crisis*, 83, 170–71; Levitats, *Jewish Community in Russia*, 202–3; Zborowski and Herzog, *Life Is with People*, 219–20.

39. Katz, *Tradition and Crisis*, 87–88, 106–10; Elazar, *Kinship and Consent*, 39. While this description applies to Eastern Europe, Jewish communities in the Islamic world also had democratic and competitive elements in their internal governance; see S. D. Goitein, "Political Conflict and the Use of Power in the World of the Ge-

niza," in *Kinship and Consent: The Jewish Political Tradition and Its Contemporary Uses*, ed. Daniel Elazar (University Press of America, 1983), 169–81.

40. Haim H. Cohn, *Human Rights in Jewish Law* (Ktav, 1984), 17–19 and passim. A more cautious view toward the inference of human rights from legal duties is presented by Aaron Kirschenbaum, in a review of R. Konvitz, ed., *Judaism and Human Rights* (W. W. Norton, 1972), in *Israel Yearbook on Human Rights* 2 (1972): 357–64. On the safeguards in judicial procedures, see Kirschenbaum, "Human Rights Revisited," *Israel Yearbook on Human Rights* 6 (1976): 228–38; Kirschenbaum also points out (232) that in a day and age when torture was routine in most legal systems, it was "virtually unheard of" in Jewish courts.

41. Lederhendler, *Road to Modern Jewish Politics*, 82–83, 112–13, 132–33. According to Steven Zipperstein, the *Haskala* "offered a haven for Jews caught between an inaccessible, larger cultural world and an unacceptable, Jewish one"; Zipperstein, *Elusive Prophet: Ahad Ha'am and the Origins of Zionism* (University of California Press, 1993), 12.

42. Levitats, *Jewish Community in Russian*, 70–71, see also 204–5; Baron, *Russian Jew*, 100.

43. Zborowski and Herzog, *Life Is with People*, 214; Katz, *Tradition and Crisis*, 93–94, 116–17.

44. Avineri, "Historical Roots of Israeli Democracy," 8.

45. Lehman-Wilzig, " 'Am K'shei Oref': Oppositionism in the Jewish Heritage," *Judaism* 40 (Winter 1991): 16–38; see also Amos Elon, *The Israelis: Founders and Sons* (Holt, Rinehart and Winston, 1971), 298; and Segre, "The Jewish Political Tradition as a Vehicle for Jewish Auto-Emancipation," in *Kinship and Consent: The Jewish Political Tradition and Its Contemporary Uses*, ed. Daniel J. Elazar (University Press of America, 1983) 300–301.

46. Eisenstadt, *Jewish Civilization*, 75.

47. Sprinzak, *Every Man Whatsoever Is Right in His Own Eyes—Illegalism in Israeli Society* (in Hebrew) (Sifriat Po'alim, 1986), 28–29: Sprinzak, "Illegalism in Israeli Political Culture: Theoretical and Historical Footnotes to the Pollard Affair and the Shin Beth Cover Up," in *Israel after Begin*, ed. Gregory S. Mahler (State University of New York Press, 1990), 55–57; Katz, *Exclusiveness and Tolerance*, 52; Zborowski and Herzog, *Life Is with People*, 232–33.

48. This theme has been developed most notably by Yehezkel Dror, especially in *To Build a State* (in Hebrew) (Akademon, 1989).

49. Elazar, *Israel: Building a New Society*, 3; Yonathan Shapiro, *Democracy in Israel* (in Hebrew) (Masada, 1977), 29.

50. Baron, *Russian Jew*, 106–7; Zborowski and Herzog, *Life Is with People*, 194, 202–3.

51. Katz, *Exclusiveness and Tolerance*, 196.

52. Roth, *Halakha and Politics*, 124–25; Cohn, *Human Rights*, 164–66. Traditional interpretations accepted Christians and Muslims as observers of the seven Noahide laws; see Kirschenbaum, "Human Rights Revisited," 229–31.

53. *Gittin*, 60a; *Avoda Zara*, 26a.

54. Cohn, *Human Rights*, 164–66; Maimonides, *Yad, Hilchot Melakhim*, 1:4–5; Roth, *Halakha and Politics*, 134.

55. Katz, *Tradition and Crisis*, 36; see also Katz, *Exclusiveness and Tolerance*, 54.

3. THE ZIONIST REVOLUTION

1. Shmuel Ettinger, "The Modern Period," in *A History of the Jewish People,* ed. Haim Hillel Ben-Sasson (Harvard University Press, 1976), 790–93.

2. This thesis is developed by Shlomo Avineri, *The Making of Modern Zionism: The Intellectual Origins of the Jewish State* (Basic Books, 1981), 5–13.

3. Jacob Katz, *Emancipation and Assimilation: Studies in Modern Jewish History* (Gregg International Publishers, 1972), 143; among the many concurring analysts, see especially Yonathan Shapiro, *Democracy in Israel* (in Hebrew) (Masada, 1977), chap. 1, on the dominance of "the national principle" over other components in Israeli society; and Baruch Kimmerling, "Between the Primordial and Civil Definitions of the Collective Identity: Eretz Yisrael or the State of Israel," in M. Lissak, E. Cohen, and U. Almagor, eds., *Comparative Social Dynamics: Essays in Honor of Shmuel Eisenstadt* (Westview Press, 1984), 265, who describes secular nationalism as "the main conceptual system within which Zionism could operate."

4. Biale, *Power and Powerlessness in Jewish History* (Schocken Books, 1986), 206.

5. Benyamin Neuberger, "Does Israel Have a Liberal-Democratic Tradition?" *Jewish Political Studies Review* 2, nos. 3 and 4 (Fall 1990): 94–95.

6. A. L. Patkin, *The Origins of the Russian-Jewish Labour Movement* (F. W. Cheshire, 1947), 247–48, 265–66; Sam Lehman-Wilzig, "'Am K'shei Oref': Oppositionism in the Jewish Heritage," *Judaism* 40 (Winter 1991): 36–37; Shapiro, *Democracy in Israel,* chap. 1.

7. For a full statement of this thesis, see Robert J. Brym, *The Jewish Intelligentsia and Russian Marxism: A Sociological Study of Intellectual Radicalism and Ideological Divergence* (Macmillan, 1978), esp. 5–6, 113; see also Calvin Goldscheider and Alan S. Zuckerman, *The Transformation of the Jews* (University of Chicago Press, 1984), 122.

8. Howard Morley Sachar, *The Course of Modern Jewish History* (Dell, 1958), 296; see also 287–90.

9. Quoted in ibid., 289.

10. Goldscheider and Zuckerman, *Transformation,* 123–25.

11. Patkin, *Origins,* 216–17; see the chapters on Hess, Syrkin, and Borochov in Avineri, *Making of Modern Zionism.*

12. For a fuller elaboration of Labor Zionist ideology (labeled "kibbutz ideology") and its role in Israeli thinking through the 1960s, see Alan Arian, *Ideological Change in Israel* (Case Western Reserve University Press, 1968).

13. On the contributions of socialism to Zionism, see Kimmerling, "Between the Primordial and Civil Definitions," 264–65.

14. Itzhak Galnoor, *Steering the Polity: Communication and Politics in Israel* (Sage, 1982), 304; Kimmerling, "Between the Primordial and Civil Definitions," 265–66; Neuberger, "Does Israel Have a Liberal-Democratic Tradition?" 88.

15. Shapiro, *Democracy in Israel,* 38. This is elaborated below and in chapter 4.

16. Vital, *Zionism: The Formative Years* (Clarendon Press, 1982), 41. See discussion in the following section.

17. Ibid., 5, 349–50; Vital, *Zionism: The Crucial Phase* (Clarendon Press, 1987), vii; see also Biale, *Power and Powerlessness,* 4. On Zionism as collective assimilation, see Boas Evron, *Jewish State or Israeli Nation?* (Indiana University Press, 1995), 108, 207.

18. Jacques Kornberg, *Theodore Herzl: From Assimilation to Zionism* (Indiana University Press, 1993), 21, 66, 154, 162.

19. Brenner, "From Here and There," *Collected Writings* (in Hebrew), vol. 2 (Kibbutz Hame'uhad, 1977), 1280; Evron, *Jewish State or Israeli Nation?* 102–3, 193.

20. Haim Hazaz, "The Sermon," in *Seething Stones: Stories, Collected Writings of Haim Hazaz* (in Hebrew), ed. Haim Hazaz (Am Oved, 1970); for an analysis from a right-wing perspective, see Dov Landau, "Who's Afraid of Yudkeh's Sermon?" (in Hebrew), *Nativ* 2 , no. 7 (January 1989): 71–81.

21. Ben Halpern, *The Idea of the Jewish State,* 2nd ed. (Harvard University Press, 1969), 4. Halpern presents the case for seeing Zionism as a "reconstruction" of tradition, in opposition to modern Western ideology; see 20–21, 57.

22. Nachman Syrkin, "The Jewish Problem and the Socialist-Jewish State," in Arthur Hertzberg, *The Zionist Idea: A Historical Analysis and Reader* (Atheneum, 1973), 349; see also Katz, *Emancipation and Assimilation,* 145; Daniel Elazar, *Israel: Building a New Society* (Indiana University Press, 1986), 15; Shmuel Almog, *Zionism and History: The Rise of a New Jewish Consciousness* (St. Martin's Press and Magnes Press, 1987), 66.

23. Vital, *Zionism: The Formative Years,* 228–29, 356–57.

24. Almog, *Zionism and History,* 309; see also 305–8.

25. Vital, *Zionism: The Formative Years,* 353; see also Kornberg, *Theodore Herzl,* 131, 160–61.

26. Ahad Ha'am, "The Jewish State and the Jewish Problem" (1897), in *Nationalism and the Jewish Ethic: Basic Writings of Ahad Ha'am,* ed. Hans Kohn (Schocken Books, 1962), 79; see also Steven Zipperstein, *Elusive Prophet: Ahad Ha'am and the Origins of Zionism* (University of California Press, 1993), 138–39.

27. Vital, *Zionism: The Formative Years,* 172–73; Elazar, *Israel: Building a New Society,* 134. Elazar maintains that, given the intensity of their ideological fervor, "only their common Jewishness, which led them to certain perceptions about the necessity for unity at some point and which gave them a useful cultural inheritance for the promotion of the requisite unity, kept them from going the divisive or repressive way of their non-Jewish peers from the same Eastern European milieu" (40).

28. Katz, *Emancipation and Assimilation,* 142.

29. *Aliya* (pl. *aliyot*) literally means "ascent" and is used uniquely to describe Jewish immigration to Eretz Yisrael.

30. Vital, *The Origins of Zionism* (Clarendon Press, 1975), 150; see also Elazar, *Israel: Building a New Society,* 22; and Elazar, "Covenant as the Basis of the Jewish Political Tradition," in *Kinship and Consent: The Jewish Political Tradition and Its Contemporary Uses,* ed. Daniel J. Elazar (University Press of America, 1983), 35–36. Vital also describes the early Hibbat Zion structure as "analogous to the old pattern of the informal rabbinical hierarchy" (155). While often observant religiously, the new settlers were still regarded as *maskilim* by Orthodox Jews of the "old *yishuv*"and came into conflict with them over such issues as *shmita* (the biblical injunction to let fields lay fallow every seventh year); see Richard Cohen, *The Return to the Land of Israel* (Zalman Shazar Center for Jewish History, 1986), 75–81.

31. Vital, *Origins,* 175, 293; Vital, *Zionism: The Formative Years,* 348–49; Shmuel Eisenstadt, *The Transformation of Israeli Society* (Westview Press, 1985), 507; Galnoor,

Steering the Polity, 302–3; Shapiro, *Democracy,* 40; Jay Y. Gonen, *A Psychohistory of Zionism* (Mason/Charter, 1975), 59; Elazar, 35–37; Neuberger, "Does Israel Have a Liberal-Democratic Tradition?" 80.

32. Shlomo Avineri, "The Historical Roots of Israeli Democracy," Second Annual Guest Lecture, Kaplan Center for Jewish Studies and Research, University of Cape Town, March 31, 1985, 7.

33. Amos Elon, *Herzl* (Holt, Rinehart and Winston, 1975), 154.

34. Ibid., 181.

35. Ernst Pawel, *The Labyrinth of Exile: A Life of Theodor Herzl* (Farrar, Straus & Giroux, 1989), 303.

36. Samuel Sager, *The Parliamentary System of Israel* (Syracuse University Press, 1985), 3.

37. Proportional representation had been proposed during the French Revolution and first applied to public elections in Adelaide, South Australia, in 1839. The first national proportional elections were held in Denmark in 1856, but after 1866 the principle was applied there only to the upper house and indirectly. The party list system of proportional representation was introduced in two Swiss cantons in 1891 and 1892, and first applied on a national level, in Serbia and Belgium, in 1899. Only an additional five states adopted the system before World War I, and it became widespread only after the war. Clarence Gilbert Hoag and George Hervey Hallett, *Proportional Representation* (Macmillan, 1926), 65–66, 162–67, 171–75.

38. *Stenographisches Protokoll der Verhandlung des III Zionisten-Kongresses,* 20–22, quoted by Vital, *Zionism: The Formative Years,* 206.

39. Vital, *Zionism: The Formative Years,* 222–23.

40. Ibid., 220, 304–5; Pawel, *Labyrinth of Exile,* 507; Mitchell Cohen, *Zion and State: Nation, Class and the Shaping of Modern Israel* (Basil Blackwell, 1987), 69.

41. Yosef Gorny, *Zionism and the Arabs, 1882–1948: A Study in Ideology* (Clarendon Press, 1987), vii.

42. Elazar, *Israel: Building a New Society,* 10.

43. Elon, *Herzl,* 290.

44. *Israel Government Yearbook 1952* (Government Printer, 1953), 21, quoted in Don Peretz, "Early State Policy towards the Arab Population, 1948–1955," in *New Perspectives on Israeli History: The Early Years of the State,* ed. Laurence J. Silberstein (New York University Press, 1991), 87.

45. Gorny, *Zionism and the Arabs,* 103–4.

46. Ibid., 42–43.

47. See the ideas of Shlomo Lavie, a second *aliya* pioneer, in Amos Elon, *The Israelis: Founders and Sons* (Holt, Rinehart and Winston, 1971), 165. A variant on this theme, promoted only by a handful, was the idea of assimilating Jewish settlement to the Arab context rather than the reverse.

48. Gorny, *Zionism and the Arabs,* 275; Susan Lee Hattis, *The Bi-National Idea in Palestine during Mandatory Times* (Shikmona, 1970).

49. Gorny, *Zionism and the Arabs,* 33–35, 110.

50. Quoted in Elon, *Herzl,* 312; see also Baruch Kimmerling, *Zionism and Territory: The Socio-Territorial Dimensions of Zionist Politics,* Research Series No. 51 (Institute of International Studies, University of California, 1983), 197.

51. This is the necessary background for understanding the description of Pal-

estine as "a land without a people for a people without a land" often attributed to early Zionist leaders. The phrase was actually used by Israel Zangwill (who, paradoxically, later became leader of the Territorialist movement), though it was used before him by two "Christian Zionist" figures (one as early as 1853). It was not used by other Zionist leaders, but in any event the meaning was that Palestine was a land not identified with a specific nation (as was indeed true at the time), not that it was uninhabited. As this discussion has demonstrated, Zionist leaders were well aware that there were people in Palestine, even when (like Herzl) they sometimes avoided the subject. See the definitive article by Adam M. Garfinkle, "On the Origin, Meaning, Use, and Abuse of a Phrase," *Middle East Studies* 27 (October 1991): 539–50.

52. Quoted in Elon, *The Israelis,* 156.

53. Gorny, *Zionism and the Arabs,* 40–77; Israel Kolatt, "The Zionist Movement and the Arabs," in Shmuel Almog, *Zionism and the Arabs: Essays* (The Historical Society of Israel and the Zalman Shazar Center for Jewish History, 1983), 2.

54. Henry Baker, *The Legal System of Israel* (Israel Universities Press, 1968), 60–63; Daniel Friedmann, *The Effect of Foreign Law on the Law of Israel* (Israel Law Review Association, 1975), 20–21; Shlomo Avineri, "Israel as a Democratic State," *Skira Hodshit* (May 1973); Gregory Mahler, *The Knesset: Parliament in the Israeli Political System* (Fairleigh Dickinson University Press, 1981), 34–35.

55. Dan Horowitz, "Before the State: Communal Politics in Palestine under the Mandate," in *The Israeli State and Society: Boundaries and Frontiers,* ed. Baruch Kimmerling (State University of New York Press, 1989), 28–65.

56. Sager, *Parliamentary System,* 10–21.

57. Peter Medding, *The Founding of Israeli Democracy, 1948–1967* (Oxford University Press, 1990), 10.

58. Gorny, "Zionist Voluntarism in the Political Struggle: 1939–1948," *Jewish Political Studies Review* 2 (Spring 1990): 85.

59. M. Cohen, *Zion and State,* 147–48, 177–78.

60. On consociationalism see Dan Horowitz and Moshe Lissak, *Origins of the Israeli Polity: Palestine under the Mandate* (University of Chicago Press, 1978), 12–13, 228–29; Horowitz, "Before the State," 30, 45–46; Eisenstadt, *Transformation,* 120–21; Medding, *Founding of Israeli Democracy,* 10; Shapiro, *Democracy,* 43–46; Galnoor, *Steering the Polity,* 368–69; Ehud Sprinzak, *Every Man Whatsoever Is Right in His Own Eyes—Illegalism in Israeli Society* (in Hebrew) (Sifriat Po'alim, 1986), 47. "Compound polity" appears in the writings of Daniel Elazar; see, for example, Elazar, *Israel: Building a Society,* 59–82. Mitchell Cohen applies "segmented pluralism" in a similar sense; see M. Cohen, *Zion and State,* 128–29, 185.

61. Nathan Yanai, "Ben-Gurion's Concept of *Mamlachtiut* and the Forming Reality of the State of Israel," *Jewish Political Studies Review* 1 (Spring, 1989): 169; Avineri, "Israel as a Democratic State"; Elazar, *Israel: Building a New Society,* 38.

62. Sarah Honig, "The Ben-Gurion History Overlooked," *Jerusalem Post,* June 26, 1989. Ben-Gurion's enthusiasm for the Soviet example was dampened by a visit there in 1923.

63. Elazar, *Israel: Building a New Society,* 23.

64. Gorny, "Changes in the Social and Political Structure of the Second Aliya between 1904 and 1940," in *Zionism: Studies in the History of the Zionist Movement and of the Jewish Community in Palestine* (in Hebrew), ed. Daniel Caspi and Gedalia Yogev,

vol. 1 (Tel Aviv University and Massada Publishing, 1975), 49–101, cited by Elazar, *Israel: Building a New Society,* 25.

65. Elazar, *Israel: Building a New Society,* 32.

66. Eliezer Rieger, *Professional Education in the Jewish Yishuv of Eretz Yisrael* (in Hebrew)(Publishing Society of the Hebrew University, 1945), 6, cited by Shapiro, *Democracy,* 32.

67. This thesis is developed primarily by Joel Migdal, "The Crystallization of the State and the Struggles over Rulemaking: Israel in Comparative Perspective," in *The Israel State and Society: Boundaries and Frontiers,* ed. Baruch Kimmerling (State University of New York Press, 1989), 1–27.

68. On the puzzle of Labor dominance generally, see Ze'ev Tshor, *The Roots of Israeli Politics* (in Hebrew)(Hakibbutz Hame'uhad, 1987); M. Cohen, *Zion and State,* esp. 74–75, 177; Gorny, "Zionist Voluntarism," 69–70; Myron Aronoff, *Israel Visions and Divisions* (Transaction Publishers, 1989), 1–2.

69. Itzhak Galnoor, *The Partition of Palestine: Decision Crossroads in the Zionist Movement* (State University of New York Press, 1994).

70. Gorny, *Zionism and the Arabs,* 306–7.

71. Speech at the Seventeenth Zionist Congress (1931), in Jabotinsky, *Speeches 1927–1940,* 117, 122, cited in Gorny, *Zionism and the Arabs,* 234.

72. Gorny, *Zionism and the Arabs,* 207–8.

73. Enzo Sereni and R. E. Ashery, eds., *Jews and Arabs in Palestine: Studies in a National and Colonial Problem* (Hechalutz Press, 1936), 149, quoted by Peretz, "Early State Policy," 9.

74. Gorny, *Zionism and the State,* 291, 310.

75. Ibid., 152–55; Michael Shalev, "Jewish Organized Labor and the Palestinians: A Study of State/Society Relations in Israel," in *The Israeli State and Society: Boundaries and Frontiers,* ed. Baruch Kimmerling (State University of New York Press, 1989), esp. 94–95, 102–3. Shalev emphasizes the role of labor market factors in the exclusion of Arab workers; whatever their relative weight, competition for jobs, traditional Jewish separatism, and "Zionist logic" worked together in this case to overwhelm the ideology of class solidarity.

76. Gorny, *Zionism and the State,* 132, 212–13, 218.

77. On the fleeting and qualified role of the "transfer" concept in Zionist thinking generally, see Shabtai Teveth, *The Evolution of 'Transfer' in Zionist Thinking,* Occasional Paper No. 107, Moshe Dayan Center for Middle Eastern and African Studies, The Shiloah Institute, Tel Aviv University, May 1989.

78. Gabriel Sheffer, "The Confrontation between Moshe Sharett and David Ben-Gurion," in *Zionism and the Arabs: Essays,* ed. Shmuel Almog (The Historical Society of Israel and the Zalman Shazar Center for Jewish History, 1983), 95–147; see also Shabtai Teveth, *Ben-Gurion and the Palestinian Arabs: From Peace to War* (Oxford University Press, 1985).

4. BUILDING A CIVIC STATE

1. For example, the definitive study of the period by Peter Y. Medding, *The Founding of Israeli Democracy, 1948–1967* (Oxford University Press, 1990); see also Noah Lucas, *The Modern History of Israel* (Praeger, 1975); Itzhak Galnoor, *Steering the*

Polity: Communication and Politics in Israel (Sage, 1982), esp. 371–72; and Galnoor, "Israeli Democracy in Transition," *Studies in Contemporary Jewry* 5 (1989): 140–41.

2. Avraham Brichta, *Democracy and Elections: On Changing the Electoral and Nomination Systems in Israel* (in Hebrew) (Am Oved, 1977), 65–68.

3. Medding, *Founding of Israeli Democracy,* 135; Lea Ben-Dor, "Ben-Gurion on '*Mamlachtiut*'," *Jerusalem Post,* 28 May 1965.

4. Ben-Gurion, *Vision and Path* (in Hebrew), vol. 3 (Mapai, 1952), 159, quoted by Nathan Yanai, "Ben-Gurion's Concept of *Mamlachtiut* and the Forming Reality of the State of Israel," *Jewish Political Studies Review* 1, nos. 1 and 2 (Spring 1989): 155.

5. Yanai, "Ben-Gurion's Concept," 152; Medding, *Founding of Israeli Democracy,* 135–36.

6. The relationship of Ben-Gurion's *mamlachtiut* to traditional sources is explored by Eliezer Don-Yehiya, "*Mamlachtiut* and Judaism in Ben-Gurion's Thought and Policy" (in Hebrew), *Hatsionut* 14 (1989): 51–88.

7. Ben-Gurion, *Vision and Path,* 48, quoted by Yanai, "Ben-Gurion's Concept," 166.

8. For general accounts of the campaign for *mamlachtiut,* see Yanai, "Ben-Gurion's Concept"; and Medding, *Founding of Israeli Democracy,* 134–77.

9. Amnon Rubinstein, *The Constitutional Law of the State of Israel* (in Hebrew) (Schocken, 1980), 10; see also Eli Nahmias, "The Constitutional Status of the Declaration of Independence" (in Hebrew), *Basha'ar,* no. 156 (1981): 40–42.

10. Medding, *Founding of Israeli Democracy,* 32. The absence of a constitution is usually listed as one of the majoritarian features of a government, since it leaves unfettered supremacy to a minimal legislative majority; this is questioned below, in the following section, and in chapter 6.

11. Daniel Friedmann, *The Effect of Foreign Law on the Law of Israel* (Israel Law Review Association, 1975), 102–3. The reference is to the "Who is a Jew?" controversy; in two decisions of the Israel Supreme Court (Rufeisen v. Minister of the Interior, 1962, and Shalit v. Minister of the Interior, 1969), and in a Knesset amendment to the Law of Return (1970), the government of Israel accepted definitions of Jewishness at variance with the Orthodox religious interpretation.

12. Martin Edelman, "The Judicial Elite of Israel," *International Political Science Review* 13 (July 1992): 244–45; Elyakim Rubinstein, *Judges of the Land* (Schocken, 1980), 136–42, 192–94.

13. When the government official in charge of rationing during the early days of statehood convened judges in order to press for stiffer sentences on black marketeers, he was told in sharp language that the judges were "as free as the birds among the trees"; Sraya Shapiro, "Must Disaster Threaten before We Act Sanely?" *Jerusalem Post,* 19 May 1985.

14. Asher Arian, *Politics in Israel: The Second Generation,* rev. ed. (Chatham House, 1989), 194.

15. The Lavon affair involved a security mishap in Egypt in 1954, for which then-Defense Minister Pinhas Lavon was first blamed and later exonerated. What made it into Israel's bitterest and longest-running contretemps, however, was Prime Minister Ben-Gurion's continued push, over several years, for a reinvestigation of the entire matter. In time, "the affair" acquired broader connotations as a "Lavonist" resistance to what was seen as Ben-Gurion's dictatorial style of rule.

16. Aaron S. Klieman, *Israel and the World after 40 Years* (Pergamon-Brassey's, 1989), 24, 32–33, 42–45, 88, 166, 169, 173, 177–78.

17. Yanai, "Ben-Gurion's Concept," 158.

18. Arend Lijphart, in *Democracies: Patterns of Majoritarian and Consensus Government in Twenty-One Countries* (Yale University Press, 1984), 178, noted that 96 percent of Israel tax revenues were going to the central government, which put Israel second of the twenty-one democracies in his study in this measure of centralization. Israeli municipalities have, however, become increasing independent of the fiscal control of the national government, both by systematic overspending of their budgets and by developing an independent tax base (property tax).

19. Medding, *Founding of Israel Democracy*, 135; on the importance of parties see Nathan Yanai, *Party Leadership in Israel: Maintenance and Change* (Turtledove Publishing, 1981).

20. The importance of collective responsibility in the Ben-Gurion system is a key point in Medding's analysis in *Founding of Israeli Democracy* (see especially 35–37).

21. Asher Arian, *Politics in Israel*, 173.

22. Sharett, *Personal Diary* (in Hebrew), vol. 1 (Am Oved, 1978), 255, quoted in Galnoor, *Steering the Polity*, 165.

23. See Shmuel Eisenstadt, *Israeli Society* (Weidenfeld and Nicolson, 1967), 332 ff.; Leonard Fein, *Politics in Israel* (Little, Brown, 1967), 228–29; Alan Arian, *The Choosing People* (Case Western Reserve University Press, 1973), 37–60.

24. Medding, *Founding of Israeli Democracy*, 63–65.

25. The identification of these three dimensions as the areas of salient issues in Israeli politics is confirmed by Lijphart, *Democracies*, 130; Alan Arian, *Ideological Change in Israel* (Case Western Reserve University Press, 1968), 48–49, presents the statistical backing for separate scales on economic and foreign policy issues; see also Daniel Shimshoni, *Israeli Democracy: The Middle of the Journey* (The Free Press, 1982), 432–33; Sammy Smooha, *Israel: Pluralism and Conflict* (University of California Press, 1978), 100–101.

26. Alan Arian, *Ideological Change*, 55.

27. Chaya Zuckerman-Bareli, "The Religious Factor in Opinion Formation among Israeli Youth," in *On Ethnic and Religious Diversity*, ed. Solomon Poll and Ernest Krausz (Bar-Ilan University, 1975), 57; see also Medding, *Founding of Israeli Democracy*, 224–25; Itzhak Galnoor, "Secrecy," in *Government Secrecy in Democracies*, ed. Itzhak Galnoor (Harper and Row, 1977), 190.

28. See the analysis by Baruch Kimmerling, "Boundaries and Frontiers of the Israeli Control System: Analytical Conclusions," in *The Israeli State and Society: Boundaries and Frontiers*, ed. Baruch Kimmerling (State University of New York Press, 1989), 271–72.

29. Alan Arian, *Ideological Change*, 36, 43, 52–53.

30. The classic portraits of the generation split are Amos Elon, *The Israelis: Founders and Sons* (Holt, Rinehart and Winston, 1971) and Yonathan Shapiro, *The Successor Generation* (in Hebrew)(Sifriat Po'alim, 1984).

31. Mitchell Cohen, *Zion and State: Nation, Class and the Shaping of Modern Israel* (Basil Blackwell, 1987), 248–49, 256–57.

32. Medding, *Founding of Israeli Democracy*, 151–52.

33. Ben-Dor, "Ben Gurion on '*Mamlachtiut*'."

34. Shevah Weiss, "Feudalism for Ever!" *Jerusalem Post*, 22 December 1985; see also Amitai Etzioni, "Alternative Ways to Democracy: The Example of Israel," *Political Science Quarterly* 74, no. 2 (June 1959): 196–214.

35. Gregory Mahler, *The Knesset: Parliament in the Israeli Political System* (Fairleigh Dickinson University Press, 1981), 157.

36. Asher Arian, *Politics in Israel*, 121, 123; Asher Arian, "Israeli Democracy 1984," *Journal of International Affairs* 38 (Winter, 1985): 262; Shimshoni, *Israeli Democracy*, 442–43.

37. Steven A. Hoffman, "Candidate Selection in Israel's Parliament: The Realities of Change," *Middle East Journal* 34 (1980): 149–52.

38. Lijphart, *Democracies*, 61. Lijphart gives a figure of 82 percent for the 1945–1980 period; adding ten years of more-than-minimal coalitions during 1980 to 1990, and six years of minimal coalitions from 1990 to 1996, lowers this to 76 percent.

39. Susan Hattis Rolef, ed., *Political Dictionary of the State of Israel* (Jerusalem Publishing House, 1993), 128–30, 369.

40. The spoils system is discussed in the context of illegalism by Ehud Sprinzak, *Every Man Whatsoever Is Right in His Own Eyes—Illegalism in Israeli Society* (in Hebrew) (Sifriat Po'alim, 1986), 104–15. The quotation from an unnamed Liberal Party minister is from Akiva Eldar, "National Government of Appointments" (in Hebrew), *Ha'aretz*, 1 October 1986 , quoted by Sprinzak, *Every Man Whatsoever*, 113.

41. According to Samuel Sager, 94 percent of the bills enacted in the 1978–1984 period were initiated by the government, and government-sponsored measures accounted for 87 percent of the legislation adopted in the 1961–1985 period; Sager, *The Parliamentary System of Israel* (Syracuse University Press, 1985), 164, 175.

42. Mahler, *The Knesset*, 89–99, 170–72, 202; Sager, *Parliamentary System*, 120.

43. Mahler, *The Knesset*, 193; see also pp. 102–3.

44. The definitive analysis of interest groups in Israel is Yael Yishai, *Land of Paradoxes: Interest Politics in Israel* (State University of New York Press, 1991); see also Marcia Drezon-Tepler, *Interest Groups and Political Changes in Israel* (State University of New York Press, 1990).

45. Daniel Elazar, *Israel: Building a New Society* (Indiana University Press, 1986), 195–96; see also 189, 197.

46. Eva Etzioni-Halevy with Rina Shapira, *Political Culture in Israel* (Praeger, 1977), 208; Sprinzak, *Every Man Whatsoever*, 33–41; Shimshoni, *Israeli Democracy*, 427.

47. Esther Golan, "Political Culture in Israel: A Case Study" (Master's thesis, University of Haifa, 1977), 38, 48; Gabriel Almond and Sydney Verba, *The Civic Culture: Political Attitudes and Democracy in Five Nations* (Princeton University Press, 1963), 94, 96. On a comparable comparison of political knowledge, Shamir and Sullivan found that 87 percent of Israelis knew the correct answer as against only 53 percent of the U.S. respondents; Michal Shamir and John Sullivan, "The Political Context of Tolerance: The United States and Israel," *American Political Science Review* 77 (December 1983): 911–27.

48. Charles Lewis Taylor and David A. Jodice, *World Handbook of Political and Social Indicators*, 3rd ed. (Yale University Press, 1983), 22–46.

49. Golan, "Political Culture," 60, 75.

50. Asher Arian, *Politics in Israel*, 284–85; Etzioni-Halevy with Shapira, *Political Culture*, 70, 77–78; Golan, "Political Culture," 91–93; Almond and Verba, *Civic Culture*, 181; Galnoor, *Steering the Polity*, 330, 373.

51. David Nahmias and David Rosenblum, *Bureaucratic Culture: Citizens and Administrators in Israel* (St. Martin's Press, 1978), 176; see also Gerald Caiden, *Israel's Administrative Culture* (Institute of Government Studies, University of California, 1970), 17–19; Mahler, *The Knesset*, 184–85.

52. The first report is recounted by Sprinzak, *Every Man Whatsoever*, 12–13; the second, from an interview with Shalom Cohen, is in David J. Schnall, *Radical Dissent in Contemporary Israeli Politics: Cracks in the Wall* (Praeger, 1979), 168.

53. Sprinzak, *Every Man Whatsoever*, 15.

54. Ibid., 23–25 and passim.

55. Ibid., 77–92.

56. Arend Lijphart, *Democracy in Plural Societies: A Comparative Exploration* (Yale University Press, 1977), 129–34; Lijphart, *Democracies*, 215–21; Medding, *Founding of Israeli Democracy*, 204–10.

57. Shmuel N. Eisenstadt, *Jewish Civilization: The Jewish Historical Experience in a Comparative Perspective* (State University of New York Press, 1992), 217.

5. THE FILTER OF SECURITY

1. Dan Horowitz and Moshe Lissak, *Trouble in Utopia: The Overburdened Polity of Israel* (State University of New York Press, 1989), 229–30.

2. Uzi Benziman, *Sharon: An Israeli Caesar* (Adama Books, 1985), 225.

3. Ze'ev Schiff and Ehud Ya'ari, *Israel's Lebanon War* (Simon and Schuster, 1984), 43.

4. Ibid., esp. 281–85; see also Aryeh Naor, *Government at War* (in Hebrew) (Lahav, 1986), on clashes between Begin and Sharon.

5. In a study by Elihu Katz and Michael Gurevitch, when asked about the basis of Jewish rights in Israel, 81 percent of the respondents mentioned the right to a refuge, while 66 percent cited Zionist settlement, 61 percent the age-old longing to return, 59 percent rights established in the Bible, 56 percent military successes, and 40 percent the UN Partition Resolution of 1947. *The Secularization of Leisure: Culture and Communication in Israel* (Harvard University Press, 1976), 322.

6. *The Military Balance 1995–1996* (The International Institute for Strategic Studies, 1995), 130–31, 134–38, 146–48. Similar figures are given in Shlomo Gazit and Ze'ev Eytan, *The Middle East Military Balance, 1993–1994* (Jaffee Center for Strategic Studies, 1994), 196–197.

7. Given the centrality of security for Israel, there are surprisingly few serious studies of the tension between security demands and democracy. Two recent studies help to fill the gap: Menachem Hofnung, *Democracy, Law, and National Security in Israel* (Dartmouth Publishing, 1996) and Gad Barzilai, *Wars, Internal Conflicts, and Political Order: A Jewish Democracy in the Middle East* (State University of New York Press, 1996).

8. Asher Arian, *Security Threatened: Surveying Israeli Opinion on Peace and War* (Cambridge University Press, 1995), 68. On basic vs. current security, see Avner Yaniv, *Deterrence without the Bomb* (Lexington Books, 1987), 99.

9. Amos Elon, *The Israelis: Founders and Sons* (Holt, Rinehart and Winston, 1971), 199. For an outsider's appreciation of how deeply the Holocaust shapes Israeli attitudes, see Conor Cruise O'Brien, *The Siege: The Saga of Israel and Zionism* (Simon and Schuster, 1986), 327–28; for an insider's analysis, see Eliezer Don-Yehiya, "Memory and Political Culture: Israeli Society and the Holocaust," *Studies in Contemporary Jewry* 9 (1993): 139–62.

10. Yoram Peri, "The Rise and Fall of Israel's National Consensus (1)," *New Outlook* 26 (May 1983): 28–31; and idem, "The Rise and Fall of Israel's National Consensus (2)," *New Outlook* 26 (June 1983): 26–32.

11. Yaniv, *Deterrence*.

12. Avi Shlaim and Avner Yaniv, "Domestic Politics and Foreign Policy in Israel," *International Affairs* 56 (April 1980): 242–62, emphasize the internal causes of a conservative, risk-averse diplomacy and especially the lack of sufficient unity within governing parties for pursuit of a coherent strategy.

13. Shlomo Aronson, *Conflict and Bargaining in the Middle East* (The Johns Hopkins University Press, 1978), chap. 1.

14. On overcompensation to past weakness, see Jay Y. Gonen, *A Psychohistory of Zionism* (Mason/Charter, 1975), 147; the cult of toughness and the symbolic importance of Meir Har-Tsion is discussed by Elon, *The Israelis*, 237.

15. Harold D. Lasswell, "The Garrison State," *American Journal of Sociology* 46 (January 1941): 455–68; Harold D. Lasswell, *National Security and Individual Freedom* (Committee for Economic Development, 1950), 23–49.

16. Baruch Kimmerling, *The Interrupted Society: Israeli Civilians in War and Routine Times* (State University of New York Press, 1985); Kimmerling, "Making Conflict a Routine: The Cumulative Effects of the Arab-Jewish Conflict upon Israeli Society," *Journal of Strategic Studies* 6, no. 3 (1983): 13–45. For overall assessments of civilian supremacy in the Israeli system, see Yoram Peri, *Between Battles or Ballots* (Cambridge University Press, 1983), and Yehuda Ben-Meir, *Civil-Military Relations in Israel* (Columbia University Press, 1995).

17. Daniel Elazar argues that this emphasis on consent and voluntary cooperation, rather than discipline and coercion, makes the army "a major embodiment of Jewish political culture"; *Israel: Building a New Society* (Indiana University Press, 1986), 188–89.

18. Lilly Weissbrod, "Protest and Dissidence in Israel," in *Cross-Currents in Israeli Culture and Politics*, ed. Myron J. Aronoff (Transaction Books, 1984), 56–59.

19. Horowitz and Lissak, *Trouble in Utopia*, 229. For an overview of this issue, see Lissak, "Paradoxes of Israeli Civil-Military Relations," in *Israeli Society and Its Defense Establishment*, ed. Moshe Lissak (Cass, 1984), 1–12.

20. Baruch Kimmerling, "Patterns of Militarism in Israel," *Archives of European Sociology* 34 (1993): 196–223.

21. Hobson, *Democracy after the War* (George Allen and Unwin, 1917), 13–19.

22. Asher Arian, *Politics in Israel: The Second Generation*, rev. ed. (Chatham House, 1989), 200 (emphasis in original).

23. U. S. Department of State, *Country Reports on Human Rights Practices* for 1996 (U. S. Government Printing Office, 1996).

24. This is the consensus among most analysts; see, for example, Asher Arian, "Israeli Democracy 1984," *Journal of International Affairs* 38 (Winter 1985): 265.

This discussion does not apply to the occupied territories of the West Bank and Gaza, which are not juridically part of Israel and are dealt with separately in chapter 10.

25. For an overview of the three mechanisms of emergency legislation, see Shimon Shetreet, "A Contemporary Model of Emergency Detention Law: An Assessment of the Israel Law," *Israel Yearbook on Human Rights* 14 (1984): 187–96, and Baruch Bracha, "Addendum: Some Remarks on Israeli Law Regarding National Security," *Israel Yearbook on Human Rights* 10 (1980): 295–97. A fuller treatment of this subject can be found in Alan Dowty, "Emergency Powers in Israel: The Devaluation of Crisis," in *Coping with Crises: How Governments Deal with Emergencies,* ed. Shao-chuan Leng (University Press of America, for the White Burkett Miller Center of Public Affairs, University of Virginia, 1990), 1–43, and in Menachem Hofnung, "States of Emergency and Ethnic Conflict in Liberal Democracies," *Terrorism and Political Violence* 6 (Autumn 1994): 340–65.

26. Bracha, "Restriction of Personal Freedom without Due Process of Law according to the Defense (Emergency) Regulations, 1945," *Israel Yearbook on Human Rights* 8 (1978): 299.

27. Professor G. I. A. D. Draper, in "Symposium on Human Rights," *Israel Yearbook on Human Rights* 1 (1971): 383. Draper adds that he and others dissuaded the British secretary of state for war from applying similar regulations later on in Cyprus, on the grounds that "they were thoroughly bad regulations."

28. *The Palestine Gazette,* No. 1422, Supplement No. 2, 27 September 1945, 1055–98.

29. Richard Crossman, *Palestine Mission: A Personal Record* (Harper and Brothers, 1947), 129.

30. Bernard Joseph, *British Rule in Palestine* (Public Affairs Press, 1948), 218–30. For severe critiques at the time by Jewish legal scholars, see M. Friedman, "Detainees under the Emergency Regulation" (in Hebrew), *Hapraklit* 2 (August 1945): 242–43; and R. Nuchimowski, "Deportations under the Defense Regulations (1)" (in Hebrew), *Hapraklit* 3 (April 1946): 104–9, and idem, "Deportations under the Defense Regulations (2)" (in Hebrew), *Hapraklit* 3 (May 1946): 134–40.

31. *Knesset Proceedings* (in Hebrew), 21 May 1951.

32. Elon, *The Israelis,* 297.

33. Dina Goren, *Secrecy and the Right to Know* (Turtledove Publishing, 1979), 164.

34. Asher Arian, *Politics in Israel,* 276; Daniel Shimshoni, *Israel Democracy: The Middle of the Journey* (The Free Press, 1982), 82–85; Goren, *Secrecy,* 94, 104, 120; U.S. Department of State, *Country Reports on Human Rights Practices for 1996.* It should be kept in mind that articles and books published abroad can usually be reprinted or quoted in the Israeli press, thus providing a convenient method of circumventing controls.

35. Goren, *Secrecy,* 112.

36. Edi Retig, "The Sting: Secret Evidence, the Burden of Proof, and Freedom of Expression" (in Hebrew), *Mishpatim* 14 (1984): 118–20, 125–26.

37. Michael Saltman, "The Use of the Mandatory Emergency Laws by the Israeli Government," *International Journal of the Sociology of Law* 10 (November 1982): 385–94; Sabri Jiryis, *The Arabs in Israel* (Monthly Review Press, 1976), 16–18, 26.

38. Saltman, "Use of the Mandatory Emergency Laws"; Avraham Poyastro, "Land

as a Mechanism of Control: Israel's Policy toward the Arab Minority 1948–1966" (in Hebrew) (Master's thesis, University of Haifa, 1985), 19–22, 37–42.

39. Alan Dershowitz, "Preventive Detention of Citizens during a National Emergency—A Comparison between Israel and the United States," *Israel Yearbook on Human Rights* 1 (1971): 303.

40. Ibid., 316–17.

41. Based on official figures collected by Jiryis, *The Arabs,* 30; Dershowitz, "Preventive Detention," 310–11, and Shetreet, "A Contemporary Model," 187.

42. Mordechai Mironi, *Return-To-Work Orders: Government Intervention in Labor Disputes through Emergency Regulations and Work Injunctions* (in Hebrew) (The Institute for Social and Labor Research, University of Tel Aviv, 1983), 26–27.

43. Shetreet, "A Contemporary Model," 191–92.

44. Yizhak Hans Klinghoffer provides a list of laws whose duration or functioning are dependent on the existence of a state of emergency. These include the Prevention of Terrorism Ordinance, 1948; the Absentee Property Act, 1950; the Prevention of Infiltration Act, 1954; the Supervision of Goods and Services Act, 1957; and a number of labor laws; "On Emergency Regulations in Israel," in *Jubilee Book for Pinhas Rosen,* ed. Haim Kohn (Mifal Hashichpul, 1962), 90.

45. Simon Shetreet, "Israeli Democracy in Wartime—The Legal Framework in Practical Perspective" (in Hebrew), *Skira Hodshit* (August–September, 1984), 48, 51.

46. Bracha, "Restriction of Personal Freedom," 311, 313; Shetreet, "A Contemporary Model," 185.

47. Bracha, "Restriction of Personal Freedom," 316–17; Rubinstein, *Judges of the Land,* 384.

6. THE EROSION OF IDEOLOGY

1. Amos Elon, *The Israelis: Founders and Sons* (Holt, Rinehart and Winston, 1971), 146, 260. Elon's book is the classic study of the generation gap.

2. As Baruch Kimmerling points out, the choice of 1967 or 1977 as the decisive turning point reflects a decision on what was critical in the change: the basic definition of the geographic unit (in 1967) or the change of elites (in 1977). There are of course others who see neither change as basic. Here both changes are regarded as important facets of a fundamental transformation that took place over an extended period and that cannot easily be represented by a single year. However, I agree with Kimmerling that the 1967 war unleashed basic forces for change and that no analysis of the post-1967 system that omits the occupied territories can be considered complete (the territories are dealt with here in chapter 10). See Kimmerling, "Sociology, Ideology and Nation Building: The Palestinians and Their Meaning in Israeli Sociology," *American Sociological Review* 57 (August 1992): 446–60.

3. Eva Etzioni-Halevy with Rina Shapira, *Political Culture in Israel* (Praeger, 1977), 30–31; see also Virginia R. Dominguez, "The Language of Left and Right in Israeli Politics," in *Cross-Currents in Israeli Culture and Politics,* ed. Myron J. Aronoff (Transaction Books, 1984), 92–93.

4. Asher Arian, *Ideological Change in Israel* (Case Western Reserve University Press, 1968), 36, 43, 52–53.

5. Yehuda Ben-Meir and Peri Kedem, "An Index of Religiosity for the Jewish

Population in Israel" (in Hebrew), *Megamot* 24 (February 1979): 353–62; Baruch Kimmerling, "Between the Primordial and Civil Definitions of the Collective Identity: Eretz Yisrael or the State of Israel?" in *Comparative Social Dynamics: Essays in Honor of Shmuel Eisenstadt,* ed. M. Lissak, E. Cohen, and U. Almagor (Westview Press, 1984), 269.

6. Abraham Diskin, "The 1977 Interparty Distances: A Three-Level Analysis," in *The Elections in Israel 1977,* ed. Asher Arian (Academic Press, 1980), 213–29; Michael Wolffsohn, *Israel: Polity, Society and Economy 1882–1986* (Humanities Press International, 1987), 42.

7. Avner Yaniv and Fabian Pascal, "Doves, Hawks and Other Birds of a Feather: The Distribution of Israeli Parliamentary Opinion on the Future of the Occupied Territories 1967–1977," *British Journal of Political Science* 10 (April 1980): 260–67.

8. Mina Zemach, *Positions of the Jewish Majority in Israel toward the Arab Minority* (Van Leer Institute, 1980); Nadav Safran, *Israel: The Embattled Ally* (Harvard University Press, 1978), 89–94; Dan Horowitz, "More than a Change in Government," *Jerusalem Quarterly* 5 (Fall 1977): 9–13; Asher Arian, "Elections 1981: Competitiveness and Polarization," *Jerusalem Quarterly* 21 (Fall 1981): 16–27; Daniel Elazar, "Israel's New Majority," *Commentary* 75 (March 1983): 33–39.

9. Wolffsohn, *Israel,* 150; see also Arnold Lewis, "Ethnic Politics and the Foreign Policy Debate in Israel," in *Cross-Currents in Israeli Culture and Politics,* ed. Myron J. Aronoff (Transaction Books, 1984), 30; for an explanation of Likud's attraction to religious voters, see Kenneth Wald and Samuel Shye, "Religious Influence in Electoral Behavior: The Role of Institutional and Social Forces in Israel," paper presented at annual meeting of the Midwest Political Science Association, Chicago, April 1993.

10. Elon, *The Israelis,* 303–4. See also Shmuel Eisenstadt, *The Transformation of Israeli Society* (Westview, 1985), 405–6; Yaacov Hasdai, *Truth in the Shadow of War,* trans. Moshe Kohn (Zmora, Bitan, Modan, 1979), 171–72; Myron J. Aronoff, *Israeli Visions and Divisions: Cultural Change and Political Conflict* (Transaction Publishers, 1989), 5–6. The classic portrait of the Labor Zionist Establishment is Yuval Elizur and Eliahu Salpeter, *Who Rules Israel?* (Harper and Row, 1973).

11. The thesis of Mapai's self-destruction in the early 1960s is developed by Avram Schweitzer, *Israel: The Changing National Agenda* (Croom Helm, 1986); on the Lavon affair, see Nathan Yanai, "The Political Affair: A Framework for Comparative Discussion," *Comparative Politics* (January 1990): 185–98.

12. Yonathan Shapiro, *The Successor Generation* (in Hebrew) (Sifriat Po'alim, 1984); see critique by Kimmerling, "Discontinuities of Elite Recruitment in Israeli Society," in *Books on Israel,* ed. Ian S. Lustick (State University of New York Press, 1988), 31–36; see also Elon, *The Israelis.*

13. This is one of the principal theses in Mitchell Cohen, *Zion and State: Nation, Class and the Shaping of Modern Israel* (Basil Blackwell, 1987).

14. For a contemporary portrait of this process see Shmuel Eisenstadt, *Israeli Society* (Weidenfeld and Nicolson, 1967), esp. 211 ff.

15. A fuller explanation for the lack of class consciousness in the development of Israeli society is given in Dan Horowitz and Moshe Lissak, *Trouble in Utopia: The Overburdened Polity of Israel* (State University of New York Press, 1989), 86–92.

16. Jay Y. Gonen, *A Psychohistory of Zionism* (Mason/Charter, 1975), 117–18.

17. Vered Krauss, "The Social Ranking of Professions in Israel" (Ph.D. dissertation, Hebrew University, 1976), cited in Wolffsohn, *Israel*, 34.

18. Horowitz and Lissak, *Trouble in Utopia*, 83–86.

19. Medding, *The Founding of Israeli Democracy, 1948–1967* (Oxford University Press, 1990), 44–47, 64–67.

20. Avner Yaniv, "Israel National Security in the 1980s: The Crisis of Overload," in *Israel after Begin*, ed. Gregory S. Mahler (State University of New York Press, 1990), 105.

21. Aronoff, *Israeli Visions*, 26; Schweitzer, *Israel*, 147–48; Itzhak Galnoor, "Israeli Society and Politics," in *The Impact of the Six-Day War*, ed. Stephen J. Roth (Macmillan, 1988), 193–94; Baruch Kimmerling, *Zionism and Territory: The Socio-Territorial Dimensions of Zionist Politics*, Research Series No. 51 (Institute of International Studies, University of California, 1983), 234–35.

22. For similar discussions see Gershon Shafir, "Ideological Politics or the Politics of Demography: The Aftermath of the Six-Day War," in *Critical Essays on Israeli Society, Politics, and Culture*, ed. Ian S. Lustick and Barry Rubin (State University of New York Press, 1991), 48–53; Gregory S. Mahler, *Israel: Government and Politics in a Maturing State* (Harcourt Brace Jovanovich, 1990), 238; Gonen, *Psychohistory*, 143–44.

23. Schweitzer, *Israel*, esp. 76.

24. Polling data from the Continuing Survey of the Israel Institute of Applied Social Research, as reported in Russell A. Stone, *Social Change in Israel: Attitudes and Events, 1967–1979* (Praeger, 1982), 149–55. See also Etzioni-Halevy with Shapira, *Political Culture*, 193.

25. Stone, *Social Change*, 265, 268–71.

26. A search of academic literature for this period uncovered only one clear prediction of the 1977 upheaval: David Nahmias, in 1976, pointed out that the right and the religious parties together were only nine seats short of a majority and that "such a coalition would end the political dominance of Labour"; Nahmias, "The Right Wing Opposition in Israel," *Political Studies* 24 (September 1976): 268–80. Don Peretz, in "The War Election and Israel's Eighth Knesset," *Middle East Journal* 28 (Spring 1974): 111–25, and Asher Arian, in "Were the 1973 Elections in Israel Critical?" *Comparative Politics* 8 (October, 1975): 152–65, also suggested this possibility.

27. Eisenstadt, *Transformation*, 505; for a critique of Eisenstadt that calls for a more pluralistic paradigm of Israeli society, see Ian S. Lustick, "The Voice of a Sociologist; the Task of an Historian; the Limits of a Paradigm," in *Books on Israel*, ed. Ian S. Lustick (State University of New York Press, 1988), 10. A contemporary study that focuses largely on the breakdown of consensus is Peter Grose, *A Changing Israel* (Vintage Books, 1985).

28. See the comparison in John L. Sullivan, Michal Shamir, Patrick Walsh, and Nigel S. Roberts, *Political Tolerance in Context: Support for Unpopular Minorities in Israel, New Zealand, and the United States* (Westview Press, 1985), 137–38; see also Itzhak Galnoor, "Israeli Democracy in Transition," *Studies in Contemporary Jewry* 5 (1989): 142–43.

29. Emanuel Gutmann, "Parliamentary Elites: Israel," in *Electoral Politics in the*

Middle East: Issues, Voters and Elites, ed. Jacob M. Landau, Ergun Ozbudun, and Frank Tachau (Croom Helm, 1980), 294. See also Yaniv and Pascal, "Doves, Hawks," 260–67.

30. Asher Arian, "The Passing of Dominance," *Jerusalem Quarterly* 5 (Fall 1977): 26–27.

31. In a Modi'in Ezrachi poll in January 1990, 75.7 percent of the respondents said they were "dissatisfied" or "very dissatisfied" with the National Unity Government (data supplied to author).

32. Ofra Seliktar, *New Zionism and the Foreign Policy System of Israel* (Southern Illinois University Press, 1986); Ilan Peleg, *Begin's Foreign Policy, 1977–1983: Israel's Move to the Right* (Greenwood Press, 1987); for a fuller picture of Begin's thinking, see his own account: Begin, *The Revolt* (Henry Schuman, 1951); and also Sasson Sofer, *Begin: An Anatomy of Leadership* (Basil Blackwell, 1988).

33. Charles Liebman and Eliezer Don-Yehiya, *Civil Religion in Israel: Traditional Judaism and Political Culture in the Jewish State* (University of California Press, 1983); Aronoff, "Political Polarization: Contradictory Interpretations of Israeli Reality," in *Cross-Currents in Israeli Culture and Politics,* ed. Myron J. Aronoff (Transaction Books, 1984), 8, and idem, *Israeli Visions,* 62.

34. Amnon Rubinstein, *The Zionist Dream Revisited* (Schocken Books, 1984), 88.

35. Kimmerling, "Between the Primordial and Civil Definitions," 266–69, 272, 276; Charles S. Liebman, "Conceptions of 'State of Israel' in Israeli Society" (in Hebrew), *Medina, Mimshal, V'yahasim Benle'umiim* [State, Government, and International Relations], no. 30 (Winter 1989): 51–60; Shmuel N. Eisenstadt, *Jewish Civilization: The Jewish Historical Experience in a Comparative Perspective* (State University of New York Press, 1992), 200–201, 214, 223.

36. Aronoff, *Israeli Visions,* 70, 73, 85–86; Shafir, "Ideological Politics," 55–56. See also chapter 10.

37. Kimmerling, "Between the Primordial and Civil Definitions," 271.

38. Similar evaluations can be found in Arnold Lewis, "Ethnic Politics," 32, 33, 35; Aronoff, *Israeli Visions,* 30, 108; and Wolffsohn, *Israel,* 155.

39. Medding, *Founding of Israeli Democracy,* 229; see also Galnoor, "Israeli Democracy," 144–45; and Nathan Yanai, "Ben-Gurion's Concept of *Mamlachtiut* and the Forming Reality of the State of Israel," *Jewish Political Studies Review* 1 (Spring 1989): 160.

40. Yosef Goell, "Likud Incompetents Are Taking Us Back to the Shtetl," *Jerusalem Post International Edition,* 11 January 1992. Goell recalls the 1950s comment of a visiting professor that the best way to understand Israeli politics "was to first get a good understanding of how a typical synagogue was run in the 'the Old Country' of Eastern Europe or in the large Jewish immigrant centers in the U.S."

41. Yair Zalmanovitch, "The Struggle over the Determination of Israeli Health Policy" (in Hebrew), paper presented at the annual meeting of the Israel Political Science Association, May 1988.

42. Itzhak Galnoor, *Steering the Polity: Communication and Politics in Israel* (Sage, 1982), 375; on "hyper-participation" see Sam Lehman-Wilzig, "Demoskraty in the Mega-Polis: Hyper-Participation in the Post-Industrial Age," in *The Future of Politics: Governance, Movements, and World Order,* ed. William Page (St. Martin's Press, 1983), 221–29.

43. Sam Lehman-Wilzig, *Stiff-Necked People, Bottle-Necked System: The Evolution and Roots of Israeli Public Protest, 1949–1986* (Indiana University Press, 1990), 27–45.

44. Sam Lehman-Wilzig, "Conflict as Communication—Public Protest in Israel, 1950–1982," in, *Conflict and Consensus in Jewish Political Life,* ed. Stuart A. Cohen and Eliezer Don-Yehiya (Bar-Ilan University Press, 1986), 128–29.

45. Wolfsfeld, *The Politics of Provocation: Participation and Protest in Israel* (State University of New York Press, 1988), 25. The Israeli data is from a survey conducted in 1984, while data on other countries is from S. M. Barnes and M. Kaase, eds., *Political Action: Mass Participation in Five Western Democracies* (Sage, 1979).

46. Lehman-Wilzig, *Stiff-Necked People,* 78 (emphasis in the original).

47. First figure from Emanuel Gutmann, "Citizen Participation in Political Life: Israel," *International Social Science Journal* 12 (1960): 55, cited in Lehman-Wilzig, *Stiff-Necked People,* 97; other figures from Asher Arian, *Politics in Israel: The Second Generation,* rev. ed. (Chatham House, 1989), 118.

48. Wolfsfeld, *Politics of Provocation,* 14, 16.

49. Lehman-Wilzig, *Stiff-Necked People,* 108–10; Wolfsfeld, *Politics of Provocation,* 13–16.

50. Ibid., 164.

51. Daniel Elazar, *Israel: Building a New Society* (Indiana University Press, 1986), 4, 85–86, 91, 100–101, 238–39; Ira Sharkansky, *What Makes Israel Tick: How Domestic Policy-Makers Cope with Constraints* (Nelson-Hall, 1985), 29.

52. The above events were reported in *Ma'ariv* and *Yediot Ahronot* (Israel's popular Hebrew-language daily newspapers) during the week of 29 May –4 June 1989.

53. For an account of private networks in various areas, see Sam Lehman-Wilzig, *Wildfire: Grassroots Protest in Israel in the Post-Socialist Era* (State University of New York Press, 1992), esp. 163; on the size of Israel's estimated "black economy," judged to be substantially larger than that of other developed states, see Ben-Zion Zilberfarb, "Estimates of the Black Economy in Israel and Overseas" (in Hebrew), *Riv'on Le'Kalkala,* no. 122 (October 1984): 320–22; on the size of private security forces see Nachman Ben-Yehuda, "The Social Meaning of Alternative Systems: Some Exploratory Notes," in *The Israeli State and Society: Boundaries and Frontiers,* ed. Baruch Kimmerling (State University of New York Press, 1989), 157–58; on a *haredi* patrol in Kiryat Sanz, Jerusalem, see Richard Primus, "On Your Walls" (in Hebrew), *Ma'ariv,* 6 August 1991.

54. Ehud Sprinzak, *Every Man Whatsoever Is Right in His Own Eyes—Illegalism in Israeli Society* (in Hebrew) (Sifriat Po'alim, 1986), 148.

55. Ibid., 14, 58–69, 93–119.

56. Menachem Hofnung, *Israel—Security Needs vs. the Rule of Law* (in Hebrew) (Nevo, 1991), 198.

57. Sullivan et al., *Political Tolerance,* 19.

58. Amos Oz, *In the Land of Israel* (The Hogarth Press, 1983), 151.

59. Aronof, *Israeli Visions,* 64; see also 13, 43, 124–25; Lilly Weissbrod, "Protest and Dissidence in Israel," in *Cross-Currents in Israeli Culture and Politics,* ed. Myron J. Aronoff (Transaction Books, 1984), 53–54, 66–67.

60. Avraham Diskin, *Elections and Voters in Israel* (Praeger, 1991), 145–46.

61. Aronof, "Political Polarization," 11; Alan S. Zuckerman, Hannah Herzog, and Michal Shamir, "The Party's Just Begun: Herut Activists in Power and after Begin," in

Israel after Begin, ed. Gregory S. Mahler (State University of New York Press, 1990), 235–55. Zuckerman, Herzog, and Shamir document the transition in Herut, with illuminating quotations from party veterans on the loss of ideological commitment.

62. For discussion of this point, see Daniel Elazar, *Israel: Building a New Society* (Indiana University Press, 1986), 185–206.

63. Shmuel N. Eisenstadt, *Israeli Society* (Basic Books, 1967), 211–14.

64. Yoram Ben-Porath, "Introduction," in *The Israeli Economy: Maturing through Crises,* ed. Yoram Ben-Porath (Harvard University Press, 1986), 1; Eitan Berglas, "Defense and the Economy: The Israeli Experience," Discussion Paper No. 83.01 (The Maurice Falk Institute for Economic Research in Israel, 1983), 41–43; idem, "Defense and the Economy," in *Israeli Economy: Maturing through Crises,* ed. Yoram Ben-Porath (Harvard University Press, 1986), 186–87; Wolffsohn, *Israel,* 248–55.

65. Berglas, *Defense and the Economy,* 176; Merrill Lynch, *The Israeli Economy* (Merrill Lynch & Co., Global Securities Research and Economics Group, International Economics Department, 1994), 18.

66. Gur Ofer, "Public Spending on Civilian Services," in *Israeli Economy: Maturing through Crises,* ed. Yoram Ben-Porath (Harvard University Press, 1986), 192–93, 199; Charles Lewis Taylor and David A. Jodice, *World Handbook of Political and Social Indicators* (Yale University Press, 1983), 28–30.

67. Horowitz and Lissak, *Trouble in Utopia,* 250–257.

68. Schweizer, *Israel,* 111; Ofer, "Public Spending," 208.

69. Ben-Porat, "Introduction," 18.

70. Ofer, "Public Spending," 194.

71. *Statistical Abstract of Israel* for years covered, reported in Merrill Lynch, *Israeli Economy,* 5.

72. *United Nations Statistical Yearbook,* 1979–1980, reported in Sharkansky, *What Makes Israel Tick,* 19.

73. See the discussion in Lehman-Wilzig, *Wildfire,* 69–70.

74. Bank of Israel, *Annual Report* (Israel Information Service, 1992; INTERNET).

75. Ibid. On developments during the 1980s see also Asaf Razin and Efraim Sadka, *The Economy of Israel: Malaise and Promise* (University of Chicago Press, 1994).

76. Israel Ministry of Finance (Israel Information Service; INTERNET).

77. Shmuel Eisenstadt, *Tradition, Change, and Modernity* (John Wiley and Sons, 1973), 3–21; see also Karl Deutsch, "Social Mobilization and Political Development," *American Political Science Review* 55 (September 1961): 17–24; Daniel Lerner, *The Passing of Traditional Society: Modernizing the Middle East* (The Free Press, 1958).

78. Eisenstadt, *Tradition, Change,* 23–25.

79. Ibid., 24.

80. Diskin, *Elections and Voters,* 142; Wolffsohn, *Israel,* 26.

81. Shulamit Har Even, "Israeli Democracy: The Current Picture" (in Hebrew), *Yediot Ahronot,* 12 October 1986; Alex Radian, "The Policy Formation—Electoral Economic Cycle 1955–1981," in *The Roots of Begin's Success,* ed. Abraham Diskin, Dan Caspi, and Emanuel Gutmann (Croom Helm and St. Martin's Press, 1984), 239.

82. Steven A. Hoffman, "Candidate Selection in Israel's Parliament: The Realities of Change," *Middle East Journal* 34 (1980): 157; Diskin, *Elections and Voters,* 164–65; Myron J. Aronoff, "Better Late than Never: Democratization in the Labor Party," in

Israel after Begin, ed. Gregory S. Mahler (State University of New York Press, 1990), 257–71.

83. Wolffsohn, *Israel,* 185–86, 213–15.

84. David Makovsky, "Poisonous Politics Are Becoming Passé," *Jerusalem Post International Edition,* 11 January 1992; Aronoff, *Israeli Visions,* xxi, 102.

85. Sprinzak, *Every Man Whatsoever,* 148–53, 159–74; Hofnung, *Israel—Security Needs,* 219, 223–24.

86. Martin Edelman, *Courts, Politics, and Culture in Israel* (University Press of Virginia, 1994), 6, 133; Albert Blaustein and Gisbert Flanz, eds., *Constitutions of the Countries of the World,* rev. ed. (Oceana Publications, 1992). The four nondemocratic countries are Oman, Qatar, Saudi Arabia, and the United Arab Emirates.

87. For a good discussion of Israel's Basic Laws see Susan Hattis Rolef, ed., *Political Dictionary of the State of Israel* (Jerusalem Publishing House, 1993), 54–56, 356.

88. Elazar, *Israel: Building a New Society,* 189–90; see also Edelman, *Courts, Politics, and Culture,* whose central thesis is that the Israeli court system must be understood in relation to the underlying political culture.

89. Elazar, *Israel: Building a New Society,* esp. 5, 119.

90. Ibid., 32, 42, 46; Edelman, "The Judicialization of Politics," *International Political Science Review* 15 (April 1994): 177–86.

91. Elazar, *Israel: Building a New Society,* 9 ff.; Samuel Sager, *The Parliamentary System of Israel* (Syracuse University Press, 1985), 41.

92. Daniel Friedmann, *The Effect of Foreign Law on the Law of Israel* (Israel Law Review Association, 1975), 119–20; Sager, *Parliamentary System,* 222–25.

93. Itzhak Galnoor, "Secrecy," in *Government Secrecy in Democracies,* ed. Itzhak Galnoor (Harper and Row, 1977), 195; Daniel Shimshoni, *Israeli Democracy: The Middle of the Journey* (The Free Press, 1982), 91–93.

94. Amnon Rubinstein, *The Constitutional Law of the State of Israel* (in Hebrew) (Schocken, 1980), 220; see analysis of law, 220–23. Also, Simon Shetreet, "A Contemporary Model of Emergency Detention Law: An Assessment of the Israeli Law," *Israel Yearbook on Human Rights* 14 (1984), esp. 186; and Hans Klinghoffer, "Preventive Detention for Reasons of Security" (in Hebrew), *Mishpatim* 11 (1981): 286–89.

95. Shetreet, "A Contemporary Model," 218–19.

96. Niall MacDermot, "Draft Intervention on Administrative Detention to the U.N. Commission on Human Rights," *ICJ Newsletter,* no. 24 (January/March 1985): 53.

97. Mordechai Mironi, *Return-to-Work Orders: Government Intervention in Labor Disputes through Emergency Regulations and Work Injunctions* (in Hebrew) (The Institute for Social and Labor Research, University of Tel Aviv, 1983), 17–18; also, *Kovetz Hatakanot* for the years involved.

98. The emergency regulations were published in the Israel press on 8 July 1985; see, for example, *Ma'ariv* and *Yediot Ahronot* of that date. The interview with the former justice minister, Haim Tsadok, is in *Davar,* 8 July 1985.

99. Rubinstein, *Constitutional Law,* 219.

100. Aronoff, *Israeli Visions,* xix; see also xxi, 37–38, 155.

101. Ibid., 133.

102. Ibid., 133–35.

103. Kimmerling, "Between the Primordial and Civil Definitions," 273, 277.

104. Yoav Peled, "Retreat from Modernity: The Ascendance of Jewish National-ism in the Jewish State," paper presented at the annual meeting, American Political Science Association, San Francisco, August 30–September 2, 1990; Wolffsohn, *Israel,* 176; Ilan Peleg, "The Peace Process and Israel's Political Culture: A Kulturkampf in the Making," paper presented at annual meeting of the American Political Science Association, Chicago, September 1–4, 1995; Joseph Agassi, *Religion and Nationality: Towards an Israeli National Identity* (in Hebrew) (Papyrus, Tel Aviv University, 1984); Boas Evron, *Jewish State or Israeli Nation?* (Indiana University Press, 1995).

105. Aronoff, *Israeli Visions,* 109–11, 114.

7. THE COMMUNAL SPLIT

1. See the discussion in Eliezer Ben-Rafael and Stephen Sharot, *Ethnicity, Religion, and Class in Israeli Society* (Cambridge University Press, 1991), 8, 45–46.

2. S. N. Eisenstadt, *The Development of the Ethnic Problem in Israeli Society: Observations and Suggestions for Research* (The Jerusalem Institute for Israel Studies, 1986), 26.

3. O'Brien, *The Siege: The Saga of Israel and Zionism* (Simon and Schuster, 1986), 347.

4. Moshe Shokeid and Shlomo Deshen, *Distant Relations: Ethnicity and Politics among Arabs and Middle Eastern Jews* (Praeger, 1982), 5; and Joseph Schwartzwald and Yehuda Amir, "Interethnic Relations and Education: An Israeli Perspective," in *Education in a Comparative Context,* ed. Ernest Krausz (Transaction Publishers, 1989), 250.

5. Sammy Smooha, *Israel: Pluralism and Conflict* (University of California Press, 1978), 366. See also discussion in Bat Yeor, *The Dhimmi: Jews and Christians under Islam* (Fairleigh Dickinson University Press, 1985), 146–50.

6. Daniel Elazar, *Israel: Building a New Society* (Indiana University Press, 1986), 158–59.

7. Moshe Shokeid, "A Case of Ethnic Myth-Making," in *Cross-Currents in Israeli Culture and Politics,* ed. Myron J. Aronoff (Transaction Books, 1984); see also Ben-Rafael and Sharot, *Ethnicity, Religion,* 45–46, 222.

8. Shlomo Deshen, "Towards an Understanding of the Special Charm of Religiosity on Eastern Jews" (in Hebrew), *Politika,* no. 24 (1989): 40–43; idem, "The Religiosity of the Eastern Jews: Public, Rabbis, and Faith" (in Hebrew), *Alpayim* 9 (1994): 44–58.

9. Judith Shuval, "The Structure and Dilemmas of Israeli Pluralism," in *The Israeli State and Society: Boundaries and Frontiers,* ed. Baruch Kimmerling (State University of New York Press, 1989), 222–23; Eisenstadt, *Development of the Ethnic Problem,* 26; Schwartzwald and Amir, "Interethnic Relations," 248; and Eliezer David Jaffe, "Ethnic and Minority Groups in Israel: Challenges for Social Work Theory, Value and Practice," *Journal of Sociology and Social Welfare* 22, no. 1 (March 1, 1995): 152. On the furtherance of negative images by Middle Eastern Jewish intellectuals themselves, see Sammy Smooha, "The Grand Collapse of the Orientals," *Ha'aretz Supplement* (February 3, 1995).

10. Sammy Smooha, "Class, Ethnic, and National Cleavages and Democracy in Is-

rael," in *Israeli Democracy Under Stress,* ed. Ehud Sprinzak and Larry Diamond (Lynne Rienner, 1993), 319; see also Shuval, "Structure and Dilemmas," 224.

11. See the discussion in Smooha, *Israel: Pluralism,* 21–25.

12. See the studies in S. N. Eisenstadt, Moshe Lissak, and Yaakov Nahon, *Communities in Israel and Their Social Standing* (in Hebrew) (Jerusalem Institute for Israel Studies, 1993): Smooha, "Class, Ethnic, and National Cleavages," 318; Smooha, "Jewish Ethnicity in Israel," in *Whither Israel? The Domestic Challenges,* ed. Keith Kyle and Joel Peters (I. B. Tauris, 1994), 164, 172–73.

13. Israel, Central Bureau of Statistics, *Statistical Abstract of Israel 1995,* 331; Ben-Rafael and Sharot, *Ethnicity, Religion,* 32.

14. The gap was greater before recent immigration from Europe: 1.17 persons per room for Jews from Africa and Asian against .84 for Jews from Europe and the Americas in 1988; *Statistical Abstract of Israel 1989,* 311; *Statistical Abstract of Israel 1995,* 341.

15. In 1994, 31.9 percent of Jews from Europe or the Americas had university training as opposed to 7.5 percent of Jews from Asia or Africa. Smooha, *Israel: Pluralism,* 179; *Statistical Abstract of Israel 1989,* 601; *Statistical Abstract of Israel 1995,* 632.

16. Shokeid and Deshen, *Distant Relations,* 155–57; Smooha, *Israel: Pluralism,* 182; Smooha, "Class, Ethnic, and National Cleavages," 324; Sharon Schwartz et al., "Separating Class and Ethnic Prejudice: A Study of North African and European Jews in Israel," *Social Psychology Quarterly* 54, no. 4 (1991): 287–98. The Schwartz study demonstrates that communal prejudices remain even when socioeconomic differences are controlled.

17. See the evidence collected in Tom Segev, *1949: The First Israelis* (The Free Press, 1986).

18. Pnina Morag-Talmon, "The Integration Processes of Eastern Jews in Israeli Society," *Studies in Contemporary Jewry* 5 (1989): 36.

19. Smooha, *Israel: Pluralism,* 77.

20. Yochanan Peres, "Ethnic Relations in Israel," *American Journal of Sociology* 76 (May 1971): 1037.

21. Ben-Rafael and Sharot, *Ethnicity, Religion,* 30, 227; Morag-Talmon, "Integration Processes," 33; Shuval, "Structure and Dilemmas," 222–23.

22. Ben-Rafael and Sharon, *Ethnicity, Religion,* 116, 214–15, 253.

23. Michael Wolffsohn, *Israel: Polity, Society and Economy 1882–1986* (Humanities Press International, 1987), 145–46.

24. The two dovish categories, accounting for the remaining respondents, were "conciliationists" and "pragmatists." Sammy Smooha, *Arabs and Jews in Israel,* vol. 1 (Westview Press, 1989), 193; Ofra Mayseless and Reuven Gal, "Hatred on the Rise," *Israeli Democracy* (Fall 1990): 23.

25. Walter Zenner, "Ethnic Factors in Israeli Life," in *Books on Israel,* ed. Ian S. Lustick (State University of New York Press, 1988), 49.

26. See, for example, the researches cited by Ben-Rafael and Sharot, *Ethnicity, Religion,* 29; and Schwartzwald and Amir, "Interethnic Relations," 262; see also Smooha, "Jewish Ethnicity," 171, and Avraham Diskin, "The Jewish Ethnic Vote: The Demographic Myth," *The Jerusalem Quarterly,* no. 35 (Spring 1985): 55; Eisenstadt, Lissak, and Nahon, *Communities in Israel.*

27. Ben-Rafael and Sharot, *Ethnicity, Religion,* 30–31; Smooha, "Class, Ethnic and National Cleavages," 167.

28. Smooha, *Israel: Pluralism,* 194–95; Shlomit Levy, Hanna Levinsohn, and Elihu Katz, *Beliefs, Observations, and Social Interaction among Israeli Jews* (The Louis Guttman Israel Institute of Applied Social Research, 1993), B-5.

29. Wolffsohn, *Israel,* 145–46.

30. Baruch Kimmerling, "Yes, Returning to the Family" (in Hebrew), *Politika,* no. 48 (March 1993): 42–43.

31. Arnold Lewis, "Phantom Ethnicity: 'Oriental Jews' in Israeli Society," in *Studies in Israeli Ethnicity: After the Ingathering,* ed. Alex Weingrod (Gordon and Breach, 1985), 150.

32. For example, the conclusion of Orit Ichilov that "Eastern adolescents . . . do not differ in their civic orientations from the general Israeli public"; Ichilov, "Citizenship Orientations of Two Israeli Minority Groups: Israel-Arab and Eastern-Jewish Youth," *Ethnic Groups* 7, no. 2 (1988): 134.

33. Ibid., 134, 136, 145–46; Schwartzwald and Amir, "Interethnic Relations," 262–63; Smooha, *Israel: Pluralism,* 149; Eisenstadt, Lissak, and Nahon, *Communities in Israel.*

34. Smooha, "Class, Ethnic, and National Cleavages," 323; see also Ben-Rafael and Sharot, *Ethnicity, Religion,* 29–30, 224; Schwartzwald and Amir, "Interethnic Relations," 255.

35. *Statistical Abstract of Israel 1987,* 105. The figures exclude marriages in which at least one partner is a third-generation Israeli or the continent of origin is unknown.

36. Calvin Goldscheider, *Israel's Changing Family* (Westview Press, 1995), chap. 10.

37. *Statistical Abstract of Israel 1995,* 95.

38. Eva Etzioni-Halevy, "Protest Politics in the Israeli Democracy," *Political Science Quarterly* 90 (Fall 1975): 514–16.

39. Smooha, *Israel: Pluralism,* 179–80.

40. Avraham Diskin, *Elections and Voters in Israel* (Praeger, 1991), 171; Samuel Sager, *The Parliamentary System of Israel* (Syracuse University Press, 1985), 58–59.

41. Smooha, "Class, Ethnic, and National Cleavages," 168–69.

42. Hanna Herzog, "Penetrating the System: The Politics of Collective Identities," in *The Elections in Israel 1992,* ed. Asher Arian and Michal Shamir (State University of New York Press, 1995), 84–89; Elazar, *Israel: Building a New Society,* 162.

43. This process is also described in Maurice M. Roumani, "Labor's Expectation and Israeli Reality: Ethnic Voting as a Means toward Political and Social Change," in *Israel Faces the Future,* ed. Bernard Reich and Gershon R. Kieval (Praeger, 1986), 57–78.

44. Efraim Ben-Zadok and Giora Goldberg, "Voting Patterns of Oriental Jews in Development Towns," *The Jerusalem Quarterly,* no. 32 (Summer 1994): 22.

45. Diskin, *Elections and Voters,* 115–16; Yochanan Peres and Sara Shemer, "The Ethnic Factor in Elections," in *The Roots of Begin's Success,* ed. Abraham Diskin, Dan Caspi, and Emanuel Gutmann (Croom Helm and St. Martin's Press, 1984), 106.

46. Yael Yishai, "Hawkish Proletariat: The Case of Israel," *Journal of Political and Military Sociology* 13 (Spring 1985): 63, 70.

47. See also Renee Taft, "Ethnic Divisions in Israel," in *Israel Faces the Future*, ed. Bernard Reich and Gershon R. Kieval (Praeger, 1986), 79–92.

48. Smooha, "Class, Ethnic, and National Cleavages," 323.

49. Baruch Kimmerling, "Boundaries and Frontiers of the Israeli Control System: Analytical Conclusions," in *The Israeli State and Society: Boundaries and Frontiers*, ed. Baruch Kimmerling (State University of New York Press, 1989), 272–74.

50. On Shas generally see Aaron P. Willis, "Shas—The Sephardic Torah Guardians: Religious 'Movement' and Political Power," in *The Elections in Israel 1992*, ed. Asher Arian and Michal Shamir (State University of New York Press, 1995), 121–39; and Willis, "Redefining Religious Zionism: Shas' Ethno-politics," *Israel Studies Bulletin* 8 (Fall 1992): 3–8.

51. Asher Arian and Michal Shamir, "Two Reversals: Why 1992 Was Not 1977," in *The Elections in Israel 1992*, ed. Asher Arian and Michal Shamir (State University of New York Press, 1995), 27–39.

52. Ibid., 38.

8. RELIGION AND POLITICS

1. Peter Grose, *A Changing Israel* (Vintage Books, 1985), 46.

2. Rita Simon, "The 'Religious Issue' in Israeli Public Life," *Israel Horizons* (Summer 1989): 29.

3. Uri Huppert, *Back to the Ghetto: Zionism in Retreat* (Prometheus Books, 1988), 183.

4. Charles S. Liebman, "Introduction," in *Conflict and Accommodation between Jews in Israel*, ed. Charles S. Liebman (Keter Publishing House, 1990), xi.

5. Shlomit Levy, Hanna Levinsohn, and Elihu Katz, *Beliefs, Observances and Social Interaction among Israeli Jews* (The Louis Guttman Israel Institute of Applied Social Research, 1993), B-3.

6. Survey by O. Cohen, cited in Sammy Smooha, *Israel: Pluralism and Conflict* (University of California Press, 1978), 196.

7. Charles Liebman and Eliezer Don-Yehiya, *Religion and Politics in Israel* (Indiana University Press, 1984), 130.

8. See discussions of this point in Asher Arian, *Politics in Israel: The Second Generation*, rev. ed. (Chatham House, 1989), 238–39; and in Alan Dowty, "Religion and Politics in Israel," *Commonweal* 110 (15 July 1983): 393–96.

9. Smooha, *Israel: Pluralism*, 43–45, 109, 143, 222.

10. Don-Yehiya, "The Resolution of Religious Conflicts in Israel," in *Conflict and Consensus in Jewish Public Life*, ed. Stuart Cohen and Eliezer Don-Yehiya (Bar-Ilan University Press, 1986), 203.

11. Martin Edelman, "The Utility of a Written Constitution: Free Exercise of Religion in Israel and the United States," paper presented at the 15th World Congress of the International Political Science Association, Buenos Aires, July 21–25, 1991.

12. Ibid., 21 ff. On freedom of religion in Israel generally see Zvi Berinson, "Freedom of Religion and Conscience in the State of Israel," *Israel Yearbook on Human Rights* 3 (1973): 223–32, and Simon Shetreet, "Some Reflections on Freedom

of Conscience and Religion in Israel," *Israel Yearbook on Human Rights* 4 (1974): 194–218.

13. See the argument by Simha Meron, "Freedom of Religion as Distinct from Freedom from Religion," *Israel Yearbook on Human Rights* 4 (1974): 219–40.

14. Dan Horowitz and Moshe Lissak, *Trouble in Utopia: The Overburdened Polity of Israel* (State University of New York Press, 1989), 144.

15. S. Zalman Abramov, *Perpetual Dilemma: Jewish Religion in the Jewish State* (World Union for Progressive Judaism, 1976), 99–100; Emile Marmorstein, *Heaven at Bay: The Jewish Kulturkampf in the Holy Land* (Oxford University Press, 1969).

16. A *haredi* is, literally, "one who trembles," meaning one who lives in fear or awe of God; the term is in common use among *haredim* themselves, while the problematic label of "ultra-Orthodox" is not. The distinction between modern Orthodox and *haredi* is explained below.

17. Abramov, *Perpetual Dilemma*, 50–51.

18. Ibid., 53.

19. Menachem Friedman, "The State of Israel as a Theological Dilemma," in *The Israeli State and Society: Boundaries and Frontiers*, ed. Baruch Kimmerling (State University of New York Press, 1989), 166; the struggle between secularization and tradition in modern Jewish history is outlined by Marmorstein, *Heaven at Bay*.

20. Martin E. Marty and R. Scott Appleby, "Introduction," in *Fundamentalisms and the State*, ed. Martin E. Marty and R. Scott Appleby (University of Chicago Press, 1993), 3; idem, "Conclusion: Remaking the State: The Limits of the Fundamentalist Imagination," 620.

21. Friedman, "State of Israel," 178, 200.

22. See the account in Amos Elon, *Herzl* (Holt, Rinehart and Winston, 1975), 237.

23. Menachem Friedman, "The Structural Foundation for Religio-Political Accommodation in Israel: Fallacy and Reality," in *Israel: The First Decade of Independence*, ed. S. Ilan Troen and Noah Lucas (State University of New York Press, 1995), 51–81; Susan Hattis Rolef, ed., *Political Dictionary of the State of Israel* (Macmillan, 1987), 287–88; Daniel Elazar, *Israel: Building a New Society* (Indiana University Press, 1986), 132; Abramov, *Perpetual Dilemma*, 127.

24. Abramov, *Perpetual Dilemma*, 140, 144; Friedman, "State of Israel," 191.

25. Don-Yehiya, "Resolution of Religious Conflicts," 206.

26. See, for example, Shubert Spero, "Who Needs Religious Political Parties?" *Jerusalem Post*, 26 May 1988.

27. Don-Yehiya, "Resolution of Religious Conflicts," 207.

28. See the discussion by Allen Shapiro, "MK Porush, Civics Instructor," *Jerusalem Post*, 24 May 1991.

29. Liebman, "Relations between *Dati* and Non-*Dati* Jews—Some Final Reflections," in *Conflict and Accommodation between Jews in Israel*, ed. Charles S. Liebman (Keter Publishing House, 1990), 216–17; Don-Yehiya, "Resolution of Religious Conflicts," 208; Shlomo Avineri, "The Violated Social Contract," *Jerusalem Post International Edition*, 28 June 1986.

30. Smooha, *Israel: Pluralism*, 223.

31. Liebman, "Jewish Fundamentalism and the Israeli Polity," in *Fundamentalisms and the State*, ed. Martin E. Marty and R. Scott Appleby (University of Chicago

Press, 1993), 76–77; Ira Sharkansky, *What Makes Israel Tick: How Domestic Policy-Makers Cope with Constraints* (Nelson-Hall, 1985), 59.

32. Poll carried out by the Smith Research Center; *Jerusalem Post*, 15 May 1986.

33. Simon, "The 'Religious Issue'," 27.

34. Liebman and Don-Yehiya, *Religion and Politics*, 99.

35. See the description of Leibowitz's thinking in Lawrence Meyer, *Israel Now: Portrait of a Troubled Land* (Delacorte Press, 1982), 369.

36. Abraham Rabinovich, "O, Jerusalem, Where Is Thy Sabbath Gone?" *Jerusalem Post Magazine* (2 June 1989): 7; see also the "scorecard" of Sam Lehman-Wilzig, "For the Sin of Ultra-Orthodox Bashing," *Sh'ma*, 9 September 1990.

37. On the Sabbath work permit controversy historically, see Peter Y. Medding, *The Founding of Israeli Democracy 1948–1967* (Oxford University Press, 1990), chap. 5.

38. Ehud Sprinzak, "Three Models of Religious Violence: The Case of Jewish Fundamentalism in Israel," in *Fundamentalisms and the State*, ed. Martin E. Marty and R. Scott Appleby (University of Chicago Press, 1993), 468.

39. *Jerusalem Post*, 15 May 1986.

40. See, for example, Elihu Katz and Michael Gurevitch, *The Secularization of Leisure: Culture and Communication in Israel* (Harvard University Press, 1976).

41. Liebman, "Introduction," xvi–xvii.

42. Ibid.

43. The slight increase in 1992 may result from better efforts to include *haredim*, who were underrepresented in earlier polls. Among the 20 percent "religious," 10 percent identified themselves as *haredim* and 10 percent as simply religious; in 1989 only 7 percent were identified as *haredim* with the religious accounting for 10 percent.

44. Charles Liebman, "The Religious Component in Israeli Ultra-Nationalism," The Eighth Annual Rabbi Louis Feinberg Memorial Lecture in Judaic Studies, University of Cincinnati, April 16, 1985. Poll results add up to 99.1 percent; the remaining .9 percent are not accounted for.

45. Levy, Levinsohn, and Katz, *Beliefs, Observances*, 330.

46. Haim Shapiro, "20% of Israeli Weddings Are Not Orthodox—Study," *Jerusalem Post International Edition*, 9 March 1996.

47. Gary S. Schiff, "Recent Developments in Israel's Religious Parties," in *Israel after Begin*, ed. Gregory S. Mahler (State University of New York Press, 1990), 273–90; Eliezer Don-Yehiya, "Religion and Ethnicity in Israeli Politics: The Religious Parties and the Elections to the 12th Knesset" (in Hebrew), *Medina, Mimshal, V'yahasim Benle'umiim* [State, Government, and International Relations], no. 32 (Spring 1990): 11–54. On the phenomenon of Shas and the development of a Sephardi-*haredi* subculture, see Friedman, "State of Israel," 175–85.

48. Haim Shapiro, "Reform Jews Charge Ministry Kept Their Strength a Secret," *Jerusalem Post*, 17 May 1989; the poll was conducted by the Guttman Institute.

49. Levy, Levinsohn, and Katz, *Beliefs, Observances*, B-4.

50. Hostility among the secular public toward the religious sector is based much more on a "lifestyle defense," reflecting broad negative perceptions of difference, than on actual threats to individual self-interest; see Kenneth Wald and Samuel Shye, "Inter-Religious Conflict in Israel," paper presented at the annual meeting of the American Political Science Association, Washington, D.C., September 2–5, 1993.

51. For a full statement of this thesis, see Charles Liebman and Eliezer Don-Yehiya, *Civil Religion in Israel: Traditional Judaism and Political Culture in the Jewish State* (University of California Press, 1983).

52. Liebman and Don-Yehiya, *Religion and Politics,* 6.

53. Elazar, *Israel: Building a New Society,* esp. 124, 143, provides a fuller description of this process; see also Grose, *A Changing Israel,* 42–44.

54. Liebman and Don-Yehiya, *Religion and Politics,* 52–53.

55. Levy, Levinsohn, and Katz, *Beliefs, Observances,* 93.

56. Survey carried out by the Guttman Institute; see Simon, "The 'Religious Issue'."

57. Yehuda Ben-Meir and Peri Kedem, "An Index of Religiosity for the Jewish Population in Israel" (in Hebrew), *Megamot* 24 (February 1979): 353–62; see also Peri Kedem, "Dimensions of Jewish Religiosity in Israel," in *Tradition, Innovation, Conflict: Jewishness and Judaism in Contemporary Israel,* ed. Zvi Sobel and Benjamin Beit-Hallahmi (State University of New York Press, 1991), 251–72.

58. Yochanan Peres, "Most Israelis Are Committed to Democracy," *Israeli Democracy* 1 (February 1987): 17–18.

59. The Knesset member was Avrum Burg, who was himself religious. Both quotations from "Shas in Zionist land," *The Jerusalem Post,* 28 May 1993.

60. Robert I. Friedman, *Zealots for Zion: Inside Israel's West Bank Settlement Movement* (Random House, 1992), 156–57.

61. This analysis of *haredi* society is taken, for the most part, from Menachem Friedman, *Haredi Society: Sources, Trends, and Processes* (in Hebrew) (Jerusalem Institute for Israel Studies, 1991); for a summary in English see Friedman, "The Ultra-Orthodox and Israeli Society," in *Whither Israel? The Domestic Challenges,* ed. Keith Kyle and Joel Peters (I. B. Tauris, 1993), 177–201. See also David Landau, *Piety and Power: The World of Jewish Fundamentalism* (Hill and Wang, 1993).

62. Liebman and Don-Yehiya, *Religion and Politics,* 122; Menachem Friedman, "'If They Are Free—They Are Not Jews'," *Israeli Democracy* 1 (February 1987): 22.

63. For an analysis of the NRP's decline, see Menachem Friedman, "The NRP in Transition—Behind the Party's Electoral Decline," in *The Roots of Begin's Success: The 1981 Israeli Elections,* ed. Dan Caspi, Avraham Diskin, and Emanuel Gutmann (Croom Helm and St. Martin's Press, 1984), 141–68.

64. Rabbi Israel Meir HaCohen, the "Hafetz Haim" (d. 1933), quoted by Friedman, "If They Are Free," 22.

65. Amnon Levi, "The *Haredi* Press and Secular Society," in *Conflict and Accommodation between Jews in Israel,* ed. Charles S. Liebman (Keter Publishing House, 1990), 27.

66. Sprinzak, "Three Models," 465.

67. Friedman, "State of Israel," 198, 208.

68. Liebman, "Jewish Fundamentalism," 71.

69. Among the *haredim* in the survey, 76 percent said that only Jews had rights to the Land of Israel, as opposed to 65 percent of the (non-*haredi*) religious, 43 percent of traditional, and 28 percent of secular Israelis. Yochanan Peres, "Religiosity and Political Positions" (in Hebrew), *Democracy* (Winter 1992): 26–31. See also Efraim Inbar, Gad Barzilai, and Giora Goldberg, "Positions on National Security of Israel's

Ultra-Orthodox Political Leadership," *International Journal of Comparative Religion* 2 (Winter 1995).

70. Itzhak Galnoor, *Steering the Polity: Communication and Politics in Israel* (Sage, 1982), 354–55.

71. See the analysis by Yosef Fund, "Agudat Yisrael Confronting Zionism and the State of Israel—Ideology and Policy" (in Hebrew), paper presented at the annual meeting of the Israel Political Science Association, Ramat Gan, May 1991; Inbar et al., "Positions on National Security."

72. See especially the study by Samuel Heilman, *Defenders of the Faith: Inside Ultra-Orthodox Jewry* (Schocken Books, 1992).

73. Joseph Shilhav and Menachem Friedman, *Growth and Segregation—The Ultra-Orthodox Community of Jerusalem* (in Hebrew) (The Jerusalem Institute for Israel Studies, 1989); Micha Odenheimer, "A Society in Flux," *Jerusalem Post International Edition*, 14 January 1989.

74. Matt Wagner, "'Modesty Patrol' Targets *Haredi* Renegades," *Jerusalem Post International Edition*, 1 January 1994; Friedman, *Haredi Society*.

75. Friedman, *Haredi Society*, 192.

76. For the religious arguments against the sacralizing of territory, see Adam Doron, *The State of Israel and the Land of Israel* (in Hebrew) (Hotsa'at Beit Berl, 1988).

77. Liebman, "Jewish Fundamentalism," 70, 72; Ian Lustick, *For the Land and the Lord: Jewish Fundamentalism in Israel* (Council on Foreign Relations, 1988), 165–68.

78. Liebman, "Jewish Fundamentalism," 73.

79. Marty and Appleby, "Conclusion: Remaking the State," 621.

80. Ibid., 622, 641.

9. ARABS IN ISRAEL

1. For an account of Bastuni's movement see Ian Lustick, *Arabs in the Jewish State: Israel's Control of a National Minority* (University of Texas Press, 1980), 116–17. For recent overviews of the Israeli Arab issue, see Ori Stendel, *The Arabs in Israel: Between Hammer and Anvil* (in Hebrew) (Academon, 1992), and Elie Rekhess, *The Arab Minority in Israel: Between Communism and Arab Nationalism* (in Hebrew) (Hakibutz Hameuhad, 1993).

2. Elihu Katz, Hannah Levinsohn, and Majid Al-Haj, "Attitudes of Israelis (Jews and Arabs) towards Current Affairs," Guttman Israel Institute of Applied Social Research Publication No. (S)EK/1129/E, January 10, 1991. See similar findings in Sammy Smooha, *Arabs and Jews in Israel: Change and Continuity in Mutual Intolerance*, vol. 2 (Westview Press, 1992), 168.

3. Smooha, *Israel: Pluralism and Conflict* (University of California Press, 1978), 263.

4. "Problems of Histadrut in the State," February 1948, Labor Party Archive, 7/69/48, quoted in Tom Segev, *1949: The First Israelis* (The Free Press, 1986), 45–46.

5. Lustick, *Arabs in the Jewish State*, 5.

6. Zionist Archive, S25, File 22200, quoted in Uzi Benziman and Atallah Mansour, *Subtenants* (in Hebrew) (Keter Publishing House, 1992), 13–14.

7. Benziman and Mansour, *Subtenants,* 11.

8. The legal expression of Israel's Jewishness is succinctly summarized by David Kretzmer, *The Legal Status of the Arabs in Israel* (Westview Press, 1990), 17–22.

9. "Problems of Education in the State," June 1948, Labor Party Archives, 7/1/48, quoted in Segev, *1949,* 45.

10. Protocol of Mapai Secretariat meeting, July 9, 1950, quoted in Benziman and Mansour, *Subtenants,* 154–55.

11. Ben-Gurion diary, January 31, 1951, cited in Benziman and Mansour, *Subtenants,* 51.

12. Ilan Pappé, "An Uneasy Coexistence: Arabs and Jews in the First Decade of Statehood," in *Israel: The First Decade of Independence,* ed. S. I. Troen and N. Lucas (State University of New York Press, 1995), 634–35.

13. Moshe Sharon, review of *Arabs in the Jewish State* by Ian Lustick, *Middle Eastern Studies* 18 (July 1982): 337; see also Don Peretz, "Early State Policy towards the Arab Populations, 1948–1955," in *New Perspectives on Israeli History: The Early Years of the State,* ed. Laurence J. Silberstein (New York University Press, 1991), 82–102.

14. See the discussions in Lustick, *Arabs in the Jewish State,* and Smooha, *Israel: Pluralism.*

15. Benziman and Mansour, *Subtenants,* 53.

16. Benziman and Mansour (ibid., 52) state that, on the basis of available evidence, three cabinet discussions took place in the 1948–1967 period, five during the 1970s, and five during the 1980s; Joseph Ginat, a former advisor on Arab affairs, recounts one preliminary discussion during Golda Meir's term as prime minister (1969–1974) and another when Ezer Weizman, as minister without portfolio during the first two years of the National Unity Government (1984–1986), dealt with Israeli Arab issues; see Ginat, "Voting Patterns and Political Behavior in the Arab Sector," in *The Arab Vote in Israel's Parliamentary Elections, 1988* (in Hebrew), ed. Jacob M. Landau (The Jerusalem Institute for Israel Studies, 1989), 15. See also Sharon, review of *Arabs in the Jewish State.*

17. Quoted by Peretz, "Early State Policy," 87.

18. See the note on his 1959 visit to Baka el-Gharbiya ("Mr. Ben-Gurion's First Visit to an Arab Community since the Establishment of the State") in "30 Years Ago," *Jerusalem Post,* 17 May 1989.

19. See the quotations in Benziman and Mansour, *Subtenants,* 19–21.

20. Grossman, *Sleeping on a Wire: Conversations with Palestinians in Israel* (Farrar, Straus & Giroux, 1993), 315.

21. Benziman and Mansour, *Subtenants,* 21.

22. Ibid., 30–35, 71–72, 198, 211–12.

23. Ibid., 32, 214.

24. Sharett to Cabinet Ministers, February 24, 1950, State Archives, Dov Yosef Archive, Correspondence and Memoranda, 703/16, quoted in Segev, *1949,* 65.

25. Interview, June 6, 1983, quoted in Segev, *1949,* 67.

26. Michael Shalev, "Jewish Organized Labor and the Palestinians: A Study of State/Society Relations in Israel," in *The Israeli State and Society: Boundaries and Frontiers,* ed. Baruch Kimmerling (State University of New York Press, 1989), 103, 107–8.

27. Lustick, *Arabs in the Jewish State,* 25–26.

28. Ibid., 78. Writing a decade later, Lustick emphasized the shift of Israeli Arabs toward a more active political role; Lustick, "The Changing Political Role of Israeli Arabs," in *The Elections in Israel 1988,* ed. Asher Arian and Michal Shamir (Westview Press, 1990), 120.

29. William Brinner, "Muslim Minorities in non-Muslim Societies," paper presented at the conference on The Arab Minority in Israel: Dilemmas of Political Orientation and Social Change, University of Tel Aviv, June 3–4, 1991; see also Smooha, *Arabs and Jews,* vol. 2, 1.

30. Fouzi El-Asmar, *To Be an Arab in Israel* (The Institute for Palestine Studies, 1978), 22; on the relationship of Israeli Arabs to Jewish political culture see Majid Al-Haj, "Strategies of Mobilization among the Arabs in Israel," in *Whither Israel? The Domestic Challenges,* ed. Keith Kyle and Joel Peters (I. B. Tauris, 1993), 140–57.

31. Azmi Bishara, as quoted in Grossman, *Sleeping on a Wire,* 296–97.

32. Writing of conversations with Israeli Arabs in the late 1980s, David Grossman notes that "the threat of transfer continued to echo, and I felt the living fear" (ibid., 324–25).

33. El-Asmar, *To Be an Arab,* 57.

34. Kretzmer, *Legal Status,* 49–76; Lustick, *Arabs in the Jewish State,* 48–49; Ofra Seliktar, "National Integration of a Minority in an Acute Conflict Situation: The Case of the Israeli Arabs," *Plural Societies* 12, nos. 3–4 (1981): 36–37; Shmuel Sandler, "Israeli Arabs and the Jewish State: The Activation of a Community in Suspended Animation," *Middle Eastern Studies* 31 (October 1995): 932–52.

35. Alouph Hareven, "Israeli Arabs as a Jewish Problem" (in Hebrew), in *One of Every Six Israelis,* ed. Alouph Hareven (The Van Leer Jerusalem Foundation, 1981), 7.

36. Sammy Smooha, *Arabs and Jews in Israel,* vol. 1, *Conflicting and Shared Attitudes in a Divided Society* (Westview Press, 1989), 141; idem, *Arabs and Jews in Israel,* vol. 2, 155.

37. See also Michal Shamir and John L. Sullivan, "Jews and Arabs in Israel," *Journal of Conflict Resolution* 29 (1985): 283–305; Asher Arian, Ilan Talmud, and Tamar Hermann, *National Security and Public Opinion in Israel,* Jaffee Center for Strategic Studies, Study No. 9 (Westview Press, 1988); and the public opinion surveys of the Israel Diaspora Institute published in the journal *Israeli Democracy* (especially Fall 1987: 35–39; Spring 1988: 15–19; Winter 1988: 42–46; and Winter 1988: 16–18). For a good summary of earlier surveys, carried out by the Israel Institute for Applied Social Research, see Russell A. Stone, *Social Change in Israel: Attitudes and Events, 1967–1979* (Praeger, 1982).

38. See the summary in Michael Wolffsohn, *Israel: Polity, Society and Economy 1882–1986* (Humanities Press International, 1987), 162; also, Hareven, "Israeli Arabs as a Jewish Problem."

39. Smooha, *Israel: Pluralism,* 199; Smooha, *Arabs and Jews,* vol. 2, 58, 149.

40. See discussion of the court case in Kretzmer, *Legal Status,* 30–31.

41. Smooha, Sammy. "Minority Status in an Ethnic Democracy: The Status of the Arab Minority in Israel," *Ethnic and Racial Studies* 13 (July 1990): 404–5; see also Smooha, *Israel: Pluralism,* 271; Smooha, *Arabs and Jews,* vol. 1, 50–51, 100–101, 109.

42. El-Asmar, *To Be an Arab*, 42.

43. Menachem Hofnung, *Israel—Security Needs vs. the Rule of Law* (in Hebrew) (Nevo, 1991), 140.

44. Ibid., 140–48.

45. Kretzmer, *Legal Status*, 66, 68, 96–97; Smooha, "Minority Status," 401.

46. The difficulty of measuring the exact extent of such expropriations is discussed by Kretzmer, *Legal Status*, 59–60; see also Hofnung, *Israel—Security Needs*, 166, 169, 173–74.

47. Regarding the concept of "present absentees," Grossman writes that "every time I write that pair of words I can't help imagining the shiver of delight that must have run through the entrails of the bureaucratic octopus when the term was first ejaculated in clerical ink. . . . Did an entire company of chalky perukes sit in intense deliberation until this dicotyledon suddenly spawned?" (*Sleeping on a Wire*, 83)

48. Jacob M. Landau, *The Arab Minority in Israel, 1967–1991* (Clarendon Press, 1993), 16; Grossman, *Sleeping on a Wire*, 314–15.

49. *Statistical Abstract of Israel 1995*, 341, 384–86, 629–30.

50. "Arabs 55 percent of Poor," *Jerusalem Post*, 20 June 1991.

51. *Statistical Abstract of Israel 1995*, 629–30.

52. Smooha, *Israel: Pluralism*, 140–41; Fanny Ginor, *Socio-Economic Disparities in Israel* (Tel Aviv University and Transaction Publishers, 1979), 207.

53. Noah Lewin-Epstein and Moshe Semyonov, *The Arab Minority in Israel's Economy: Patterns of Ethnic Inequality* (Westview Press, 1993), 57. As the authors point out (60), a similar percentage of Jewish Israelis are overeducated for the jobs they hold, but the trend in the two communities is in opposite directions.

54. Kretzmer, *Legal Status*, 170; see also Sami K. Mari, *Arab Education in Israel* (Syracuse University Press, 1978), and Majid Al-Haj, *Education, Empowerment, and Control: The Case of the Arabs in Israel* (State University of New York Press, 1995).

55. In 1994 Arabs comprised 6.2 percent of Israeli undergraduates; see *Statistical Abstract of Israel 1995*, 674.

56. Lewin-Epstein and Semyonov, *Arab Minority*; Kretzmer, *Legal Status*, 83.

57. Lewin-Epstein and Semyonov, *Arab Minority*, 25–26.

58. Baruch Kimmerling, "Boundaries and Frontiers of the Israeli Control System: Analytical Conclusions," in *The Israeli State and Society: Boundaries and Frontiers*, ed. Baruch Kimmerling (State University of New York Press, 1989), 265–84.

59. Elie Rekhess, "Israeli Arabs and the Arabs of the West Bank and Gaza: Political Affinity and National Solidarity," *Asian and African Studies* 23 (November 1989): 121–22, 147; Grossman, *Sleeping on a Wire*, 13, 63.

60. Smooha, *Arabs and Jews*, vol. 2, 129–39.

61. Avraham Diskin, "Statistical Aspects of the Vote in the Arab Sector," in *The Arab Vote in Israel's Parliamentary Elections, 1988* (in Hebrew), ed. Jacob M. Landau (The Jerusalem Institute for Israel Studies, 1989), 27; Rekhess, *Arab Minority*, 142.

62. Steve Rodan and Jacob Dallal, "A Fundamental Gamble," *Jerusalem Post International Edition*, 10 September 1994. See also Rekhess, "Israeli Arabs," 133–34; Rekhess, "Resurgent Islam in Israel," *Asian and African Studies* 27 (March/July 1993): 189–206; Grossman, *Sleeping on a Wire*, 233.

63. Dr. Massoud Eghbarieh of the Givat Haviva Center for Arab Studies, as re-

ported in Haim Shapiro, "Islamic Movement Waning," *Jerusalem Post International Edition,* 15 July 1995.

64. Landau, *Arab Minority,* 154.

65. Smooha, *Arabs and Jews,* vol. 2, 38–39; the figures are from the 1988 survey.

66. The 1976 survey is reported in Smooha, *The Orientation and Politicization of the Arab Minority in Israel,* rev. ed. (Institute of Middle Eastern Studies, University of Haifa, 1984); the 1980 survey in idem, *Arabs and Jews,* vol. 1; and the 1985 and 1988 surveys in idem, *Arabs and Jews,* vol. 2. For Smooha's response to criticism of survey data and his own in particular, see *Arabs and Jews,* vol. 1, 29–30, and vol. 2, 21.

67. Smooha, *Arabs and Jews,* vol. 2, 84.

68. Ibid., 51, 58, 163, 267.

69. Nadim Rouhana, "The Intifada and the Palestinians of Israel: Resurrecting the Green Line," *Journal of Palestine Studies* 19 (Spring 1990): 71.

70. Hanna Levinsohn, Elihu Katz, and Majid Al Haj, *Jews and Arabs in Israel: Common Values and Reciprocal Images* (Guttman Israel Institute of Applied Social Research, 1995), 22; see also Rouhana, "The Intifada and the Palestinians," 59.

71. See the figures in Rekhess, "Israeli Arabs," 126–27; see also Smooha, *Orientation and Politicization,* 3–5, 101–3; Hareven, "Israeli Arabs as a Jewish Problem," 9–10; and Orit Ichilov, "Citizenship Orientations of Two Israeli Minority Groups: Israel-Arab and Eastern-Jewish Youth," *Ethnic Groups* 7, no. 2 (1988): 132–33.

72. Smooha, *Arabs and Jews,* vol. 2, 87.

73. Ginat, "Voting Patterns," 13; Ginat, "Israeli Arabs: Some Recent Social and Political Trends," *Asian and African Studies* 23 (November 1989): 204; Grossman, *Sleeping on a Wire,* 15 (statement by Azmi Bishara); see also Rouhana, "The Intifada and the Palestinians," 59, on the emergence of Israeli Arabs as a "democratic force" in the country.

74. Atallah Mansour, as quoted by Marda Dunsky, "The Thin Green Line," *Jerusalem Post International Edition,* 24 June 1989.

75. Smooha, "The Divergent Fate of the Palestinians on Both Sides of the Green Line: The Intifada as a Test," paper presented at the conference on the Arab Minority in Israel: Dilemmas of Political Orientation and Social Change, University of Tel Aviv, June 3–4, 1991; Ginat, "Israeli Arabs," 200; Al Haj, "Strategies of Mobilization"; Emile Sahliyeh, "The PLO and the Israeli Arabs," *Asian and African Studies* 27 (March/July 1993): 85–96.

76. Ginat, "Israeli Arabs," 192; see also Smooha, "Minority Status," 398.

77. See the summary in Smooha, *Arabs and Jews,* vol. 2, 174–78, 201–5.

78. Avraham Diskin, *Elections and Voters in Israel* (Praeger, 1991), 92; Wolffsohn, *Israel,* 169.

79. Diskin, "Statistical Aspects of the Vote," 25; Lustick, "Changing Political Role," 118–19.

80. Sam Lehman-Wilzig, "Copying the Master: Patterns of Israeli-Arab Protest, 1950–1990," *Asian and African Studies* 27 (March/July 1993): 129–48.

81. Majid Al-Haj, "Kinship and Local Politics among the Arabs in Israel," *Asian and African Studies* 27 (March/July 1993): 47–66; Al-Haj, "Strategies of Mobilization," 156.

82. Nadim Rouhana, "The Political Transformation of the Palestinians in Israel:

From Acquiescence to Challenge," *Journal of Palestine Studies* 18 (Spring 1989): 46.

83. Majid Al-Haj and Henry Rosenfeld, "The Emergence of an Indigenous Political Framework in Israel: The National Committee of Chairmen of Arab Local Authorities," *Asian and African Studies* 23 (November 1989): 205–44.

84. Rouhana, "Political Transformation of the Palestinians," 60–61, 64.

85. Ibid., 64, 67–68, 72; Majid Al-Haj, "Elections in the Arab Street during the Intifada: Propaganda and Results," in *The Arab Vote in Israel's Parliamentary Elections, 1988*, ed. Jacob M. Landau (The Jerusalem Institute for Israel Studies, 1989), 35–49; Yitzhak Reiter, "The Arab Democratic Party and its Place in the Orientation of Israeli Arabs," in ibid., 77. Smooha's surveys for 1985 and 1988, cited above, also testify to the limited impact of the *intifada;* see Smooha, *Arabs and Jews,* vol. 2, 228–32.

86. Rekhess, "Israeli Arabs," 144–45.

87. Al Haj, "Elections in the Arab Street," 39; Reiter, "The Arab Democratic Party," 70, 72.

88. Hofnung, *Israel—Security Needs,* 148–57, 221–23; Smooha, *Arabs and Jews,* vol. 2, 8, 260–61.

89. Alouph Hareven, "Equality and Integration: An Annual Progress Report 1992/1993" (Sikkuy, 1993): 7, 19.

90. Alouph Hareven and As'ad Ghanem, eds., *Equality and Integration: Retrospect and Prospects 1992–1996* (Sikkuy, 1996), 9–10.

91. Kretzmer, *Legal Status,* 176.

92. Smooha, "Minority Status," 391; Smooha, *Arabs and Jews,* vol. 2, 13.

93. Peled, "Ethnic Democracy and the Legal Construction of Citizenship: Arab Citizens of the Jewish State," *American Political Science Review* 86 (June 1992): 432–43.

94. Louis L. Snyder, *Encyclopedia of Nationalism* (Paragon House, 1990), 230.

95. Roger Scruton, *A Dictionary of Political Thought,* 2nd ed. (Harper and Row, 1982), 313.

96. This includes some states that also recognize *jus solis;* a partial list would include Belgium, Bulgaria, Finland, France, Germany, Hungary, Liberia, Poland, Sri Lanka, Switzerland, and the United Kingdom as well as the Soviet Union and most Soviet successor states. Donner, *The Regulation of Nationality in International Law,* 2nd ed. (Transnational Publishers, 1994), 32, 69, 114–19; UN Legal Department, *Laws Concerning Nationalities* (UN ST/LEG/ser.B/4, 1954), 222–24, 386–87. The Israeli Law of Return can also be defended as a policy of selective immigration rather than as extension of a particular conception of citizenship; since all states practice selective immigration, the question then becomes the legitimacy of selection on ethnic grounds, and again Israel is not unique in this regard.

97. Claude Klein, *Israel as a Nation-State and the Problem of the Arab Minority: In Search of a Status* (International Center for Peace in the Middle East, 1987), 4; UN Legal Department, *Supplement to the Volume on Laws Concerning Nationality* (UN ST/LEG/ser.B/9, 1959), 118; William Rogers Brubaker, "Immigration, Citizenship, and the Nation-State in France and Germany: A Comparative Historical Analysis," *International Sociology* 5 (December 1990): 386–87, 396, 400; Manfred Steger and F. Peter

Wagner, "Political Asylum, Immigration, and Citizenship in the Federal Republic of Germany," *New Political Science* 24–25 (Spring 1993): 65, 67.

98. UN, *Laws Concerning Nationalities*, 466.

99. Based on the data in *Maps 'N' Facts* (Broderbund Software, 1994); closely related languages were grouped together and microstates were eliminated.

100. *Freedom in the World: The Annual Survey of Political Rights and Civil Liberties 1994–1995* (Freedom House, 1995), 683–84.

101. Smooha's definition specifies institutionalized dominance of one ethnic group, not just numerical predominance; however, apart from the most clearly consociational cases like Switzerland, nearly all of these twenty-six states appear to be characterized by at least some degree of institutionalized ethnic dominance.

102. Lijphart, "The Power-Sharing Approach," in *Conflict and Peacemaking in Multiethnic Societies*, ed. Joseph V. Montville (Lexington Books, 1990), 494–95, 503.

103. To strengthen the observation, linguistic divisions in Belize and Cape Verde do not appear to be politically significant, while the controversy over citizenship for Russians in Estonia and Latvia remains a contentious international issue.

104. At the end of 1994 Arabs constituted 19 percent (1.03 million) of a total population of 5.46 million. This was expected to rise to about 21 percent by 2005. Historically the higher birthrate in the Arab sector has been offset by Jewish immigration, and this birthrate has been declining with improved living standards. Consequently demographers project relative stability in the population balance within Israel. *Statistical Abstract of Israel 1994*, 90; Central Bureau of Statistics, "Israel's Population—5.46 million," Israel Information Service, December 29, 1994, INTERNET; Calvin Goldscheider, "The Demographic Embeddedness of the Arab-Jewish Conflict in Israeli Society," *Middle East Review* 21 (Spring 1989): 21.

105. Cynthia Enloe, *Ethnic Soldiers: State Security in Divided Societies* (University of Georgia Press, 1980), 54–63, 78–82, 136, 182–83, 189–90.

106. This argument is developed by Oren Yiftachel, "The Concept of 'Ethnic Democracy' and Its Applicability to the Case of Israel," *Ethnic and Racial Studies* 15 (January 1992): 125–36.

107. The exchange between Shammas and Yehoshua is in Grossman, *Sleeping on a Wire*, esp. 257, 270–71.

108. Alex Weingrod, "Shadow Games: Ethnic Conflict and Political Exchange in Israel," *Regional Politics and Policy* 3 (Spring 1993): 190–209.

109. Smooha, *Arabs and Jews*, vol. 2, 113.

110. Klein, *Israel as a Nation-State*, 24; see also Sammy Smooha, "Class, Ethnic, and National Cleavages and Democracy in Israel," in *Israeli Democracy under Stress*, ed. Ehud Sprinzak and Larry Diamond (Lynne Rienner, 1993), 325–26; Smooha, "Minority Status," 409–10.

111. Smooha, *Arabs and Jews*, vol. 2, 112, 168; Levinsohn, Katz, and Al Haj, *Jews and Arabs in Israel*, 23.

112. For example, Faisal al-Husseini, quoted in Smooha, *Arabs and Jews*, vol. 2, 412.

113. The likely impact of a peace agreement on Jewish-Arab relations within Israel is surveyed in Sammy Smooha, "Arab-Jewish Relations in Israel in the Peace Era," *Israel Affairs* 1 (Winter 1994): 227–44; see also Rouhana, "The Intifada and the

Palestinians," 73; Elie Rekhess, "Israel's Arab Citizens and the Peace Process," in *Israel under Rabin,* ed. Robert O. Friedman (Westview Press, 1995), 189–204; and Clyde Haberman, "Israeli Arabs Say P.L.O. Pact Is a Path to First-Class Status," *New York Times,* 24 November 1993.

10. THE IMPACT OF THE WEST BANK AND GAZA

1. Baruch Kimmerling, "Boundaries and Frontiers of the Israeli Control System: Analytical Conclusions," in *The Israeli State and Society: Boundaries and Frontiers,* ed. Baruch Kimmerling (State University of New York Press, 1989), 265–84.

2. Julius Stone, *Israel and Palestine: Assault on the Law of Nations* (The Johns Hopkins University Press, 1981), 693; Yoram Dinstein, "The International Law of Belligerent Occupation and Human Rights," *Israel Yearbook on Human Rights* 8 (1978): 104–43; Moshe Drori, "The Legal System in Judea and Samaria: A Review of the Previous Decade with a Glance at the Future," *Israel Yearbook on Human Rights* 8 (1978): 144–77.

3. For a statement of this claim see Stone, *Israel and Palestine,* 119, and Yehuda Blum, "The Missing Reversioner: Reflections on the Status of Judea and Samaria," *Israel Law Review* 2 (1968): 279, 289–291.

4. See the well-reasoned argument in Esther Rosalind Cohen, *Human Rights in the Israeli-Occupied Territories 1967–1982* (Manchester University Press, 1985), 52–53. The Geneva Convention also has a one-year time limit on the applicability of some of its provisions, but Israel has not invoked this clause (ibid., 50–51). See also Theodor Meron, "West Bank and Gaza: Human Rights and Humanitarian Law in the Period of Transition," *Israel Yearbook on Human Rights* 9 (1979): 106–20.

5. Michael Goldstein, "Israeli Security Measures in the Occupied Territories: Administrative Detention," *Middle East Journal* 32, no. 1 (Winter 1978): 37 (summarizing the claims made by the UN Special Committee to Investigate Israeli Practices Affecting Human Rights of the Population of the Occupied Territories). The applicability of the Defense Regulations to the Golan Heights or Sinai was altogether dubious, as neither had been part of Palestine, but in both cases the affected population was small and the question became moot (in Sinai by the return to Egyptian sovereignty, and on the Golan Heights by the extension of Israeli law).

6. Dov Shefi, "The Protection of Human Rights in Areas Administered by Israel: United Nations Findings and Reality," *Israel Yearbook on Human Rights* 3 (1973): 344–45; Fania Domb, "Judicial Decisions: Supreme Court of Israel," *Israel Yearbook on Human Rights* 9 (1979): 343–44; Israel National Section of the International Commission of Jurists, *The Rule of Law in the Areas Administered by Israel* (1981), 68 (includes citations of the Jordanian court cases); Menachem Hofnung, *Israel—Security Needs vs. the Rule of Law* (in Hebrew) (Nevo, 1991), 317.

7. Gerhard Von Glahn, *The Occupation of Enemy Territory* (Minneapolis: University of Minnesota Press, 1957), 57; see also Dinstein, "International Law of Belligerent Occupation," and Drori, "Legal System in Judea and Samaria."

8. Cohen, *Human Rights,* 285; Stone, *Israel and Palestine,* 693–722; Von Glahn, *Occupation of Enemy Territory,* 54, 62–63, 98, 100, 110–11, 139–41; Geoffrey Best, *Humanity in Warfare: The Modern History of the International Law of Armed Conflicts* (Methuen, 1983), 297–98.

9. Von Glahn, *Occupation of Enemy Territory,* 264; for a description of the extreme

measures used under the laws of war by the Germans in Belgium during World War I, see Best, *Humanity in Warfare,* 226–27.

10. Cohen, *Human Rights,* 95; Emma Playfair, *Administrative Detention in the Occupied West Bank* (Al-Haq [Law in the Service of Man], 1986), 11; Hofnung, *Israel—Security Needs,* 317.

11. For a good statement of the low-profile policy see the chapter by Raphael Vardi, one of the key Israeli figures in occupation policy, "Israeli Administration and Self-Rule in the Territories: The Israeli Perspective," in *Judea, Gaza, and Samaria: Views on the Present and Future,* ed. Daniel Elazar (American Enterprise Institute, 1982), 171–80.

12. See in particular the annual reports issued by the West Bank Data Project, as well as Meron Benvenisti and Shlomo Khayat, *The West Bank and Gaza Atlas* (West Bank Data Project, 1988).

13. Israel Ministry of Defense, Office of the Co-ordinator of Government Operations in Judea, Samaria and Gaza District, *Judea, Samaria, and the Gaza District, 1967–1987: Twenty Years of Civil Administration* (Carta, 1987), 45–46, 53, 54.

14. Ibid., 14, 17, 84.

15. Ibid., 25; Benvenisti and Khayat, *The West Bank and Gaza Atlas,* 42.

16. Particularly the ownership of durable goods; see Israel Central Bureau of Statistics, *Statistical Abstract of Israel 1994,* 802.

17. Statement by Israel Defense Forces (IDF) spokesperson, *Ha'aretz,* 28 October 1993, reported in B'tselem [The Israeli Information Center for Human Rights in the Occupied Territories], *Human Rights Violations in the Occupied Territories 1992/1993* (B'tselem, n. d.), 46.

18. Cohen, *Human Rights,* 76–92.

19. O'Brien, *Law and Morality in Israel's War with the PLO* (Routledge, 1991), 254.

20. Statement by the Ministry of Justice in B'tselem, *Human Rights Violations,* 142; O'Brien, *Law and Morality,* 135.

21. Inge Genefke, "Evidence of the Use of Torture," in *Torture: Human Rights, Medical Ethics and the Case of Israel,* ed. Neve Gordon and Ruchama Marton (Zed Books for the Association of Israeli-Palestinian Physicians for Human Rights, 1995), 98.

22. Also confirmed by the results of a survey of 700 ex-detainees reported in Eyad El-Serraj, "Torture and Mental Health: A Survey of the Experience of Palestinians in Israeli Prisons," in Gordon and Marton, *Torture,* 105.

23. The Israeli government responded that the form was only being used experimentally at one prison and that its use would not be continued; see Ruchama Marton, "The White Coat Passes like a Shadow: The Health Profession and Torture in Israel," in Gordon and Marton, *Torture,* 37, 39.

24. U.S. Department of State, *Country Reports on Human Rights Practices 1996,* INTERNET; Amnesty International, *Amnesty International Report 1996,* 186; see also B'tselem, *Human Rights Violations,* 131–44; Hofnung, *Israel—Security Needs,* 128–29, 276.

25. U.S. Department of State, *Country Reports 1996.*

26. Virgil Falloon, *Excessive Secrecy, Lack of Guidelines: A Report on Military Censorship in the West Bank* (Al-Haq [Law in the Service of Man], 1986), 8–18.

27. The 1979 court case is Sakhwil et al. v. Commander of the Judea and

Samaria Region, H. C. 434/79, 34(1) P.D. 464; see Domb, "Judicial Decisions: Judgments of the Supreme Court of Israel Relating to the Administered Territories," *Israel Yearbook on Human Rights* 10 (1980): 345–46. The 1990 case is Israel Civil Rights Association v. Commander of Southern Region, H. C. 4112/90, 44(4) P.D. 626. For a definitive analysis see David Kretzmer, "High Court of Justice Review of the Demolition and Sealing of Houses in the Territories," in *Klinghoffer Book on Public Law* (in Hebrew) (Faculty of Law, Hebrew University of Jerusalem, 1993), 305–57; see also Cohen, *Human Rights*, 103; O'Brien, *Law and Morality*, 243–45.

28. Ann M. Lesch, "Israeli Deportation of Palestinians from the West Bank and the Gaza Strip, 1967–1978," *Journal of Palestine Studies* 8 (Winter 1979): 102–3; the Israeli figure is given in *Financial Times*, 9 December 1977.

29. Attorney General Meir Shamgar, "The Observance of International Law in the Administered Territories," *Israel Yearbook on Human Rights* 1 (1971): 274–75; Shefi, "Protection of Human Rights," 348–49; Thomas S. Kuttner, "Israel and the West Bank: Aspects of the Law of Belligerent Occupation," *Israel Yearbook on Human Rights* 7 (1977): 213–14, 216.

30. For a definitive statement of the illegality of deportation under the Fourth Geneva Convention, see Yoram Dinstein, "The Israel Supreme Court and the Law of Belligerent Occupation: Deportations," *Israel Yearbook on Human Rights* 23 (1993): 1–26; see also Cohen, *Human Rights,* 110–11.

31. The key court case was Abd el Afu et al. v. Commander of the IDF Forces in the West Bank et al., H.C. 785/87, 42(2) P.D. 4, published in English in *Israel Yearbook on Human Rights* 23 (1993): 277–86; see Dinstein, *Israel Supreme Court,* 12–22.

32. H.C. 5973/92, The Association for Civil Rights in Israel et al. v. Minister of Defense et al., published in English in *Israel Yearbook on Human Rights* 23 (1993): 353–61.

33. Playfair, *Administrative Detention,* 3–5; Goldstein, "Israeli Security Measures," 44.

34. Itzak Zamir, "Directives of the Attorney General on the Matter of the Emergency Powers (Detention) Law, 5739—1979," *Israel Law Review* 18 (Winter 1983): 157–58.

35. Kuttner, "Israel and the West Bank," 211–12; Playfair, *Administrative Detention,* 14–15, 19; Cohen, *Human Rights,* 128, presents the case for a qualified acceptance of administrative detention as a legal measure.

36. See, for example, Stone, *Israel and Palestine,* 123, 177–81.

37. Cohen, *Human Rights,* 162–63.

38. Moshe Drori, "The Israeli Settlement in Judea and Samaria and its Organizational and Municipal Structure: Legal Aspects" (in Hebrew), *City and Region* 4, no. 3 (1981): 28–45; Hofnung, *Israel—Security Needs,* 294–95.

39. The Beit El case is Ayub v. Minister of Defense, H. C. 606/78, 33(2) P.D. 113; Elon Moreh is Dweikat et al. v. the Government of Israel et al., H. C. 390/79, 34(1) P.D. 1; see Domb, "Judicial Decisions: Supreme Court of Israel," 345–49.

40. Cohen, *Human Rights,* 138–39.

41. B'tselem, *Human Rights Violations,* 110; *Amnesty International Report, 1996,* 186; also data supplied by B'tselem.

42. Al-Haq [Law in the Service of Man], personal communication, February 17, 1996; B'tselem, *Human Rights Violations,* 67, 79–82; U.S. Department of State, 1996.

43. Menachem Friedman, "The State of Israel as a Theological Dilemma," in *The Israeli State and Society: Boundaries and Frontiers,* ed. Baruch Kimmerling (State University of New York Press, 1989), 206.

44. On Gush Emunim as a revitalization movement see Myron J. Aronoff, "Gush Emunim: The Institutionalization of a Charismatic, Messianic, Religious-Political Revitalization Movement in Israel," in *Religion and Politics,* vol. 3 of *Political Anthropology,* ed. Myron J. Aronoff (Transaction Books, 1984), 63–84. See also chapter 6.

45. Charles S. Liebman, "Jewish Fundamentalism and the Israeli Polity," in *Fundamentalisms and the State,* ed. Martin E. Marty and R. Scott Appleby (University of Chicago Press, 1993), 74. For overall studies of Gush Emunim and related movements see Ehud Sprinzak, *The Ascendance of Israel's Radical Right* (Oxford University Press, 1991), and Ian S. Lustick, *For the Land and the Lord: Jewish Fundamentalism in Israel* (Council on Foreign Relations, 1988).

46. See the analysis by Eliezer Don-Yehiya, "Jewish Messianism, Religious Zionism and Israeli Politics: The Impact and Origins of Gush Emunim," *Middle East Studies* 23 (April 1987): 215–34; and by Sprinzak, *Ascendance,* 12–21.

47. Charles S. Liebman and Eliezer Don-Yehiya, *Religion and Politics in Israel* (Indiana University Press, 1984), 135–36.

48. The Hess article is quoted by Yoram Peri, "Expulsion Is Not the Final Solution" (in Hebrew), *Davar,* 3 August 1984; on the law against "strangers in the land," see article by Yisrael Ariel in *Nekuda* 79 (2 November 1984): 24.

49. Rael Jean Isaac, *Israel Divided: Ideological Politics in the Jewish State* (The Johns Hopkins University Press, 1976), 134.

50. The IIASR, now known as the Guttman Israel Institute of Applied Social Research, carried out 204 surveys in the 1967–1992 period. There are four major polling organizations in Israel using sophisticated survey methods that produce results similar enough to each other to instill some degree of confidence; all use stratified sampling techniques and a sample size (generally around 1,200) that gives a 3 to 4 percent margin of error. The polls reported here cover only the adult Jewish population within Israel proper, not Arabs within Israel nor Jewish settlers in the territories. Earlier IIASR data is summarized in Russell A. Stone, *Social Change in Israel: Attitudes and Events, 1967–1979* (New York: Praeger, 1982); for more recent years, see Jacob Shamir and Michal Shamir, *The Dynamics of Israeli Public Opinion on Peace and the Territories,* Research Report No. 1 (The Tami Steinmetz Center for Peace Research, 1993), 5–12; Asher Arian, *Security Threatened: Surveying Israeli Opinion on Peace and War* (Cambridge University Press, 1995), 95–96.

51. Elihu Katz and Hannah Levinsohn, "Too Good To Be True: Notes on the Israel Elections of 1988," *International Journal of Public Opinion Research* 1, no. 2 (1989): 117.

52. Yaniv, "Israel National Security in the 1980s: The Crisis of Overload," in *Israel after Begin,* ed. Gregory S. Mahler (State University of New York Press, 1990), 107.

53. *Ha'aretz,* 27 June 1975; reported, with a comment on the dovish push in the question, by Isaac, *Israel Divided,* 150. Polls conducted by Modi'in Ezrachi during the 1980s consistently showed more hawkish attitudes, by about 10 percent, than other polls, and the wording of the questions seems relevant; for example, Modi'in

Ezrachi offered the option of *tsiruf* ("joining together") rather than the more blatant *sipuah* ("annexation") to describe the permanent incorporation of the territories into Israel.

54. The April 1987 poll was conducted by Modi'in Ezrachi and reported in *Ma'ariv,* 12 May 1987.

55. Survey conducted by the Dahaf Research Institute in July 1984 and reported in Asher Arian, "Israeli Democracy 1984," *Journal of International Affairs* 38 (Winter 1985): 268–69.

56. Benvenisti and Khayat, *The West Bank and Gaza Atlas,* 32; Herb Keinon, *Israeli Settlements: A Guide* (Anti-Defamation League, 1995), 4–5.

57. By 1996 the number of settlers grew to around 140,000 to 145,000, including 15,000 on the Golan Heights, according to best estimates; on problems of estimation amidst conflicting claims, see Keinon, *Israeli Settlements,* 15–18.

58. The annual Arab population increase in the mid-1990s was between 75,000 and 80,000; *Statistical Abstract of Israel 1994,* 786.

59. Keinon, *Israeli Settlements,* 48.

60. Ian Lustick, in *Unsettled States, Disputed Lands* (Cornell University Press, 1993), analyzes Israel's attempt to integrate the West Bank in the framework of a general theory of state expansion and contraction, making use of comparison with the British in Ireland and the French in Algeria.

61. Israel, Central Bureau of Statistics, *Projections of Population in Judea, Samaria and Gaza Area up to 2002* (Central Bureau of Statistics, 1987). For fuller discussion of "the demographic dilemma" see the writings of Arnon Soffer: *On the Demographic and Geographic Situation in the Land of Israel: End of the Zionist Dream?* (in Hebrew) (Gestlit Press, 1988); "Population Projections for the Land of Israel," *Middle East Review* 20 (Summer 1988): 43–49; "Demography and the Shaping of Israel's Borders," *Contemporary Jewry* 10, no. 2 (1989): 91–105. See also the various publications of the West Bank Data Project, which include a wide range of population data and projections.

62. See, for example, the interview with Sari Nusseibeh in *Koteret Rashit,* 13 November 1985 (in Hebrew).

63. For responses to Netanyahu see A. Schweizer, "Statistics on the Brain" (in Hebrew), *Ha'aretz,* 22 July 1988; and Don Petreanu, "Numbers and Politics," *Jerusalem Post International Edition,* 27 August 1988; also, the cited works by Arnon Soffer and *Statistical Abstract of Israel 1994,* 786.

64. Elyakim Ha'etzni, quoted by Yair Kotler, *Heil Kahane* (Adama Books, 1986), 177.

65. Sergio DellaPergola, "Will There Be More Mass Immigration?" in *On the Way to Year 2000: More War or Progress to Peace?* (in Hebrew), ed. Alouph Hareven (Van Leer Institute, 1988), 58; see also DellaPergola, "On the Differential Frequency of Western Migration to Israel," *Studies in Contemporary Jewry* 1 (1984): 292–315; and Della Pergola, "*Aliya* and Other Jewish Migrations: Toward an Integrated Perspective," in *Studies in the Population of Israel,* ed. Usiel O. Schmelz and Gad Nathan (Scripta Hierosolymitana 30, Magnes Press, Hebrew University, 1986), 172–209.

66. This is developed most completely by Raphael Israeli, *Palestinians Between Israel and Jordan* (Praeger, 1991).

67. Meir Kahane, *They Must Go* (Grosset and Dunlap, 1981), 102.

68. Dahaf Research Institute poll reported in *Davar,* 3 August 1984; Hanoch Smith poll, *Jerusalem Post,* 2 October 1986; Modi'in Ezrachi poll, *Ma'ariv,* 15 July 1987.

69. Frankel, "A Pogrom Situation in the West Bank," *Jerusalem Post,* 23 July 1987.

70. Soffer, "Population Projections, 10–23.

71. Quoted in Lawrence Meyer, *Israel Now: Portrait of a Troubled Land* (Delacorte Press, 1982), 384.

72. Israelis have written extensively on the impact of occupation on Israeli democracy; see, in particular, Alon Pinkas, "Garrison Democracy: The Impact of the 1967 Occupation of Territories on Institutional Democracy in Israel," in *Democracy, Peace, and the Israeli-Palestinian Conflict,* ed. Edy Kaufman, Shukri B. Abed, and Robert L. Rothstein (Lynne Rienner, 1993), 61–83; Hofnung, *Israel—Security Needs,* esp. 281–347; and Asher Arian, "Israeli Democracy 1984," 259–76.

73. For an excellent collation of evidence on this score, see Edy Kaufman, "War, Occupation, and the Effects on Israeli Society," in Kaufman et al., *Democracy, Peace, and the Israeli-Palestinian Conflict,* 85–133; see also Yoram Peri, "The Arab-Israeli Conflict and Israeli Democracy," in *Israeli Democracy under Stress,* ed. Ehud Sprinzak and Larry Diamond (Lynne Rienner, 1993), 343–57.

74. On settler violence see David Weisburd and Vered Vinitzky, "Vigilantism as Rational Social Control: The Case of the Gush Emunim Settlers," in *Cross-Currents in Israeli Culture and Politics,* ed. Myron J. Aronoff (Transaction Books, 1984), 69–87.

75. Moshe Zemer, "Halacha and Occupation," *Jerusalem Post,* 20 May 1995.

76. Harkabi, *The Bar-Kochba Syndrome* (Rossell Books, 1983). Harkabi wrote voluminously for two decades against Israeli expansionism; see in particular *The Fateful Hour* (Harper and Row, 1988). On the traditional Jewish critique of power, see Shlomo Avineri, "The Historical Roots of Israeli Democracy." (Second Annual Guest Lecture, Kaplan Center for Jewish Studies and Research, University of Cape Town, March 31, 1985), 8–9. More radical Israeli critiques discussed the "original sins" of Zionism against the Palestinians; see Benjamin Beit-Hallahmi, *Original Sins: Reflections on the History of Zionism and Israel* (Pluto Press, 1992).

77. On security policy see Avner Yaniv, *Deterrence without the Bomb* (Lexington Books, 1987), and idem, "Israel National Security," 93–109.

78. Gad Barzilai and Ilan Peleg, "Israel and Future Borders: An Assessment of a Dynamic Process," *Journal of Peace Research* 31, no. 1 (1994): 69; for a vivid portrait of this period of transition see Glenn Frankel, *Beyond the Promised Land: Jews and Arabs on the Hard Road to a New Israel* (Simon and Schuster, 1994).

79. Asher Arian, *Security Threatened,* 68–69.

80. Ibid., 263.

81. Goldberg, Barzilai, and Inbar, *The Impact of Intercommunal Conflict: The Intifada and Israeli Public Opinion,* Policy Studies No. 43 (The Leonard Davis Institute for International Relations, 1991), 12.

82. *Jerusalem Post,* 21 June 1992.

83. Asher Arian, *Security Threatened,* 97–98, 274.

84. Smith Research Center, as reported in *Jerusalem Post,* 2 October 1986; *Near East Report,* 25 July 1988; and *New York Times,* 2 April 1989. Similar figures are reported by Asher Arian, *Security Threatened,* 106.

85. Elihu Katz, Hanna Levinsohn, and Majid Al-Haj, "Attitudes of Israelis (Jews

and Arabs) towards Current Affairs," Guttman Israel Institute of Applied Social Research Publication No. (S)EK/1129/E, January 10, 1991; Asher Arian, "Security and Political Attitudes in Israel: 1986–1991," *Public Opinion Quarterly* 56 (Spring 1992), 125.

86. Inbar and Goldberg, "Is Israel's Political Élite Becoming More Hawkish?" *International Journal* 45 (Summer 1990): 631–60; Goldberg, "The Likud: Moving toward the Center," in *Israel at the Polls, 1988–1989,* ed. Daniel J. Elazar and Shmuel Sandler (Wayne State University Press, 1992), 45–66.

87. Asher Arian, "Security and Political Attitudes," 125.

88. Goldberg, Barzilai, and Inbar, *Impact of Intercommunal Conflict,* 48–49, 53, 56; Gad Barzilai, Giora Goldberg, and Efraim Inbar, "Israeli Leadership and Public Attitudes toward Federal Solutions for the Arab-Israeli Conflict before and after Desert Storm," *Publius: The Journal of Federalism* 21 (Summer 1991): 206. In the first of these two studies (49), the authors even delineate a profile of Likud doves, who are generally older, more educated, less religious, and with higher incomes than the average Likud supporter.

89. For an analysis of the gap between elite (Labor) opinion and the general public during this period see Asher Arian, *Ideological Change in Israel* (Case Western Reserve University Press, 1968), 36, 43, 52–53.

90. The potential for shaping of opinion by leaders is a major theme in Asher Arian's summary study of Israeli attitudes on security; see Arian, *Security Threatened,* esp. 256–61.

91. This theme is developed by Gad Barzilai and Ilan Peleg, "Israel and Future Borders," 63–64.

92. On PLO talks and the return of territory: Arian, *Security Threatened,* 100, 107. On the peace process and Oslo: 1995 monthly polling data supplied by the Tami Steinmetz Center for Peace Research, Tel Aviv University.

93. Tami Steinmetz Center for Peace Research, Tel Aviv University.

94. Arian, *Security Threatened,* 104.

95. Joseph Alpher, "Settlements and Borders" (in Hebrew), in *Final Status Issues: Israel-Palestinians,* Study No. 3, (Jaffee Center for Strategic Studies, Tel Aviv University, November, 1994), 36–41, 62 (map 10).

96. Polls of March 27 and April 25, 1995, supplied by the Tami Steinmetz Center.

97. For a more extended, and somewhat less optimistic, view of the clash of values within Israel, see Ilan Peleg, "The Peace Process and Israel's Political Culture: A Kulturkampf in the Making," paper presented at annual meeting of the American Political Science Association, Chicago, September 1–4, 1995.

EPILOGUE

1. Myron J. Aronoff and Pierre M. Atlas, "The Peace Process and Competing Challenges to the Dominant Zionist Discourse," in *The Israel-Palestinian Peace Process: Interdisciplinary Perspectives,* ed. Ilan Peleg (State University of New York Press, 1996).

2. See Arend Lijphart, "Israeli Democracy and Democratic Reform in Comparative Perspective," in *Israeli Democracy under Stress,* ed. Ehud Sprinzak and Larry Diamond (Lynne Rienner, 1993), 107–23.

3. These terms are from, respectively, Ilan Peleg, "The Peace Process and Israel's Political Culture: A Kulturkampf in the Making," paper presented at the annual meeting of the American Political Science Association, Chicago, September 1–4, 1995; Erik Cohen, "Israel as a Post-Zionist Society," *Israel Affairs* 1 (Spring 1995): 211; Zeev Ben-Sira, *Zionism at the Close of the Twentieth Century: A Dilemma* (The Edwin Mellen Press, 1993), 102.

4. Myron J. Aronoff, "Political Polarization: Contradictory Interpretations of Israeli Reality," in *Cross-Currents in Israeli Culture and Politics,* ed. Myron J. Aronoff (Transaction Books, 1984), 20.

5. Boas Evron, *Jewish State or Israeli Nation?* (Indiana University Press, 1995), 210.

6. Oz, "The Secret of the Zionist Magic," in idem, *Under the Blazing Light* (in Hebrew) (Sifriat Po'alim, 1979), 155.

7. Steven J. Zipperstein, *Elusive Prophet: Ahad Ha'am and the Origins of Zionism* (University of California Press, 1993), xix, xxiv.

8. "Zionism Now: Land for People," *The Economist,* 11 July 1992, 26.

9. Charles S. Liebman and Steven M. Cohen, *Two Worlds of Judaism: The Israeli and American Experiences* (Yale University Press, 1990), 175.

10. See Uri Regev, "Israel: The Real Challenge—A Response," CCAR Journal: A Reform Jewish Quarterly (Spring/Summer 1996): 1–17.

11. E.A. (Election Appeal) 2/88 Ben Shalom v. Chairman of Central Elections Committee 43(2) P.D. 221.

12. Letter from Hannah Arendt to Karl Jaspers, September 4, 1947, in Lotte Kohler and Hans Saner, eds., *Hannah Arendt—Karl Jaspers: Correspondence, 1926–1969,* quoted in "The Idea of the 'Chosen People': An Exchange," *New York Times,* 19 September 1992.

13. Fein, *Where Are We? The Inner Life of America's Jews* (Harper and Row, 1988), 168.

BIBLIOGRAPHY

Abramov, S. Zalman. *Perpetual Dilemma: Jewish Religion in the Jewish State.* World Union for Progressive Judaism, 1976.

Agassi, Joseph. *Religion and Nationality: Towards an Israeli National Identity* (in Hebrew). Papyrus, Tel Aviv University, 1984.

Al-Haj, Majid. *Education, Empowerment, and Control: The Case of the Arabs in Israel.* State University of New York Press, 1995.

———. "Elections in the Arab Street during the Intifada: Propaganda and Results." In *The Arab Vote in Israel's Parliamentary Elections, 1988,* edited by Jacob M. Landau, 35–49. The Jerusalem Institute for Israel Studies, 1989.

———. "Kinship and Local Politics among the Arabs in Israel." *Asian and African Studies* 27 (March/July 1993): 47–66.

———. "The Political Behavior of the Arabs in Israel in the 1992 Elections: Integration versus Segregation." In *The Elections in Israel 1992,* edited by Asher Arian and Michal Shamir, 141–160. State University of New York Press, 1995.

———. "Strategies of Mobilization among the Arabs in Israel." In *Whither Israel? The Domestic Challenges,* edited by Keith Kyle and Joel Peters, 140–157. I. B. Tauris, 1993.

Al Haj, Majid, Elihu Katz, and Samuel Shye. "Arab and Jewish Attitudes toward a Palestinian State." *Journal of Conflict Resolution* 37 (December 1993): 619–32.

Al-Haj, Majid, and Henry Rosenfeld. "The Emergence of an Indigenous Political Framework in Israel: The National Committee of Chairmen of Arab Local Authorities." *Asian and African Studies* 23 (November 1989): 205–44.

Almog, Shmuel. *Zionism and History: The Rise of a New Jewish Consciousness.* St. Martin's Press and Magnes Press, 1987.

Almond, Gabriel A., and Sidney Verba. *The Civic Culture: Political Attitudes and Democracy in Five Nations.* Princeton University Press, 1963.

Alpher, Joseph. "Settlements and Borders" (in Hebrew). In *Final Status Issue: Israel-Palestinians,* Study No. 3. Jaffee Center for Strategic Studies, Tel Aviv University, November 1994.

Antonovsky, Aaron, and Alan Arian. *Hopes and Fears of Israelis: Consensus in a New Society.* Jerusalem Academic Press, 1972.

Aran, Gideon. "Eretz Israel: Between Politics and Religion: The Movement to Stop the Withdrawal from Sinai" (in Hebrew). The Jerusalem Institute for Israel Studies, 1985.

Arian, Alan. *The Choosing People: Voting Behavior in Israel.* Case Western Reserve University, 1973.

———. *Ideological Change in Israel.* Case Western Reserve University Press, 1968.

Arian, Asher. "Elections 1981: Competitiveness and Polarization." *Jerusalem Quarterly* 21 (Fall 1981): 16–27.

———. "Israeli Democracy 1984." *Journal of International Affairs* 38 (Winter 1985): 259–76.

———. "The Passing of Dominance." *Jerusalem Quarterly* 5 (Fall 1977): 20–32.

———. *Politics in Israel: The Second Generation.* Rev. ed. Chatham House Publishers, 1989.

———. "Security and Political Attitudes in Israel: 1986–1991." *Public Opinion Quarterly* 56 (Spring 1992): 116–28.

———. *Security Threatened: Surveying Israeli Opinion on Peace and War.* Cambridge University Press, 1995.

Arian, Asher, and Michal Shamir. "Two Reversals: Why 1992 Was Not 1977." In *The Elections in Israel 1992,* edited by Asher Arian and Michal Shamir, 17–53. State University of New York Press, 1995.

Arian, Asher, Michal Shamir, and Raphael Ventura. "Public Opinion and Political Change: Israel and the Intifada." *Comparative Politics* 24 (April 1992): 317–35.

Arian, Asher, Ilan Talmud, and Tamar Hermann. *National Security and Public Opinion in Israel,* Jaffee Center for Strategic Studies, Study No. 9. Westview Press, 1988.

Aronoff, Myron J. "Better Late than Never: Democratization in the Labor Party." In *Israel after Begin,* edited by Gregory S. Mahler, 257–71. State University of New York Press, 1990.

———. "Gush Emunim: The Institutionalization of a Charismatic, Messianic, Religious-Political Revitalization Movement in Israel." In *Religion and Politics,* vol. 3 of *Political Anthropology,* edited by Myron J. Aronoff, 63–84. Transaction Books, 1984.

———. *Israeli Visions and Divisions: Cultural Change and Political Conflict.* Transaction Publishers, 1989.

———. "Political Polarization: Contradictory Interpretations of Israeli Reality." In *Cross-Currents in Israeli Culture and Politics,* edited by Myron J. Aronoff, 1–23. Transaction Books, 1984.

Aronoff, Myron J., and Pierre Atlas. "The Peace Process and Competing Challenges to the Dominant Zionist Discourse." In *The Israel-Palestinian Peace Process: Interdisciplinary Perspectives,* edited by Ilan Peleg. State University of New York Press, 1996.

Aronson, Shlomo. *Conflict and Bargaining in the Middle East.* The Johns Hopkins University Press, 1978.

Avineri, Shlomo. "The Historical Roots of Israeli Democracy." Second Annual Guest Lecture, Kaplan Center for Jewish Studies and Research, University of Cape Town, March 31, 1985.

————. "Israel as a Democratic State" (in Hebrew). *Skira Hodshit* (May 1973): 25–37.

————. *The Making of Modern Zionism: The Intellectual Origins of the Jewish State*. Basic Books, 1981.

————. "The Violated Social Contract." *Jerusalem Post International Edition*, 28 June 1986.

Avishai, Bernard. *The Tragedy of Zionism*. Farrar, Straus & Giroux, 1985.

Avruch, Kevin. "Jewish Fundamentalism in Israel." In *Critical Essays on Israeli Politics, Society, and Culture*, edited by Ian Lustick and Barry Rubin, 129–143. State University of New York Press, 1991.

Avruch, Kevin A. "Gush Emunim: Politics, Religion, and Ideology in Israel." *Middle Eastern Review* 11, no. 2 (Winter 1978–1979): 26–31.

Baker, Henry. *The Legal System of Israel*. Israel Universities Press, 1968.

Bar, Haviva, and Jaaber Asakleh. "Allocation of Time by Senior Government Officials to Jewish and Arab Local Authorities." Guttman Israel Institute for Applied Social Research, 1992.

Bar-Siman-Tov, Ya'akov. "Value Complexity in Shifting from War to Peace: The Israeli Peace-Making Experience with Egypt." *Political Psychology* 16, no. 3 (1995): 545–65.

Baron, Salo W. *The Russian Jew under Tsars and Soviets*. 2nd ed. Macmillan, 1976.

Barzilai, Gad. *Wars, Internal Conflicts, and Political Order: A Jewish Democracy in the Middle East*. State University of New York Press, 1996.

Barzilai, Gad, Giora Goldberg, and Efraim Inbar. "Israeli Leadership and Public Attitudes toward Federal Solutions for the Arab-Israeli Conflict before and after Desert Storm." *Publius: The Journal of Federalism* 21 (Summer 1991): 191–209.

Barzilai, Gad, and Ilan Peleg. "Israel and Future Borders: An Assessment of a Dynamic Process." *Journal of Peace Research* 31, no. 1 (1994): 59–73.

Begin, Menachem. *The Revolt*. Henry Schuman, 1951.

Beit-Hallahmi, Benjamin. *Original Sins: Reflections on the History of Zionism and Israel*. Pluto Press, 1992.

Beit-Hallahmi, Benjamin. "Religion and Politics in Israel." In *Books on Israel*, edited by Ian S. Lustick, 107–11. State University of New York Press, 1988.

Ben-Dor, Lea. "Ben-Gurion on 'Mamlachtiut'." *Jerusalem Post*, 28 May 1965.

Ben-Meir, Yehuda. *Civil-Military Relations in Israel*. Columbia University Press, 1995.

Ben-Meir, Yehuda, and Peri Kedem. "An Index of Religiosity for the Jewish Population in Israel" (in Hebrew). *Megamot* 24 (February 1979): 353–62.

Ben-Porath, Yoram. "Introduction." In *The Israeli Economy: Maturing through Crises*, edited by Yoram Ben-Porath, 1–23. Harvard University Press, 1986.

Ben-Rafael, Eliezer, and Stephen Sharot. *Ethnicity, Religion, and Class in Israeli Society*. Cambridge University Press, 1991.

Ben-Sira, Zeev. *Zionism at the Close of the Twentieth Century: A Dilemma*. Edwin Mellen Press, 1993.

Ben-Yehuda, Nachman. "The Social Meaning of Alternative Systems: Some Exploratory Notes." In *The Israeli State and Society: Boundaries and Frontiers*, edited by Baruch Kimmerling, 152–64. State University of New York Press, 1989.

Ben-Zadok, Efraim, and Giora Goldberg. "Voting Patterns of Oriental Jews in Development Towns." *The Jerusalem Quarterly*, no. 32 (Summer 1994): 15–27.

Benvenisti, Meron. *Intimate Enemies: Jews and Arabs in a Shared Land.* University of California Press, 1995.

Benvenisti, Meron, and Shlomo Khayat. *The West Bank and Gaza Atlas.* The West Bank Data Base Project, 1988.

Benyamini, Kalman. "When Principles Conflict with Emotion and Reality." *Israeli Democracy* (Fall 1990): 24–26.

Benziman, Uzi. *Sharon: An Israeli Caesar.* Adama Books, 1985.

Benziman, Uzi, and Atallah Mansour. *Subtenants* (in Hebrew). Keter Publishing House, 1992.

Berglas, Eitan. "Defense and the Economy." In *The Israeli Economy: Maturing through Crises,* edited by Yoram Ben-Porath, 173–91. Harvard University Press, 1986.

———. "Defense and the Economy: The Israeli Experience." Discussion Paper No. 83.01. The Maurice Falk Institute for Economic Research in Israel, 1983.

Berinson, Zvi. "Freedom of Religion and Conscience in the State of Israel." *Israel Yearbook on Human Rights* 3 (1973): 223–32.

Best, Geoffrey. *Humanity in Warfare: The Modern History of the International Law of Armed Conflicts.* Methuen, 1983.

Biale, David. *Power and Powerlessness in Jewish History.* Schocken Books, 1986.

Blum, Yehuda. "The Missing Reversioner: Reflections on the Status of Judea and Samaria." *Israel Law Review* 3 (April 1968): 279–301.

Bracha, Baruch. "Addendum: Some Remarks on Israeli Law Regarding National Security." *Israel Yearbook on Human Rights* 10 (1980): 289–98.

Bracha, Baruch. "Restriction of Personal Freedom without Due Process of Law according to the Defence(Emergency) Regulations, 1945." *Israel Yearbook on Human Rights* 8 (1978): 296–323.

Brecher, Michael. *The Foreign Policy System of Israel: Setting, Images, Processes.* Oxford University Press, 1972.

Brichta, Avraham. *Democracy and Elections: On Changing the Electoral and Nomination Systems in Israel* (in Hebrew). Am Oved, 1977.

———. "Selection of Candidates to the Tenth Knesset: The Impact of Centralization." In *Israel at the Polls, 1981: A Study of the Knesset Elections,* edited by Howard R. Penniman and Daniel J. Elazar, 18–35. American Enterprise Institute for Public Policy Research and Indiana University Press, 1986.

———. "Women in the Knesset." *Parliamentary Affairs* 28 (1974–1975): 31–50.

Brinner, William. "Muslim Minorities in non-Muslim Societies." Paper presented at conference on The Arab Minority in Israel: Dilemmas of Political Orientation and Social Change, University of Tel Aviv, June 3–4, 1991.

Brym, Robert J. *The Jewish Intelligentsia and Russian Marxism: A Sociological Study of Intellectual Radicalism and Ideological Divergence.* Macmillan, 1978.

Cohen, Erik. "Israel as a Post-Zionist Society." *Israel Affairs* 1 (Spring 1995): 211–14.

Cohen, Esther Rosalind. *Human Rights in the Israeli-Occupied Territories 1967–1982.* Manchester University Press, 1985.

Cohen, Michael J. *The Origins and Evolution of the Arab-Zionist Conflict.* University of California Press, 1987.

Cohen, Mitchell. *Zion and State: Nation, Class and the Shaping of Modern Israel.* Basil Blackwell, 1987.

Cohen, Richard. *The Return to the Land of Israel.* Zalman Shazar Center for Jewish History, 1986.

Cohen, Saul. *The Geopolitics of Israel's Border Question.* Jaffee Center for Strategic Studies, Study No. 7. Westview Press, 1986.

Cohn, Haim H. *Human Rights in Jewish Law.* Ktav, 1984.

Crossman, Richard. *Palestine Mission: A Personal Record.* Harper and Brothers, 1947.

Czudnowski, Moshe. "Legislative Recruitment under Proportional Representation in Israel: A Model and a Case Study." *Midwest Journal of Political Science* 14 (May 1970): 216–48.

———. "Socio-Cultural Variables and Legislative Recruitment." *Comparative Politics* 4, no. 4 (July 1972): 561–87.

Dahaf Research Institute. "Political and Social Attitudes among Youth" (in Hebrew). April 1986.

———. "The Popularity of Different Electoral Lists among Youth: Interim Report" (in Hebrew). May 1985.

Dahl, Robert A. *Polyarchy, Participation, and Observation.* Yale University Press, 1971.

DellaPergola, Sergio. "*Aliya* and Other Jewish Migrations: Toward an Integrated Perspective." In *Studies in the Population of Israel,* edited by Usiel O. Schmelz and Gad Nathan, 172–209. Scripta Hierosolymitana 30, Magnes Press, Hebrew University, 1986.

———. "On the Differential Frequency of Western Migration to Israel." *Studies in Contemporary Jewry* 1 (1984): 292–315.

———. "Will There Be More Mass Immigration?" (in Hebrew). In *On the Way to Year 2000: More War or Progress to Peace?* edited by Alouph Hareven, 37–58. Van Leer Institute, 1988.

Dershowitz, Alan. "Preventive Detention of Citizens during a National Emergency— A Comparison between Israel and the United States." *Israel Yearbook on Human Rights* 1 (1971): 295–321.

Deshen, Shlomo. "The Religiosity of the Eastern Jews: Public, Rabbis, and Faith" (in Hebrew). *Alpayim* 9 (1994): 44–58.

———. "Towards an Understanding of the Special Charm of Religiosity on Eastern Jews" (in Hebrew). *Politika,* no. 24 (1989): 40–43.

Dinstein, Yoram. "The International Law of Belligerent Occupation and Human Rights." *Israel Yearbook on Human Rights* 8 (1978): 104–43.

———. "The Israel Supreme Court and the Law of Belligerent Occupation: Deportations." *Israel Yearbook on Human Rights* 23 (1993): 1–26.

Diskin, Abraham. "The 1977 Interparty Distances: A Three-Level Analysis." In *The Elections in Israel 1977,* edited by Asher Arian, 213–29. Academic Press, 1980.

———. "The Competitive Multi-Party System of Israel (1949–1973)" (in Hebrew). Ph.D. diss., Hebrew University, 1976.

Diskin, Avraham. *Elections and Voters in Israel.* Praeger, 1991.

———. "The Jewish Ethnic Vote: The Demographic Myth." *The Jerusalem Quarterly,* no. 35 (Spring 1985): 53–60.

———. "Statistical Aspects of the Vote in the Arab Sector" (in Hebrew). In *The Arab Vote in Israel's Parliamentary Elections, 1988,* edited by Jacob M. Landau, 22–34. The Jerusalem Institute for Israel Studies, 1989.

Domb, Fania. "Judicial Decisions: Judgments of the Supreme Court of Israel Relating to the Administered Territories." *Israel Yearbook on Human Rights* 10 (1980): 330–46.

———. "Judicial Decisions: Supreme Court of Israel." *Israel Yearbook on Human Rights* 9 (1979): 335–56.

Dominguez, Virginia R. "The Language of Left and Right in Israeli Politics." In *Cross-Currents in Israeli Culture and Politics,* edited by Myron J. Aronoff, 89–109. Transaction Books, 1984.

Don-Yehiya, Eliezer. "Festivals and Political Culture: Independence Day Celebrations." *Jerusalem Quarterly,* no. 45 (Winter 1988): 61–84.

———. "Jewish Messianism, Religious Zionism and Israeli Politics: The Impact and Origins of Gush Emunim." *Middle East Studies* 23 (April 1987): 215–34.

———. "*Mamlachtiut* and Judaism in Ben-Gurion's Thought and Policy" (in Hebrew). *Hatsionut* 14 (1989): 51–88.

———. "Memory and Political Culture: Israeli Society and the Holocaust." *Studies in Contemporary Jewry* 9 (1993): 139–62.

———. "Religion and Ethnicity in Israeli Politics: The Religious Parties and the Elections to the 12th Knesset" (in Hebrew). *Medina, Mimshal, V'yahasim Benle'umiim* [State, Government, and International Relations], no. 32 (Spring 1990): 11–54.

———. "The Resolution of Religious Conflicts in Israel." In *Conflict and Consensus in Jewish Public Life,* edited by Stuart Cohen and E. Don-Yehiya, 203–18. Bar-Ilan University Press, 1986.

Donner, Ruth. *The Regulation of Nationality in International Law.* 2nd ed. Transnational Publishers, 1994.

Dowty, Alan. "The Arab-Israel Conflict: Options and Dilemmas." *Continuum* 1 (Autumn 1990): 171–77.

———. "Building a Civic State: Israel's First Decade." In *Israel: The First Decade of Independence,* edited by S. Ilan Troen and Noah Lucas. State University of New York Press, 1994.

———. "Confidence Building: The Israeli Domestic Dimension." In *Confidence and Security Building Measures in the Middle East,* edited by Gabriel Ben-Dor and David Dewitt. Westview Press, 1994.

———. "Emergency Powers in Israel: The Devaluation of Crisis." In *Coping with Crises: How Governments Deal with Emergencies,* edited by Shao-chuan Leng, 1–43. University Press of America, for the White Burkett Miller Center of Public Affairs, University of Virginia, 1990.

———. "Israel: The Deadlock Persists." *Current History* 90 (January 1991): 14–17, 34–35.

———. "Jewish Political Traditions and Contemporary Israeli Politics." *Jewish Political Studies Review* 2 (Fall 1990): 55–84.

———. "Jewish Politics and Israeli Democracy." *Mosaic,* no. 10 (Spring 1991): 32–47.

———. "Minority Rights, Jewish Political Traditions, and Zionism." *Shofar* 10 (Fall 1991): 23–48.

———. "Religion and Politics in Israel." *Commonweal* 110 (15 July 1983): 393–96.

————. "Religious-Secular Accommodation in Israeli Politics." In *Jewish Sects, Religious Movements, and Political Parties*, edited by Menachem Mor, 393–414. Creighton University Press, 1992.

————. "The Use of Emergency Powers in Israel." *Middle East Review* 21 (Fall 1988): 34–46.

Drezon-Tepler, Marcia. *Interest Groups and Political Change in Israel*. State University of New York Press, 1990.

Dror, Yehezkel. "Can We Maintain a State?" (in Hebrew). Paper presented at annual meeting of the Israel Political Science Association, Jerusalem, May 23, 1989.

Drori, Moshe. "The Israeli Settlement in Judea and Samaria and its Organizational and Municipal Structure: Legal Aspects" (in Hebrew). *City and Region* 4, no. 3 (1981): 28–45.

————. "The Legal System in Judea and Samaria: A Review of the Previous Decade with a Glance at the Future." *Israel Yearbook on Human Rights* 8 (1978): 144–77.

Edelman, Martin. *Courts, Politics, and Culture in Israel*. University Press of Virginia, 1994.

————. "The Judicial Elite of Israel." *International Political Science Review* 13 (July 1992): 235–48.

————. "The Judicialization of Politics in Israel." *International Political Science Review* 15 (April 1994): 177–86.

————. "The Utility of a Written Constitution: Free Exercise of Religion in Israel and the United States." Paper presented at the XV World Congress of the International Political Science Association, Buenos Aires, July 21–25, 1991.

Eidelberg, Paul. "Demophrenia: Democracy in a Madman's Straightjacket" (in Hebrew). *Nativ* 4, no. 3 (May 1991): 46–51.

Eisenstadt, S. N. *The Development of the Ethnic Problem in Israeli Society: Observations and Suggestions for Research*. The Jerusalem Institute for Israel Studies, 1986.

————. *Israeli Society*. Weidenfeld and Nicolson, 1967.

————. *Jewish Civilization: The Jewish Historical Experience in a Comparative Perspective*. State University of New York Press, 1992.

————. *Tradition, Change, and Modernity*. John Wiley and Sons, 1973.

————. *The Transformation of Israeli Society*. Westview Press, 1985.

Eisenstadt, S. N., Moshe Lissak, and Yaakov Nahon. *Communities in Israel and Their Social Status* (in Hebrew). Jerusalem Institute for Israel Studies, 1993.

El-Asmar, Fouzi. *To Be an Arab in Israel*. The Institute for Palestine Studies, 1978.

Elazar, Daniel. *Israel: Building a New Society*. Indiana University Press, 1986.

————. "Israel's New Majority." *Commentary* 75 (March 1983): 33–39.

Elazar, Daniel J. "Covenant as the Basis of the Jewish Political Tradition." In *Kinship and Consent: The Jewish Political Tradition and Its Contemporary Uses*, edited by Daniel J. Elazar, 21–51. University Press of America, 1983.

Elazar, Daniel J. "Future Directions." In *Kinship and Consent: The Jewish Political Tradition and Its Contemporary Uses*, edited by Daniel J. Elazar, 389–92. University Press of America, 1983.

————. "Introduction: The Jews' Rediscovery of the Political and its Implications." In *Kinship and Consent: The Jewish Political Tradition and its Contemporary Uses*, edited by Daniel J. Elazar, 1–17. University Press of America, 1983.

————. "The Kehillah: From its Beginning to the End of the Modern Epoch." In *Public Life in Israel and the Diaspora*, edited by Sam N. Lehman-Wilzig and Bernard Susser, 23–63. Bar-Ilan University Press, 1981.

Elazar, Daniel J., and Stuart Cohen. *The Jewish Polity: Jewish Political Organization from Biblical Times to the Present*. Indiana University Press, 1985.

Eldad, Yisrael. "Zionism against Democracy" (in Hebrew). *Nativ* 2, no. 1 (1989): 54–60.

Elizur, Yuval, and Eliahu Salpeter. *Who Rules Israel?* Harper and Row, 1973.

Elon, Amos. *Herzl*. Holt, Rinehart and Winston, 1975.

————. *The Israelis: Founders and Sons*. Holt, Rinehart and Winston, 1971.

El-Serraj, Eyad. "Torture and Mental Health: A Survey of the Experience of Palestinians in Israeli Prisons." In *Torture: Human Rights, Medical Ethics, and the Case of Israel*, edited by Neve Gordon and Ruchama Marton, 104–07. Zed Books for the Association of Israeli-Palestinians Physicians for Human Rights, 1995.

Enloe, Cynthia. *Ethnic Conflict and Political Development*. Little, Brown, 1973.

————. *Ethnic Soldiers: State Security in Divided Societies*. University of Georgia Press, 1980.

Ettinger, Shmuel. "Rule of the Mob and Leadership That Looks Out for Itself" (in Hebrew). *Migvan* (September 1982): 14–18.

Etzioni, Amitai. "Alternative Ways to Democracy: The Example of Israel." *Political Science Quarterly* 74, no. 2 (June 1959): 196–214.

Etzioni-Halevy, Eva. "Protest Politics in the Israeli Democracy." *Political Scienbce Quarterly* 90 (Fall 1975): 514–16.

Etzioni-Halevy, Eva, with Rita Shapira. *Political Culture in Israel*. Praeger, 1977.

Evron, Boas. *Jewish State or Israeli Nation?* Indiana University Press, 1995.

Falloon, Virgil. *Excessive Secrecy, Lack of Guidelines: A Report on Military Censorship in the West Bank*. Al-Haq [Law in the Service of Man], 1986.

Fein, Leonard. *Politics in Israel:* Little, Brown, 1967.

Feller, S. Z. "The Applicability of Israeli Criminal Law According to Emergency Regulations" (in Hebrew). *Hapraklit* 36 (April 1985): 262–81.

Finkelstein, Louis. *Jewish Self-Government in the Middle Ages*. Greenwood Press, 1972.

Frankel, Glenn. *Beyond the Promised Land: Jews and Arabs on the Hard Road to a New Israel*. Simon & Schuster, 1994.

Frankel, William. *Israel Observed: An Anatomy of the State*. Thames and Hudson, 1980.

Friedlander, Dov, Eliyahu Ben-Moshe, and Yonah Schelekens. "Regional Demographic Changes in Israel" (in Hebrew). Research Report No. 3. Jerusalem Institute for Israel Studies, 1989.

Friedlander, Dov, and Calvin Goldscheider. "Israel's Population: The Challenge of Pluralism," *Population Bulletin* 39, no. 2 (April 1984).

Friedman, M. "Detainees under the Emergency Regulations" (in Hebrew). *Hapraklit* 2 (August 1945): 242–43.

Friedman, Menachem. *Haredi Society: Sources, Trends, and Processes* (in Hebrew). Jerusalem Institute for Israel Studies, 1991.

————. "'If They Are Free—They Are Not Jews'." *Israeli Democracy* 1 (February 1987): 22–24.

————. "The NRP in Transition—Behind the Party's Electoral Decline." In *The Roots of Begin's Success: The 1981 Israeli Elections*, edited by Dan Caspi, Abraham

Diskin, and Emanuel Gutmann, 141–68. Croom Helm and St. Martin's Press, 1984.

———. "Religious Zealotry in Israeli Society." In *On Ethnic and Religious Diversity in Israel,* edited by Solomon Poll and Ernest Krausz, 91–109. Bar-Ilan University, 1975.

———. "The State of Israel as a Theological Dilemma." In *The Israeli State and Society: Boundaries and Frontiers,* edited by Baruch Kimmerling, 165–215. State University of New York Press, 1989.

———. "The Structural Foundation for Religio-Political Accommodation in Israel: Fallacy and Reality." In *Israel: The First Decade of Independence,* edited by S. Ilan Troen and Noah Lucas, 51–81. State University of New York Press, 1995.

———. "The Ultra-Orthodox and Israeli Society." In *Whither Israel? The Domestic Challenges,* edited by Keith Kyle and Joel Peters, 177–201. I. B. Taurus, 1993.

Friedman, Robert I. *Zealots for Zion: Inside Israel's West Bank Settlement Movement.* Random House, 1992.

Friedman, Rabbi Natan Zvi. "Guidelines of Democracy and Jewish Law" (in Hebrew). *Tehumin* 4 (1982–1983): 255–58.

Friedmann, Daniel. *The Effect of Foreign Law on the Law of Israel.* Israel Law Review Association, 1975.

Frisch, Hillel. "The Arab Vote in the 1992 Elections: The Triviality of Normality; the Significance of Electoral Power." In *Israel at the Polls 1992,* edited by Daniel J. Elazar and Shmuel Sandler, 103–25. Rowman and Littlefield, 1995.

Fund, Yosef. "Agudat Yisrael Confronting Zionism and the State of Israel—Ideology and Policy" (in Hebrew). Paper presented at the annual meeting of the Israel Political Science Association, Ramat Gan, May 1991.

Galnoor, Itzhak. "Israeli Democracy in Transition." *Studies in Contemporary Jewry* 5 (1989): 126–47.

———. "Israeli Society and Politics." In *The Impact of the Six-Day War,* edited by Stephen J. Roth, 171–96. Macmillan, 1988.

———. *The Partition of Palestine: Decision Crossroads in the Zionist Movement.* State University of New York Press, 1994.

———. "Secrecy." In *Government Secrecy in Democracies,* edited by Itzhak Galnoor, 176–200. Harper and Row, 1977.

———. *Steering the Polity: Communication and Politics in Israel.* Sage, 1982.

Garfinkle, Adam M. "On the Origin, Meaning, Use and Abuse of a Phrase." *Middle Eastern Studies* 27 (October 1991): 539–50.

Gastil, Raymond. "The Past, Present, and Future of Democracy." *Journal of International Affairs* 38 (Winter 1985): 161–79.

Genefke, Inge. "Evidence of the Use of Torture." In *Torture: Human Rights, Medical Ethics, and the Case of Israel,* edited by Neve Gordon and Ruchama Marton, 97–103. Zed Booksfor the Association of Israeli-Palestinian Physicians for Human Rights, 1995.

Geva, Yehuda, and Jack Habib. "The Development of the Transfer System and the Redistribution of Income." In *The Israeli Economy: Maturing Through Crises,* edited by Yoram Ben-Porath, 209–220. Harvard University Press, 1986.

Gil, B. *Chronicles of Aliya: Thirty Years of Aliya to the Land of Israel, 1919–1949* (in Hebrew). Jewish Agency for the Land of Israel, 1949–1950.

Ginat, Joseph. "Israeli Arabs: Some Recent Social and Political Trends." *Asian and African Studies* 23 (November 1989): 183–204.

———. "Voting Patterns and Political Behavior in the Arab Sector" (in Hebrew). In *The Arab Vote in Israel's Parliamentary Elections, 1988,* edited by Jacob M. Landau, 3–21. The Jerusalem Institute for Israel Studies, 1989.

Ginor, Fanny. *Socio-Economic Disparities in Israel.* Tel Aviv University and Transaction Publishers, 1979.

Gitelman, Zvi. "Comparative Politics and the Jewish Political Experience." *Jewish Political Studies Review* 1 (Fall 1989): 77–88.

Goitein, S. D. "Political Conflict and the Use of Power in the World of the Geniza." In *Kinship and Consent: The Jewish Political Tradition and its Contemporary Uses,* edited by Daniel Elazar, 169–181. University Press of America, 1983.

Golan, Esther. "Political Culture in Israel: A Case Study" (in Hebrew). Master's thesis, University of Haifa, 1977.

Goldberg, Giora. "The Likud: Moving toward the Center." In *Israel at the Polls, 1988–1989,* edited by Daniel J. Elazar and Shmuel Sandler, 45–66. Wayne State University Press.

Goldberg, Giora, Gad Barzilai, and Efraim Inbar. *The Impact of Intercommunal Conflict: The Intifada and Israeli Public Opinion.* Policy Studies No. 43. The Leonard Davis Institute for International Relations, 1991.

Goldscheider, Calvin. "The Demographic Embeddedness of the Arab-Jewish Conflict in Israeli Society." *Middle East Review* 21 (Spring 1989): 15–24.

———. *Israel's Changing Family.* Westview Press, 1995.

———. *Israel's Changing Society: Population, Ethnicity, and Development.* Westview Press, 1996.

Goldscheider, Calvin, and Alan S. Zuckerman. *The Transformation of the Jews.* University of Chicago Press, 1984.

Goldstein, Michael. "Israeli Security Measures in the Occupied Territories: Administrative Detention." *Middle East Journal* 32, no. 1 (Winter 1978): 35–44.

Gonen, Jay Y. *A Psychohistory of Zionism.* Mason/Charter, 1975.

Goren, Dina. "The Communication Media and Democracy in Israel" (in Hebrew). *Skira Hodshit* (August–September 1984): 57–65.

Goren, Dina. *Secrecy and the Right to Know.* Turtledove Publishing, 1979.

Gorny, Yosef. *The State of Israel in Jewish Public Thought: The Quest for Collective Identity.* New York University Press, 1994.

———. *Zionism and the Arabs, 1882–1948: A Study in Ideology.* Clarendon Press, 1987.

———. "Zionist Voluntarism in the Political Struggle: 1939–1948." *Jewish Political Studies Review* 2 (Spring 1990): 67–104.

Greenbaum, Charles W., Leon Mann, and Shoshana Harpaz. "Children's Perceptions of Minority Rights: Israel in a Cross-National Perspective." In *The Israeli State and Society: Boundaries and Frontiers,* edited by Baruch Kimmerling, 134–151. State University of New York Press, 1989.

Grose, Peter. *A Changing Israel.* Random House, Vintage Books, 1985.

Grossman, David. *Jewish and Arab Settlements in the Tulkarm Sub-District.* West Bank Data Base Project, 1986.

Grossman, David. *Sleeping on a Wire: Conversations with Palestinians in Israel.* Farrar, Straus & Giroux, 1993.

Gutman, Yehiel. *The Attorney General Against the Government* (in Hebrew). Idanim, 1981.

Gutmann, Emanuel. "Citizen Participation in Political Life: Israel." *International Social Science Journal* 12, no. 1 (1960): 53–62.

———. "Parliamentary Elites: Israel." In *Electoral Politics in the Middle East: Issues, Voters and Elites,* edited by Jacob M. Landau, Ergun Ozbudun, and Frank Tachau, 273–97. Croom Helm, 1980.

———. "Parties and Blocs—Stability and Change" (in Hebrew). In *The Israeli Political System,* edited by Moshe Lissak and Emanuel Gutmann, 122–70. Am Oved, 1977.

Ha'am, Ahad. "The Jewish State and the Jewish Problem" (1897). In *Nationalism and the Jewish Ethic: Basic Writings of Ahad Ha'am,* edited by Hans Kohn, 66–89. Schocken Books, 1962.

Hadad, Suhaila, R. D. McLaurin, and Emile Nakhleh. "Minorities in Containment: The Arabs of Israel." In *The Political Role of Minority Groups in the Middle East,* edited by R. D. McLaurin, 76–108. Praeger, 1979.

Halper, Jeff. "The Intifada and Israeli Society." *Association for Israel Studies Newsletter* 4 (Fall 1988): 10–13.

Halpern, Ben. *The Idea of the Jewish State.* 2nd ed. Harvard University Press, 1969.

Hareven, Alouph. "Equality and Integration: An Annual Progress Report 1992–1993." Sikkuy [The Association for the Advancement of Equal Opportunity], 1993.

———. "Israeli Arabs as a Jewish Problem" (in Hebrew). In *One of Every Six Israelis,* edited by Alouph Hareven, 3–13. The Van Leer Jerusalem Foundation, 1981.

Hareven, Alouph, ed. "Equality and Integration: Annual Progress Report 1993/1994." Sikkuy, 1994.

Hareven, Alouph, and As'ad Ghanem. *Equality and Integration: Retrospect and Prospects 1992–1996.* Sikkuy, 1996.

Harkabi, Yehoshafat. *The Bar Kochba Syndrome.* Rossell Books, 1983.

———. *Israel's Fateful Hour.* New York: Harper and Row, 1988.

Hasdai, Yaacov. *Truth in the Shadow of War.* Translated by Moshe Kohn. Zmora, Bitan, Modan, 1979.

Hattis, Susan Lee. *The Bi-National Idea in Palestine during Mandatory Times.* Shikmona, 1970.

Hazaz, Haim. "The Sermon" (in Hebrew). In *Seething Stones: Stories, Collected Writings of Haim Hazaz,* edited by Hazaz, 219–237. Am Oved, 1970.

Heilman, Samuel. *Defenders of the Faith: Inside Ultra-Orthodox Jewry.* Schocken Books, 1992.

Herzog, Hanna. "Penetrating the System: The Politics of Collective Identities." In *The Elections in Israel 1992,* edited by Asher Arian and Michal Shamir, 81–102. State University of New York Press, 1995.

Hoag, Clarence Gilbert, and George Hervey Hallett. *Proportional Representation.* Macmillan, 1926.

Hobson, J. A. *Democracy after the War.* George Allen and Unwin, 1917.

Hoffman, Steven A. "Candidate Selection in Israel's Parliament: The Realities of Change." *Middle East Journal* 34 (1980): 285–301.

Hofnung, Menachem. *Democracy, Law, and National Security in Israel.* Dartmouth Publishing, 1996.

———. *Israel—Security Needs vs. the Rule of Law* (in Hebrew). Nevo, 1991.

———. "States of Emergency and Ethnic Conflict in Liberal Democracies." *Terrorism and Political Violence* 6 (Autumn 1996): 340–65.

Hornstein, N. "Entrenching Provisions in the Basic Law" (in Hebrew). *Hapraklit* 25 (October 1969): 648–55.

Horowitz, Dan. "Before the State: Communal Politics in Palestine under the Mandate." In *The Israeli State and Society: Boundaries and Frontiers,* edited by Baruch Kimmerling, 28–65. State University of New York Press, 1989.

Horowitz, Dan. "More than a Change in Government." *Jerusalem Quarterly* 5 (Fall 1977): 9–13.

Horowitz, Dan, and Moshe Lissak. *Origins of the Israeli Polity: Palestine under the Mandate.* University of Chicago Press, 1978.

Horowitz, Dan, and Moshe Lissak. *Trouble in Utopia: The Overburdened Polity of Israel.* State University of New York Press, 1989.

Hunter, Robert E. "Seeking Middle East Peace." *Foreign Policy* 73 (Winter 1988–1989): 3–21.

Ichilov, Orit. "Citizenship Orientations of Two Israeli Minority Groups: Israel-Arab and Eastern-Jewish Youth." *Ethnic Groups* 7, no. 2 (1988): 113–36.

Inbar, Efraim, and Giora Goldberg. "Is Israel's Political Elite Becoming More Hawkish?" *International Journal* 45 (Summer 1990): 632–60.

Inbar, Efraim, and Shmuel Sandler. "Israel's Deterrence Strategy Revisited." *Security Studies* 3, no. 2 (1994): 330–58.

Inglehart, Ronald. *Culture Shift in Advanced Industrial Society.* Princeton University Press, 1990.

Inkeles, Alex, ed. *On Measuring Democracy.* Transaction Books, 1991.

Iris, Mark, and Avraham Shama. "Political Participation and Ethnic Conflict in Israel." Paper read at the annual meeting of the Midwest Political Science Association, Chicago, May 1–3, 1975.

Isaac, Rael Jean. *Israel Divided: Ideological Politics in the Jewish State.* The Johns Hopkins University Press, 1976.

Israel, Central Bureau of Statistics. *Immigration to Israel, 1987.* Special Series No. 833. Central Bureau of Statistics, 1988.

———. *Projections of Population in Judea, Samaria, and Gaza Area up to 2002.* Special Series No. 802. Central Bureau of Statistics, 1987.

Israel, Ministry of Defense, Office of the Co-ordinator of Government Operations in Judea, Samaria and Gaza District. *Judea, Samaria, and the Gaza District, 1967–1987: Twenty Years of Civil Administration.* Carta, 1987.

Israel, National Section of the International Commission of Jurists. *The Rule of Law in the Areas Administered by Israel.* National Section of the International Commission of Jurists, 1981.

Israeli, Raphael. *Palestinians Between Israel and Jordan.* Praeger, 1991.

Jaffe, Eliezer David. "Ethnic and Minority Groups in Israel: Challenges for Social Work Theory, Value and Practice." *Journal of Sociology and Social Welfare* 22, no. 1 (1 March 1995): 149–71.

Jiryis, Sabri. *The Arabs in Israel.* Monthly Review Press, 1976.

Joseph, Bernard. *British Rule in Palestine.* Public Affairs Press, 1948.

Kahane, Meir. *They Must Go.* Grosset and Dunlap, 1981.

Katz, Ehud. "The Words of the Wise: Ultra-Orthodox Hierarchies and the Fate of the Nation." *Israel Scene* (April/May 1990): 3–4.

Katz, Elihu, and Majid Al-Haj. "Options: Dovish, Hawkish and Local Arab." In *Research Report, 1988 & 1989,* edited by Haya Gratch, 17–19. Guttman Israel Institute of Applied Social Research, 1990.

Katz, Elihu, and Michael Gurevitch. *The Secularization of Leisure: Culture and Communication in Israel.* Harvard University Press, 1976.

Katz, Elihu, and Hannah Levinsohn. "How the Intifada Is Perceived in Public Opinion" (in Hebrew). In *The Seventh War: The Effects of the Intifada on Israeli Society,* edited by Reuven Gal, 45–54. Hakibbutz Hame'uhad, 1990.

———. "Too Good To Be True: Notes on the Israel Elections of 1988." *International Journal of Public Opinion Research* 1, no. 2 (1989).

Katz, Elihu, Hanna Levinsohn, and Majid Al-Haj. "Attitudes of Israelis (Jews and Arabs) towards Current Affairs." Guttman Israel Institute of Applied Social Research Publication No. (S)EK/1129/E, January 10, 1991.

Katz, Jacob. *Emancipation and Assimilation: Studies in Modern Jewish History.* Gregg International Publishers, 1972.

———. *Exclusiveness and Tolerance: Studies in Jewish-Gentile Relations in Medieval and Modern Times.* Oxford University Press, 1961.

———. *Out of the Ghetto: The Social Background of Jewish Emancipation, 1770–1870.* Harvard University Press, 1973.

———. *Tradition and Crisis: Jewish Society at the End of the Middle Ages.* Schocken Books, 1971.

Kaufman, Edy. "War, Occupation, and the Effects on Israeli Society." In *Democracy, Peace, and the Israeli-Palestinian Conflict,* edited by Edy Kaufman, Abed B. Shukri and Robert L. Rothstein, 85–133. Lynne Rienner, 1993.

Kaufman, Gerald. *Inside the Promised Land: A Personal View of Today's Israel.* Wildwood House, 1986.

Kaufmann, Yadin. "Israel's Flexible Voters." *Foreign Policy* 61 (Winter 1985–1986): 109–24.

Kedem, Peri. "Dimensions of Jewish Religiosity in Israel." In *Tradition, Innovation, Conflict: Jewishness and Judaism in Contemporary Israel,* edited by Zvi Sobel and Benjamin Beit-Hallahmi, 251–72. State University of New York Press, 1991.

Keinon, Herb. *Israeli Settlements: A Guide.* Anti-Defamation League, 1995.

Kesse, Tsvi. "Anti-Democracy at the Gate" (in Hebrew). *Migvan* (September, 1981): 53–56.

Kimmerling, Baruch. "Between the Primordial and Civil Definitions of the Collective Identity: Eretz Yisrael or the State of Israel?" In *Comparative Social Dynamics: Essays in Honor of Shmuel Eisenstadt,* edited by M. Lissak, E. Cohen, and U. Almagor, 262–83. Westview Press, 1984.

———. "Boundaries and Frontiers of the Israeli Control System: Analytical Conclusions." In *The Israeli State and Society: Boundaries and Frontiers,* edited by Baruch Kimmerling, 265–84. State University of New York Press, 1989.

———. "Discontinuities of Elite Recruitment in Israeli Society." In *Books on Israel,* edited by Ian S. Lustick, 31–36. State University of New York Press, 1988.

————. *The Interrupted Society: Israeli Civilians in War and Routine Times.* State University of New York Press, 1985.

————. "Making Conflict a Routine: The Cumulative Effects of the Arab-Jewish Conflict upon Israeli Society." *Journal of Strategic Studies* 6 (1983): 13–45.

————. "Patterns of Militarism in Israel." *Archives of European Sociology* 34 (1993): 196–223.

————. "Sociology, Ideology and Nation Building: The Palestinians and Their Meaning in Israeli Sociology." *American Sociological Review* 57 (August 1992): 446–60.

————. "Yes, Returning to the Family" (in Hebrew). *Politika,* no. 48 (March 1993): 40–45.

————. *Zionism and Territory: The Socio-Territorial Dimensions of Zionist Politics.* Research Series No. 51. Institute of International Studies, University of California, 1983.

Kirschenbaum, Aharon. "Human Rights Revisited." *Israel Yearbook on Human Rights* 6 (1976): 228–38.

————. Review of *Judaism and Human Rights,* ed. R. Konvitz. *Israel Yearbook on Human Rights* 2 (1972): 357–64.

Klein, Claude. *Israel as a Nation-State and the Problem of the Arab Minority: In Search of a Status.* International Center for Peace in the Middle East, 1987.

Klieman, Aaron S. *Israel and the World after 40 Years.* Pergamon-Brassey's, 1989.

Klinghoffer, Yizhak Hans. "On Emergency Regulations in Israel" (in Hebrew). In *Jubilee Book for Pinhas Rosen,* edited by Haim Kohn, 86–121. Mifal Haschichpul, 1962.

Kolatt, Israel. "The Zionist Movement and the Arabs." In *Zionism and the Arabs: Essays,* edited by Shmuel Almog, 1–34. The Historical Society of Israel and the Zalman Shazar Center for Jewish History,1983.

Kornberg, Jacques. *Theodore Herzl: From Assimilation to Zionism.* Indiana University Press, 1993.

Kotler, Yair. *Heil Kahane.* Adama Books, 1986.

Kretzmer, David. "High Court of Justice Review of the Demolition and Sealing of Houses in the Territories" (in Hebrew). In *Klinghoffer Book on Public Law,* 305–57. Faculty of Law, Hebrew University of Jerusalem, 1993.

Kretzmer, David. *The Legal Status of the Arabs in Israel.* Westview Press, 1990.

Kuttab, Jonathan, and Raja Shehadeh. *Civilian Administration in the Occupied West Bank.* Al-Haq [Law in the Service of Man], 1982.

Kuttner, Thomas S. "Israel and the West Bank: Aspects of the Law of Belligerent Occupation." *Israel Yearbook on Human Rights* 7 (1977): 166–221.

Landau, David. *Piety and Power: The World of Jewish Fundamentalism.* Hill and Wang, 1993.

Landau, Dov. "Who's Afraid of Yudkeh's Sermon?" (in Hebrew) *Nativ* 2, no. 7 (January 1989): 71–81.

Landau, Jacob M. *The Arab Minority in Israel, 1967–1991.* Clarendon Press, 1993.

————. *The Arabs in Israel: A Political Study.* Oxford University Press, 1969.

Landau, Moshe. "A Constitution as Supreme Law for the State of Israel?" (in Hebrew) *Hapraklit* 27 (March 1971): 30–36.

Lasswell, Harold D. "The Garrison State." *American Journal of Sociology* 46 (January 1941): 455–68.

———. *National Security and Individual Freedom.* Committee for Economic Development, 1950.

Lederhendler, Eli. *The Road to Modern Jewish Politics.* Oxford University Press, 1989.

Lehman-Wilzig, Sam. "'Am K'shei Oref' : Oppositionism in the Jewish Heritage." *Judaism* 40 (Winter 1991): 16–38.

———. "Conflict as Communication—Public Protest in Israel, 1950–1982." In *Conflict and Consensus in Jewish Political Life,* edited by Stuart A. Cohen and Eliezer Don-Yehiya, 128–45. Bar-Ilan University Press, 1986.

———. "Copying the Master: Patterns of Israeli-Arab Protest, 1950–1990." *Asian and African Studies* 27 (March/July 1993): 129–48.

———. "Demoskraty in the Mega-Polis: Hyper-Participation in the Post-Industrial Age." In *The Future of Politics: Governance, Movements, and World Order,* edited by William Page, 221–29. St. Martin's Press, 1983.

———. "For the Sin of Ultra-Orthodox Bashing." *Sh'ma* (7 September 1990).

———. *Stiff-Necked People, Bottle-Necked System: The Evolution and Roots of Israeli Public Protest, 1949–1986.* Indiana University Press, 1990.

———. *Wildfire: Grassroots Protest in Israel in the Post-Socialist Era.* State University of New York Press, 1992.

Lehman-Wilzig, Sam N. "Public Protest and Systemic Stability in Israel: 1960–1979." In *Public Life in Israel and the Diaspora,* edited by Sam N. Lehman-Wilzig and Bernard Susser, 171–210. Bar-Ilan University Press, 1981.

Lesch, Ann M. "Israeli Deportation of Palestinians from the West Bank and the Gaza Strip, 1967–1978." *Journal of Palestine Studies* 8, no. 3 (Spring 1979): 81–112.

———. "Israeli Deportation of Palestinians from the West Bank and the Gaza Strip, 1967–1978." *Journal of Palestine Studies* 8, no. 2 (Winter 1979): 101–31.

Levi, Amnon. "The *Haredi* Press and Secular Society." In *Conflict and Accommodation between Jews in Israel,* edited by Charles S. Liebman, 21–44. Keter Publishing House, 1990.

Levinsohn, Hanna, Elihu Katz, and Majid Al-Haj. *Jews and Arabs in Israel: Common Values and Reciprocal Images.* Guttman Israel Institute of Applied Social Research, 1995.

Levitats, Isaac. *The Jewish Community in Russia, 1844–1917.* Posner and Sons, 1981.

Levy, Shlomit, Hana Levinsohn, and Elihu Katz. *Beliefs, Observances and Social Interaction among Israeli Jews.* Guttman Israel Institute of Applied Social Research, 1993.

Lewin-Epstein, Noah. "The Arab Minority in Israel's Economy: An Israeli Dilemma." *Israel Studies Bulletin* 9 (Fall 1993): 3–7.

Lewin-Epstein, Noah, and Moshe Semyonov. *The Arab Minority in Israel's Economy: Patterns of Ethnic Inequality.* Westview Press, 1993.

Lewis, Arnold. "Ethnic Politics and the Foreign Policy Debate in Israel." In *Cross-Currents in Israeli Culture and Politics,* edited by Myron J. Aronoff, 25–38. Transaction Books, 1984.

———. "Phantom Ethnicity: 'Oriental Jews' in Israeli Society." In *Studies in Israeli Ethnicity: After the Ingathering,* edited by Alex Weingrod, 133–57. Gordon and Breach, 1985.

Liebman, Charles, and Eliezer Don-Yehiya. *Civil Religion in Israel: Traditional Judaism and Political Culture in the Jewish State.* University of California Press, 1983.

Liebman, Charles S. "Conceptions of 'State of Israel' in Israeli Society" (in Hebrew). *Medina, Mimshal, V'yahasim Benle'umiim* [State, Government, and International Relations], no. 30 (Winter 1989): 51–60.

———. "Introduction." In *Conflict and Accommodation between Jews in Israel,* edited by Charles S. Liebman, xi-xviii. Keter Publishing House, 1990.

———. "Jewish Fundamentalism and the Israeli Polity." In *Fundamentalisms and the State,* edited by Martin E. Marty and R. Scott Appleby, 68–87. University of Chicago Press, 1993.

———. "Relations between *Dati* and Non-*Dati* Jews—Some Final Reflections." In *Conflict and Accommodation between Jews in Israel,* edited by Charles S. Liebman, 215–31. Keter Publishing House, 1990.

———. "The Religious Component in Israeli Ultra-Nationalism," Eighth Annual Rabbi Louis Feinberg Memorial Lecture in Judaic Studies. Judaic Studies Program, University of Cincinnati, April 16, 1985.

Liebman, Charles S., and Steven M. Cohen. *Two Worlds of Judaism: The Israeli and American Experiences.* Yale University Press, 1990.

Liebman, Charles S., and Eliezer Don-Yehiya. *Religion and Politics in Israel.* Indiana University Press, 1984.

Lijphart, Arend. "Democracies: Forms, Performance, and Constitutional Engineering." *European Journal of Political Research* 25 (January 1994): 1–17.

———. *Democracies: Patterns of Majoritarian and Consensus Government in Twenty-One Countries.* Yale University Press, 1984.

———. *Democracy in Plural Societies: A Comparative Exploration.* Yale University Press, 1977.

———. "Democratic Political Systems: Types, Cases, Causes, and Consequences." *Journal of Theoretical Politics* 1, no. 1 (1989): 33–48.

———. "Israeli Democracy and Democratic Reform in Comparative Perspective." In *Israeli Democracy Under Stress,* edited by Ehud Sprinzak and Larry Diamond, 107–23. Lynne Rienner, 1993.

———. *The Politics of Accommodation: Pluralism and Democracy in the Netherlands.* University of California Press, 1968.

———. "The Power-Sharing Approach." In *Conflict and Peacemaking in Multiethnic Societies,* edited by Joseph V. Montville, 491–509. Lexington Books, 1990.

Lissak, Moshe. "Paradoxes of Israeli Civil-Military Relations." In *Israeli Society and Its Defense Establishment,* edited by Moshe Lissak, 1–12. Cass, 1984.

Lucas, Noah. *The Modern History of Israel.* Praeger, 1975.

Luebbert, Gregory M. *Comparative Democracy: Policymaking and Governing Coalitions in Europe and Israel.* Columbia University Press, 1986.

Lustick, Ian. *Arabs in the Jewish State: Israel's Control of a National Minority.* University of Texas Press, 1980.

———. "The Changing Political Role of Israeli Arabs." In *The Elections in Israel 1988,* edited by Asher Arian and Michal Shamir, 115–31. Westview Press, 1990.

———. "Stability in Deeply Divided Societies: Consociationalism versus Control." *World Politics* 31 (April 1979): 325–44.

Lustick, Ian S. *For the Land and the Lord: Jewish Fundamentalism in Israel.* Council on Foreign Relations, 1988.

————. *Unsettled States, Disputed Lands.* Cornell University Press, 1993.

————. "The Voice of a Sociologist; the Task of an Historian; the Limits of a Paradigm." In *Books on Israel,* edited by Ian S. Lustick, 9–16. State University of New York Press, 1988.

Mahler, Gregory. *Bibliography of Israeli Politics.* Westview Press, 1985.

————. *The Knesset: Parliament in the Israeli Political System.* Fairleigh Dickinson University Press, 1981.

————. *Israel: Government and Politics in a Maturing State.* Harcourt Brace Jovanovich, 1990.

Manicas, Peter T. *War and Democracy.* Basil Blackwell, 1989.

Mari, Sami K. *Arab Education in Israel.* Syracuse University Press, 1978.

Marmorstein, Emile. *Heaven at Bay: The Jewish Kulturkampf in the Holy Land.* Oxford University Press, 1969.

Marton, Ruchama. "The White Coat Passes like a Shadow: The Health Profession and Torture in Israel." In *Torture: Human Rights, Medical Ethics, and the Case of Israel,* edited by Neve Gordon and Ruchama Marton, 33–40. Zed Books for the Association of Israeli-Palestinian Physicians for Human Rights, 1995.

Marty, Martin E, and R. Scott Appleby. "Conclusion: Remaking the State: The Limits of the Fundamentalist Imagination." In *Fundamentalisms and the State,* edited by Martin E. Marty and R. Scott Appleby, 620–43. University of Chicago Press, 1993.

————. "Introduction." In *Fundamentalisms and the State,* edited by Martin E. Marty and R. Scott Appleby, 1–9. University of Chicago Press, 1993.

Mayseless, Ofra, and Reuven Gal. "Hatred on the Rise." *Israeli Democracy* (Fall 1990): 21–23.

McLaurin, R. D. "Majorities as Minorities: The Arabs in Israeli Occupied Territory." In *The Political Role of Minority Groups in the Middle East,* edited by R. D. McLaurin, 221–39. Praeger, 1979.

Medding, Peter Y. *The Founding of Israeli Democracy, 1948–1967.* Oxford University Press, 1990.

Mendelsohn, Ezra. *On Modern Jewish Politics.* Oxford University Press, 1993.

Mendes-Flohr, Paul. "The Chosen People Concept and Zionism." Paper read at conference on Religion and Nationalism: Chosen People Themes in Western Nationalist Movements, 1880–1920. German Historical Institute and Harvard Divinity School, June 13–16, 1991.

Meron, Simha. "Freedom of Religion as Distinct from Freedom from Religion." *Israel Yearbook on Human Rights* 4 (1974): 219–40.

Meron, Theodor. "West Bank and Gaza: Human Rights and Humanitarian Law in the Period of Transition." *Israel Yearbook on Human Rights* 9 (1979): 106–20.

Merrill Lynch. *The Israeli Economy.* Merrill Lynch & Co., Global Securities Research and Economics Group, International Economics Department, 1994.

Meyer, Lawrence. *Israel Now: Portrait of a Troubled Land.* Delacorte Press, 1982.

Migdal, Joel. "The Crystallization of the State and the Struggles over Rulemaking: Israel in Comparative Perspective." In *The Israeli State and Society: Boundaries and Frontiers,* edited by Baruch Kimmerling, 1–27. State University of New York Press, 1989.

Mironi, Mordechai. *Return-to-Work Orders: Government Intervention in Labor Disputes through Emergency Regulations and Work Injunctions* (in Hebrew). The Institute for Social and Labor Research, University of Tel Aviv, 1983.

Morag-Talmon, Pnina. "The Integration Processes of Eastern Jews in Israeli Society." *Studies in Contemporary Jewry* 5 (1989): 25–38.

Nahmias, David. "The Right Wing Opposition in Israel." *Political Studies* 24 (September 1973): 268–80.

Nahmias, David, and David Rosenblum. *Bureaucratic Culture: Citizens and Administrators in Israel.* St. Martin's Press, 1978.

Nahmias, Eli. "The Constitutional Status of the Declaration of Independence" (in Hebrew). *Basha'ar,* no. 156 (1981): 40–42.

Neuberger, Benjamin. "Does Israel Have a Liberal-Democratic Tradition?" *Jewish Political Studies Review* 2, nos. 3 and 4 (Fall 1990): 85–97.

———. "Israel's Democracy and Comparative Politics." *Jewish Political Studies Review* 1 (Fall 1989): 67–75.

Nisan, Mordechai. "The Zionist Sacrifice to the Moloch of Democracy" (in Hebrew). *Nativ* 3, no. 4 (July 1990): 16–21.

Nordlinger, Eric A. *Conflict Regulation in Divided Societies.* Center for International Affairs, Harvard University, 1972.

Nuchimowski, R. "Deportations under the Defence Regulations (1)" (in Hebrew). *Hapraklit* 3 (April 1946): 104–9.

———. "Deportations under the Defence Regulations (2)" (in Hebrew). *Hapraklit* 3 (May 1946): 134–40.

O'Brien, Conor Cruise. *The Siege: The Saga of Israel and Zionism.* Simon & Schuster, 1986.

O'Brien, William V. *Law and Morality in Israel's War with the PLO.* Routledge, 1991.

Ofer, Gur. "Public Spending on Civilian Services." In *The Israeli Economy: Maturing Through Crises,* edited by Yoram Ben-Porath, 192–208. Harvard University Press, 1986.

Oz, Amos. *In the Land of Israel.* The Hogarth Press, 1983.

———. *Under This Blazing Light.* Sifriat Po'alim, 1979 (in Hebrew); Cambridge University Press, 1995.

Pach, Arie. "Human Rights in West Bank Military Courts." *Israel Yearbook on Human Rights* 7 (1977): 222–52.

Pappé, Ilan. "An Uneasy Coexistence: Arabs and Jews in the First Decade of Statehood." In *Israel: The First Decade of Independence,* edited by S. Ilan Troen and Noah Lucas, 617–58. Ithaca: State University of New York Press, 1995.

———. "Pandora's Box Syndrome—Israeli Policy-Makers' Fear of a Comprehensive Settlement for the Arab-Israeli Conflict." Paper presented at annual meeting of the International Society of Political Psychology. Tel Aviv, June 18–22, 1989.

Patkin, A. L. *The Origins of the Russian-Jewish Labour Movement:* F. W. Cheshire, 1947.

Pawel, Ernst. *The Labyrinth of Exile: A Life of Theodor Herzl.* Farrar, Straus & Giroux, 1989.

Peled, Yoav. "Ethnic Democracy and the Legal Construction of Citizenship: Arab Citizens of the Jewish State." *American Political Science Review* 86 (June 1992): 432–43.

———. "Retreat from Modernity: The Ascendance of Jewish Nationalism in the

Jewish State." Paper presented at the annual meeting, American Political Science Association, San Francisco, August 30–September 2, 1990.

Peleg, Ilan. *Begin's Foreign Policy, 1977–1983: Israel's Move to the Right.* Greenwood Press, 1987.

———. "The Legacy of Begin and Beginism for the Israeli Political System." In *Israel after Begin,* edited by Gregory S. Mahler, 19–49. State University of New York Press, 1990.

———. "The Peace Process and Israel's Political Culture: A Kulturkampf in the Making." Paper presented at annual meeting of the American Political Science Association. Chicago, September 1–4, 1995.

Peres, Yochanan. "Ethnic Relations in Israel." *American Journal of Sociology* 76 (May 1971): 1021–47.

———. "Most Israelis Are Committed to Democracy." *Israeli Democracy* 1 (February 1987): 16–19.

———Peres, Yochanan. "Religiosity and Political Positions" (in Hebrew). *Israeli Democracy* (Winter 1992): 26–31.

———. "Tolerance—Two Years Later." *Israeli Democracy* (Winter 1990): 16–18.

Peres, Yochanan, and Mira Freund. "Tolerance Israeli Style." *Israeli Democracy* 1, no. 3 (Fall 1987): 35–39.

Peres, Yochanan, and Sara Shemer. "The Ethnic Factor in Elections." In *The Roots of Begin's Success,* edited by Dan Caspi, Abraham Diskin, and Emanuel Gutmann, 89–111. Croom Helm and St. Martin's Press, 1984.

Peres, Yochanan, and Ephraim Ya'ar. "Postscript: Democracy under Fire." *Israeli Democracy* (Spring 1991): 26–29.

Peretz, Don. "Early State Policy towards the Arab Population, 1948–1955." In *New Perspectives on Israeli History: The Early Years of the State,* edited by Laurence J. Silberstein, 82–102. New York University Press, 1991.

———. "Scholarship on Jewish-Arab Relations: Fifty Years Ago and Today." In *Books on Israel,* edited by Ian S. Lustick, 83–89. State University of New York Press, 1988.

Peri, Yoram. "The Arab-Israeli Conflict and Israeli Democracy." In *Israeli Democracy under Stress,* edited by Ehud Sprinzak and Larry Diamond, 343–57. Lynne Rienner, 1993.

———. *Between Battles and Ballots: Israeli Military in Politics.* Cambridge University Press, 1983.

———. "The Rise and Fall of Israel's National Consensus (1)." *New Outlook* 26 (May 1983): 28–31.

———. "The Rise and Fall of Israel's National Consensus (2)." *New Outlook* 26 (June 1983): 26–32.

Pinkas, Alon. "Garrison Democracy: The Impact of the 1967 Occupation of Territories on Institutional Democracy in Israel." In *Democracy, Peace, and the Israeli-Palestinian Conflict,* edited by Edy Kaufman, Shukri B. Abed, and Robert L. Rothstein, 61–83. Lynne Rienner, 1993.

Playfair, Emma. *Administrative Detention in the Occupied West Bank.* Al-Haq [Law in the Service of Man], 1986.

Powell, G. Bingham. *Contemporary Democracies: Participation, Stability, and Violence.* Harvard University Press, 1982.

Poyastro, Avraham. "Land as a Mechanism of Control: Israel's Policy toward the

Arab Minority 1948–1966" (in Hebrew). Master's thesis, University of Haifa, 1985.

Rabushka, Alvin, and Kenneth A. Shepsle. *Politics in Plural Societies: A Theory of Democratic Instability.* Charles E. Merrill Publishing, 1972.

Radian, Alex. "The Policy Formation—Electoral Economic Cycle 1955–1981." In *The Roots of Begin's Success,* edited by Dan Caspi, Abraham Diskin, and Emanuel Gutmann, 219–43. Croom Helm and St. Martin's Press, 1984.

Ram, Uri. *The Changing Agenda of Israeli Sociology.* State University of New York Press, 1995.

Razin, Assaf, and Efraim Sadka. *The Economy of Modern Israel: Malaise and Promise.* University of Chicago Press, 1994.

Regev, Uri. "Israel: The Real Challenge—A Response." *CCAR Journal: A Reform Jewish Quarterly* (Spring/Summer 1996): 1–17.

Reich, Bernard. *Israel: Land of Tradition and Conflict.* Westview Press and Croom Helm, 1985.

Reiter, Yitzhak. "The Arab Democratic Party and Its Place in the Orientation of Israeli Arabs" (in Hebrew). In *The Arab Vote in Israel's Parliamentary Elections, 1988,* edited by Jacob M. Landau, 63–84. The Jerusalem Institute for Israel Studies, 1989.

———. "Forming Their Identity." *Israeli Democracy* (Fall 1989): 31–34.

Rekhess, Elie. "The Arab Minority and the 1992 Election: Integration or Alienation?" In *Israel at the Crossroads,* edited by Efraim Karsh and Gregory Mahler, 150–67, 246–48. British Academic Press, 1994.

———. "The Arab Minority in Israel" (in Hebrew). In *Hebrew Encyclopedia,* 480–510: Sifriat Po'alim, 1993.

———. *The Arab Minority in Israel: Between Communism and Arab Nationalism* (in Hebrew). Hakibbutz Hame'uchad, 1993.

———. "Initial Israeli Policy Guidelines towards the Arab Minority, 1948–1949." In *New Perspectives on Israeli History: The Early Years of the State,* edited by Laurence J. Silberstein, 103–123. New York University Press, 1991.

———. "Israeli Arabs and the Arabs of the West Bank and Gaza: Political Affinity and National Solidarity." *Asian* and *African Studies* 23 (November 1989): 119–54.

———. "Israel's Arab Citizens and the Peace Process." In *Israel under Rabin,* edited by Robert O. Freedman, 189–204. Westview Press, 1995.

———. "Resurgent Islam in Israel." *Asian and African Studies* 27 (March/July, 1993): 189–206.

Retig, Edi. "The Sting: Secret Evidence, the Burden of Proof, and Freedom of Expression" (in Hebrew). *Mishpatim* 14 (1984): 108–26.

Revel, Jean-Francois. *How Democracies Perish.* Doubleday and Company, 1984.

Roberts, Adam, Boel Joergensen, and Frank Newman. "Academic Freedom under Israeli Military Occupation." In *Report of WUS/ICJ Mission of Enquiry into Higher Education in the West Bank and Gaza.* World University Service (UK) and International Commission of Jurists, 1984.

Rolef, Susan Hattis. "A Threat to Democracy is a Threat to Zionism." *Jerusalem Post,* 20 May 1991.

Rolef, Susan Hattis, ed. *The Dilemma of Religion and Politics: Attitudes and Positions within the Israeli Labor Movement on Religious Pluralism.* Semana Publishing, 1986.

————. *Political Dictionary of the State of Israel.* Jerusalem Publishing House, 1993.

Romann, Michael. *Jewish Kiryat Arba Versus Arab Hebron.* West Bank Data Base Project, 1986.

Rosenbaum, Aaron D. "Tehiya as a Permanent Nationalistic Phenomenon." In *Israel after Begin,* edited by Gregory S. Mahler, 71–90. State University of New York Press, 1990.

Roth, Sol. *Halakha and Politics: The Jewish Idea of a State.* Ktav and Yeshiva University Press, 1988.

Rouhana, Nadim. "The Intifada and the Palestinians of Israel: Resurrecting the Green Line." *Journal of Palestine Studies* 19 (Spring 1990): 58–75.

————. "The Political Transformation of the Palestinians in Israel: From Acquiescence to Challenge." *Journal of Palestine Studies* 18 (Spring 1989): 38–59.

Roumani, Maurice M. "Labor's Expectation and Israeli Reality: Ethnic Voting as a Means toward Political and Social Change." In *Israel Faces the Future,* edited by Bernard Reich and Gershon R. Kieval, 57–78. Praeger, 1986.

Rubin, Barry. "Israeli Foreign Policy." In *Books on Israel,* edited by Ian S. Lustick, 55–61. State University of New York Press, 1988.

Rubinstein, Amnon. *The Constitutional Law of the State of Israel* (in Hebrew). Schocken, 1980.

————. "The Need for Amendment of Defense Regulations" (in Hebrew). *Hapraklit* 38 (July 1973): 486–99.

————. *The Zionist Dream Revisited.* Schocken Books, 1984.

Rubinstein, Dani. "The Relationship of the Majority to the Minority—in Practice" (in Hebrew). In *One of Every Six Israelis,* edited by Alouph Hareven, 96–101. The Van Leer Jerusalem Foundation, 1981.

Rubinstein, Elyakim. *Judges of the Land* (in Hebrew). Schocken, 1980.

————. "Zionist Attitudes on the Jewish-Arab Conflict until 1936." In *Zionism and the Arabs: Essays,* edited by Shmuel Almog, 35–72. The Historical Society of Israel and the Zalman Shazar Center for Jewish History, 1983.

Rudolph, Harold. "The Judicial Review of Administrative Detention Orders in Israel." *Israel Yearbook on Human Rights* 14 (1984): 148–81.

Rustow, Dankwart A. *A World of Nations: Problems of Political Modernization.* The Brookings Institution, 1967.

Sachar, Howard Morley. *The Course of Modern Jewish History.* Dell, 1958.

Safran, Nadav. *Israel: The Embattled Ally.* Harvard University Press, 1978.

Sager, Samuel. *The Parliamentary System of Israel.* Syracuse University Press, 1985.

————. "Pre-State Influences on Israel's Parliamentary System." *Parliamentary Affairs* 25 (1972): 29–49.

Sahliyeh, Emile. "The PLO and the Israeli Arabs." *Asian and African Studies* 27 (March/July 1993): 85–96.

Salmon, Yosef. "The Emergence of a Jewish Collective Consciousness in Eastern Europe during the 1860s and 1870s." *Association for Jewish Studies Review* 16 (Spring/Fall 1991): 107–32.

Saltman, Michael. "The Use of the Mandatory Emergency Laws by the Israeli Government." *International Journal of the Sociology of Law* 10 (November 1982): 385–94.

Sandler, Shmuel. "Israeli Arabs and the Jewish State: The Activation of a Community in Suspended Animation." *Middle Eastern Studies* 31 (October 1995): 932–52.

Schiff, Gary S. "Recent Developments in Israel's Religious Parties." In *Israel after Begin*, edited by Gregory S. Mahler, 273–90. State University of New York Press, 1990.

Schiff, Ze'ev. "The Spectre of Civil War in Israel." *The Middle East Journal* 39 (Spring 1985): 231–45.

Schiff, Ze'ev, and Ehud Ya'ari. *Israel's Lebanon War.* Simon & Schuster, 1984.

Schild, Ozer. "Comments on the Survey of Political and Social Attitudes among Youth" (in Hebrew). The Van Leer Jerusalem Institute, May 1986.

Schnall, David J. *Radical Dissent in Contemporary Israeli Politics: Cracks in the Wall.* Praeger, 1979.

Schwartz, Sharon, Bruce G. Link, Bruce P. Dohrenwend, Guedalia Naveh, Itzhak Levav, and Patrick Shrout. "Separating Class and Ethnic Prejudice: A Study of North African and European Jews in Israel." *Social Psychology Quarterly* 54, no. 4 (1991): 287–98.

Schwartzwald, Joseph, and Yehuda Amir. "Interethnic Relations and Education: An Israeli Perspective." In *Education in a Comparative Context*, edited by Ernest Krausz, 245–68. Transaction Publishers, 1989.

Schweid, Eliezer. "Relations between Religious and Secular Citizens in the State of Israel" (in Hebrew). *Skira Hodshit* 33, nos. 2 and 3 (5 November 1986).

Schweitzer, Avram. *Israel: The Changing National Agenda.* Croom Helm, 1986.

Segev, Tom. *1949: The First Israelis.* The Free Press, 1986.

Segre, Dan V. *A Crisis of Identity: Israel and Zionism.* Oxford University Press, 1980.

———. "The Jewish Political Tradition as a Vehicle for Jewish Auto-Emancipation." In *Kinship and Consent: The Jewish Political Tradition and Its Contemporary Uses*, edited by Daniel J. Elazar, 293–307: University Press of America, 1983.

Seliktar, Ofira. "National Integration of a Minority in an Acute Conflict Situation: The Case of the Israeli Arabs." *Plural Societies* 12, nos. 3–4 (1981): 25–40.

———. *New Zionism and the Foreign Policy System of Israel.* Southern Illinois University Press, 1986.

Shachar, Rina. "The Attitudes of Israeli Youth toward Inter-Ethnic and Intra-Ethnic Marriage: 1975 and 1990." *Ethnic and Racial Studies* 16 (October 1993): 683–95.

Shafir, Gershon. "Ideological Politics or the Politics of Demography: The Aftermath of the Six-Day War." In *Critical Essays on Israeli Society, Politics, and Culture*, edited by Ian S. Lustick and Barry Rubin, 41–61. State University of New York Press, 1991.

———. "Institutional and Spontaneous Settlement Drives: Did Gush Emunim Make a Difference?" In *The Impact of Gush Emunim: Politics and Settlement in the West Bank*, edited by David Newman, 153–71. Croom Helm, 1985.

———. *Land, Labor and the Origins of the Israeli-Palestinian Conflict 1882–1914.* Cambridge University Press, 1989.

Shalev, Michael. "Jewish Organized Labor and the Palestinians: A Study of State/Society Relations in Israel." In *The Israeli State and Society: Boundaries and Frontiers*, edited by Baruch Kimmerling, 93–133. State University of New York Press, 1989.

Shamgar, Meir. "The Observance of International Law in the Administered Territories." *Israel Yearbook on Human Rights* 1 (1971): 262–77.

Shamir, Jacob, and Michal Shamir. *The Dynamics of Israeli Public Opinion on Peace and the Territories.* Research Report No. 1. The Tami Steinmetz Center for Peace Research, 1993.

Shamir, Michal. "Political Intolerance among Masses and Elites in Israel: A Reevaluation of the Elitist Theory of Democracy." *The Journal of Politics* 53 (November 1991): 1018–43.

Shamir, Michal, and John L. Sullivan. "Jews and Arabs in Israel: Everybody Hates Somebody, Sometime." *Journal of Conflict Resolution* 29 (June 1985): 283–305.

———. "The Political Context of Tolerance: The United States and Israel." *American Political Science Review* 77 (December 1983): 911–27.

Shapiro, Yonathan. *Democracy in Israel* (in Hebrew). Masada, 1977.

———. *The Successor Generation* (in Hebrew). Sifriat Po'alim, 1984.

Sharkansky, Ira. *What Makes Israel Tick: How Domestic Policy-Makers Cope with Constraints.* Nelson-Hall, 1985.

Sharon, Moshe. Review of *Arabs in the Jewish State: Israel's Control of a National Minority* by Ian Lustick. *Middle Eastern Studies* 18 (July 1982): 336–44.

Shcffer, Gabriel. "The Confrontation Between Moshe Sharett and David Ben-Gurion." In *Zionism and the Arabs: Essays,* edited by Shmuel Almog, 95–147. The Historical Society of Israel and the Zalman Shazar Center for Jewish History, 1983.

———. *Moshe Sharett: Biography of a Political Moderate.* Clarendon Press, 1996.

Shefi, Dov. "The Protection of Human Rights in Areas Administered by Israel: United Nations Findings and Reality." *Israel Yearbook on Human Rights* 3 (1973): 337–61.

Sheftler, M. "Thoughts on Constitutional Questions" (in Hebrew). *Hapraklit* 26 (February 1970): 6–16.

Shehadeh, Raja, and Jonathan Kuttab. *The West Bank and the Rule of Law.* International Commission of Jurists and Al-Haq [Law in the Service of Man], 1980.

Shetreet, Simon. "A Contemporary Model of Emergency Detention Law: An Assessment of the Israeli Law." *Israel Yearbook on Human Rights* 14 (1984): 182–220.

———. "Israeli Democracy in Wartime—The Legal Framework in Practical Perspective" (in Hebrew). *Skira Hodshit* (August–September 1984): 46–56.

———. "A Rejoinder." *Israel Yearbook on Human Rights* 4 (1974): 241–44.

———. "Some Reflections on Freedom of Conscience and Religion in Israel." *Israel Yearbook on Human Rights* 4 (1974): 194–218.

Shilhav, Joseph, and Menachem Friedman. *Growth and Segregation—The Ultra-Orthodox Community of Jerusalem* (in Hebrew). Jerusalem Institute for Israel Studies, 1989.

Shimoni, Gidon. *The Zionist Ideology.* Brandeis University Press, 1995.

Shimshoni, Daniel. *Israeli Democracy: The Middle of the Journey.* Free Press, 1982.

Shipler, David K. *Arab and Jew: Wounded Spirits in a Promised Land.* Times Books, 1989.

Shlaim, Avi, and Avner Yaniv. "Domestic Politics and Foreign Policy in Israel." *International Affairs* 56 (April 1980): 242–62.

Shokeid, Moshe. "A Case of Ethnic Myth-Making." In *Cross-Currents in Israeli Culture and Politics,* edited by Myron J. Aronoff, 39–49. Transaction Books, 1984.

Shokeid, Moshe, and Shlomo Deshen. *Distant Relations: Ethnicity and Politics among Arabs and Middle Eastern Jews.* Praeger, 1982.

Shuval, Judith. "The Structure and Dilemmas of Israeli Pluralism." In *The Israeli State and Society: Boundaries and Frontiers,* edited by Baruch Kimmerling, 216–36. State University of New York Press, 1989.

Sicker, Martin. *The Judaic State: A Study in Rabbinical Political Theory.* Praeger, 1988.

———. *What Judaism Says about Politics: The Political Theology of the Torah.* Jason Aronson, 1994.

Siegel, Judy. "Jerusalem a Step Nearer Soccer Stadium." *Jerusalem Post,* 22 April 1987.

Simon, Rita J. "Assessing Israel's Record on Human Rights." *The Annals of the American Academy of Political and Social Science,* no. 506 (November 1989): 115–28.

———. "The 'Religious Issue' in Israeli Public Life." *Israel Horizons* (Summer 1989): 25–29.

Simon, Rita J., Jean M. Landis, and Menachem Amir. "Public Support for Civil Liberties in Israel." *Middle East Review* 21 (Summer 1989): 2–8.

Smith, Hanoch, and Rafi Smith. *Judaism in the Jewish State: A 1989 Survey of Attitudes of Israeli Jews.* American Jewish Committee, Institute of Human Relations, 1989.

Smooha, Sammy. "Arab-Jewish Relations in Israel in the Peace Era." *Israel Affairs* 1 (Winter 1994): 227–44.

———. *Arabs and Jews in Israel.* Vol. 1: *Conflicting and Shared Attitudes in a Divided Society.* Westview Press, 1989.

———. *Arabs and Jews in Israel.* Vol. 2: *Change and Continuity in Mutual Intolerance.* Westview Press, 1992.

———. "Class, Ethnic, and National Cleavages and Democracy in Israel." In *Israeli Democracy under Stress,* edited by Ehud Sprinzak and Larry Diamond, 309–42. Lynne Rienner, 1993.

———. "The Divergent Fate of the Palestinians on Both Sides of the Green Line: The Intifada as a Test." Paper presented at conference on the Arab Minority in Israel: Dilemmas of Political Orientation and Social Change, University of Tel Aviv, June 3–4, 1991.

———. *Israel: Pluralism and Conflict.* University of California Press, 1978.

———. "Jewish Ethnicity in Israel." In *Whither Israel? The Domestic Challenges,* edited by Keith Kyle and Joel Peters, 161–76. I. B. Tauris, 1994.

———. "Minority Status in an Ethnic Democracy: The Status of the Arab Minority in Israel." *Ethnic and Racial Studies* 13 (July 1990): 389–413.

———. *The Orientation and Politicization of the Arab Minority in Israel.* Rev. ed. Institute of Middle Eastern Studies, University of Haifa, 1984.

Smooha, Sammy, and Ora Cibulski. *Social Research on Arabs in Israel 1948–1976: Trends and an Annotated Bibliography.* Turtledove Publishing, 1978.

Sofer, Sasson. *Begin: An Anatomy of Leadership.* Basil Blackwell, 1988.

Soffer, Arnon. "The Changing Situation of Majority and Minority and its Spatial Expression—The Case of the Arab Minority in Israel." In *Pluralism and Political Geography: People, Territory and State,* edited by Nurit Kliot and Stanley Waterman, 80–99. Croom Helm and St. Martin's Press, 1983.

———. "Demography and the Shaping of Israel's Borders." *Contemporary Jewry* 10, no. 2 (1989): 91–105.

———. *On the Demographic and Geographic Situation in the Land of Israel: The End of the Zionist Dream?* (in Hebrew). Gestlit Press, 1988.

———. "Population Projections for the Land of Israel." *Middle East Review* 20 (Summer 1988): 43–49.

Sprinzak, Ehud. *The Ascendance of Israel's Radical Right.* Oxford University Press, 1991.

———. *Every Man Whatsoever Is Right in His Own Eyes—Illegalism in Israeli Society* (in Hebrew). Sifriat Po'alim, 1986.

———. "Gush Emunim: The Tip of the Iceberg." *Jerusalem Quarterly* 21 (Fall 1981): 28.

———. "Illegalism in Israeli Political Culture: Theoretical and Historical Footnotes to the Pollard Affair and the Shin Beth Cover Up." In *Israel after Begin,* edited by Gregory S. Mahler, 51–69. State University of New York Press, 1990.

———. "Three Models of Religious Violence: The Case of Jewish Fundamentalism in Israel." In *Fundamentalisms and the State,* edited by Martin E. Marty and R. Scott Appleby, 462–90. University of Chicago Press, 1993.

Stendel, Ori. *The Arabs in Israel: Between Hammer and Anvil* (in Hebrew). Academon, 1992.

Stone, Julius. *Israel and Palestine: Assault on the Law of Nations.* The Johns Hopkins University Press, 1981.

———. *Legal Controls of International Conflict:* Maitland Publications, 1959.

Stone, Russell A. *Social Change in Israel: Attitudes and Events, 1967–1979.* Praeger, 1982.

Sullivan, John L., Michal Shamir, Nigel S. Roberts, and Patrick Walsh. "Political Intolerance and the Structure of Mass Attitudes." *Comparative Political Studies* 17 (October 1984): 319–44.

Sullivan, John L., Michal Shamir, Patrick Walsh, and Nigel S. Roberts. *Political Tolerance in Context: Support for Unpopular Minorities in Israel, New Zealand, and the United States.* Westview Press, 1985.

Susser, Bernard. "Jewish Political Theory." In *Public Life in Israel and the Diaspora,* edited by Sam N. Lehman-Wilzig and Bernard Susser, vol. 1 of *Comparative Jewish Politics.* Bar-Ilan University Press, 1981.

Syrkin, Nachman. "The Jewish Problem and the Socialist-Jewish State." In *The Zionist Idea: A Historical Analysis and Reader,* edited by Arthur Hertzberg. Atheneum, 1973.

Taft, Renee. "Ethnic Divisions in Israel." In *Israel Faces the Future,* edited by Bernard Reich and Gershon R. Kieval, 79–92. Praeger, 1986.

Taylor, Charles Lewis, and David A. Jodice. *World Handbook of Political and Social Indicators.* 3rd ed. Yale University Press, 1983.

Teveth, Shabtai. *Ben-Gurion and the Palestinian Arabs: From Peace to War.* Oxford University Press, 1985.

———. *The Evolution of 'Transfer' in Zionist Thinking.* Occasional Paper No. 107. Moshe Dayan Center for Middle Eastern and African Studies, The Shiloah Institute, Tel Aviv University, May 1989.

Tsemah, Mina, and Ruth Tsin. "Attitudes of Youth toward Democratic Values" (in Hebrew). The Van Leer Jerusalem Institute, September 1984.

Tshor, Ze'ev. *The Roots of Israeli Politics* (in Hebrew). Hakibbutz Hame'uhad, 1987.

United Nations Legal Department. *Laws Concerning Nationality.* UN ST/LEG/ser.B/4, 1954.

———. *Supplement to the Volume on Laws Concerning Nationality.* UN ST/LEG/ser.B/9, 1959.

Van den Berghe, Pierre. "Pluralism and the Polity: A Theoretical Exploration." In *Pluralism in Africa*, edited by Leo Kuper and M. G. Smith, 67–81. University of California Press, 1969.

Vardi, Raphael. "Israeli Administration and Self-Rule in the Territories: The Israeli Perspective." In *Judea, Gaza, and Samaria: Views on the Present and Future*, edited by Daniel Elazar, 171–79. American Enterprise Institute, 1982.

Vital, David. *The Origins of Zionism*. Clarendon Press, 1975.

——. *Zionism: The Formative Years*. Clarendon Press, 1982.

——. *Zionism: The Crucial Phase*. Clarendon Press, 1987.

Von Glahn, Gerhard. *The Occupation of Enemy Territory*. University of Minnesota Press, 1957.

Wald, Kenneth, and Samuel Shye. "Inter-Religious Conflict in Israel." Paper presented at the annual meeting of the American Political Science Association, Washington, D.C., September 2–5, 1993.

——. "Religious Influence in Electoral Behavior: The Role of Institutional and Social Forces in Israel." Paper presented at the annual meeting of the Midwest Political Science Association, Chicago, April 15–17, 1993.

Weingrod, Alex. "Shadow Games: Ethnic Conflict and Political Exchange in Israel." *Regional Politics and Policy* 3 (Spring 1993): 190–209.

Weinshal, Theodore D. "How to Change Government Administration in Israel: The Socio-Cultural Structure in Israel" (in Hebrew). *Al Haperek: Hamishtar V'ha'ezrah* (1975–1976): 40–51.

Weisburd, David, and Vered Vinitzky. "Vigilantism as Rational Social Control: The Case of the Gush Emunim Settlers." In *Cross-Currents in Israeli Culture and Politics*, edited by Myron J. Aronoff, 69–87. Transaction Books, 1984.

Weiss, Shevach. "Israeli Democracy after the Test of a Generation" (in Hebrew). *Skira Hodshit* (December 1978): 28–34.

Weissbrod, Lilly. "From Labour Zionism to New Zionism: Ideological Change in Israel." *Theory and Society* 10 (November 1981): 777–803.

——. "Protest and Dissidence in Israel." In *Cross-Currents in Israeli Culture and Politics*, edited by Myron J. Aronoff, 51–68. Transaction Books, 1984.

Wieseltier, Leon. "The Demons of the Jews." *The New Republic* (11 November 1985): 15–25.

Willis, Aaron. "Redefining Religious Zionism: Shas' Ethno-politics." *Israel Studies Bulletin* 8 (Fall 1992): 3–8.

Willis, Aaron P. "Shas—The Sephardic Torah Guardians: Religious 'Movement' and Political Power." In *The Elections in Israel 1992*, edited by Asher Arian and Michal Shamir, 121–39. State University of New York Press, 1995.

Wolffsohn, Michael. *Israel: Polity, Society and Economy 1882–1986:* Humanities Press International, 1987.

Wolfsfeld, Gadi. *The Politics of Provocation: Participation and Protest in Israel*. State University of New York Press, 1988.

Wurmser, Meyrav, ed. "Playing Partisan Games: Elite Ideas and Foreign Policy in Israel." Paper presented at annual meeting of the American Political Science Association. Chicago, September 1–4, 1995.

Ya'ar, Ephraim, and Yochanan Peres. "Democracy Index." *Israeli Democracy* 2, no. 4 (Winter 1988): 15–19.

Yanai, Nathan. "Ben-Gurion's Concept of *Mamlachtiut* and the Forming Reality of the State of Israel." *Jewish Political Studies Review* 1 (Spring 1989): 151–77.

———. *Party Leadership in Israel: Maintenance and Change.* Turtledove Publishing, 1981.

———. "The Political Affair: A Framework for Comparative Discussion." *Comparative Politics* 22 (January 1990): 185–98.

Yaniv, Avner. *Deterrence without the Bomb.* Lexington Books, 1987.

———. "Israel National Security in the 1980s: The Crisis of Overload." In *Israel after Begin,* edited by Gregory S. Mahler, 93–109. State University of New York Press, 1990.

———. "A Strange Thing Has Happened to Israeli Deterrence" (in Hebrew). *Politika* 26 (May 1989): 6–9.

Yaniv, Avner, and Fabian Pascal. "Doves, Hawks and Other Birds of a Feather: The Distribution of Israeli Parliamentary Opinion on the Future of the Occupied Territories 1967–1977." *British Journal of Political Science* 10 (April 1980): 260–67.

Yaniv, Avner, and Yael Yishai. "Israeli Settlements in the West Bank: The Politics of Intransigence." *Journal of Politics* 43 (November 1981): 1105–28.

Yiftachel, Oren. "The Concept of 'Ethnic Democracy' and Its Applicability to the Case of Israel." *Ethnic and Racial Studies* 15 (January 1992): 125–36.

———. "The State, Ethnic Relations and Democratic Stability: Lebanon, Cyprus, and Israel." *GeoJournal* 28 (1 November 1992): 319–22.

Yishai, Yael. "Hawkish Proletariat: The Case of Israel." *Journal of Political and Military Sociology* 13 (Spring 1985): 53–73.

———. *Land of Paradoxes: Interest Politics in Israel.* State University of New York Press, 1991.

Yuchtman-Ya'ar, Ephraim. "The Test of Israel's Arab Minority." *Israeli Democracy* 2, no. 1 (Spring 1988): 42–46.

Yuchtman-Ya'ar, Ephraim, and Yochanan Peres. "Public Opinion and Democracy after Three Years of Intifada." *Israeli Democracy* (Spring 1991): 21–25.

Zborowski, Mark, and Elizabeth Herzog. *Life Is with People: The Culture of the Shtetl.* Schocken Books, 1952.

Zemach, Mina. *Positions of the Jewish Majority in Israel toward the Arab Minority.* Van Leer Institute, 1980.

Zenner, Walter. "Ethnic Factors in Israeli Life." In *Books on Israel,* edited by Ian S. Lustick, 47–54. State University of New York Press, 1988.

Zipperstein, Steven J. *Elusive Prophet: Ahad Ha'am and the Origins of Zionism.* University of California Press, 1993.

Zuckerman, Alan S., Hannah Herzog, and Michal Shamir. "The Party's Just Begun: Herut Activists in Power and after Begin." In *Israel after Begin,* edited by Gregory S. Mahler, 235–55. State University of New York Press, 1990.

Zuckerman-Bareli, Chaya. "The Religious Factor in Opinion Formation among Israeli Youth." In *On Ethnic and Religious Diversity,* edited by Solomon Poll and Ernest Krausz, 53–89. Bar-Ilan University, 1975.

INDEX

Compositor: Prestige Typography
Text: 10/12 Baskerville
Display: Baskerville
Printer and Binder: BookCrafters, Inc.